VICTORIAN MATERIAL CULTURE

VICTORIAN MATERIAL CULTURE

General Editors:
Tatiana Kontou and Victoria Mills

Volume V

Fashionable Things

Edited by Tatiana Kontou
and Kara Tennant

Routledge
Taylor & Francis Group
LONDON AND NEW YORK

First published 2023
by Routledge
4 Park Square, Milton Park, Abingdon, Oxon OX14 4RN

and by Routledge
605 Third Avenue, New York, NY 10158

Routledge is an imprint of the Taylor & Francis Group, an informa business

British Library Cataloguing-in-Publication Data
A catalogue record for this book is available from the British Library

Library of Congress Cataloging-in-Publication Data
A catalog record has been requested for this book

ISBN: 978-1-138-22526-8 (set)
eISBN: 978-1-315-40038-9 (set)
ISBN: 978-1-138-22538-1 (volume V)
eISBN: 978-1-315-39998-0 (volume V)

DOI: 10.4324/9781315399980

Typeset in Times New Roman
by Apex CoVantage, LLC

Publisher's Note
References within each chapter are as they appear in the original complete work

CONTENTS

VOLUME V Fashionable Things

EDITED BY TATIANA KONTOU AND KARA TENNANT

ACKNOWLEDGEMENTS

The following images have been reproduced in this volume courtesy of the Victoria and Albert Museum, London, UK: photograph of Crinolette, Great Britain, ca. 1870 made; photograph by Julia Margaret Cameron, 'Dora as the Bride' (sitter Annie Chinery Cameron), albumen print, 1869; Edward Killingworth Johnson, drawing depicting a young widow holding her wedding dress (water-colour and gouache on paper, 1877); photograph of cut-steel chatelaine with attachments, England, ca. 1863–1885. The image titled 'Mourning brooches containing the hair of a deceased relative' is reproduced here courtesy of the Wellcome Collection. Attribution 4.0 International (CC BY 4.0) as well as the photograph by Julia Margaret Cameron, 'A young woman in mourning dress', 1868/1872. G. W. Hunt, 'Dolly Varden' (music title page), Boston: Oliver Ditson & Co., has been reproduced courtesy of the Newberry Library, Chicago.

The editors would like to offer heartfelt thanks to Claire Cock-Starkey, who has been a kind and generous research assistant at an especially demanding time during the pandemic.

Tatiana Kontou would like to offer enormous thanks to Jenny Bourne Taylor, Andrew Mangham, Barbara Giraud and Sofia Pelendridis, who have been with her from the beginning of this volume and offered suggestions, advice and inspiring conversations. Special thanks are due to Chryssa Marinou for suggesting useful references. Tatiana would like to offer thanks to her friends for unfailing love and support, too many to be named here, they know who they are. Finally, special thanks are due to David Tucker, who offered practical advice when needed.

Kara Tennant is very grateful to family: to her partner, Richard Blann, and his parents, June and Lionel; and to her mother, Lee Davies, for all their love and generosity. Sincere thanks are also due to friends and colleagues: in particular to Fiona Howells for her empathy and support; to Harriet Posner, for her kindness, her pertinent questions and her willingness to listen; to Lee Thomas, for the opportunity to teach new and hugely-beneficial scholarly areas; to Simon Thomas, for his wisdom and sound advice during this work; and to Steven Wright, for his insight and unwavering interest in the project. Many thanks are also due to Nadine Pittard for her tenacity and professionalism in tracking down some key and invaluable critical material. Finally, Kara would like to thank Tatiana for inviting her onto this project, and for being the absolute best of teammates and collaborators throughout the process – I know that I speak for us both in saying that we are now life-long friends.

BIBLIOGRAPHY

Further Primary Sources

Amaranth, 'Mourning', *Hearth and Home*, 18 August 1892, pp. 461–462.
[Anon], 'Chignons Defended', *Sheffield Independent*, 12 March 1867, p. 7.
[Anon], 'A Defence of Ladies' Dresses', *Punch*, 26 September 1857, p. 128.
[Anon], 'Designs for Mourning Jewellery', *The Englishwoman's Domestic Magazine*, 1 September 1879, p. 140.
[Anon], 'The Dress of Englishwomen', *Pall Mall Gazette*, 10 March 1869, p. 11.
[Anon], ('[e]dited by Madame Elise'), 'The Secret of Beauty', *Bow Bells*, 7 April 1875, p. 332.
[Anon], 'False Jewellery', *The Dundee Courier*, 14 November 1898, p. 6
[Anon], 'Fashion in Mourning', *Bow Bells*, 30 November 1894, pp. 545–546.
[Anon], 'Fashionable Hobbies', *Punch*, 17 March 1849, p. 107.
[Anon], 'Fashionable Jewellery', *The Englishwoman's Domestic Magazine,* June 1869, p. 319.
[Anon], 'Fashions in Feathers', *The London Journal*, 1 April 1894, pp. 12–13.
[Anon], 'Fashions in Furs', *Bow Bells*, 1 February 1889, p. 72.
[Anon], 'Fashions in Jewellery', *The Country Gentleman, Sporting Gazette, and 'The Man About Town'*, 1 October 1898, p. 1292.
[Anon], 'The Female Art Gallery', *The Englishwoman's Domestic Magazine*, 1 November 1869, p. 237.
[Anon], 'Fur Rugs and Robes', *Bow Bells*, 28 December 1888, p. 408.
[Anon], 'Gloves and Loves', *Fun*, 24 July 1878, p. 33.
[Anon], 'Home Hobbies. IV. – Diaphanie', *The Children's Friend* [1893?], pp. 106–108.
[Anon], 'Jewellery Notions', *The Dundee Courier and Argus*, 9 May 1895, p. 4.
[Anon], 'The Latest in Mourning', *The London Journal*, 1 July 1893, p. 5.
[Anon], 'A Luminous Toe', *The London Journal*, 13 March 1897, p. 226.
[Anon], 'Mourning as a Fashion', *London Reader*, 17 February 1877, p. 376.
[Anon], 'Mourning Orders For Court and Public', *The Daily News*, 30 October 1897, p. 6.
[Anon], 'My Chignon', *The Girl of the Period Miscellany*, [August 1869?], p. 185.
[Anon], 'Never Wear False Hair!', *Twice a Week*, 25 June 1862, p. 115. [NB: this article notes that it is reproduced from *The Queen*]
[Anon], 'Potichomanie', *The Englishwoman's Domestic Magazine*, [n.d.; Vol. 3, 1855?], p. 303.
[Anon], 'Sealskin Coats, Alive and Dead', *Chambers's Journal*, 27 November 1886, pp. 753–756.
[Anon], 'The Secret of "Beauty;" Or, The Ugly Girl Who Tried to Make Herself Beautiful', *Young Folks Paper*, 26 May 1888, pp. 324–325.

[Anon], 'Small White Elephants', *Chambers's Journal*, 27 August 1864, pp. 545–547.

[Anon], 'Terrific Accident', *Punch*, 19 December 1857, p. 25.

[Anon], 'Wedding Extravagances', *Chambers's Journal*, 11 May 1878, p. 303.

[Anon], 'The Wedding Ring. A Tale.', *Chambers' Edinburgh Journal*, 15 September 1849, pp. 163–165.

[Anon], 'What a Ridiculous Fashion!', *Punch*, 21 August 1858, p. 79.

[Anon], 'Woman's Crowning Glory', *The London Journal*, 27 March 1875, p. 200.

[Anon], 'A Young Lady's Lament', *Punch*, 14 June 1856, p. 243.

Beatrice, 'Notes on London Fashions', *The London Journal*, 1 December 1884, p. 2.

T. Bull, 'Sect. V. – Dress', in *Hints to Mothers, for the Management of Health During the Period of Pregnancy, and in the Lying-In Room; with an Exposure of Popular Errors in Connexion with Those Subjects, Etc. And Hints Upon Nursing.* (*London: Longman, Brown, Green, and Longmans*, 1849 [6th edition]), pp. 26–29.

S. F. A. Caulfeild, 'Occupations for the Holidays', *Silver Sails: Being the Holiday No. of the Girl's Own Paper* [1882?], pp. 23–24.

P. H. Chavasse, 'Clothing', in *Advice To A Wife on the Management of Herself; During the Periods of Menstruation, Pregnancy, Labour, and Suckling. With an Introductory Chapter, specially addressed to a Young Wife*, 3rd edition (London: Longman, Brown, Green and Longmans; Simpkin, Marshall, and Co.; R. Davies, Birmingham, 1854), pp. 48–49.

W. Collins, *No Name*, ed. with an Introduction and Notes by Mark Ford (London: Penguin Classics, 1994)

C. Darwin, *The Descent of Man, and Selection in Relation to Sex*, 2 vols. (London: John Murray, 1888 [2nd edition, Revised and Augmented])

H. Gray, 'Fashion's Phases', *Tinsleys' Magazine*, June 1888, pp. 456–464.

T. G. Hake, 'The Wedding Ring', *Merry England*, October 1887, pp. 341–342.

L. Housman, 'Petticoat Government', *The Contemporary Review*, November 1913, pp. 663–672. Reproduced in L. Delap, M. DiCenzo and L. Ryan (eds.), *Feminism and the Periodical Press, 1900–1918* (Volume II) (London and New York: Routledge, no date [first published Abingdon, Routledge: 2006]), n.pag.

H. James, *The Portrait of a Lady*, ed. with an Introduction by Geoffrey Moore and Notes by Patricia Crick (London: Penguin, 2003 [Penguin Classics])

E. Kerr, *The Mystery of Grange Drayton* (Ludgate Circus Bldgs., E.C.: Wesleyan Methodist Sunday-School Union, 1884)

Dr. A. Kingford, *Health, Beauty and the Toilet. Letters to Ladies from a Lady Doctor* (London and New York: Frederick Warne and Co., 1886)

Pauline, 'The Sable Muff, Or the Vanquished Belle', *The World Of Fashion*, 1 February 1844, pp. 29–31.

[L. Sambourne], 'As Birds' Feathers and Train Dresses are all the go, Miss Swellington adopts one of Nature's Own Designs', *Punch*, 21 December 1867, p. 256.

[L. Sambourne], 'History Repeats Itself', *Punch*, 18 June 1870, p. 248.

[L. Sambourne], '"I Would I Were A Bird —"', *Punch*, 23 April 1870, p. 167.

[L. Sambourne], 'Mr. Punch's Designs After Nature', *Punch*, 1 April 1871, p. 127.

SENEX, 'The Chatelaine of the Haunted House. A Tale of Fashion', *Punch*, [13 January 1849], p. 22.

The Silkworm, 'Spinnings Out of Town', *The Englishwoman's Domestic Magazine*, April 1868, pp. 209–211.

A. Thorn, 'Coloured Clothes', *The Englishwoman's Domestic Magazine*, [June 1860], p. 58.

Victoria and Albert Museum,'Dress (1868–9)'. V&A Collections. Available at: https://collections.vam.ac.uk/item/O1387342/dress/ [accessed 21 June 2021]

Victoria and Albert Museum, 'Dress: ca. 1894 (made)'. V&A Collections. Available at: https://collections.vam.ac.uk/item/O15543/dress-liberty--co/ [accessed 10 July 2021]

Secondary Sources

W. Abberley, *Mimicry and Display in Victorian Literary Culture: Nature, Science and the Nineteenth-Century Imagination* (Cambridge: Cambridge University Press, 2020)

A. Adburgham, *Women in Print: Writing Women and Women's Magazines From the Restoration to the Accession of Victoria* (London: George Allen and Unwin, 1972)

R. Aindow, *Dress and Identity in British Literary Culture, 1870–1914* (Farnham, Surrey, and Burlington, VT: Ashgate, 2010)

J. M. Allan, 'Health and Hygiene: "Monster top-knots and balloon chignons" Purity and Contamination in the False Hair Trade', in S. Heaton (ed.), *A Cultural History of Hair in the Age of Empire* (Volume 5) (London: Bloomsbury, 2018), pp. 83–100.

S. Amato, *Beastly Possessions: Animals in Victorian Consumer Culture* (Toronto, Buffalo and London: University of Toronto Press, 2015)

K. Anderson, 'Coral Jewellery', *Victorian Review*, 34(1), (Spring 2008), pp. 47–52.

J. Arnold, *Victorian Jewelry, Identity, and the Novel: Prisms of Culture* (Farnham, Surrey, and Burlington, VT: Ashgate, 2011)

J. Ashelford (with Special Photography by Andreas von Einsiedel), *The Art of Dress: Clothes Through History 1500–1914* (London: The National Trust, 1996)

R. Barthes, *Camera Lucida: Reflections on Photography* (trans. by Richard Howard) (New York: Hill and Wang: 1980)

R. Barthes, *The Fashion System* (trans. by Matthew Ward and Richard Howard) (Berkeley and Los Angeles: University of California Press, 1990)

A. Beaujot, *Victorian Fashion Accessories* (London and New York: Berg, 2012)

S. A. Bedikian, 'The Death of Mourning: From Victorian Crepe to the Little Black Dress', *Omega*, 57(1), (2008), 35–52.

M. Beetham, *A Magazine of Her Own? Domesticity and Desire in the Woman's Magazine, 1800–1914* (London and New York: Routledge, 1996)

M. Beetham and K. Boardman, *Victorian Women's Magazines: An Anthology* (Manchester and New York: Manchester University Press, 2001)

B. Bell, 'Taken From Life: the unsettling art of death photography'. BBC News, 4 June 2016. Available at: https://bbc.co.uk/news/uk-england-36389581 [accessed 10 July 2021]

S. D. Bernstein, 'Designs after Nature: Evolutionary Fashions, Animals, and Gender', in D. D. Morse and Martin A. Danahay (eds.), *Victorian Animal Dreams: Representations of Animals in Victorian Literature and Culture* (London and New York: Routledge, 2017 [first published in 2007 by Ashgate Publishing]), pp. 65–79.

N. Bown, Empty Hands and Precious Pictures: Post-mortem Portrait Photographs of Children, *Australasian Journal of Victorian Studies*, 14(2), (2009), pp. 8–24.

A. Braida and G. Pieri, 'Introduction', in A. Braida and G. Pieri (eds.), *Image and Word: Reflections of Art and Literature from the Middle Ages to the Present* (Oxford: European Humanities Research Centre of the University of Oxford, in conjunction with the Modern Humanities Research Association, 2003), pp. 1–14.

C. Breward, *The Culture of Fashion: A New History of Fashionable Dress* (Manchester and New York: Manchester University Press, 1995)

A. Briefel, 'Cosmetic Tragedies: Failed Masquerade in Wilkie Collins's *The Law and the Lady*', *Victorian Literature and Culture*, 37(2), (2009), pp. 463–81.

J. Burnett (ed.), *Useful Toil: Autobiographies of Working People from the 1820s to the 1920s* (Abingdon and New York: Routledge, 1994 [first published in 1974 by Allen Lane/Penguin Books])

S. Bury, *Jewellery, 1789–1910: The International Era* (Woodbridge, Suffolk: Antique Collectors' Club, 1991)

A. Calahan, *Fashion Plates: 150 Years of Style* (New Haven, Connecticut: Yale University Press, 2015)

M. Carter, *Fashion Classics from Carlyle to Barthes* (Oxford and New York: Berg, 2003)

L. M. de Carvalho, F. M. Fernandes, M. de Fátima Nunes and J. Brigola, 'Whitby Jet Jewels in the Victorian Age', *Harvard Papers in Botany*, 18(2), (2013), pp. 133–136.

T. Cave, *Mignon's Afterlives: Crossing Cultures from Goethe to the Twenty-First Century* (Oxford: Oxford University Press, 2011)

S. Cheang, 'Ethnicity', in D. A. Baxter (ed.), *A Cultural History of Dress and Fashion in the Age of Empire* (London and New York: Bloomsbury Academic, 2017), pp. 141–164.

A. A. Cheng, 'Ornamentalism: A Feminist Theory for the Yellow Woman', *Critical Enquiry*, 44(3), (Spring 2018), pp. 415–446.

Y. Chiba, 'Japonisme: East-West Renaissance in the Late 19th Century', *Mosaic: a Journal for the Interdisciplinary Study of Literature,* 31(2), (1998), pp. 1–20.

J. P. Clark, *The Business of Beauty: Gender and the Body in Victorian London* (London and New York, Bloomsbury, 2020)

M. Clarke, *Fashionability, Exhibition, Culture and Gender Politics: Fair Women* (London: Routledge, 2020)

G. E. Cummins and N. D. Taunton, *Chatelaines: Utility to Glorious Extravagance* (Woodbridge: Antique Collectors' Club, 1994)

S. Daly, *The Empire Inside: Indian Commodities in Victorian Domestic Novels* (Ann Arbor: The University of Michigan Press, 2011)

M. A. Danahay, 'Nature Red in Hoof and Paw: Domestic Animals and Violence in Victorian Art', in D. D. Morse and M. A. Danahay (eds.), *Victorian Animal Dreams: Representations of Animals in Victorian Literature and Culture* (London and New York: Routledge, 2017 [first published in 2007 by Ashgate Publishing]), pp. 97–119.

A. M. David, *Fashion Victims: The Dangers of Dress Past and Present* (London and New York: Bloomsbury Visual Arts, 2015)

L. Davidoff and C. Hall, *Family Fortunes: Men and Women of the English Middle Class, 1780–1850* (London: Routledge, 1997 [first published in 1987 by Hutchinson Education])

D. Denisoff, *Sexual Visuality from Literature to Film, 1850–1950* (Houndsmill, Basingstoke, Hampshire and New York: Palgrave Macmillan, 2004)

D. M. Dove, 'Dickens, Death, and the Dolly Varden Dress', *Victoriographies*, 12(1), (2022), pp. 31–51.

Y. C. Draznin, *Victorian London's Middle-Class Housewife: What She Did All Day* (Westport, Connecticut, and London: Greenwood, 2001)

E. Ehrman, 'Frith and Fashion', in M. Bills and V. Knight (eds.), *William Powell Frith: Painting the Victorian Age* (New Haven and London: Yale University Press in association with Guildhall Art Gallery, City of London, and The Mercer Art Gallery, Harrogate Museum and Arts, 2006), pp. 111–129.

S. Eliot, 'Books and their Readers – Part 1', in D. Walder (ed.), *The Nineteenth-Century Novel: Identities* (London: Routledge, 2001), pp. 157–188.

E. Ewing, *Fur in Dress* (London: Batsford, 1981)

J. Flanders, *The Victorian House: Domestic Life from Childbirth to Deathbed* (London: HarperCollins, 2003)

M. Flower (with a foreword by J. Biggs and a chapter on collecting by D. L. Moore), *Victorian Jewellery* [Revised ed.] (London: Cassell, 1967)

C. Ford, *Julia Margaret Cameron: A Critical Biography* (Los Angeles: The J. Paul Getty Museum, 2003)

H. Fraser, 'Women and the Modelling of Victorian Sculptural Discourse', *Visual Resources*, 33(1–2), (2017), pp. 74–93.

H. Fraser, S. Green and J. Johnston, *Gender and the Victorian Periodical* (Cambridge: Cambridge University Press, 2003)

E. Freedgood, 'FRINGE', *Victorian Literature and Culture*, 30(1), (2002), pp. 257–263.

N. Gauld, 'Victorian Bodies: The Wild Animal as Adornment', *The British Art Journal*, 6(1), (Spring/Summer 2005), pp. 37–42.

C. Gere and J. Rudoe, *Jewellery in the Age of Queen Victoria: A Mirror to the World* (London: British Museum Press, 2010)

C. Gere and J. Rudoe, 'Jewellery at the 1862 Exhibition', *The Journal of the Decorative Arts Society 1850 to the Present*, 38, (2014), pp. 82–105.

A. Gernsheim, *Victorian and Edwardian Fashion: A Photographic Survey* (New York: Dover, 1981)

S. Gilmartin, 'The Sati, the Bride, and the Widow: Sacrificial Woman in the Nineteenth Century', *Victorian Literature and Culture,* 25(1), (1997), pp. 141–158.

E. G. Gitter, 'The Power of Women's Hair in the Victorian Imagination', *PMLA*, 99(5), (October 1984), pp. 936–954.

D. Gorham, *The Victorian Girl and the Feminine Ideal* (London: Croom Helm, 1982)

S. Granata, 'The Dark Side of the Tank: The Marine Aquarium in the Victorian Home', in H. Kingstone and K. Lister (eds.), *Paraphernalia! Victorian Objects* (New York and Abingdon: Routledge [Taylor & Francis], 2018), pp. 81–98.

S. Granata, *The Victorian aquarium: literary discussions on nature, culture, and science* (Manchester: Manchester University Press, 2021)

K. Hadjiafxendi and P. Zakreski (eds.), *Crafting the Woman Professional in the Long Nineteenth Century: Artistry and Industry in Britain* (Farnham, Surrey, and Burlington, VT: Ashgate, 2013)

J. R. Harpley, 'Glittering Baubles: An Examination of Chatelaines in Britain, 1839–1900', *The Journal of Dress History,* 4(3), (Autumn 2020), pp. 45–71.

L Hart, *Fatal Women: Lesbian Sexuality and the Mark of Aggression* (London: Routledge, 1994)

K. Heath, *Aging by the Book: The Emergence of Midlife in Victorian Britain* (Albany: State University of New York Press, 2009)

J. Hedgecock, *The Femme Fatale in Victorian Literature: the Danger and the Sexual Threat* (Cambria Press: Amherst, New York, 2008)

J. Heffernan, 'Ekphrasis and representation', *New Literary History*, 22, (1991), pp. 297–316.

C. Hibbert, *Edward VII: The Last Victorian King* (New York and Houndsmills: Palgrave Macmillan, 2007)

H. Hind, 'Pondering on that little circle of plaited hair': Hairwork, Materiality, and Identity in Wilkie Collins's Hide and Seek (1854)', *Wilkie Collins Journal*, 17, September 2019. Available at: https://wilkiecollinssociety.org/pondering-on-that-little-circle-of-plaited-hair-hairwork-materiality-and-identity-in-wilkie-collinss-hide-and-seek-1854/ [accessed 14 July 2021]

S. Hiner, 'Feminized Commodities, Female Communities: The Colin Sisters and the Stealthy Work of the Fashion Plate', *French Historical Studies*, 43(2), (2020), pp. 223–252.

V. Holland, *Hand Coloured Fashion Plates 1770–1899* (London: B. T. Batsford, 1988)

A. Hollander, *Feeding the Eye: Essays* (Berkeley and Los Angeles, California and London: University of California Press, 1999 [paperback edition published 2000])

C. Hughes, *Dressed in Fiction* (Oxford and New York: Berg, 2006)

G. B. Hughes, 'Georgian and Victorian Chatelaines', *Country Life*, 4 October 1956, pp. 727–731.

K. Hughes, *The Victorian Governess* (London and New York: Hambledon and London, 2001 [1993])

S. Hyde, *Exhibiting Gender* (Manchester and New York: Manchester University Press, 1997)

C. Ingraham, *White Weddings: Romancing Heterosexuality in Popular Culture* (2nd edition) (New York and London: Routledge, 2008)

C. Ives, 'Japonisme' [Essay; Heilbrunn Timeline of Art History], MET Museum, October 2004. Available at: https://metmuseum.org/toah/hd/jpon/hd_jpon.htm [accessed 8 July 2021]

The J. Paul Getty Museum, *In Focus: Julia Margaret Cameron: Photographs from the J. Paul Getty Museum* (Los Angeles: The J. Paul Getty Museum, 1996)

A. Jackson (with M. Hinton), *The V&A Guide to Period Styles* (London: V&A Publications, 2002)

P. Jalland, *Death in the Victorian Family* (Oxford: Oxford University Press, 1996)

L. Johnston (with M. Kite and H. Persson), *Nineteenth-Century Fashion in Detail* (London: V&A Publications, 2005)

C. B. Kortsch, *Dress Culture in Late Victorian Women's Fiction* (London and New York: Routledge, 2016 [originally published by Ashgate Publishing in 2009])

D. Kunzle, *Fashion and Fetishism: Corsets, Tight-Lacing & Other Forms of Body-Sculpture* (Stroud: Sutton Publishing, 2004)

E. Langland, *Nobody's Angels: Middle-Class Women and Domestic Ideology in Victorian Culture* (Ithaca and London: Cornell University Press, 1995)

J. Laver, *Costume and Fashion: A Concise History* (4th edition with a concluding chapter by A. de la Haye and A. Tucker) (London: Thames & Hudson World of Art, 2002)

G. E. Lavery, *Quaint, Exquisite: Victorian Aesthetics and the Idea of Japan* (Princeton, NJ and Oxford: Princeton University Press, [2019])

K. Ledbetter, *Victorian Needlework* ([Victorian Life and Times Series] Santa Barbara, California; Denver, Colorado, and Oxford, England: Praeger [an imprint of ABC-CLIO, LLC], 2012)

S. Lee, '1840 – Queen Victoria's Wedding Dress', *Fashion History Timeline*, 28 January 2020. Available at: https://fashionhistory.fitnyc.edu/1840-queen-victorias-wedding-dress/ [accessed 23 September 2021]

S. Lennox, 'The Beautified Body: Physiognomy in Victorian Beauty Manuals', *Victorian Review*, 42(1), (Spring 2016), pp. 9–14.

L. A. Loeb, *Consuming Angels: Advertising and Victorian Women* (New York and Oxford: Oxford University Press, 1994)

T. Logan, *The Victorian Parlour: A Cultural Study* (Cambridge: Cambridge University Press, 2001)

J. Long, 'Portable Pets: Live and Apparently Live Animals in Fashion, 1880–1925', *Costume*, 43, (2009), pp. 109–126.

C. Lupton, The Knowing Book: Authors, It-Narratives, and Objectification in the Eighteenth Century', *NOVEL: A Forum on Fiction*, 39(3), (2006), pp. 402–420.

D. Lutz, 'The Dead Still Among Us: Victorian Secular Relics, Hair Jewelry, and Death Culture', *Victorian Literature and Culture*, 39, (2011), pp. 127–142.

D. Lutz, *The Brontë Cabinet: Three Lives in Nine Objects* (New York and London: W. W. Norton and Co., 2015)

D. Lutz, *Relics of Death in Victorian Literature and Culture* (Cambridge: Cambridge University Press, 2015)

J. M. MacLachlan, '"As if I Had Wings To Fly: The Victorian "Cult of Feminine Beauty" Through the Lens of Julia Margaret Cameron's Pre-Raphaelite Camera', Master of Arts Thesis, Department of English, University of Alberta, 1999. National Library of Canada. Available at: https://nlc-bnc.ca/obj/s4/f2/dsk2/ftp03/MQ46987.pdf [accessed 15 July 2021]

R. Mahawatte, 'Hair and Fashioned Femininity in Two Nineteenth-Century Novels', in G. Biddle-Perry and S. Cheang (eds.) *Hair: Styling, Culture and Fashion* (Oxford: Berg, 2008), pp. 193–203.

S. Marcus, 'Reflections on Victorian Fashion Plates', *Differences: a Journal in Feminist Studies,* 14(3), (2003), pp. 4–33.

M. W. Marien, *Photography: A Cultural History* (London: Laurence King Publishing, 2006)

G. Marshall, *Actresses on the Victorian Stage: Feminine Performance and the Galatea Myth* (Cambridge: Cambridge University Press, 1998)

C. T. Matthews, 'Form and Deformity: the Trouble with Victorian Pockets', *Victorian Studies*, 52(4), (2010), pp. 561–590.

A. McClintock, *Imperial Leather: Race, Gender and Sexuality in the Colonial Contest* (New York: Routledge, 1995)

A. McEwan, 'The antimacassar in fact and fiction: how textual resources reveal a domestic textile', in M. Hayward and E. Kramer (eds.), *Textiles and Text: Re-establishing the Links between Archival and Object-based Research: Postprints* [AHRC Research Centre for Textile Conservation and Textile Studies: Third Annual Conference 11–13 July 2006], (London: Archetype Publications, 2007), pp. 164–172.

J. Miller, 'Fiction, Fashion and the Victorian Seal Fur Hunt' in K. L. Edwards, D. Ryan, and J. Spencer (eds.), *Reading Literary Animals: Medieval to Modern* (London: Routledge: 2019), pp. 212–226.

L. Miskin, 'The Victorian "Cameo Craze": Cameos, Femininity, and the Fashioning of Britain's Imperial Identity', *Victorian Review,* 42(1), (Spring 2016), pp. 167–184.

R. N. Mitchell, 'Death Becomes Her: On the Progressive Potential of Victorian Mourning', *Victorian Literature and Culture*, 41, (2013), 595–620.

R. N. Mitchell, *Fashioning the Victorians: a Critical Sourcebook* (London: Bloomsbury Visual Arts, 2018)

R. N. Mitchell, 'Victorian Faddishness: The Dolly Varden from Dickens to *Patience*', *Journal of Victorian Culture*, 26(2), 2021, pp. 153–171.

S. Mitchell, *Daily Life in Victorian England* (Westport: Greenwood Press, 1996)

D. L. Moore, *Fashion Through Fashion Plates 1771–1970* (London: Ward Lock, 1971)

L. Nayder, *The Other Dickens: A Life of Catherine Hogarth* (Ithaca and London: Cornell University Press, 2011)

L. Nead, *Victorian Babylon: People, Streets and Images in Nineteenth-Century London* (New Haven and London: Yale University Press, 2000)

C. Nicklas, 'Splendid Hues: Colour, Dyes, Everyday Science and Women's Fashion, 1840–1875'. Doctoral thesis, University of Brighton, (2009). Available at: https://cris.

brighton.ac.uk/ws/portalfiles/portal/318269/C+Nicklas+Thesis+Final.pdf [accessed 13 July 2021]

J. Nunn, *Fashion in Costume 1200–2000*, 2nd edition (London: Herbert Press, 2000 [first published in 1984])

G. Ofek, *Representations of Hair in Victorian Literature and Culture* (Farnham, Surrey, and Burlington, VT: 2009)

B. Palmer, *Women's Authorship and Editorship in Victorian Culture: Sensational Strategies* (Oxford: Oxford University Press, 2011)

C. Palmer, 'Colour, Chemistry and Corsets: Mary Philadelphia Merrifield's *Dress as a Fine Art*', *Costume*, 47(1), (2013), pp. 3–27.

A. Pert, *Red Cactus: The Life of Anna Kingsford* (Watsons Bay NSW, Australia: Books & Writers Network, 2007)

J. Phegley, *Courtship and Marriage in Victorian England* (Santa Barbara, California; Denver, Colorado; and Oxford, England: Praeger [an imprint of ABC-CLIO, LLC, 2012])

M. Pointon, 'Materializing Mourning: Hair, Jewellery and the Body', in M. Kwint, C. Breward and J. Aynsley (eds.), *Material Memories* (Oxford: Berg, 1999), pp. 39–57.

M. Pointon, 'Wearing Memory: Mourning, Jewellery and the Body', in G. Ecker (ed.), *Trauer Trager – Trauer Zeigen: Inszenierungen der Geschlecter* (Munich: Fink, 1999), pp. 65–81.

R. Poliquin, *The Breathless Zoo: Taxidermy and the Cultures of Longing* (University Park, Pennsylvania: The Pennsylvania State University Press, 2012)

L. de Propris and L. Lazzeretti, 'Measuring the Decline of a Marshallian Industrial District: The Birmingham Jewellery Quarter', *Regional Studies*, 43(09), (2009), pp. 1135–1154.

Public Health England, *Hydrogen Chloride/Hydrochloric Acid: Incident Management*. August 2019 [first published June 2016; full document updated August 2019]. Available at: https://assets.publishing.service.gov.uk/government/uploads/system/uploads/attachment_data/file/825230/Hydrogen_Chloride_incident_management_PHE_2019.pdf [accessed 15 July 2021]

P. Pulham, *The Sculptural Body in Victorian Literature and Culture: Encrypted Sexualities* (Edinburgh: Edinburgh University Press, 2020)

T. Puri, 'Fabricating Intimacy: Reading the Dressing Room in Victorian Literature', *Victorian Literature and Culture*, 41, (2013), pp. 503–525.

L. Pykett, *The 'Improper' Feminine: The Women's Sensation Novel and the New Woman Writing* (London and New York: Routledge, 1992)

H. Rappaport, *Queen Victoria: A Biographical Companion* (Santa Barbara, California; Denver, Colorado; and Oxford: ABC-CLIO, 2003)

E. Richards, *Darwin and the Making of Sexual Selection* (Chicago and London: The University of Chicago Press, 2017)

D. Roberts, 'The Paterfamilias of the Victorian Governing Classes' in A. S. Wohl (ed.), *The Victorian Family: Structures and Stresses* (London and New York: Routledge, 2016 [first published in 1978 by Croom Helm]), pp. 59–81.

T. Sakai, 'The "Dolly Varden" Polonaise at the Seaside: A Fashion Revival in the early 1870s', *The Dickensian*, 114(506), (Winter 2018), pp. 252– 256.

T. Schaffer, *Novel Craft: Victorian Domestic Handicraft and Nineteenth-Century Fiction* (Oxford: Oxford University Press, 2011)

C. Schmitt, 'Victorian Beetlemania', in D. D. Morse and M. A. Danahay (eds.), *Victorian Animal Dreams: Representations of Animals in Victorian Literature and Culture* (London and New York: Routledge, 2017 [first published in 2007 by Ashgate Publishing]), pp. 35–51.

V. Sherrow, *Encyclopedia of Hair: A Cultural History* (Westport, Connecticut, and London: Greenwood Press, 2006)

A. B. Shteir, '"Fac-similes of Nature": Victorian Wax Flower Modelling', *Victorian Literature and Culture,* 35, (2007), pp. 649–661.

G. Simmel, 'Adornment', in D. Frisby and M. Featherstone (eds.), *Simmel on Culture: Selected Writings* (London, Thousand Oaks, CA and New Delhi: 1997), pp. 206–210.

C. Sloan, 'Possessing Dresses: Fashion and Female Community in *The Woman in White*', *Victorian Literature and Culture*, (44), (2016), pp. 801–816.

M. Smith, *Literary Realism and the Ekphrastic Tradition* (University Park: The Pennsylvania State University Press, 1995)

K. Staniland, *In Royal Fashion: The Clothes of Princess Charlotte of Wales & Queen Victoria 1796–1901* (London: Museum of London, 1997)

K. Staniland and S. M. Levey, 'Queen Victoria's Wedding Dress and Lace', *Costume*, 17(1), (1983), pp. 1–32.

V. Steele, *Fashion and Eroticism: Ideals of Feminine Beauty from the Victorian Era to the Jazz Age* (New York and Oxford: Oxford University Press, 1985)

V. Steele, *Paris Fashion: A Cultural History* [2nd edition; revised and updated] (Oxford and New York: Berg, 1998)

V. Steele, *The Corset: A Cultural History* (New Haven and London: Yale University Press, 2001)

E. L. Steere, '"I thought you was an evil spirit": The Hidden Villain of *Lady Audley's Secret*', *Women's Writing*, 15(3), (2008), 300–319.

L. Summers, *Bound to Please: A History of the Victorian Corset* (Oxford and New York: Berg, 2001)

L. Talairach-Vielmas, *Moulding the Female Body in Victorian Fairy Tales and Sensation Novels* (London and New York: Routledge, 2016 [First published in 2007 by Ashgate Publishing])

L. Taylor, *Mourning Dress: A Costume and Social History* (Abingdon and New York: Routledge, 2009 [first published in 1983 by George Allen & Unwin Ltd])

K. Tennant, '"Graceful Expression and Useful Purpose": Mid-Victorian Fashionable Femininity'. Doctoral thesis, 2010, Cardiff University.

K. Tennant, 'The Discerning Eye: Viewing the Mid-Victorian "Modern" Woman', in I. Parkins and E. M. Sheehan (eds.) *Cultures of Femininity in Modern Fashion* (Durham, New Hampshire: University of New Hampshire Press, 2011), pp. 103–123.

K. Tennant, 'Female Space, Feminine Grace: Ladies and the Mid-Victorian Railway', in K. Hill (ed.), *Britain and the Narration of Travel in the Nineteenth Century: Texts, Images, Objects* (Farnham: Ashgate, 2016), pp. 53–72.

K. Tennant, '"Buying in Style": sartorial sensibilities and Victorian popular fiction', in J. Hatter and N. Moody (eds.), *Fashion and Material Culture in Victorian Fiction and Periodicals* (Brighton: Edward Everett Root Publishers, 2019), pp. 87–100.

J. Thomas, *Pictorial Victorians: The Inscription of Values in Word and Image* (Athens, OH: Ohio University Press, 2004)

M. Tolini, '"Beetle Abominations" and Birds on Bonnets: Zoological Fantasy in Late-Nineteenth-Century Dress', *Nineteenth-Century Art Worldwide*, 1(1), (Spring 2002). Available at: http://19thc-artworldwide.org/spring02/206-qbeetle-abominationsq-and-birds-on-bonnets-zoological-fantasy-in-late-nineteenth-century-dress [accessed 23 June 2021]

D. Trotter, 'Dickens and Frith', in M. Bills and V. Knight (eds.), in *William Powell Frith: Painting the Victorian Age* (New Haven and London: Yale University Press in association with Guildhall Art Gallery, City of London, and The Mercer Art Gallery, Harrogate Museum and Arts, 2006), pp. 29–39.

M. Turda and M. S. Quine, *Historicizing Race* (London and New York: Bloomsbury Academic, 2017)

A. Turner-Bishop, 'Livesey, Joseph (1794–1884)', in J. S. Blocker Jr., D. M. Fahey, and I. R. Tyrrell (eds.), *Alcohol and Temperance in Modern History: An International Encyclopedia* (Vol. I A-L) (Santa Barbara, California, Denver, Colorado, and Oxford, England, ABC: Clio, 2003), p. 383.

T. Veblen, *The Theory of the Leisure Class: An Economic Study in the Evolution of Institutions* (New York: Macmillan Co., 1899)

Victoria and Albert Museum, 'Fashioned from the animal kingdom' [from *Fashioned from Nature* exhibition, 21 April 2018 – 27 January 2019]. Available at: https://vam.ac.uk/articles/fashioned-from-animals [accessed 23 June 2021]

A. K. Wettlaufer, *In the Mind's Eye: The Visual Impulse in Diderot, Baudelaire and Ruskin* (Amsterdam and New York: Rodopi, 2003)

C. Wilcox, *Bags* (London: V&A Publications, 1999)

S. Wolf (with contributions by S. Lipscomb, D. N. Mancoff, and P. Rose), *Julia Margaret Cameron's Women* (Chicago: The Art Institute of Chicago, and New Haven and London: Yale University Press, 1998)

J. Wosk, *Women and the Machine: Representations from the Spinning Wheel to the Electronic Age* (Baltimore and London: Johns Hopkins University Press, 2001)

D. Wynne, *Women and Personal Property in the Victorian Novel* (Farnham, Surrey, and Burlington, VT: Ashgate, 2010)

S. Yan, 'The Art of Working in Hair: Hair Jewellery and Ornamental Handiwork in Victorian Britain', *The Journal of Modern Craft*, 12(2), (2019), pp. 123–139.

M. Yoshihara, *Embracing the East: White Women and American Orientalism* (Oxford and New York, Oxford University Press, 2003)

L. Young, *Middle Class Culture in the Nineteenth Century: America, Australia and Britain* (Houndmills and New York: Palgrave Macmilan, 2003)

INTRODUCTION TO VOLUME V

Fashionable Things

In Wilkie Collins' *No Name* (1862), a pivotal episode occurs whereby the protagonist, Magdalen Vanstone, 'seat[s] herself at the opposite side of the table, and move[s] the candles so as to obtain a clear and uninterrupted view of her servant's face'.[1] What follows is a shift in the dynamic between lady and servant when the two women discuss dressing up and dressing down. Magdalen, the dispossessed daughter of a country squire, is hatching a plan to regain what should have been her inheritance. The plan has temerity. Magdalen, an accomplished actress in provincial theatricals, asks her servant, Louisa, to teach her the duties of a '[parlour-maid]'.[2]

Her motivation is to enter the house of a distant relative, who has a predilection for pretty, young maids, and search for a will that she believes will enable her to reinstate her and her sister's financial status. In turn, Louisa is shocked at the audacity of the plan, as Magdalen further suggests that she and Louisa exchange positions so that Magdalen will wait on Louisa, whilst Louisa will undertake the role of the lady. Perhaps it is humility, or the sense of the dangers inherent in challenging the established social hierarchy, that makes Louisa tremble at the prospect, knowing that she is 'not a lady' and fearing being 'found out'.[3] Yet, Magdalen's riposte is bold and assertive:

> Shall I tell you what a lady is? A lady is a woman who wears a silk gown, and has a sense of her own importance. I shall put the gown on your back, and the sense in your head. You speak good English – you are naturally quiet, and self-restrained – if you can only conquer your timidity, I have not the least fear of you. There will be time enough, in the new lodging, for you to practise your character, and for me to practise mine. There will be time enough to make some more dresses.[4]

No Name centres around the slipperiness of identity when possessions and names are taken away. Like many sensation novels, *No Name* also negotiates cultural anxieties about the authenticity of identity and the fixity of class, exposing, through Magdalen's brazen assertions, what a lady is 'made of' – primarily, expensive dresses and self-awareness.[5] In Collins' narrative, the dress makes the 'lady' visible, while the use of language and comportment breathe life into the part. Consequently, class becomes

DOI: 10.4324/9781315399980-1

embodied in accoutrements and etiquette. The narrative urges us to conclude that if 'dress' acts as an instantaneous sign of one's social position, then it is a sign that can be easily made manifest – a trope used all too often in sensation fiction. And, as many critics have shown, Victorian fashionable dress could prove a marker of misidentification, but also provide a means to finding comfort and solace. In Collins' earlier novel, *The Woman in White* (1859), for example, the mysterious character Anne Catherick dresses all in white, enabling her to embody an earlier version of herself, dressed thus by the motherly figure Mrs Fairlie, who also donned white garments.[6] Anne's white outfit keeps her past – and those no longer living – literally next to her skin, and through dress, her attachment to Mrs Fairlie becomes visibly evident.

Unable to cover all aspects of Victorian fashionable culture in terms of class, gender, race, ethnicity and age in a single volume, we have deliberately narrowed our scope to the material culture of the middle-class woman. *Fashionable Things* aims to elaborate on Magdalen's definition of a lady by discussing objects that are representative of both 'fashionability' and middle-class taste. With a focus on middle-class fashionable women, who were often the key signifiers of family status and wealth,[7] our sources create narratives around the messages that women endeavoured to convey about themselves and about their lifestyles. How were women of limited or restricted financial means able to follow fashion? How were upper-class tastes understood and appropriated through more affordable objects and items of clothing? What were the appropriate fabrics, accessories and ornaments that 'respectable' ladies should wear, and on what occasions should they wear them? The ideas about fashionability and femininity discussed in our selected sources also forge links with other volumes in the collection, as raw materials were turned into jewellery and underwear, debates surrounding the arts influenced fabrics and styles of dresses (be they manufactured or shop-bought), and advancements in textile dyes widened the palette of dressmakers and milliners.

Our selections convey how ideas about popular crazes became material objects as, for example, an interest in amateur natural history could be commodified into the form of a domestic bird-cage or an aquarium, leisure time was 'realised' in beadwork, and beauty ideals were achieved through technological devices such as the corset and the crinolette.

Our sources also reveal how empire and colonialism were important contexts for a discussion of fashionable artefacts and ideas of beauty, for example, as notions of race primitivism are considered in relation to modern jewellery in some of our selected material,[8] and critiques of women's tiny boots are flippantly discussed using the language of race essentialism.[9] Indeed, our selected extracts include vocabulary, expressions and attitudes in relation to gender, nationality, race and ethnicity that, while reflective of certain Victorian attitudes, are highly troubling, inappropriate, unacceptable and offensive to a modern readership. Some of the widely-known sources are placed alongside more obscure Victorian material to demonstrate the complexity and versatility of Victorian fashionability. But while the volume draws upon important work by critics who have focused on particular items of clothing and ornaments, it is not an examination of the history of Victorian fashion theory and culture, nor does it intend to make a comprehensive survey of Victorian middle-class costume.[10] *Fashionable Things* dialogues with Rebecca N. Mitchell's illuminating critical sourcebook *Fashioning the Victorians* (2018), which includes selections on the corset, the crinoline, Victorian weddings and mourning dress. Mitchell's volume also plots developments in dress alongside cultural, political and social ideas, whilst ours has a sharp focus on the materiality of fashionability and on the ways that both cultural and social ideas infused objects.[11] The four sections that make up our collection, 'Embodying Fashionability'; 'Dressing Up'; 'Animal and Insect Accessories; Home Decoration'; and 'Handicraft' can be described as object-focused vignettes exploring the porosity of boundaries between women's bodies and their fashionable accoutrements; between animals and accessories; and between self and handcrafted object. Our sections examine a range of sources that discuss objects for enhancing or concealing one's physical characteristics, including dresses worn to celebrate marital unions; the 'garbs of woe' that acknowledged great losses; alongside adornments such as taxidermied hats and jewellery. The final section turns to the domestic artefacts produced by women as tangible examples of female craftsmanship as a form of leisure activity.

Yet fashion was often perceived as incompatible with traditional ideals of womanhood, and as the nineteenth century progressed, the relationship between fashionability and femininity became increasingly uneasy.[12] Many texts warn against too intense an interest in modish clothing, drawing attention to the widening gulf between fashionability and 'feminine' values. In this way, a paradox emerged, with a contradictory, self-referential logic. Although dress was central to constructions of identity, women were, conversely, discouraged from too overt or marked an interest in sartorial matters. And while commentators often maintained that the material culture of clothing possessed little intrinsic value or meaning, it was used to construct a model of modest womanhood and social respectability.

In this way, women were engaged in a continual balancing act: while on the one hand they should be wary of succumbing to clothing's supposedly trivial lure, on the other, huge importance was placed upon getting the details right. As Tara Puri writes, clothing could prove to be a social danger as well as a pleasure; female dress was not merely seen as 'a frivolous pursuit but had been transformed into a serious occupation, for the wrong shade of colour or texture of fabric could end in a social mishap'.[13] The implication here is that dress is not something to be enjoyed for its own sake, but rather, to be studied in order for a woman to present herself appropriately to the world, and to evade accusations of 'vulgarity'. For this reason, in our first section we include a number of sources that engage with these debates, including Mrs Merrifield's 'How Far Should the Fashions be Followed?', Caroline Stephen's 'Thoughtfulness in Dress' and Emily Pfeiffer's 'The Tyranny of Fashion'.

Our sources show that it was not necessarily improper to be fashionable but, rather, to be *ridiculous*. The fear of ridicule is present in much Victorian dress discourse, and accordingly, our selections within this volume acknowledge the fickle yet ever-present 'anxious struggle[s]'[14] presented by dress. They also capture some of the sprawling, contradictory questions about how readers negotiated their sartorial decisions while resisting ever-changing fashion trends. The tension between fashionability, conspicuousness, indifference and adherence underscores much writing and thinking about dress during this period. While in one sense, modishness represented an unwholesome drift towards frivolity, in another, it signified social standing. Many writers on fashion were therefore concerned with inadvertently tipping from stylishness into absurdity.

'Fashionability', as Meaghan Clarke observes, 'in its most expansive sense encompassed the presentation and interpretation of fashion through diverse cultural forms'.[15] Such forms are present in this volume through selections derived from etiquette manuals, advice columns, fashion plates, advertisements, engravings, photographic portraits, drawings, popular fiction, music sheets, and catalogues. The dissemination of information about fashionable clothes, ornaments and even hobbies were often conveyed through fashion periodicals. Many women's magazines, for example, included illustrations of dresses and accessories through fashion plates and engravings. The fashion plate was a crucial method through which ideas about fashion were circulated during the nineteenth century, and became increasingly significant in shaping notions of Victorian womanhood.[16] Through its form, which usually combined an engraving with a portion of descriptive text, it presented a visual image of fashionable femininity to a rapidly widening readership.[17] A lady's maid, for example, might peruse fashion periodicals and, in some cases, perhaps even wear her employer's handed-down outfits.[18] In this way, the illustrations of fashionable clothes and accessories enabled women to participate in a shared visual culture of dress, even though lower-class women did not typically have the means to purchase the items pictured.

Fashion plates first appeared in eighteenth-century periodicals such as *The Lady's Magazine* (1770–1834) and Nicolaus von Heideloff's *Gallery of Fashion*, which ran between 1794 and 1803.[19] As Valerie Steele details, fashion plates were created from a watercolour sketch, which was turned into a black-and-white print by an engraver.[20] Colour was then included by painters (usually women), with '[e]ach worker', as Steele notes, '[applying] solid blocks of colour without tonal variation'.[21] Once complete, the finished illustration was included in the periodical, often at the very beginning of the issue, where it might be physically divorced from the written text that described it. This format was highly successful and was adopted by numerous successors throughout the nineteenth century, most notably the French *Le Follet*, which was founded in 1846 (and was also available in English translation), the 1858–1895 *Ladies' Treasury*, and Samuel and Isabella Beeton's mid-century enterprise, *The Englishwoman's Domestic Magazine* –[22] all three of which are represented within this volume.

Our selections are drawn from a range of sources, and are designed to give a sense of the breadth and variety of contemporary perspectives and debates surrounding fashionability. Unsurprisingly, many female-orientated texts were concerned with both fashion and domestic issues, such as *The Englishwoman's Domestic Magazine*, *The Ladies' Treasury*, *The Lady's Newspaper* and *Le Follet*. Alongside these, we draw upon magazines aimed at a unisex readership such as *London Society*, *Bow Bells*, *Belgravia* and *The Cornhill Magazine*, as well as upon magazines aimed specifically at older children or young women, such as *The Girl's Own Paper*. Readers uncertain of sartorial practicalities might turn to didactic writings in the form of so-called guidebooks, conduct books and etiquette manuals. Popular from the 1830s, these works advised on correct and proper dress during a period of gradually increasing social freedom and class mobility.[23] In contrast, we also incorporate opinion pieces that speak to a more entrenched view of traditional femininity that appeared in periodicals including *The Cornhill Magazine*, more tongue-in-cheek articles from *Chambers's Journal,* and overtly satirical pieces from periodicals such as *Punch*, its aptly named competitor *Judy*, and *Fun*, which provide a biting commentary on contemporary modes and behaviours, and sometimes blatantly communicate misogyny. Literary sources, particularly those drawn from periodicals and sensation fiction, are included as powerful indicators of the figurative uses of fashionable dress and ornament.[24]

Our selections are not strictly divided by material or theoretical focus. This distinction is discussed by Roland Barthes in *The Fashion System* (1967), and is a key concept explored by Julia Thomas in relation to Victorian visual culture.[25] In *The Fashion System*, Barthes identifies three different types of garment as depicted in fashion journalism. Two of these can be represented on paper: the 'image' garment, which he describes as 'the one presented to [the reader] as photographed or drawn',[26] and the 'written' garment, which constitutes the accompanying text. Finally, there is the 'real' garment or 'the actual dress they both refer to'.[27] Despite the differences between the written and image garments, Barthes emphasises that they 'refer to the same reality' in the form of the real garment, which, he claims, allows them to 'recover a single identity'.[28] Its logic imposes a linear trajectory upon the process of representation, whereby the real garment must be produced *before* the image garment, in order to create the photograph.

But for the majority of Victorian fashion images, there was no photographic representation of the 'image' garment. While photography was used from the 1850s to produce fashionable portraits (as included in our volume) and images such as the *carte-de-visite*,[29] photographic images did not generally appear in fashion magazines until the early twentieth century. Rather, the fashion plate was the preferred method of modish illustration throughout the nineteenth century. This meant that while there was usually a 'written' and an 'image' garment in the form of the fashion plate and its accompanying text, the real garment did not exist in the Barthesian sense, as Victorian fashion illustrators did not necessarily have any contact with the garments that they were commissioned to depict. In addition, fashion plates were frequently removed from periodicals, perhaps by readers wishing to retain the image or, alternatively, by dressmakers, who might display the latest fashion plates in their shops, even recreating the look presented in the image using fabric from their own stock of material.[30] Not only does this process challenge the Barthesian categories, but it also suggests the potential for multiple meanings, as the fashionable image is separated from its original context. If modified according to the purchaser's own preference, the fashion plate also highlights a woman's own ability to dress herself in the latest fashions according to her own taste and budget. Thus, while some of our sources replicate material objects in written and visual forms, others constitute imaginative constructions of the objects they present. Many of the objects represented in fashion plates, therefore, have only ever been held in the mind's eye.

While our series focuses on material 'things', the selections included in this volume enable us to enter into an imaginary rendering of emotional responses of subjects to objects, and to illustrate the kinds of 'psychic' and 'cultural work' performed by sartorial details that might otherwise seem a 'superfluous' addition to clothing.[31] In this fashion engraving from *The Ladies' Treasury* from around the late 1870s (Figure 1),[32] an elegant lady is pictured in *medias res*, putting on a glove as she prepares to go out. As we explore in our section on Mourning attire, illustrations of mourning and 'half-mourning' wear frequently appeared in women's magazines, and presented readers with fashionable representations of recently-bereaved middle-class Victorian ladies. This woman wears 'half-mourning', indicating that some period between the present and the time of the physical bereavement has

Figure 1 "HALF MOURNING DRESS."

elapsed. The image invites the reader to observe her whilst she looks at herself in the mirror, a replication of gazes that is presented by the mirror on the dressing-table. The contemporary reader/viewer would have pored over these images and their descriptions in order to fashion herself according to the latest modes, but also to consider the display of her own emotions at times of loss, calibrated according to the most recent etiquette books. In this way, women were obliged to consider the loss of loved ones through the lens of the practicalities of how to dress, and what was considered acceptable in mourning wear. The details, and even the trimmings of these dresses, might also be interpreted as containing or framing the mourner within the world that continues to exist after a private loss.[33]

Our selections, then, enable us to explore the reverie that a Victorian woman might experience while viewing fashionable images. Some of our sources feature photographs of actual objects, while others are photographic portraits of women in fashionable wedding dresses or mourning wear. However, we also include a wide variety of written sources on fashionable dress and adornments, laden with detailed descriptions of fabrics, patterns, pleats and fringes. While this might seem an unexpected choice in a volume so engaged with the immediate tactility of clothes, adornments or handcrafted objects, we, alongside the other volumes' editors, wish to convey as vividly as possible the power of words made into 'things' – through the trope of ekphrasis.

Ekphrasis, from the Greek for to 'speak out', is a slippery term. It has a long and varied history, originally used as a rhetorical construct applying to many kinds of vivid description.[34] Ekphrasis is characterized by an energising impulse to transfer mental images as accurately and vividly as possible to the mind of the reader, and is rhetorically known as 'enargeia'. Enargeia provides the drive to create the object; to make it speak for itself, and captures some of the 'weight' and tangibility of dress and ornaments that fill this volume, momentarily suspended between states of materiality and reverie. With the ekphrastic potential of these sources in mind, we wished to show our readers how material culture might be realised through printed words on the page, and how women's consumption of ekphrastic fashionability created for them an interiority, a reverie filled with things. To this effect, fashionable women were not only publicly visible but also, as in a form of heautoscopy, dressed themselves in ekphrastic clothing for their own enjoyment and imaginative pleasure. Drawing on Sharon Marcus' work on fashion plates and the homoerotics of the female gaze, we might suppose that the female reader not only 'saw the image of a woman who like herself was looking at a fashionable woman',[35] but took pleasure from reading descriptions of fashionable clothes and their wearers, and relished immersing herself in words that might provoke feelings of joy and delight.

In relation to the 'lives' of things, Deborah Lutz confesses, 'as much as I favor the idea of inanimate things having lives concealed from us, I still feel that an object's meaning – its slumbering life – comes from our own desires and passions, the shadows we let play over it'.[36] In this way, the material culture of fashionability was enlivened by the desires, aspirations and reveries of the women who consumed it. Indeed, the journalist and dress reformer Mrs Mary Eliza Haweis, whose 1878 work *The Art of Beauty* is represented in our selections, writes that '[d]ress is the second self, a dumb self, yet a most eloquent expositor of the person'.[37] And, at the opening of the twentieth century, the cultural critic Georg Simmel made a comparable point on fine jewellery when he proposed that, '[t]he radiations of adornment, the sensuous attention it provokes, supply the personality, so to speak, with such an enlargement or intensification of its sphere: the personality, *is* more when it is adorned'.[38] Lutz, Haweis and Simmel suggest that 'things' and their owners are never truly severed of their connections – particularly when it comes to fashionable things – but rather, they symbiotically co-create each other.

Some of our sources also emphasise the porosity of boundaries between non-human animals and human beings that is evident in contemporary debates about fashionable clothes and adornment. They illustrate how, alongside aesthetically transforming women, there was an element of 'playfulness', whereby animal and woman would merge through fashionable objects. Indeed, as critics have noted, it seems no coincidence that these ideas emerged in the wake of Charles Darwin's 1859 *On the Origin of Species* and his 1871 *The Descent of Man*.[39] One way in which this was manifest, as Susan David Bernstein and Evelleen Richards argue, was through the imaginative blurring of women and birds, particularly within *Punch*'s cartoons. These present an extreme, and arguably disturbing, satire of the contemporary fashion for feathers and other animal accoutrements, most dramatically realised in the cartoonist Edward Linley Sambourne's 'Designs After Nature' series, which appeared in *Punch* in the late 1860s and 1870s. Some of these are ostensibly light-hearted, such as 'As Birds' Feathers and Train Dresses are all the go' (Figure 2),[40] published on 21 December 1867. This makes a humorous commentary on the foolishness of female fashion by featuring a young woman, 'Miss Swellington', confidently parading through a fashionable park adorned, as its caption notes, in an ensemble that conflates the contemporary fashions for 'Birds, Feathers and Train Dresses'. The woman glides along, attracting the attention of a languid young man of the 'Swell' type.[41] The image initially serves to draw attention to gender difference, the man looking, while the woman is figured as an object of display.[42]

Yet the scene is not as simple as it may initially appear. Bernstein notes that the woman is adorned in feathers specific to the *male* peacock,[43] reading her as a 'gender-blurring' figure,[44] an interpretation that is further reinforced by her name, which clearly recalls the male 'Swell' stereotype. Such cartoons of women dressed in the latest fashions prefigure, reflect and visually parody Darwin's theories on sexual selection, published in *The Descent of Man*. In this work, Darwin proposes that the ornamental beauty of 'males display[ing] their attractions with elaborate care in the presence of females' is part of the 'sexual struggle' for the most appropriate mate, but in the human, fashionable, world, this ritual is reversed.[45]

Figure 2 "AS BIRDS' FEATHERS AND TRAIN DRESSES ARE ALL THE GO, MISS SWELLINGTON ADOPTS ONE OF NATURE'S OWN DESIGNS."

The image also hints at physical conflations between humans and non-human animals in its depiction of the woman's clothing, as the the back portion and train of her skirt are revisioned so as to resemble birds' wings and a (male) peacock's tail. Other cartoons, however, were more overt in their suggestions. One image, entitled 'Mr. Punch's Designs After Nature',[46] published, as Richards notes, 'just a few weeks' after Darwin's *The Descent of Man*,[47] depicts a young and modish woman 'viewed from behind',[48] affording a view of 'the whole peacock she wears on her head'[49] and her hair, which '[blends] with her long, loose tresses'.[50] Another illustration, published the previous year, in 1870, and entitled 'I Would I Were A Bird', pictures a rather determined-looking young woman striding along a pier, fully decked out in black-and-white feathers.[51] While the image does not indicate any troubling merging of animal and human, what it does suggest is her rather inexplicable ambition for an avian transformation.

Ideas about the relationship between humans and non-human animals continue to circulate in the later part of the nineteenth century across a wide range of cultural production. The manipulative character Madame Merle, in Henry James' *The Portrait of a Lady* (1882), suggests a merging between selfhood and things, drawing on the image of a 'shell' to create a very modern theory of identity:

> [E]very human being has his shell and [. . .] you must take the shell into account. By the shell I mean the whole envelope of circumstances. There's no such thing as an isolated man or woman; we're each of us made up of some cluster of appurtenances. What shall we call our 'self'? Where does it begin? where does it end? It overflows into everything that belongs to us – and then it flows back again. I know a large part of myself is in the clothes I choose to wear. I've a great respect for *things*! One's self – for other people – is one's expression of one's self; and one's house, one's furniture, one's garments, the books one reads, the company one keeps – these things are all expressive.[52]

Madame Merle's exposition conveys an understanding of the self as a kind of 'composite object' comprised not just of material parts, but of intentions and acts. To this end, the objects discussed in this volume do not represent *the* 'middle-class' fashionable lady, but the middle-class lady as a 'composite object' herself.

Notes

1 W. Collins, *No Name*, ed. with an Introduction and Notes by Mark Ford (London: Penguin Classics, 1994) p. 499.
2 Collins, *No Name*, p. 503.
3 Collins, *No Name*, p. 503.
4 Collins, *No Name*, p. 503.
5 See K. Tennant, 'The Discerning Eye: Viewing the Mid-Victorian "Modern" Woman', in I. Parkins and E. M. Sheehan (eds.), *Cultures of Femininity in Modern Fashion* (Durham, NH: University of New Hampshire Press, 2011), pp. 103–123 (pp. 117–118) for consideration of the perceived distinction between 'lady' and maid. See also L. Nead, *Victorian Babylon: People, Streets and Images in Nineteenth-Century London* (New Haven and London: Yale University Press, 2000), pp. 62–64, for further fascinating exploration of the confusions that might arise between so-called 'respectable' women (p. 64) and prostitutes within the urban environment. Here we might refer to the concept of the 'Girl of the Period' trope, coined by the journalist Mrs Eliza Lynn Linton during the late 1860s, which we discuss in the Headnotes to our sections on Context and Cosmetics. See also L. Nead, *Victorian Babylon*, pp. 66, 75–76, for discussion of Mrs Linton in this context.
6 Casey Sloan makes a similar point, arguing that 'Anne's emphatic rejection of socially acceptable garb in favor of a dress rich with interpersonal meaning further emphasizes the text's attempt to form communities of women that transcend economic separation. Like Laura's choice of dress, Anne's also symbolically undermines class hierarchies in order to construct a community based on friendship and shared experience.' See C. Sloan, 'Possessing Dresses: Fashion and Female Community in *The Woman in White*', *Victorian Literature and Culture*, (44), (2016), pp. 801–816, (p. 811). For further discussion of the significance of dress within the novel, see C. Hughes, *Dressed in Fiction* (Oxford and New York: Berg, 2006), Chapter 5: 'The Woman in White and the

Woman in Colour: Wilkie Collins's *Woman in White* and Mary Braddon's *Lady Audley's Secret*', pp. 70–88.

7 For a theorization of women as a visible marker of economic prosperity and status, see T. Veblen, *The Theory of the Leisure Class: An Economic Study in the Evolution of Institutions* (New York: Macmillan Co., 1899). Although this text focuses mainly upon the affluent classes, it also demonstrates how the impulses of conspicuous consumption pervade both middle-class womanhood and middle-class aspirations. For further consideration of Veblen's work within the context of dress, see R. N. Mitchell, *Fashioning the Victorians: a Critical Sourcebook* (London: Bloomsbury Visual Arts, 2018), p. 28. Mitchell's anthology also includes Veblen's previous article 'The Economic Theory of Woman's Dress', published in *Popular Science Monthly* of 1894 (see *Fashioning the Victorians*, pp. 53–59). See also M. Carter, Chapter 3: 'Thorstein Veblen's Leisure Class', in *Fashion Classics from Carlyle to Barthes* (Oxford and New York: Berg, 2003), pp. 41–58, and L. Young, *Middle Class Culture in the Nineteenth Century: America, Australia and Britain* (Houndmills and New York: Palgrave Macmillan, 2003), p. 160. Additionally, while some of our selections, such as Sylvia's *How To Dress Well On A Shilling a Day* (an extract from which is included in our section on Mourning attire), attempt to set financial definitions for their readers, we have not been prescriptive in our definition of the middle-class woman. Rather, in our volume we focus upon the Victorian ideology of the middle classes as a social aspiration. For further discussion of Victorian female readerships, see M. Beetham, *A Magazine of Her Own? Domesticity and Desire in the Woman's Magazine, 1800–1914* (London and New York: Routledge, 1996); M. Beetham and K. Boardman, *Victorian Women's Magazines*: An Anthology (Manchester and New York: Manchester University Press, 2001), and of class, see L. Davidoff and C. Hall, *Family Fortunes: Men and Women of the English Middle Class, 1780–1850* (London and New York: Routledge, 1997 [first published in 1987 by Hutchinson Education]); and Y. C. Draznin, *Victorian London's Middle-Class Housewife: What She Did All Day* (Westport, Connecticut, and London: Greenwood, 2001).

8 See, for example, S. Daly, *The Empire Inside: Indian Commodities in Victorian Domestic Novels* (Ann Arbor, MI: The University of Michigan Press, 2011). In this study, Daly explores the significance of the unmounted diamond in Wilkie Collins' novel *The Moonstone*, reading it as a trope for conveying the means by which foreign treasures become domestic jewellery. See Chapter 3: 'Plunder as Property: Diamonds', pp. 61–83.

9 For a comprehensive understanding of how 'race' is created through cultural and scientific discourses, see M. Turda and M. S. Quine, *Historicizing Race* (London and New York: Bloomsbury Academic, 2018). Although not explicitly dealing with fashionable dress, this study is helpful in evaluating and understanding Victorian writings on fashion and references to racial hierarchies. For a nuanced analysis of the intersections between race, gender and class, particularly in relation to commodity fetishism and material culture, see A. McClintock, *Imperial Leather: Race, Gender and Sexuality in the Colonial Contest* (New York: Routledge, 1995). Examining the production and consumption of material culture in the late nineteenth and early twentieth centuries, McClintock showcases ways in which advertising was creating a culture of imperialism, even within the domestic space, and her analysis can be incisive when thinking about the sources reproduced here. For a discussion of how the dressed body was used to convey ethnic identity, see S. Cheang, 'Ethnicity', in D. A. Baxter (ed.), *A Cultural History of Dress and Fashion in the Age of Empire* (London and Oxford: Bloomsbury, 2017), pp. 141–164.

10 The volume draws upon and extends the work of critics, including S. Amato, *Beastly Possessions: Animals in Victorian Consumer Culture* (Toronto: University of Toronto Press, 2015); J. Arnold, *Victorian Jewelry, Identity, and the Novel: Prisms of Culture* (Farnham, Surrey and Burlington, VT, 2011); A. Beaujot, *Victorian Fashion Accessories* (London and New York: Berg, 2012); Beetham, *A Magazine of Her Own?*;

C. Breward, *The Culture of Fashion: A New History of Fashionable Dress* (Manchester and New York: Manchester University Press, 1995); A. A. Cheng, 'Ornamentalism: A Feminist Theory for the Yellow Woman', *Critical Enquiry*, 44(3), (Spring 2018), pp. 415–446; J. Flanders, *The Victorian House: Domestic Life from Childbirth to Deathbed* (London: HarperCollins, 2003); A. Gernsheim, *Victorian and Edwardian Fashion: A Photographic Survey* (New York: Dover, 1981); S. Granata, 'The Dark Side of the Tank: The Marine Aquarium in the Victorian Home', in H. Kingstone and K. Lister (eds.), *Paraphernalia! Victorian Objects* (New York and Abingdon: Routledge/Taylor & Francis, 2018), pp. 81–98; P. Jalland, *Death in the Victorian Family* (Oxford: Oxford University Press, 1996); J. R. Harpley, 'Glittering Baubles: An Examination of Chatelaines in Britain, 1839–1900', *The Journal of Dress History,* 4(3), (Autumn 2020), pp. 45–71; L. Johnston (with M. Kite and H. Persson), *Nineteenth-Century Fashion in Detail* (London: V&A Publications, 2005); C. B. Kortsch, *Dress Culture in Late Victorian Women's Fiction* (London and New York: Routledge, 2016 [originally published by Ashgate Publishing in 2009]); D. Kunzle, *Fashion and Fetishism: Corsets, Tight-Lacing & Other Forms of Body-Sculpture* (Stroud: Sutton Publishing, 2004), pp. 100–101; J. Laver, *Costume and Fashion: A Concise History*, 4th edition, with a concluding chapter by A. de la Haye and A. Tucker (London: Thames & Hudson World of Art, 2002); T. Logan, *The Victorian Parlour: A Cultural Study* (Cambridge: Cambridge University Press, 2001); J. Long, 'Portable Pets: Live and Apparently Live Animals in Fashion, 1880–1925', *Costume*, 43, (2009), pp. 109–126; D. Lutz, *Relics of Death in Victorian Literature and Culture* (Cambridge: Cambridge University Press, 2015); S. Marcus, 'Reflections on Victorian Fashion Plates', *Differences: a Journal in Feminist Studies,* 14(3), (2003), pp. 4–33; R. N. Mitchell, *Fashioning the Victorians*; D. L. Moore, *Fashion Through Fashion Plates 1771–1970* (London: Ward Lock, 1971); G. Ofek, *Representations of Hair in Victorian Literature and Culture* (Farnham, Surrey, and Burlington, VT: Ashgate, 2009); J. Phegley, *Courtship and Marriage in Victorian England* (Santa Barbara, CA, Denver, CO, and Oxford, England: Praeger [an imprint of ABC-CLIO, LLC], 2012); R. Poliquin, *The Breathless Zoo: Taxidermy and the Cultures of Longing* (University Park, PA: The Pennsylvania State University Press, 2012); V. Steele, *Fashion and Eroticism: Ideals of Feminine Beauty from the Victorian Era to the Jazz Age* (New York and Oxford: Oxford University Press, 1985); V. Steele, *The Corset: A Cultural History* (New Haven and London: Yale University Press, 2001); L. Taylor, *Mourning Dress: A Costume and Social History* (Abingdon and New York: Routledge, 2009 [originally published in 1983 by George Allen & Unwin Ltd.]); J. Thomas, *Pictorial Victorians: The Inscription of Values in Word and Image* (Athens, OH: Ohio University Press, 2004); M. Tolini, '"Beetle Abominations" and Birds on Bonnets: Zoological Fantasy in Late-Nineteenth-Century Dress', *Nineteenth-Century Art Worldwide*, 1(1), (Spring 2002), available at: http://19thc-artworldwide.org/spring02/206-qbeetle-abominationsq-and-birds-on-bonnets-zoological-fantasy-in-late-nineteenth-century-dress [accessed 23 June 2021]; and J. Wosk, *Women and the Machine: Representations from the Spinning Wheel to the Electronic Age* (Baltimore and London: Johns Hopkins University Press, 2001).

11 Also relevant is Beetham and Boardman, *Victorian Women's Magazines*, in relation to Victorian print culture.

12 The reactionary early-Victorian commentator Mrs. Ellis, for example, identified fashion as a potentially corrupting influence, writing in 1842 that '[t]he young girl cannot too scrupulously shroud her modest feelings from [its] unsparing test'. Rather, she suggests that 'the highest standard at which a right-minded woman can aim with regard to dress, is, that it should be becoming, and not conspicuous' (p. 128). Mrs. [Sarah Stickney] Ellis, *The Daughters of England, their Position in Society, Character and Responsibilities* (1842; New York: D. Appleton & Co. and Philadelphia: George S. Appleton, 1843), p. 128. See K. Tennant, '"Graceful Expression and Useful Purpose" : Mid-Victorian Fashionable Femininity' (Doctoral Thesis, 2010, Cardiff University), p. 26,

and Tennant, 'The Discerning Eye', which considers the perceived threat of 'modernity' as manifest in female fashion, conduct and deportment. In this chapter, Tennant considers the disjunction between supposedly '"old" and "new" modes of [Victorian] femininity', exploring the links with dress (p. 107).

13 See T. Puri, 'Fabricating Intimacy: Reading the Dressing Room in Victorian Literature', *Victorian Literature and Culture*, 41, (2013), pp. 503–525 (p. 503).

14 [C. Stephen], 'Thoughtfulness in Dress', *The Cornhill Magazine*, September 1868, pp. 281–298 (p. 281).

15 M. Clarke, *Fashionability, Exhibition, Culture and Gender Politics: Fair Women* (London: Routledge, 2020), p. xii. This observation derives from Clarke's exploration of the 1894 portrait exhibition entitled *Fair Women*, held at London's Grafton Galleries. Described by Clarke as 'the Victorian equivalent of a contemporary blockbuster' (p. ix), Clarke's study focuses on fashion, modernity and gender politics. Her definition of 'fashionability' within the culture of female collectors also aptly describes our understanding of the term, which we borrow here for our volume.

16 For further details, see Tennant, '"Graceful Expression and Useful Purpose"', which deals explicitly with the fashion plate (see Introduction, specifically pp. 35–37).

17 For further discussion of the readerships of nineteenth-century women's magazines, see Beetham, *A Magazine of Her Own?*. With specific reference to *The Englishwoman's Domestic Magazine,* Beetham points out that, while the periodical adhered to the traditional notion that 'a woman should dress appropriately to her situation and income (p. 78), somewhat paradoxically, the magazine simultaneously opened up the 'exclusive and elite' world of fashion to 'as wide a readership as possible' (p. 76). See also C. Breward, *The Culture of Fashion*, p. 152 (cited in Tennant, '"Buying in Style" : sartorial sensibilities and Victorian popular fiction', in J. Hatter and N. Moody (eds.), *Fashion and Material Culture in Victorian Fiction and Periodicals* (Brighton: Edward Everett Root Publishers, 2019), pp. 87–100, p. 90). In addition, Simon Eliot suggests that middle-class periodicals seem to have been purchased and perused by upper-working-class women. He writes that nineteenth-century magazines were 'specialized' in identifying and assimilating their readers' needs and preferences, wryly noting that 'a magazine that targets the upper and upper middle classes will not be read exclusively by such a clientele' but also made provision for the 'socially aspiring' element of its readership. See S. Eliot, 'Books and their Readers – Part 1', in D. Walder (ed.), *The Nineteenth-Century Novel: Identities* (London: Routledge, 2001), pp. 157–188 (p. 161).

18 However, while there were clearly social distinctions between a lady and her maid, this role required a high level of knowledge of fashion and the visual appearance of fashionability. This is discussed in Tennant, 'The Discerning Eye', pp. 117–118. For further consideration of the role of the lady's-maid (including the practice of receiving 'her mistress's cast-off clothes', see S. Mitchell, *Daily Life in Victorian England* (Westport: Greenwood Press, 1996), pp. 54–55 (p. 54); K. Hughes, *The Victorian Governess* (London and New York: Hambledon and London, 2001 [1993])), p. 95); and J. Burnett (ed.), *Useful Toil: Autobiographies of Working People from the 1820s to the 1920s* (Abingdon and New York: Routledge, 1994 [first published in 1974 by Allen Lane/Penguin Books]), p. 145. For a fictional example, the maid Phœbe in M. E. Braddon's *Lady Audley's Secret* marries in a gown donated by her mistress; see Tennant, '"Buying in Style"' for a brief mention of this episode (p. 91).

19 For further discussion of eighteenth-century ladies' periodicals, see A. Adburgham, *Women in Print: Writing Women and Women's Magazines From the Restoration to the Accession of Victoria* (London: George Allen and Unwin, 1972), pp. 204–217.

20 V. Steele, *Paris Fashion: A Cultural History* [2nd edition; revised and updated] (Oxford and New York: Berg, 1998), p. 112.

21 Steele, *Paris Fashion*, p. 112.

22 For further discussion of these periodicals, see Beetham, *A Magazine of Her Own?*, pp. 59–88. The married couple Samuel and Isabella Beeton were prolific publishers and

editors of periodicals and books, notably *The Englishwoman's Domestic Magazine*, and perhaps most famously, the domestic manual *Mrs. Beeton's Book of Household Management* (1861). As Tennant details, *The Englishwoman's Domestic Magazine* featured the writer known as 'The Silkworm', the pseudonym of Matilda Browne, who later founded *Myra's Journal*, selections from which are included within this volume. See Tennant, '"Buying in Style", p. 99. As noted within this piece, see also Beetham, *A Magazine of Her Own?*, pp. 79–81, and B. Palmer, *Women's Authorship and Editorship in Victorian Culture: Sensational Strategies* (Oxford: Oxford University Press, 2011), p. 34.

23 For further discussion of these texts, see E. Langland, *Nobody's Angels: Middle-Class Women and Domestic Ideology in Victorian Culture* (Ithaca, NY, and London: Cornell University Press, 1995), pp. 25–28, and Davidoff and Hall, *Family Fortunes*, p. 156. While they were often overtly gendered, with some aimed at men, Langland nonetheless argues that, in general, 'these texts focus upon women rather than men' (*Nobody's Angels*, p. 25).

24 For an illuminating consideration of the significance of fashion within a literary sense, see Hughes, *Dressed in Fiction*. Tennant also explores this overall area within '"Graceful Expression and Useful Purpose"'.

25 R. Barthes, *The Fashion System*, trans. by Matthew Ward and Richard Howard (Berkeley and Los Angeles: University of California Press, 1990). For further details, see Tennant, '"Graceful Expression and Useful Purpose"', pp. 46–48. See also Thomas, *Pictorial Victorians*, p. 79.

26 Barthes, *The Fashion System*, p. 3.

27 Barthes, *The Fashion System*, p. 4.

28 Barthes, *The Fashion System*, pp. 3, 4.

29 The *carte-de-visite* was a small, head-and-shoulders or full-length portrait photograph, usually taken in a studio. The name, however, is misleading: they are different from calling cards, which were engraved with the holder's name and exchanged and distributed as part of Victorian middle- and upper-class social life. For further discussion of the *carte-de-visite*, see M. W. Marien, *Photography: A Cultural History* (London: Laurence King Publishing, 2006), pp. 84–85, and Mitchell, *Daily Life in Victorian England*, pp. 150–151, for an account of the conventions associated with the calling card.

30 In *Hand Coloured Fashion Plates*, Vyvyan Holland notes that, as early as the 1770s, dressmakers adapted or customized fashion plates 'to give a better idea of the appearance of the dresses'. V. Holland, *Hand Coloured Fashion Plates 1770–1899* (London: B. T. Batsford, 1988), p. 48.

31 See E. Freedgood, 'FRINGE.', *Victorian Literature and Culture*, 30(1), (2002), pp. 257–263 (pp. 259, 262, 258). In this article, Freedgood contends that in the Victorian period, fringes and 'trimming performed symbolic work for a culture whose anxieties seemed to gather at edges – of clothing, of furniture, of nations, of empires, and eventually, of selves' (p. 257).

32 [Anon], 'Half Mourning Dress', *The Ladies' Treasury*, [c. late 1870s], p. 706.

33 See E. Freedgood, 'FRINGE.'

34 For a history of the term, definitions and analysis see M. Smith, *Literary Realism and the Ekphrastic Tradition* (University Park, PA: The Pennsylvania State University Press, 1995). See also A. Braida and G. Pieri, 'Introduction', in A. Braida and G. Pieri (eds.), *Image and Word: Reflections of Art and Literature from the Middle Ages to the Present* (Oxford: European Humanities Research Centre of the University of Oxford, in conjunction with the Modern Humanities Research Association, 2003), pp. 1–14 (p. 11). Here Braida and Pieri reference J. Heffernan, 'Ekphrasis and representation', *New Literary History*, 22, (1991), pp. 297–316 (p. 304). See also A. K. Wettlaufer, *In the Mind's Eye: The Visual Impulse in Diderot, Baudelaire and Ruskin* (Amsterdam and New York: Rodopi, 2003), pp. 57–58.

35 S. Marcus, 'Reflections on Victorian Fashion Plates', p. 15.

36 D. Lutz, *The Brontë Cabinet: Three Lives in Nine Objects* (New York and London: W. W. Norton and Co., 2015), p. 13.
37 Mrs H. R. [Mary Eliza] Haweis, *The Art of Beauty* (New York: Harper & Brothers, 1878), p. 11. Also quoted in Gernsheim, *Victorian and Edwardian Photographs*, p. 66, and V. Steele, *Fashion and Eroticism*, p. 132. For further discussion of Haweis, see Gernsheim, pp. 66–67. An extract from Haweis' later work *The Art of Dress* (1879) is also reproduced, along with invaluable discussion, in Mitchell, *Fashioning the Victorians*, pp. 63–66 (discussion of Haweis) and pp. 71–76 (extract from *The Art of Dress*). See also Tennant, 'The Discerning Eye', p. 106), for a brief discussion of this issue, and Steele, *Fashion and Eroticism*, for further consideration of the notion of Victorian dress as 'an "index of the mind" and "character" of the wearer' (p. 132).
38 G. Simmel, 'Adornment', in D. Frisby and M. Featherstone (eds.), *Simmel on Culture: Selected Writings* (London, Thousand Oaks, CA, and New Delhi: SAGE Publications, 1997), pp. 206–210 (p. 207). See also Carter, *Fashion Classics*, Chapter 4: 'Georg Simmel: Clothes and Fashion', pp. 59–81, for further consideration of Simmel's writings on fashion.
39 C. Darwin, *The Descent of Man, and Selection In Relation to Sex*, 2 vols. (London: John Murray, 1888 [Second Edition, Revised and Augmented]). See E. Richards, *Darwin and the Making of Sexual Selection* (Chicago and London: The University of Chicago Press, 2017), Chapter 8: 'Flirting with Fashion', pp. 221–257, and S. D. Bernstein, 'Designs after Nature: Evolutionary Fashions, Animals, and Gender', in D. D. Morse and M. A. Danahay (eds.), *Victorian Animal Dreams: Representations of Animals in Victorian Literature and Culture* (London and New York: Routledge, 2017 [first published in 2007 by Ashgate Publishing]), pp. 65–79. Bernstein's essay also discusses our *Cornhill Magazine* selection, 'Thoughtfulness in Dress', attributing the article to Caroline Stephen (p. 68).
40 [L. Sambourne], 'As Birds' Feathers and Train Dresses are all the go, Miss Swellington adopts one of Nature's Own Designs', *Punch*, 21 December 1867, p. 256. Also reproduced in Morse and Danahay, *Victorian Animal Dreams* [listed as Figure 6].
41 Bernstein describes this figure as 'a young swell ogling a woman' ('Designs after Nature', p. 65).
42 See also Tennant, 'The Discerning Eye', for further consideration of the fashionable cultural phenomenon of 'seeing and being seen' within this type of context (pp. 113–115).
43 Bernstein, 'Designs after Nature', p. 65.
44 Bernstein, 'Designs after Nature', p. 69.
45 Darwin, *The Descent of Man*, Vol. II, pp. 435, 433.
46 [L. Sambourne], 'Mr. Punch's Designs After Nature', *Punch*, 1 April 1871, p. 127. Reproduced in Richards, *Darwin and the Making of Sexual Selection*, p. 249, and in Morse and Danahay, *Victorian Animal Dreams* [listed as Figure 8].
47 Richards, *Darwin and the Making of Sexual Selection*, p. 248.
48 Richards, *Darwin and the Making of Sexual Selection*, p. 248.
49 Richards, *Darwin and the Making of Sexual Selection*, p. 248.
50 Richards, *Darwin and the Making of Sexual Selection*, p. 248.
51 [L. Sambourne], '"I Would I Were A Bird –"', *Punch*, 23 April 1870, p. 167. This image is also reproduced and briefly discussed in Richards, *Darwin and the Making of Sexual Selection*, p. 247.
52 H. James, *The Portrait of a Lady*, ed. with an Introduction by Geoffrey Moore and Notes by Patricia Crick (London: Penguin, 2003 [Penguin Classics]), p. 253. For further discussion of this episode, see R. Aindow, *Dress and Identity in British Literary Culture, 1870–1914* (Farnham, Surrey, and Burlington, VT: Ashgate, 2010), p. 9.

PART 1

Embodying Fashionability

1.1

Context

DOI: 10.4324/9781315399980-3

1.1 Context

The Victorian female experience was inextricably linked with that of clothing, but, as we outline in our Introduction, this often proved a tricky relationship. While too marked an interest in fashion was often seen to represent a damaging character weakness, dress was also interpreted as a 'reflection' of the character and social status of the wearer, and frequently became the subject of close scrutiny, commentary and criticism.

These ideas are conveyed within our selections for this volume, which demonstrate how the materiality of dress was 'translated' into social concerns. They capture tensions that ran through Victorian dress discourse and, in some cases, that still resonate in modern fashion media. This is certainly the case for our first selection. Enigmatically titled 'A Complaint' and written by a woman whose acronym, H. R. H., echoes royalty, this letter appeared in *The Lady's Newspaper* of January 1847. It raises a very modern problem: H. R. H. writes to the magazine's editor that its fashionable images feature only 'elegant' women 'on whom dresses cannot choose but look well'.[1] Claiming that her own 'dumpy' form does not reflect these body shapes, she owns that she feels 'constantly mortified' that there is 'nothing to suit [*her*]'. The magazine's editor gives an equally modern response. Disregarding the woman's candid self-deprecation, they urge that she 'wrongs herself cruelly', and furthermore, that with a little effort, she might modify the styles so as to flatter her own figure. In this way, the female body is figured in itself as artefact, functioning as a symbol of material disappointment, and failing to concord with the ideals represented by both fashionable clothing and images – themselves realised in material form.

Our next extract is an article by the 'multi-skilled Victorian intellectual' Mrs Mary Philadelphia Merrifield,[2] who, as Caroline Palmer writes, 'exploited her considerable knowledge of art and science in order to validate the study of fashion and to raise it in seriousness as a topic'.[3] Entitled 'How Far Should the Fashions Be Followed?' and published in *The Lady's Newspaper* around eight years later in 1855, this article advises readers on how to navigate the balance between the perceived social need to follow the general direction of contemporary fashion, while adapting this to the particulars of the wearer's own body.

This is followed by a column from *The Ladies' Treasury* of June 1857. Named 'Conduct and Carriage', this formed part of a series that presented the reader with a set of 'Rules to Guide a Young Lady in Points of Etiquette and Good Breeding in her Intercourse with the World'. Written in the form of scripted dialogues between an idealised mother and daughter, the columns focus upon the young Geraldine Vernon's navigation of London 'Society', fashionability, courtship, bereavement and, in a subsequent series, motherhood.[4] What is interesting about this article is that, like Mrs Merrifield two years earlier, it advised cautious adherence to the prevailing modes: Mrs. Vernon urges the young Geraldine to '[b]e always in the fashion, but never in the extreme of the fashion', emphasising that '[s]ingularity in dress is always to be avoided'.[5] Nonetheless, however 'odious' or 'ridiculous' her daughter might consider the fashions,[6] she is instructed to obediently follow the example set by ladies of her own social status. Our next selection, entitled 'Thoughtfulness in Dress' and attributed to Caroline Stephen, continues to treat the 'problem' of how to dress the female body.[7] While the approach verges into the philosophical and the more abstract nature of beauty, the advice is nonetheless rooted in materiality. Readers are advised, for example, to be mindful of the moral necessity to avoid 'sham or deceptive imitation' and even cautioned to avoid supposedly 'unnatural' fashions, such as wearing artificial flowers out of season.[8] Wider issues of class and social status are also raised, whereby female dress should not only reflect 'the social position which one actually holds rather than the next above it', but also maintain consistency if one should come into contact with others of varying status.[9]

Our next source, which appeared in the lively periodical *London Society* of 1869, addresses an apparently pressing and ubiquitous matter, namely, 'A Lady's Question: What Shall We Wear?'. Posed from a specifically gendered perspective, this article addresses issues of class, economy and taste, acknowledging the stereotype that Englishwomen supposedly dressed in a less stylish manner than their French counterparts.[10] Here the article light-heartedly pinpoints a central conundrum of Victorian fashion, as the social pressure for economy results in 'an inferior arrangement "made to do"', and the embarrassment of knowing that the wearer 'is not *well* dressed after all'.[11] But the article also touches upon a growing contemporary fear that was expounded in Mrs Linton's much-cited 'Girl of the Period' article of March 1868, namely, that a woman might be mistaken for being 'fast', a term used to denote a woman whose dress, appearance and deportment was troublingly forthright, forward and direct.[12]

With these fears in mind, it is hardly surprising that our next selection, 'The Tyranny of Fashion', appeared in *The Cornhill Magazine* around ten years later. Attributed to Emily Pfeiffer, this piece details the social dangers of those women seemingly trapped by 'the fantastic dance of fashion'.[13] Noting that men had already felt 'relief' from its 'foolish oppression',[14] the writer laments the social expectations exerted upon women, linking these directly with the technical requirements of contemporary dressmaking. Referring to the close fit of the garments of the late 1870s, which had moved far from the expansive crinolines of twenty years earlier, the writer points out that,

> [t]he manufacture of the simplest-looking modern gown, closely sheathing two-thirds of the body [. . .] has become an affair demanding not only an inordinate degree of skill in the fitter, but a ruinous amount of time, patience and money on the part of the person fitted.[15]

From here, Pfeiffer passionately likens the female form to that of an inanimate plaything, 'bound and trussed until it looked as dead as a wooden doll',[16] allowing herself to speculate about a world in which simpler, more comfortable and less costly garments were both available and socially accepted.

We then move to a more overt and detailed treatise, an extract from the author Mrs Haweis' 1878 *The Art of Beauty*. In this text, Haweis proclaims the importance of dress when articulating identity, asserting the importance of individualism when presenting dress as an art form. While much of the work focuses upon such areas as colour, detail, form and proportion of dress, this extract is concerned with its wider ideology. To this end, Haweis addresses the concern raised by the *London Society* writer about the supposed lack of sartorial discernment demonstrated by Englishwomen, who apparently preferred to defer to their milliner rather to rely upon their own judgement. Haweis also poses a bold and deceptively radical question: '[w]hy is one's individuality, so clear within, to be so confused without?'[17]

Our final extract, taken from *The Rational Dress Society's Gazette*, is derived from a publication specifically geared towards dress reform.[18] Taking up concerns previously raised by Haweis, this editorial unambiguously opposed garments that it perceives as threatening to health, or those which undermined either movement or the body's natural form. To this effect, fashionable items like the crinoline and crinolette, narrow, tiny boots, heavy clothing and stiff corsets – the very materials of a fashionable lady – are deemed cumbersome, 'ugly and deforming'.[19]

Notes

1 H. R. H., 'A Complaint', *The Lady's Newspaper*, 9 January 1847, p. 26.

2 C. Palmer, 'Colour, Chemistry and Corsets: Mary Philadelphia Merrifield's *Dress as a Fine Art*', *Costume*, 47(1), 2013, pp. 3–27 (p. 4).

3 Palmer, abstract to 'Colour, Chemistry and Corsets', p. 3.

4 See K. Tennant, 'Female Space, Feminine Grace: Ladies and the Mid-Victorian Railway', in K. Hill (ed.), *Britain and the Narration of Travel in the Nineteenth Century: Texts, Images, Objects* (Farnham: Ashgate, 2016), pp. 53–72 (p. 58), for further consideration of this series. In this chapter, a different instalment is discussed from that which we include in this volume, namely, that published in August 1857. It is also worth noting that there was some inconsistency within the 'Conduct and Carriage' series in other installments; while in our selection on Mourning attire, the series' young protagonist is named Gertrude, elsewhere she is called Geraldine.

5 [Anon], 'Conduct and Carriage; Or, Rules to Guide a Young Lady on Points of Etiquette and Good Breeding in her Intercourse with the World', *The Ladies' Treasury*, June 1857, pp. 119–120 (p. 120).

6 [Anon], 'Conduct and Carriage', p. 120.

7 [C. Stephen], 'Thoughtfulness in Dress', *The Cornhill Magazine*, September 1868, pp. 281–298. The article is attributed to Stephen by sources including S. D. Bernstein, 'Designs after Nature: Evolutionary Fashions, Animals, and Gender', in D. D. Morse and M. A. Danahay (eds.), *Victorian Animal Dreams: Representations of Animals in Victorian Literature and Culture* (London and New York: Routledge, 2017 [first published in 2007 by Ashgate Publishing]), pp. 65–79 (p. 68).

8 [Stephen], 'Thoughtfulness in Dress', pp. 287, 292.
9 [Stephen], 'Thoughtfulness in Dress', p. 290.
10 For a brief consideration of 'the much-revered style' of French ladies, see K. Tennant, '"Buying in Style": sartorial sensibilities and Victorian popular fiction', in J. Hatter and N. Moody (eds.), *Fashion and Material Culture in Victorian Fiction and Periodicals* (Brighton: Edward Everett Root Publishers, 2019), pp. 87–100 (p. 90).
11 [Anon], 'A Lady's Question: What Shall We Wear?', *London Society*, May 1869, pp. 410–414 (p. 412).
12 [Anon], [Mrs Eliza Lynn Linton], 'The Girl of the Period', *The Saturday Review*, 14 March 1868, pp. 339–340 (p. 340). This article is introduced and reproduced in Mitchell, pp. 65–70. Linton's article is discussed in K. Tennant, 'The Discerning Eye: Viewing the Mid-Victorian "Modern" Woman', in I. Parkins and E. M. Sheehan (eds.), *Cultures of Femininity in Modern Fashion* (Durham, NH: University of New Hampshire Press, 2011), pp. 103–123 (p. 107); this chapter also addresses the concept of 'fastness', pp. 106–111. Tennant also very briefly addresses 'fastness' in 'Female Space, Feminine Grace', p. 59. For further discussion of Linton and 'The Girl of the Period', see H. Fraser, S. Green, and J. Johnston, *Gender and the Victorian Periodical* (Cambridge: Cambridge University Press, 2003), pp. 21–26, as well as V. Steele, *Fashion and Eroticism: Ideals of Feminine Beauty from the Victorian Era to the Jazz Age* (New York and Oxford: Oxford University Press), pp. 128–130.
13 E. P. [Emily Pfeiffer], 'The Tyranny of Fashion', *The Cornhill Magazine*, July 1878, pp. 83–94. As Rosy Aindow notes, the article is generally agreed to have been authored by Pfeiffer. See R. Aindow, *Dress and Identity in British Literary Culture, 1870–1914* (Farnham, Surrey, and Burlington, VT: Ashgate, 2010), p. 57.
14 [Pfeiffer], 'The Tyranny of Fashion', p. 83.
15 [Pfeiffer], 'The Tyranny of Fashion', p. 84.
16 [Pfeiffer], 'The Tyranny of Fashion', p. 85.
17 Haweis, Mrs. H. R. [Mary Eliza], 'Importance of Dress', in *The Art of Beauty* (New York: Harper & Brothers, Publishers, 1878), p. 16.
18 Mitchell's anthology includes an illuminating section on dress reform; see R. N. Mitchell, *Fashioning the Victorians: a Critical Sourcebook* (London: Bloomsbury Visual Arts, 2018), pp. 61–64, as well as for an article by Florence Pomeroy, who was President of the Rational Dress Society (pp. 77–83).
19 [Anon], Statement and 'Editorial Note', *The Rational Dress Society's Gazette*, January 1889, p. 1. Also included within this extract is an 'Editorial Note' that refers to Miss [Lydia] Becker, advocate for women's suffrage and editor of the *Women's Suffrage Journal*. Yet, as Christine Bayles Kortsch notes, Becker 'took a conservative stance on dress', opposing the abolition of the corset, directing women to 'stick to [their] stays' [corsets] and, as our extract details, only advising against tight-lacing. See C. B. Kortsch, *Dress Culture in Late Victorian Women's Fiction* (London and New York: Routledge, 2016 [originally published by Ashgate Publishing in 2009]), p. 91. See also V. Steele, *The Corset: A Cultural History* (New Haven and London: Yale University Press, 2001), p. 59.

1

H. R. H., 'A COMPLAINT.'

The Lady's Newspaper, 9 January 1847, p. 26

TO THE EDITOR OF THE LADY'S NEWSPAPER.

"Sir, – A point to which I would call your attention is this: – In nearly all books of fashion, the ladies are represented as tall elegant figures, on whom dresses cannot choose but look well. Now, I belong to the "dumpy" class, and am constantly mortified at finding nothing to suit *me*. Again, my hair is not of the graceful, redundant and flowing character, so prettily described in your pages; I have lost much during severe illness, but as it is growing again, and as I[]want yet three years of thirty, I am unwilling to begin to wear caps, but I should like to see a *neat, ladylike, morning head dress*, equally opposed to the formal seoigné, and the tawdry compound of laces, ribbon, and bugles, with which our shop windows are ornamented. May I hope to find in your paper a satisfactory reply to these queries?

"Your's [*sic*] obediently,
"H. R. H."

***

We beg to assure our fair correspondent that in the art of dressing well, one of the most important points is the just adaptation of the style and make of the dress to the person of the wearer. We more than suspect – nay, we are quite convinced that H. R. H. wrongs herself cruelly in her use of the epithet "dumpy." We are willing to believe that she may, perhaps, be somewhat *petite* in stature, and a little inclined to *embon point;* and if so, there is no reason why the prevailing fashions, with appropriate modification, may not be worn as gracefully by her as by ladies of tall and slender figure. For example, if *five* flounces are prescribed by the bulletins of fashion, we would recommend H. R. H. to confine herself to *four,* or if she must have five, let them all be a little narrower than those worn by her tall friends. The same rule of proportion is applicable to every article of female costume; but the neglect of it is, we grieve to say, a sin of frequent occurrence. A tasteful and judicious adaptation

DOI: 10.4324/9781315399980-4

of the *general* fashion to the person of the *individual* wearer gives to the Parisian ladies that air of grace and gentility for which they are so justly admired. "H. R. H." shall very soon see a morning cap which we have no doubt will please her. – ED.

2

MRS MERRIFIELD, 'HOW FAR SHOULD THE FASHIONS BE FOLLOWED?'

The Lady's Newspaper, 7 July 1855, p. 12

The subject proposed for present consideration is, how far it is advisable to follow the fashions. The golden rule on this point is generally admitted to be, that no lady who wishes to avoid singularity, should adopt a fashion until it becomes more singular not to adopt it than to follow it. It is always safer to follow than to lead a fashion; indeed, as the changes of fashion are generally in extremes, it requires frequently great personal attractions to reconcile us to a new mode. Any change of costume excites attention; and this attention is unavoidably transferred from the dress to the wearer, whose beauties or defects are thus brought prominently into notice. The same thing occurs when a person persists in wearing a mode which has become obsolete. The old-fashioned body is quite as remarkable, though in a different way, as the lady who sets the fashion. On the one we are too apt to look with astonishment or admiration, on the other with contempt or ridicule.

Our golden rule is, however, too general to be adopted by every one without some modification. Although it must be the aim of every lady who wishes to be well-dressed, to follow, to a certain extent, the costume generally worn, yet it must always be with a proper consideration for her own stature and proportions, age, rank in life, and complexion; and especially for health and decorum. The same costume which may become the tall, slight girl of eighteen, will be probably quite unsuited to a short, stout woman of fifty; and the colours which are becoming to the fair, must be inappropriate to the florid or the brunette neither is a carriage-costume adapted to the humble pedestrian. Propriety must be studied before fashion. We must study not merely the form of a garment, or the style of a trimming, but also whether the one or the other is suited to our own particular person. Every lady should make herself acquainted with the norma[l] proportions and beauties of the female figure, which she should compare with her own individual proportions, features, and complexion. She should then, as far as she can consistently with propriety, select such a style of dress as will display her person to the greatest advantage. This will answer the double purpose of setting off any beauties she may happen to possess, while it will draw the attention of the spectator

DOI: 10.4324/9781315399980-5

from the consideration of her defects. In common parlance, a style of dress which accomplishes these objects, is said to be "becoming." We admire the beauties of the lady, while her less favourable points are judiciously kept in the background.

In order to avoid being misunderstood, the reader is requested to bear in mind that the great principle in dress is to develop beauties by appropriate treatment of costume and decoration, not to conceal any defects which may unfortunately be found on our persons. Whatever is false or artificial is as reprehensible in dress as in morals. Pearl powder and rouge, false and dyed hair, are falsehoods addressed to the eye instead of the ear; and, like other untruths, seldom escape detection and contempt. In spite of the skill with which they are employed, their artificiality is betrayed by their utter want of harmony with the surrounding parts. I have heard of a lady who, from mere caprice, and without any intention to deceive, used frequently to change the colour of her hair. Sometimes she would appear with flaxen curls, and perhaps the following week would surprise her acquaintance by her luxuriant ringlets of glossy black; then, tired of this sable hue, she would resume her own brown locks; so that the colour of her hair was as variable as the weather. This, perhaps, is an extreme case, yet there was a time when flaxen hair was all the rage in London, and was adopted by fashionable ladies without any reference to their complexion, or to the known colour of their own hair.

Scarcely less absurd than this is the present fashion of wearing small bonnets at the back of the head. It is unnecessary to allude to the chances of getting rheumatism in the head from the unusual exposure of the upper part of it to the vicissitudes of the weather. Sufficient reasons for repudiating this mode are to be found in the acknowledged fact that it is extremely unbecoming to most people. Custom has, in some degree, reconciled us to it; still, the introduction is so recent, that we can all remember how these small bonnets were laughed at when they were first worn – resting, not on the head, but on the nape of the neck, or, as *Punch* says, "running to waste (waist)." Let us devote a few lines to consider in what respects this fashion is deserving of the ridicule which has been thrown upon it. In the first place, the use of a bonnet is admitted to be to protect the head from the weather, and to screen the face from the sun. Now the fashionable bonnet cannot be said to do either, for it neither covers the head, nor shades the face. In the next place, where the crown of the bonnet is thrown so low behind, it makes the wearer appear short-necked; this fact, we are sure, cannot have escaped observation. A short neck, all our readers must be aware, is considered almost as a deformity, and quite incompatible with grace and elegance. Viewed in front, perhaps the only point in which a lady sees her own face in a bonnet, there is no objection to the fashion as far as concerns the form of the brim; but this circumstance is calculated rather to mislead, and to withdraw attention from the ungracefulness of the lines which form the profile, especially where the lady has a well-developed forehead. Every artist knows how much beauty depends upon the form and direction of the lines of which a figure is composed. It is admitted that lines should be long, flowing, and undulating. Now, let any unprejudiced person sketch in profile a lady's head in a fashionable bonnet, and fill the outline with ink; in this case, there cannot, I think, be two opinions as to the ungracefulness of the outline. The only way to ascertain whether a fashion is really becoming or not, is to strip it of adventitious ornaments and trimmings, to reduce it to a simple outline, and then to observe whether the lines formed by the drapery with the figure are graceful. If these satisfy the eye of taste, and there is nothing in the fashion which militates against propriety, decorum, and health, the fashion may be safely adopted, otherwise, it should be resolutely discountenanced by all women of sense.

3

[ANON], 'CONDUCT AND CARRIAGE; OR, RULES TO GUIDE A YOUNG LADY ON POINTS OF ETIQUETTE AND GOOD BREEDING IN HER INTERCOURSE WITH THE WORLD.'

The Ladies' Treasury [June 1857], pp. 119–120

[In order to make the following hints agreeable and amusing, as well as instructive and improving, it has been deemed advisable to convey them in the popular form of a dialogue between a mother and daughter.]

Scene. – *A Drawing room at the Elms, near Windsor. – Time, evening. –* Mrs. Vernon *embroidering a collar,* Miss Vernon, *a pretty girl of eighteen, reading to her*.

Mrs. V. Put down your book, Geraldine. It has struck nine, and as you leave me at eight to-morrow morning, all I have to say to you I must say to-night.

Geraldine, *putting down the book, drawing an ottoman to her mother's arm-chair, sinking down upon it, and taking Mrs. Vernon's hand in both her own.*

Ger. Oh, mamma! as the time draws near, I wish you had not accepted my aunt's invitation for me. I am terrified when I think of the morning visits I shall have to pay and to receive, the dinner parties and balls at which I must appear; and that without you, dearest and best of mothers, to turn to, to consult, I shall not know what to wear, what to say, what to do, how to act. Even in this dear, quiet home, I have never done anything without your sanction and counsel; and now I am to go alone into the wide, wide world to think for myself, act for myself, speak for myself, and, I fear, make myself very ridiculous and my aunt very angry.

Mrs. V. (*embracing her*) Geraldine, I should have ill fulfilled my duty as your mother – your sole surviving parent, alas! – were you, indeed, so ignorant how to conduct yourself in society as your present natural timidity makes you fancy you are. But I am certain you will find yourself, when

DOI: 10.4324/9781315399980-6

introduced and called upon to play your part in the great drama of life, quite equal to the occasion. Every thorough-bred, well-informed woman does. It is only the ill-informed, half-bred, and vulgar that are really awkward in society. But a little timidity and reserve, at eighteen, is not unbecoming either in the daughter of a countess or a curate.

Ger. No, mamma, I dare say not; but there are so many little things I do not know, and when I have not you to ask, I shall be so puzzled what to decide, and shall be almost sure to decide wrong. Now though dear papa was a quiet country clergyman, and "remote from towns he led his godly life," you were a baronet's daughter, and saw a great deal of the *beau monde* in your youth; and have kept up some intercourse with it all your life, indeed, till quite lately. You can tell me all I want to know; only it is as the occasions arise that I shall be at such a loss for your directions, mamma.

Mrs. V. You can write to me daily, my love! Indeed, I hope you will; and I ask you, too, conscientiously to keep a diary of events, thoughts, feelings, and a short account of your every outlay, small and great. But I dare say I can give you a few general rules and hints now. And though fashion, on minute points of manners, customs, and etiquette, is almost as fickle as it is in those of taste and dress; yet, with the habits you have (in common with all ladies) already acquired, and with the instinct, courtesy, and innate grace of a young English gentlewoman, you cannot go far wrong. Now, what puzzles you at this moment?

Ger. Well, mamma, I will tell you. If I see any gentleman in the park whom I have sat by at dinner, or dined with the night before, am I to bow to him, or to wait for him to recognise me?

Mrs. V. The lady must bow first. The Queen and the Princesses of the blood royal are the only ladies to whom a gentleman pays the homage of raising his hat without the sanction of a bend or a bow.

Ger. And what about shaking hands, mamma?

Mrs. V. In that you must be guided by circumstances and feelings. As a general rule, a young lady should not be too ready to give her hand – to members of the unfair sex especially. Her doing so may be misconstrued; particularly by the vain, young, middle-aged, and even old coxcombs who frequent balls, dinner-parties, concerts, public places, and, above all, the park and gardens. Such men fancy every lady is either smitten with them or trying to smite, and any unwonted cordiality or approach to an advance is sure to be misconstrued, and, perhaps, ridiculed in that sarcastic, sneering spirit which is the bane of English society. But if I would have you, my Geraldine, beware of giving your hand too readily to those, I would warn you still more earnestly against refusing it ungraciously, or granting it coldly and with insolent nonchalance, as some young ladies do, to any friends of your aunt's or our own, – any sensible, steady, superior men, older and wiser than yourself, who, in shaking hands with a young girl, mean kindly to encourage you to confide in them, would be ineffably disgusted and estranged were they not met with a graceful and cordial deference and sympathy.

Ger. I think I know what you mean, mamma; and on that point (and it has puzzled me much) I feel now quite at my ease. If I meet young Hanton at a ball, I shall not shake hands with him, even if he deigns to remember me and our pleasant pic-nic in Windsor Forest; but if I should see dear Mr. Allgood or Dr. Fathom, I shall shake hands cordially with them, for they cannot misconstrue my doing so.

Mrs. V. Again, about gloves. I would not have you extravagant, but the best gloves are the cheapest in the end; and a soiled glove, or one with a hole or a palpable repair, is quite inadmissible where you are paying a visit or frequenting a public place. However, your aunt tells me the great expense of your cousin's gloves, white ones especially, is much diminished by a plan they have adopted of having them cleaned. There are places, it seems, where, for twopence a pair, they are cleaned so as to look like new, and free from the offensive smell which used to distinguish this process. When you are in Harley-street you can inquire about this. In the meantime I have provided you, dearest, with a good stock of the best French kid gloves, white and coloured, and a few pairs of fancy mittens for *demie toilette.*

Ger. Thank you, kind, dear mamma. But should I wear white kid gloves at dinner? – a grand dinner, I mean.

Mrs. V. Certainly not, nor should you ever take your gloves off at church or in public places. I was distressed to see you last Sunday untie your bonnet strings and take off your gloves in church.

Ger. It was so hot, mamma.

Mrs. V. No matter, my love. Unless actually in fear of fainting – which, as it alarms, gives trouble, and has other evil consequences, you must avoid at all events, if possible – you should never interfere with your dress, put on or take off anything, when once you are completely dressed. Some ladies have a habit of smoothing their hair, settling their brooches or bracelets, putting a scarf or cloak, gloves or mittens off or on; that is all bad. It arises either from vanity or *mauvaise honte,* both equally incompatible with perfect elegance of mind and manners. Once drest as carefully, neatly, and becomingly as your taste and your means allow, try to forget all about it. Never endeavour to catch a glimpse of yourself in the pier-glasses or mirrors that abound in those temples of vanity, modern drawing-rooms. But do not pointedly avoid your own reflection, if brought suddenly in contact with it; that would be affected and prudish. Pay no compliments to other ladies on their looks or toilets. It is a common artifice to direct attention to your own charms and attire. Be always in the fashion, but never in the extreme of the fashion.

Ger. And must I, then, adopt the odious hooped petticoats and crinolines so caricatured in *Punch,* and in which our neighbours, the Greens, look so ridiculous?

Mrs. V. If you find them generally worn by ladies of your own rank in life, you must adopt them. Singularity in dress is always to be avoided. If hoops are worn (odious as I abstractedly think such monstrous devices), the loveliest creature in the world would, in general society, look a dowdy without them.

Ger. And what about my hair, mamma? My cousins, you know, wear theirs *à l'Eugénie,* strained off their faces; and they say no other way is really stylish.

Mrs. V. I do not agree to that. It is bold, masculine, and, to most faces, very disfiguring. Your beautiful, glossy, and abundant hair, braided simply as you wear it now, will not be *outré* even in London, for the Queen still wears hers in that style, and the Queen can do no wrong!

Ger. You know, mamma, I have several loves of aprons; may I wear them when we have morning visitors calling at my aunt's?

Mrs. V. No, dearest! they would have too jaunty an air; they would make you look like a waiting-maid in a play. An apron is out of place as an ornament, and I always think it as silly to embroider an apron as to gild the handle of a broom.

Ger. Another thing, mamma; if I meet lords and ladies of title at my aunt's (and she visits a great many, you know), I don't know how to address them. Should I say, "my lord," and "your lordship" – "my lady," and "your ladyship," at every turn?

Mrs. V. You may just once now and then do so, to show these great people that you are fully aware who and what they are. But to repeat their titles often or obtrusively would be to copy the servility of landlords hoping for their patronage, and tradespeople for their custom. You will find your aunt, my sister, though only the widow of a colonel in the guards, yet so intimate, and so completely at her ease and on an equality with the *élite* of the nobility, that she calls them (as ladies of their own rank do) by their names, such as "Clanricarde," "Aberdeen," "Brougham," "Clarendon," &c. &c.; but, of course, that can only be done by women extremely intimate with them, and of a certain age and position.

Ger. When I go out in the carriage, mamma, where ought I to sit?

Mrs. V. As a rule, a young lady in the presence of her elders should always take the least convenient, comfortable, and desirable place; but if your aunt, or any other lady you are going out with, points out any other place, don't, out of mistaken humility or mock-modesty, dispute the point. I have seen young girls keep a whole party shivering on the door-steps because they would not place themselves at once where their chaperons directed them. Remember, Louis XVIII. said, the best-bred man he had ever met with was Lord Stair, because when Louis XVIII. directed him to precede him, he, without hesitating and drawing back, obeyed at once.

Ger. I am very much obliged to you, dear mamma, and the hints you have given me have made me feel more at my ease; but still I shall not know how to dress for the different parties to which I shall be invited.

Mrs. V. A girl of sense and perception sees at a glance what people of good taste do, and takes them as her guide. As a general rule, young people should not be over-dressed. White muslin – tarlatan, as it is called – is suitable for a small party or a grand ball. Whatever Fashion and your mantua-maker may suggest, let true modesty decide on the cut of your corsage. Whenever you can do so, adopt the pretty lace jacket now in vogue; but when that is inadmissible, as in full dress it may be, remember "the modest tucker" of blonde or lace takes nothing from the grace of your attire, and, to the eye of taste and sentiment, lends it that additional charm "the angel of the flowers" bestowed on the rose, when he threw over its blushing beauties a "veil of moss – – "

Ger. (*in tears*) My own dear mamma! I hope in all things to do right, because I shall ever have present to my mind the thought, "What would my mother like? – what would she approve?"

Mrs. V. I have only a few more general rules to give you, and then you must go at once to bed, my darling. Don't fret at this, our first parting. Three weeks will soon pass, and then I shall come and fetch my child, and hope to find her as pure and more polished than she leaves me now. You have ready wit, repartee, and a dangerous talent for mimicry. Never let your wit betray you into sarcasm, nor your repartee into impertinence. Remember Lord Lyttelton's excellent advice to the woman he loved and wedded:

"Nor make to dangerous wit a vain pretence,
But simply rest content with common sense;
For wit, like wine, intoxicates the brain,
Too strong for feeble woman to sustain.
Of those who claim it, more than half have none,
And half of those who have it are undone."

With regard to mimicry, it is the talent of the ape. Leave it, then, to that "libel upon man."

Ger. Oh, mamma, you little understand my feelings, if you think I, in the terrible ordeal that awaits me, shall be disposed to show off my wit, indulge in repartee, or dream of taking any one off. If I can get on decently myself, and not disgrace my own mamma, I shall be quite content.

Mrs. V. All this awe of the world will vanish when you are behind the scenes. You will then see that the actors wear tinsel, not gold, and "drink large draughts of nothing out of pasteboard goblets." Very, very soon, you will be quite at your ease, quite yourself, – and *osez partout être vous-même* – your better self. Never boast, never flatter; I need not say, never falsify.

Remember there are no white lies; they are all black as their father himself. Be punctual to a moment, in all engagements, small and great – with a marchioness, a music-mistress, or a milliner. Keep "the whiteness of your soul," even in the great black Babel to which I send you with a blessing and a prayer. There is no perfect lady who is not a good Christian. It was a quaint remark of an old divine, that the most finished gentleman that ever appeared on earth was our blessed Saviour. Humility, charity, integrity, dignity, gentleness, and patient self-control – these constitute the Christian character, and that of the true gentleman and lady. – One thing more: be orderly in all your pursuits, and, as far as possible, be still an early riser. In three weeks I shall fetch you from Harley-street to sojourn with your Aunt Burton in St. John's Wood – a true lady, though a brewer's widow. There you will see a new world; but, though small etiquettes may vary, good breeding and its laws are immutable.

4

[CAROLINE STEPHEN], 'THOUGHTFULNESS IN DRESS.'

The Cornhill Magazine, September 1868, pp. 281–298

IT is no doubt easier to find fault than to suggest remedies, and the two processes are generally about equally unpleasant to the person for whose benefit they are intended; but for the sake of variety it is as well to employ them alternately. As we have lately heard so much about the faults of women's dress, I may perhaps be allowed to offer some practical suggestions as to the principles upon which it ought to be regulated. It will at any rate afford me some consolation to embody in this form the result of many years' anxious struggle with the difficulties of the problem. Those difficulties are greater than can be imagined by any outsider. By outsiders I mean in the first place men, who, whatever their own cares and anxieties in the matter of dress, have at any rate to deal with a far less complicated system than ours; and in the next place all women who by reason of their wealth and beauty are raised above, or through poverty or indifference to personal appearance have sunk below, the ordinary level of careful contrivance. The first of these two classes of women, who have no need to plan their dress with care, will of course never be very large, and may be left out of our consideration altogether; but the second is recruited by many who might by proper measures be reclaimed from it, and who collectively might thus be induced to make a considerable contribution to the beauty of the world. Considering that every human being must dress somehow, and that most people's clothes pass in the course of every day before the eyes of a large number of their fellow-creatures, to almost all of whom they convey, or at least may convey some impression either of pleasure or pain, the sum of the effects produced by dress is by no means unimportant. As things are at present it is hard to say whether we should gain or lose most if it were decreed by Act of Parliament that we should all wear a uniform, or if some discovery were made by which the human race could be clothed with fur or plumage. The effect might be monotonous, but it would at least be inoffensive. It would be something like compounding for the extermination of barrel-organs by the abolition of concerts and choral services, and I think it very doubtful whether a majority might not be obtained in favour of such a compromise. However this may be, there is no doubt much room for improvement in the matter of dress, in respect of beauty, significance, and fitness.

DOI: 10.4324/9781315399980-7

The root of the evil is the want of thought; women no doubt care enough, talk enough, dream enough, and spend enough (both of time and money) about dress, but they do not generally put enough thought into it; and the result appears in the wretchedly meaningless and inharmonious toilettes which fill our houses and streets. The defect is common to all classes, from the maid-of-all-work, whose imitation of her betters is as unreasoning as that of a monkey, to the lady of fashion who spends hundreds a year in producing a result which suggests nothing but Marshall and Snelgrove's.

The subject ought, I think, to be recognized as a branch, however humble, of women's education. The natural love of dress is too strong to be ignored or extinguished, and might be made not only a part, but an instrument of education, if the principles of reason and fitness upon which it really rests were better ascertained, and a knowledge of them were more generally diffused. It would be easy to suggest plans for the diffusion of such knowledge, but the first requisite is that the fact and the importance of its existence should be recognized. People are too apt to think of dress either as a mere amusement, not worth studying seriously, or else as a mysterious art which cannot be reduced to language.

This last opinion is indeed true with respect to a part, but by no means the most important part, of the subject. With regard to mere beauty, apart from significance or fitness, it is very difficult to lay down any principles in words. Beauty of form, colour, and texture can scarcely be reduced to language, except in so far as it depends upon fitness, and fitness (even when understood as including becomingness, or adaptation to the wearer's personal appearance) is very far from constituting the whole difference between beautiful and ugly dress. Without pretending to offer any opinion upon the vexed metaphysical questions respecting abstract beauty, I may safely say that there is an important element of beauty which is addressed rather to the eye than to the mind, and which can therefore be taught, if at all, only by means of that gradual education of the eye which is involved in the study of good models, whether natural or artificial. In respect of such merely sensuous beauty, it is no doubt true that there is no disputing about tastes. Preferences which cannot be justified by reason can have no more weight than that which public opinion may assign to the taste of the persons experiencing them. It is notorious that public opinion does give considerable weight to individual tastes in proportion to the degree of cultivation which they are known to have received; and that there is a sufficient agreement among such generally acknowledged judges to make their criticisms valuable in influencing the education of other eyes. But any verbal instructions must be confined to questions of harmony (or adaptation of parts to each other) and fitness (or adaptations whether of parts, or the whole of any dress to the conditions under which it is to be worn). A full statement of the principles which ought to be observed in these respects would contain all that part of the art of dress which can be put into words. I will attempt to give a sketch of those leading principles which I should especially wish to see impressed upon the minds of students.

A perfect dress, as it seems to me, would be one in which every part was harmoniously combined so as to produce a whole perfectly adapted to the wearer's personal appearance, character, and circumstances, due regard being at the same time had to time, place, fashion, convenience, and economy.

On each of these heads I have a few words to say.

First, with regard to the combination of parts. This is one of the great difficulties of dress in all cases where expense is not a matter of indifference. A woman's outdoor attire, for instance, must be considered as consisting of at least three parts, – bonnet or hat, mantle (using the word as a generic term for all outdoor garments), and gown. If these were bought in equal numbers, so as to be bound together in life-long alliances, things would be comparatively easy; but it is not so. Their average longevity is different. That of bonnets is by far the shortest, while the extraordinary variations in the duration of shawls introduce a disturbing element into our calculations in respect of outdoor garments; and in the case of gowns, the question of their probable duration is complicated by the necessity of providing for all sorts of contingencies; so that no one can count upon reserving any one of these articles as the inseparable companion of any other, and the difficulty, therefore, of securing that each of the three parts of the outdoor costume shall bear witness of intentional adaptation to the other two is considerable. Some precautions may be suggested for the prevention of the most glaring inconsistencies. For instance, with respect to colour, there are two ways of lessening the danger: either the wearer may choose some one colour, with which every separate article of dress she buys shall harmonise, or she may decide in which of the three parts of her costume variation of colour shall be allowed, restricting herself in the other two parts sternly to neutral tints. These two plans may be in a measure combined, and after a certain experience has been acquired, a compromise between them is perhaps the best arrangement; but beginners should practise each separately. For instance, the choice of some one fundamental colour with which all the separate articles of dress should more or less severely harmonise, is, for every reason, worth making early in life; and for a time (at any rate until the wardrobe shall have been thoroughly weeded from unmanageable colours) it is wise to allow no departure from this rule. But not only does the eye naturally demand and enjoy more variety than a strict observance of this rule through life would allow, but the rule alone is insufficient to secure the object of perfect harmony even in colour between the parts of a toilette. Colours which harmonise with the same colour do not necessarily harmonise with each other. Besides this, regard must be had to the quantity and situation of each colour. Two colours which, if combined in very unequal proportions, are perfectly harmonious, may even as mere colour be intolerable in equal quantities. Again, the rule that two of these principal divisions of the outdoor costume shall be of neutral tint would, if severely followed, produce an unduly sombre effect, and would afford no further security against the very dangers just described. These rules, as I have said, only aim at preventing some of the worst catastrophes in mere colour, and leave many other very important questions – that of light and shade among others – quite untouched. Another point in which harmony is to be observed is that of texture. A very common error is to put on a mantle of more delicate or richer texture than is suitable to the gown, as, for instance, lace over woollen stuff; the opposite error is less offensive because it may always be supposed that the mantle is thrown on by way of *bonâ fide* protection to the gown, and is related to it in some degree as the husk is to the kernel. Discrepancies between the bonnet and mantle are obviously more inexcusable than discrepancies between these and the gown, because the two former are understood to be assumed or laid aside together, whereas the gown may have to be worn for a greater number of hours, and under different circumstances. But this consideration, though it may excuse, cannot alter the want of harmony, which is always a serious defect.

I have but pointed out a few among the multitude of ways in which dress may be discordant. It is needless to give further instances, for in what I shall say about the different objects to which dress should be adapted, I shall be enumerating as many points in which harmony may be observed or violated. Each of these various considerations should influence consistently all the separate parts of a toilette; each one therefore introduces a fresh element of difficulty into the problem. It is obvious that in so complicated a process there are but two ways of securing unfailing consistency: one is an unlimited wardrobe, the other a steady adherence to fixed principles.

I have said that dress should be adapted to the wearer's (1) personal appearance, (2) character, and (3) circumstances.

1. *Personal Appearance.* – On the simple principle that harmony is in itself better than discord, and beauty better than ugliness, I should wish to see every dress adapted, as perfectly as can conveniently be done, to the colouring, the shape, and the size of the wearer. Words are so inadequate to describe colour that it is scarcely possible to lay down any rules about the becomingness of particular colours to particular complexions. Everything depends upon variations of tint too slight to be translated into language. The great thing, therefore, to be impressed upon the students under this head will be that they must choose their colours by the eye, and by that alone, never allowing themselves to act upon any theory without constant reference to it. Mr. Ruskin, in his *Elements of Drawing,* advises his pupils, if any one tells them that two colours are discordant, to take the earliest opportunity of combining them, in the conviction that they will afford a peculiarly lovely result. Without going quite so far as this, I think every artist would agree that some of the most unusual and, so to speak, unrecognized combinations are, in skilful hands, the most beautiful. But then the hands must be really skilful, and it is perhaps more dangerous to recommend than to forbid such combinations. One common notion, however, I must protest against, viz., that two different tints of the same nominal colour, – for instance, turquoise and French blue, – should never be combined. All the most brilliant effects, not only of nature, but of oriental colouring, are produced by such subtle combinations, or rather gradations of colour; but the more subtle and lovely the more difficult they are to manage, and the more carefully the quantity, as well as the exact quality of each tint, must

be chosen. The different effect of the same colours in different materials is very remarkable, and should be carefully pointed out to students. It is perhaps safe to say, as a general rule (but not without exceptions), that delicate colours, (such as lavender, dove colour, sea-green, pale blue, &c.) require fine materials. They not only soon fade and get spoilt in common or rough materials; but even when new such colours are apt to look washy and unsatisfactory in coarse stuffs, – their beauty often depends upon a sort of bloom which is to be seen only in silk or other fine textures. The principal combination of colour will, in some cases, be between the dress on the one hand, and the colouring of the wearer on the other; while in other cases the colouring of the wearer is so neutral or insignificant that the whole interest of the effect, in point of colour, must be obtained by combinations between the different parts of the dress itself. In every case, however, it is important to take care that the dress shall not overpower the wearer, either in colour or in any other respect.

In adapting the dress to the shape and size of the wearer, a certain knowledge of drawing and of the proper proportions of the figure is of course the chief help. There are, however, a few well-ascertained rules which may safely be taught. One, for instance, is that transverse shapes generally tend to lessen height and increase breadth, while longitudinal forms have the opposite effect. Another well-known rule (which I believe is easily explained by a reference to optical science) is the tendency of light colours to increase apparent size, and *vice versâ*. People of more than average size should be cautious about wearing white or very light colours for this reason, although it must always be remembered that proportion and colour impress the eye so much more sensibly than mere scale that this rule is a very subordinate one, and only to be applied after those more important subjects have been thoroughly considered. It should, however, be remembered that more than average size necessarily involves a certain degree of conspicuousness, which makes any peculiarity of dress doubly undesirable in such cases. A small person may wear with impunity both colours and shapes which would be inexcusably striking on a large figure. Nothing goes so far to redeem unusual size as complete repose both in form and colour. Much trimming, loose ends and streamers, frills and furbelows, and caprices of all kinds, are apt to become intolerable when magnified, while on a small scale they may please, by a certain fluttering airiness which is in keeping with the impression of a tiny creature. But here also proportion may almost reverse the effect of scale. A short heavy figure may even more imperatively need quietness in dress than one of twice its actual volume which has run up into slenderness. And this naturally leads me to the second respect in which dress should be adapted to the wearer, namely, character; which, indeed, is scarcely separable from the form on which it is impressed, and according to which such questions as the last should mainly be decided.

2. *Character*. – It is as hard to draw the line between person and dress as between mind and matter, and there is, perhaps, no form of matter into which, and by which, mind can infuse a more subtle and incalculably radiating influence than it does by and into dress. Dress which is not informed and animated by individual

character is to that which truly expresses the mind of the wearer what a dead body is to a living one. This life of dress, individuality, is, perhaps, not quite extinct in any one, being to some extent independent of the will, but all its vigour depends upon the degree in which dress is the result of the real working of the wearer's own mind. It is therefore generally seen in the greatest perfection in the dress of women who are neither very rich nor very poor. Like animal life, it depends for its health upon a due balance of restraint and abundance: wealth overlays it, and poverty cramps it. A woman who has no need to think of the price of her clothes, must have a singularly strong natural tendency to the use of dress as a means of self-expression, if she does not leave a good deal of the arrangement of her toilette to her maid and her dressmaker, merely to save herself trouble; and the succession of the articles of which her wardrobe is composed is so rapid as to make each one worth much less thought to her than it would be to a woman who expected to spend a longer time within it: and, on the other hand, it is a task beyond ordinary powers to express one's mind fully within the limits of a very narrow purse. On this subject, therefore, great allowances must be made for individual difficulties, and great credit should be given for any clear indication of real inventive power or even of real thought and adaptation. The best advice which can be given to students on this head is that they should never set aside any instinctive preference of their own in regard to particular shapes and colours, unless for a definite assignable reason. As in the choice of wholesome food, inclination is to a person in good health a better guide than any rules of diet, so, in dress, a woman who has a genuine instinctive preference for any particular colour will generally be safe in indulging it in the absence of any distinct reason to the contrary; and though, no doubt, the free play of individual tastes would at first give rise to a fresh crop of mistakes, yet those very blunders have in them an element of life and progress which is utterly absent in the dull uniformity of merely imitative dress. There is a broad distinction between mistakes prompted by real pleasure in colour, even if uncultivated, and those which are the results of a desire to attract attention, or of mere carelessness; and we ought to beware lest in our desire to discourage vulgarity we crush the germs of growth by too unrelenting a spirit of criticism. As to the manner of indicating character, that will no doubt be as various as character itself; but some general correspondences might be pointed out, as, for instance, that between gravity of temperament and quietness of colouring; and the distinction between the quietness of severity, which, in dress, means cold and hard colours, such as steel grey, black, dark brown, and the quietness of simplicity, represented by the use of primary or very delicate colours – for instance, pure blue, white, or clear soft grey, and the quietness of a balanced and self-controlled character, which seems to me to indicate the fitness of deep full colours, such as violet, deep blue, maroon or crimson. But any colours may be either quiet, or the contrary, according to their quantity and treatment, especially as to trimming. Perhaps the chief point to be observed for obtaining quietness of colouring, is that the trimming should be either of the same colour as the dress, (a difference in shade, great enough to be perceptibly intentional and yet not sufficient to produce an actual contrast, is perhaps the best calculated to give a subdued effect to the whole,) or else in sufficient quantity, and sufficiently mixed ("united," as painters say,) with the colour of the ground, to be almost confounded with it, as is best seen in the case of lace; or else in such a very small quantity as to escape observation, merely producing a sense of finish, and perhaps a slight glow or shade, the cause of which must be sought for to be perceived. But quietness, though it is one of the safest and most inexhaustibly charming characteristics which can belong to dress, is not the only quality which we should wish to see expressed by it. Delicacy, freshness, simplicity, liveliness, elaborateness, sternness, dignity, caprice, cheerfulness, gloom, evenness or variability of temperament – all these and countless other varieties of character and disposition have their appropriate influence on dress – and no toilette is fairly entitled to the praise of individuality which does not distinctly reflect some such quality really characteristic of the wearer.

And here I must give a distinct place to one virtue which at the present time needs to be specially encouraged in dress, namely, truthfulness, which implies an utter contempt for any sort of sham or deceptive imitation whatever. To wear any such things appears to me to be not only in every case to symbolize, but in very many to commit, an act of dishonesty; and whatever may be the practice of a discreditably notorious few, I am sure that the immense though silent majority of English ladies repudiate any such practices with abhorrence – at least in theory. It is of course even more difficult to draw the precise line between truth and falsehood in dress than in language; but there is no need to lay down such precise lines. We all know the difference in ordinary cases, and those who really care to be honest, have not much difficulty in steering clear of the doubtful places. There is but one other virtue against which offences can be actually committed in dress, namely, modesty; and on that subject, also, some means of bringing to bear upon the young and thoughtless the better judgment of older and more cultivated minds might really promote important ends.

3. *Circumstances*. – That dress should be adapted to the circumstances of the wearer is a sufficiently obvious, not to say trite remark, but it is not only constantly disregarded in practice, but also very insufficiently developed in theory. The wearer's circumstances may be considered under the heads of age, rank, and domestic relations. It is often supposed that care in the choice of dress is appropriate only to the young, or that at most it becomes later in life a painful necessity, and a struggle to lessen as much as possible disfigurements which cannot be repaired. It would lead me too far to attempt to combat this opinion, or even to enumerate the differences in feeling which are implied by a dissent from it. But I may just explain, without attempting to establish, my own view of the way in which the advance of age should affect dress, and modify our attitude with regard to it. At the two ends of life it of course happens, though for different reasons, that dress is a matter in which the wearer is comparatively passive. It is then to a considerable extent the business of other hands; and at both these times, for this, among other reasons, the great things to be aimed at are freshness and simplicity; in childhood the simplicity of innocence, and in old age the simplicity of gravity.

But at every age a large part of the impression made upon others by any person depends upon his or her dress; and I do not think that at any age it ought to be a matter of indifference whether that impression is pleasing or otherwise. And it seems to me that the sum of the impressions produced upon the mind through the eye by an aged person, may be as pleasing as that produced upon the mind through the eye by the same person at any other age, although the mere pleasure to the eye itself is no doubt almost always less. This, of course, implies that the balance is redressed by a corresponding increase of beauty of expression in age; and surely this is often the case, – surely there is in some old countenances a spiritual beauty, and an accumulation of interest in the records of past experience written in their lines, which surpasses any beauty which the same countenances can have exhibited earlier in life. It is true that this is the rarest of all kinds of beauty. I may be mistaken in thinking it also the highest; it certainly requires some degree of responsive power in the observer for its appreciation; but to deny its existence would be, I think, to write oneself down blind and insensible. I am, however, in danger of straying from my immediate subject. I have alluded to this beauty only to explain why I should wish to see it reverently attired in garments such as shall harmonize with and not distract the attention from its solemn pathos. To succeed in this is surely worth some thought and care in those on whom the task devolves; and it is the less difficult since mere beauty in the dress itself becomes gradually more and more unimportant, as complete subordination to the spiritual or intellectual interest of the wearer's countenance gradually absorbs all other considerations. Black, white, and grey are the only tints which seem thoroughly appropriate to the very latest period of life; and there cannot be much difficulty in arranging these. Besides this process of simplification, the traditions of the wearer's life can hardly fail to have supplied some characteristic and becoming types; and a slight adherence to these, in disregard of the progress of fashion, gives at once a graceful touch of quaintness to the costume of an old lady which has a special charm for younger generations.

Perhaps a more discouraging period to deal with is that vaguely called "elderly;" when the obvious beauty of youth has not yet been replaced by the picturesqueness, the cultivated significance, or the pathos of old age. Yet even at this age there is a difference, and an important difference, between a well-dressed and an ill-dressed woman; and the importance of the art of dress may surely quite as reasonably be supposed to vary in a direct, as in an inverse proportion to the difficulty of the problem. That the difficulty of the problem does increase somewhere about the middle period of life, I fully admit. But that very difficulty affords the greatest scope for skill in the choice of those delicate gradations by which a woman may adapt her costume to her years; and the wisdom of such a well-considered and carefully executed adaptation to the facts of the case, instead of any attempt to disguise or ignore them, is evident on the grounds both of morality and policy. If it were only for the sake of the perpetuation of interest which results from the necessity of continual adaptation to a changing position, it would be worth while to recognize the lapse of time; and it is, of course, unnecessary to point out how essential to the moral propriety and dignity of a woman's appearance it is that her dress should be suitable to her age. The general tendency of the alteration of style suitable to middle age is towards elaborateness in trimmings and appointments and richness of materials. Complicated and intricate patterns and trimmings seem to shadow forth the complexity and intricacy which is the distinguishing characteristic of the middle period of life. They also, if well arranged, bear witness to the gradually increasing mastery in the art which has been acquired since the early days, when to plan a simple white dress was enough for the beginner; while, later in life, any such elaborate arrangements would become burdensome or lifeless, and a return to some degree of simplicity naturally accompanies the gradual withdrawal from the multiform activities of middle life. The richness of material, however, which becomes especially suitable when the first youth is passed, need never be laid aside, and indeed seems, in a sense, especially appropriate to those who are no longer exposed to the wear and tear of the busiest years of existence.

Dress also has to be, in some respects, adapted to the social position of the wearer; and on this subject it is very difficult to lay down any very well-defined rules. For there is no saying beforehand what social position any individual may assign to herself; nor is it easy to say exactly what, in the way of dress, is due to any particular assignable rank; still less how the rival claims of rank and wealth ought to be adjusted. But some general principles may be laid down with confidence. One is, that no every-day costume (*i.e.,* no costume which is not avowedly planned with a view to some special festivity) should be such as to be manifestly unsuitable to any company in which the wearer is liable to find herself. A perfect costume for the wife of a London clergyman, for instance, would be one in which she might receive a visit from a duchess, or pay one to a washerwoman, without disrespect to either. Black silk and white muslin are the typical representatives of the kind of gowns which can hardly be unsuitable in any company. And the same result is always more or less promoted by a dependence for effect rather upon perfection of finish than upon splendour of design. We ought also to encourage by every means the disposition to mark by one's dress the social position which one actually holds rather than the next above it; impressing upon students how much more real respect is due to (for instance) a servant who dresses consistently like a servant, than to one who succeeds (even if by rare good fortune she does succeed now and then) in looking like a lady; showing how impossible it is that any such attempts to assume the appearance of a class above one's own should be consistently carried out in everything, and how peculiarly unladylike is the inevitable failure. The same lesson is fully as much required higher up in the social scale. It would be better, for instance, for a barrister's wife to dress consistently, if only up to the point which might be pronounced suitable for the wife of an attorney, than that she should oscillate between the costumes suitable to the wives of judges and of barristers' clerks respectively. The important truth is that the thing which really gives an impression of refinement and good-breeding is not the particular *pitch* of dress chosen, but the degree in which that pitch, be it what it may, is sustained by perfect finish and "keeping" in every detail. It is obvious that the higher the style aimed at the more difficult and expensive it will be to carry it out in this sustained manner, and therefore the most really refined women in each class will generally be those who pitch their dress lowest for that class, – they having the highest standard of completeness, and the keenest sense of its necessity.

Under the head of domestic relations come all such questions as those respecting the appropriate distinctions between the dress of young ladies before and after their entrance into society, between that of married and unmarried women, and questions respecting mourning and the use of costumes generally. I think that, as a general rule, the more significant dress can be made the better; and I would therefore encourage every attempt to indicate the circumstances of the wearer by appropriate diversities of style. But any sort of costume depends for all its effect upon common consent. The very essence of a conventional symbol is that people should have agreed to attach a particular meaning to its use; and no degree of natural fitness will replace such conventional significations. The effect of costume depends not upon what it ought to mean, but upon what it does mean. We very much want some machinery for taking the sense of the community upon questions of dress, and for suggesting symbols which might with advantage be generally used to signify particular states and conditions of life.

The subject of mourning is one on which there is much to be said, and plausible reasons may be given for or against the whole system. It seems to me natural and inevitable, and to most people's feeling probably grateful, that there should be some such shelter from the ordinary cares of dress in times of real sorrow, and the adoption of mourning cannot be such a shelter unless it be so strictly conventional as to give no indication of the actual feelings of any individual wearer. But the form which it takes in England is to the last degree troublesome and unreasonable. The addition of so many inches of crape for every degree of affinity is irritatingly absurd. Apart from this, crape itself is a peculiarly bad material for the purpose, from its expensiveness and its liability to injury from every drop of rain. The too common addition of quantities of jet ornaments, or, still worse, of black flowers and other dismal translations of finery into funereal trappings, is both lugubrious and ill-timed, and nobody can think the result really beautiful. To lay aside one's ornaments is the natural symbol of grief, and a relief when the feeling is real. The French plan of signifying "depth" of mourning by increasing the degree of plainness of the simple black dress, and by the absence of ornaments and trimming, seems to me much the most reasonable and appropriate. The period of wearing mourning is considerably shorter than ours. I believe they never wear crape at all, and I cannot see how any one living or dead is the worse for it. The free use of white in all cases of mourning, however deep, would also be a great gain. In hot weather to condemn mourners to the use of heavy black clothes is a mild form of suttee, and should, in common charity, be abolished. But it is too much to expect that individuals should have the courage to break through such customs as these, and there seems no present prospect of any means being provided for united action in such matters. Many suggestions might be made respecting costumes for particular occasions. I will confine myself to one, which seems to me much needed, – I mean a church-going costume. The old simple idea of going to church in one's "Sunday best" had, no doubt, much to recommend it, and in small country churches where each person is familiar with every one else's wardrobe, and the same bonnet and gown does duty week after week for months together, the "Sunday best" really is a sort of church costume; but in great cities it developes into something very different and much less appropriate. A London congregation comes to church dressed very much as if for a flower-show, and the effect is anything but devotional. Good and bad toilettes are alike distracting. Now that we are so busy about the vestments of the officiating clergy, might we not reform the dress of the worshippers? A long black, white, or grey cloak, descending to the ground and worn with a hood of the same material, would be put on in a moment, and would have a very grave and suitable appearance. It would be easier to collect one's thoughts in a church so filled than in such a scene as we now worship in.

I have said that attention to the three great considerations of personal appearance, character, and circumstances, must be combined with a due regard to time, place, fashion, convenience, and economy. A few words respecting each of these will sum up the rest of what I have to say.

1. *Time*. – There is a vague code, which ought to be better defined, regulating the articles appropriate to morning, afternoon, and evening dress. The morning, of course, should be distinguished by freshness and simplicity, the evening by splendour. It may be almost an unreasonable demand in connection with most ladies, but the sentiment of morning attire appears to me to require that it should, at least in some remote degree, suggest a working dress. For this, as well as for the sake of freshness, as large a proportion as possible of it should consist of what are rather ungrammatically called "washing materials;" and it should at least look as if that part of it were washed every day. In summer, cottons and muslins make it easy to carry this out approximately; in winter, the sentiment must be represented by the collar and sleeves. Some kinds of lace are more or less, and should be stringently, set apart for evening, and some for morning use. But there is room for a good deal more definition in this branch of the subject. One anomaly calls for a passing remark – it is, that the distinction between morning and evening lace is so little regarded in bonnets, probably because they are not considered as meant to be washed. But in their present beautifully simple form what would be prettier or more easily managed than morning bonnets made of muslin and Valenciennes lace, and washed as often as their freshness was in the slightest degree impaired? And how much more ladylike such clean and simple head-dresses would be than the tulle and blonde constructions now too often worn at all hours of the day. The sentiment of evening costume is, I suppose, that it is improvised for the one occasion on which it is worn; and, therefore, no degree of flimsiness or fragility in the materials can offend one's taste, whatever one may think of them in point of economy. The afternoon is a compromise between morning and evening which it is hard to treat philosophically. To dress three times a day seems scarcely worthy of a rational creature, and this is indeed theoretically recognized by the technical

use of the word "morning dress" for everything worn before dinner. It would be well if practice were more nearly in accordance with theory in this particular.

The time of year need be noticed only as still further complicating the problem of dress for those who have to think much of expense. It is easy enough to adapt one's clothing to the temperature, if one can afford it. I may mention, however, that some regard is due to other people's eyes as well as one's own feelings, that dress should *look* cool in summer and warm in winter, even if the wearer should be abnormally indifferent to the sensations of heat and cold. Also, when artificial flowers are worn, it is essential that they should be such as are really in season, at least in greenhouses. Under the head of time we have also to consider the question of repetition. It is not only in buying new articles of dress that thought is needed, but in the daily selection of such as shall be worn together, so as to secure enough and not too much variation from day to day. Abrupt changes of the whole costume, or perfectly uniform repetitions of the same arrangement on successive days, seem to me almost equally undesirable. The most perfect arrangement, I think, is a combination of continuousness with variety by means of alterations of detail, while the foundation remains the same; and when that is changed the transition may be rendered less abrupt by the re-appearance of some familiar ornament, redeeming the new attire from strangeness. Rapid and total changes of dress destroy the web of pleasing associations which time weaves round clothes as well as round other inanimate objects.

2. In the consideration of *place* the distinction between town and country corresponds in some degree to that between morning and evening. In the country there is always a charm in what suggests rural occupations even when it is manifestly only a suggestion. A lady's outdoor dress in the country should always be one in which, if she did milk a cow or make hay, she would be picturesquely and becomingly, even if really unsuitably, dressed for the occasion. Tried by this test, silk and black lace and all sorts of gauzy materials would be condemned, and, I think, rightly, as unsuitable to the country. For the seaside a similar test might be founded upon the possibility of carrying any given costume into a boat. This test would be even more exclusive than the last; and should perhaps be less rigorously applied, though it ought never to be quite lost sight of. Some regard may be had, when it is possible, to the probable surroundings in respect of furniture, &c.; and furniture might be chosen more than is now done with a view to its relations with the dress of its owners; but it is impossible to insist very strictly upon attention to such varying combinations as these.

3. I now come to the vexed and most perplexing question of *fashion*. All theory scouts the dominion of fashion as baseless, while all practice bends to it. To the philosophical mind there is something very irritating in seeing such absolute sway exercised by a power which eludes all inquiry into its source or laws. In more ordinary minds it almost inspires a sort of superstitious awe. Like the Indian chupatties which herald a revolution, it comes nobody knows whence, it spreads nobody knows how, with more than electric rapidity. Those who have made the most energetic attempts to resist its authority know best how certain is their

ultimate defeat. I am not going to attempt to reason about this most unreasonable power; only to describe what seems to me to be the right way of regarding it. It is of no use to ignore it; it can hardly be worth any woman's while to resist it; but it need not be allowed to tyrannize everywhere, and it is mere folly for everybody to attempt to keep pace with it. Its proper function seems to me to be like that of rules in a game of skill, to give scope for ingenuity in observing it. Were there no succession of fashions, dress would sink to a mere mechanical repetition of established models. Whether this would be a moral gain or not, it would clearly destroy half the interest of the spectacle. That interest is equally destroyed when mere fashion is allowed to decide everything, as it is in too many instances. You know the fashion, and can, therefore, predict such a one's dress. The real interest is in watching the variations which may be produced in the dress of a woman who is resolutely harmonious and individual in her own style of dress, by a reference more or less distant to the varying fashions of the day. In such cases the fashion is like an air led by some unknown and invisible performer, but caught up and repeated by a number of instruments, modulated into different keys, and varied into a thousand new creations, while the original air is never lost sight of, nor too widely departed from. Let fashion be thus regarded, and instead of an unmeaning tyranny, it becomes the motive of perpetually renewed interest; and it will, at the same time, become apparent that the very object of consulting the fashion is defeated by too servile an adherence to it on the one hand, or by abortive attempts to follow it on the other. The practical difficulty remains of adjusting the respective limits of fashion and individuality. There are two or three principal considerations by which this adjustment should be influenced. In the first place, the more remote any part of a woman's dress is from her own personality the more completely it may be abandoned to fashion. Thus, the shape and length of a skirt, the choice of a flat trimming which does not alter the outline of the figure, such extraneous adjuncts as muffs, parasols, fans, &c., – all these things are the mere prey of fashion, and the variations which it may work in them are mostly too remote to disturb the stamp of individuality. But when fashion creeps up to the sleeves, and the cut of the body of a gown, its influence must be more jealously scrutinized – grave individual exigencies may begin to encounter it here; and when it comes to a question of hairdressing, the whole expression of the face being at stake, fashion should be almost the last consideration to be admitted, although, even here, it should never be ignored. Colouring also should always be determined rather by the permanent characteristics of the wearer than by any variations of fashion. Another rule always to be borne in mind is, that personal inclinations rank above fashion. No woman of fine moral sense would wear what she herself felt to be distinctly ugly in mere deference to fashion. Personal inclinations are to fashion what the individual conscience is to public opinion, – much influenced by it, but reacting upon it, and paramount while opposed to it. The eye is so much affected by habit that the sense of ugliness rarely long withstands a very strong current of fashion; and when the sense of ugliness is lost the reason for holding out is gone; but it is almost morally important that as long as it exists it should not be outraged.

It can rarely even seem necessary to do so, for there are few fashions which may not be adopted in moderation, and so discreetly adapted to the taste of the wearer as to become fresh sources of beauty. And in the course of its revolutions, fashion every now and then developes really beautiful forms, which it would be well if we could in some way stamp with public approbation, so that they might be saved from the ordinary lot of oblivion.

The last caution which I should wish to impress upon students with regard to fashion is the necessity of taking a sober measurement of the degree in which one really either can or ought to dress fashionably. To make snatches at occasional fragmentary bits of fashion when one's purse does not allow of the whole wardrobe being kept up consistently to the same degree of novelty, but would amply suffice to keep one neat and fresh in the style of a few weeks or months ago, is simply to throw away the substance for the shadow, and to make one's unavoidable deficiencies doubly glaring. Also, it must be remembered that fashionable dress is as unbecoming in a lady living in a quiet unfashionable society as the attempt to look like a lady is in her housemaid; though it is very likely that she severely condemns the latter error, while she has not strength of mind to refuse her connivance, at least, at her dressmaker's attempts to make her commit the former.

4. In turning to the subject of *convenience,* we emerge from the enchanted grounds where invisible powers exercise their mysterious authority, to the plain light of common sense and reason. That sleeves intended to be worn at meal times should be so constructed as not to dip into dishes; that outdoor gowns should either be short or capable of being shortened; that bodies and skirts, having different periods of existence, and needing to be occasionally packed up, should be separable; that gowns to be put on by human creatures should have their fastenings within reach of the human hand; that hats should be light and shady, parasols for a variable climate large enough to serve as a shelter both from sun and rain; that cloaks should be waterproof, and winter petticoats made of stout coloured stuff instead of white cambric; all these obvious truths have recently dawned upon the minds of this generation, and it is much to be hoped that we shall be able to retain our hold of them. The hope would be more consoling if the records of past fashions did not bear testimony to the extraordinary eclipses which such truths have formerly undergone. In losing sight of them we should lose not only the actual conveniences which they secure to us, but we should be giving up that manifest constructive fitness which, as we all know, is one of the most unfailing guides to the higher kinds of beauty in decorative art. A dress rationally adapted to its purpose would give a certain pleasure to rational creatures even if it were utterly devoid of beauty; but these adaptations are to decorative beauty what trellis-work is to a climbing plant. The ornaments which grow naturally upon them have a charm and a vigour which is unattainable by the pursuit of beauty as a primary object. Beauty, like pleasure, seems to have a mysterious habit of following in the wake of those who are pursuing other objects, while eluding those who turn aside to seek it.

5. All these various considerations – harmony, personal appearance, character, circumstances, time, place, fashion, and convenience, – act upon each other, restricting and promoting and complicating each other in the most incalculable manner, but they are all, like most other human affairs, subject to the last consideration on my list – that of *economy*. All the other ends might be attained by the simple expedient of boundless expenditure; but even were that expedient within the reach of all, there would be a coarse facility about the use of it which would reduce a noble sport to a mere battue. The whole interest of the pursuit, considered as an art, or at least as a game of skill, would fall to the ground if the contents of all the warehouses of London and Paris were at one's service. Even in that very improbable case there would still be a certain moral value in moderation. But the cases which in any degree approximate to this lie beyond my province. Any sum under 100*l*. a year needs careful management to be made to yield a thoroughly satisfactory crop of clothes. It is perhaps quite as difficult to lay out 100*l*. as 20*l*. a year to the best advantage, though, of course, with the larger sum one is not made to feel the consequences of one's mistakes so long or so grievously. Ordinary mortals, whose pin-money is really limited, be its limits what they may, ought to consider well with themselves in which direction they will economize, and in which they will launch out. Expense may be well bestowed in several distinct, almost opposite, ways. One plan which has its merits is to buy none but the very best – which, unfortunately, are almost invariably the most expensive – materials, on the plea, which we will not handle too roughly, that "they are the most economical in the long run." They are certainly apt to be the most beautiful. The opposite plan of a rapid succession of cheap things has also much to recommend it, (provided the cheap materials be also simple, otherwise cheapness is apt to mean tawdriness,) especially as regards freshness and the facility of keeping pace with the fashion. But this plan would be doubly expensive to any lady who was obliged to have recourse to the services of a dressmaker. Whichever branch of this alternative may be chosen, it is still necessary to consider whether the evening or the morning, the indoor or outdoor costume shall be the first object, for the sake of which the rest of one's wardrobe shall, if necessary, be stinted. This will naturally depend upon one's social habits – that time of day being most carefully provided for when one is most likely to be observed by the friends one most cares to please. I hardly know why it is that there is a certain flavour of propriety and dignity about the earlier hours of the day which makes one feel that a woman who spent her chief care and most of her money on her morning toilettes would occupy a sort of moral pedestal, raised slightly above the level of one whose pride was in her dinner-dresses. And yet even husbands, fathers, and brothers are oftener at leisure to be pleased by dress after the day's work is over than at the breakfast-table, where their attention is at best divided between it and the newspaper. Whatever the full explanation of this sentiment may be, most people certainly feel that the moral respectability of dowdiness is at its minimum in the morning and increases as the day goes on till it reaches its maximum after dinner – while the indulgence accorded by severe moralists to beauty and freshness of adornment runs an opposite course. Perhaps

the instinct of self-preservation warns these censors – who after all are themselves human, and have to provide their own or their families' wardrobes – that good taste does not allow so much money to be spent on morning as on evening toilettes, and that they are therefore a sort of safety-valve for the ineradicable love of dress inherent in the female mind. A still further subdivision may be made by which the reserve forces are directed upon some particular article of either morning or evening dress, all the rest being done as cheaply as may be, as a mere background for the display of some one favourite vanity. One lady will thus concentrate her efforts upon lace, another upon furs, a third will at all hazards indulge her love of rich silk gowns, a fourth will before everything secure dainty and appropriate garnishings. These specialities naturally arise unconsciously from strong individual tastes, but even where there is not such a natural bias it is worth while to consider whether more may not be effected by some degree of concentration than by the equal distribution of one's forces. Whatever path may ultimately be chosen, whether richness of materials, perpetual renewal of freshness, morning neatness or evening splendour, lace, fur, jewels or trimmings, be made the chief aim, it remains true that no ordinary income can suffice to accomplish them all, and that complete success in any one of these branches generally implies severe self-restraint in the others. What I have already said once or twice about the much greater effect of refinement which is produced by perfect finish of execution than by ambitious design, should be especially borne in mind in making this choice. Far better wear no lace at all than be obliged to eke out a set by the addition of pieces of a different character, or than put it upon inappropriate materials. Far better wear a complete set of bog-oak ornaments than an amethyst brooch with emerald bracelets and pearl earrings. Far better wear a linsey-wolsey gown with carefully chosen and corresponding collars, sleeves, petticoat, gloves, &c., than a rich silk with fragmentary and ill-combined appointments. But this perfect finish is about the most expensive quality that can be aimed at in dress; and it also appeals to a more cultivated taste than we can always reckon upon in spectators.

And with a short appeal to spectators I will conclude my remarks. No art can reach its utmost perfection which is not criticised with discriminating interest, and, at the same time, with a fair share of indulgence. In both these elements we too often fail as spectators. Everybody cannot be always at leisure to observe everybody else's dress: but when we do observe it, and comment upon it, we might at least take the trouble to do so intelligently; to consider the aim and the execution; to do justice to either, if either are good; and to forgive shortcomings in the one for the sake of merit in the other. Let any unprejudiced person run over the list of the topics upon which I have touched, remembering that they are but specimens of the considerations which have to be borne in mind in the choice of clothes, and say whether great indulgence be not due to those who have to reconcile them all without running into debt, or spending upon the matter an amount of time and money which any reasonable woman would be ashamed to spend upon dress. Indeed, as I think over them all, I am inclined to wonder, not at our failures – hideous and frequent though they be – but at the measure of our success. For want of thought, though the most serious and fundamental, is not the only source of failure; too much thought may be almost as dangerous and a good deal more embarrassing; for it may lead to the adoption of a style of dress which is addressed rather to the mind than the eye, and it may meet with criticisms proceeding merely from the eye. Besides, thoughtful people are very apt to get entangled in their own subtleties; or in avoiding Scylla to fall into Charybdis; or to reflect till they become desperate and act like fools; in short, their snares are in proportion to their sensitiveness. What is wanted is the combination of a clear grasp of certain fixed principles, with a knack of execution. And when we remember how rare a combination this is, we shall not be tempted to be too severe upon well-meant, though only partially successful attempts. Anything really pretty and judicious ought to meet with instant and hearty recognition; a sorrowful silence is punishment enough for most failures. My remarks have been offered partly as aids to thought, but are intended, and I hope will be accepted, also as a plea for indulgence.

5

[ANON], 'A LADY'S QUESTION: WHAT SHALL WE WEAR?'

London Society, May 1869, pp. 410–414

WHAT shall we wear? It is a question always under discussion. It is for ever being asked; and it is for the interest of human nature that it should be happily answered: also, it is a question concerning which, justly or unjustly, we have to suffer reproach. Is it true that, as a rule, English women are ill dressed? It is an accusation often enough heard, and hopelessly given in to; yet, if we apply the judgment to a particular class, it is grossly untrue. If, in the London season, you watch those who may be seen every day out of doors in walking or driving costume, with whom to dress well is a duty attached to their position, you will not anywhere find better examples of good taste and costly elegance. In these 'higher circles' of society you may find all that the most fastidious criticism can require; if there are exceptions they are among known eccentricities, and they can be accounted for: but these people have the command of money, they live under a necessity that prescribes propriety in dress, and even great splendour of costume, and what they are to wear, is a question of such magnitude as to require the advice of recognized councillors.

Immense prices are paid to dressmakers, not for sewing seams, or using scissors, but for tho judgment that results from the education of their eyes and the refinement of their taste; these great *artistes* are paid for making every customer look her best.

To take the entire management of her dress is generally a task beyond the power of a lady in the midst of the worry and work, the toil and trouble of a London season. The gowns required for evening wear are so various, the dresses for daylight must be so many, the head-gear for such a multitude of occasions so skilfully chosen, that she *must* live under instruction; she must have her prime minister in the fashionable dressmaker, and her next in council the clever waiting-woman, who reminds, suggests, sorts, and considers; who keeps up a vivid remembrance of what her mistress has worn, and *where* she has worn it; with knots in her memory as to who were there – a mental labour which must not end with the season. Of course there is a terrible list of finery that cannot survive at furthest beyond its *second* night; but other costumes last longer. By-and-by, in the round of the country houses, the perfect handmaiden will take care that the blue brocade shall not

DOI: 10.4324/9781315399980-8

be worn where the spiteful Lady X— , who never forgets anything, may see it and smile, because in London she has seen it twice already. 'Such a pretty dress, Mrs. M — , I *always* thought so.'

We knew, and greatly respected, a lady, who wrote down daily where she had been, whom she had met, and *what she had worn*; she enjoyed the reputation of being always well dressed. If she wore a dress twice following at your house it was a proof that she loved and trusted you – she never did it by mistake. But all this belongs to the world of persons who have time, money, and high positions; where ministers and prime ministers are to be had, and with whom *to dress* is really part of the serious business of life. In these upper regions there is, to say the least, as good dressing as can be found anywhere. 'No wonder!' cries the reader. Well, no wonder! we echo the thought and the words. All we assert is, that perfect taste in dress is to be found among English women, and that, unquestionably, it is *there*. We are willing, after much thought, great observation, and years of experience, to go to the utmost limits, and declare that a well-dressed English gentlewoman is the best-dressed woman in the world, and that she can walk in her silk attire better than any woman in Europe, a Spaniard alone excepted.

But if, now, we descend from these highest walks of life and fashion to the broader fields where the multitude meet, and where *the nation,* in its women, is fairly represented, how is the accusation of our being an ill-dressed people to be met? Not quite so boldly, we must confess. And for good reasons; for, indeed, we must call the reasons we are going to give in explanation, *good,* knowing motives; but they are only good because of ignorance – ignorance of better modes which are even more consistent with those most excellent motives.

Here is a list of 'good' reasons from which bad dressing results.

1. Not to appear as lightly led away by frivolous pleasures.
2. Not to yield to suggestions of personal indulgence.
3. Not to spend more money than might be convenient.
4. Not to be like lovers of change.
5. Not to be thought *fast*.

Here are five reasons, very good, when the motives are considered in a moral point of view; and very ridiculous, unsound, and, in fact, disgraceful, when examined by the mirror of truth – which every lady should keep in her dressing room – and by common sense.

To take these 'reasons' as they come, let it be at once granted that frivolity is an unbearable vice; but a woman ought to have an honest pleasure in dress, just as she should have pleasure in any successful triumph of civilisation – the perfect cooking of an every-day dish, for instance. The every-day things of life, by being habitual, are taken out of the region of frivolous pleasure. If any persons say they really do not care for dress, it is as absurd as to say they do not care for cleanliness – that they see no decency in keeping up respectable habits. To be a sloven is not meritorious; it is, probably, to be idle and lazy, and possibly to be unclean.

In 1802, when Madame Récamier, so celebrated for beauty, talents, and fashion, visited London, she walked in Kensington Gardens dressed *à l'antique;* that is, as nearly like a draped statue as possible; with her hair down her back, a white veil over her head, and scarcely as many folds in her outer garment, and almost as few under ones as you may see exhibited by the figure of Britannia on a penny. The English ladies then wore very clinging robes, and small straight bonnets, with scarfs and folded draperies, or, perhaps, a fringed, soft shawl hung on the shoulders so as to trail to the ground, and fall away from the arms, preserving as much the general effect of a draped statue as possible, wind and weather permitting. The amount of absurdity which the contemplation of such *elegantes* as Madame Récamier presented, was, however, new in the world. It is hard to believe that, only a few years before, our grandmothers were sitting to Sir Joshua Reynolds in the fascinations of a costume which must always claim admiration. The bodies wrapped, or square, the modest muslins, the hanging lace – and the faces so honest, without a line of the self-consciousness of the robed *à l'antique* period – a period when English women looped up their scanty dress on one side only, to show the low slipper and high sandalled ankle as they stood in the *pose statuesque;* and damped their flesh-coloured silk stockings to show the ankle perfectly, dying of the practice as many did. It now strikes us that it was a heavy price to pay, when to go without stockings would have been safer, as to health, and what the proprieties, other things considered, need not have boggled at. But *la frivolité* reigned, and had her victims sacrificed to her: we do not think that any woman, under the wholesomer influence of the present day, need fear being entrapped into such idolatry. Indeed, as to that worship, it no longer exists.

As to the second reason on our list, it ought to be dismissed as a mere excuse. To dress well is a trouble, and not an indulgence. Let us pass on. The fear of spending too much money is an honourable timidity, because it has its root in honesty. But it may be doubted if there is any more inconvenient extravagance than neglected dress. For six months or more the prudent lady spends 'next to nothing.' Suddenly, before the year closes, some unthought-of occasion arises when she has to be dressed. The great question comes as to what shall she wear? Money has to be spent; the very money she thought she had saved; not by little and little, when it would not have been felt, but painfully, in a lump, to her grief, for she had not laid it by; to her impoverishment, for she has to borrow from the future; and probably in her necessity, still desiring to save, and in dread of extravagance, some important details are left out – or an inferior arrangement 'made to do,' and she is not *well* dressed after all. So fails the third of our reasons, and we come to the fourth.

Let us immediately confess that not to like to be among the lovers of change is a wholesome fear, and very necessary to her who would be always and really well dressed. And so it seems like a contradiction to say that the rapidity with which English women will give in to the adoption of some particular style on the mere word of a saleswoman or a dressmaker that it will be in vogue in the season is well known. English women will never be well dressed till they learn to think for themselves. They must also learn to use their judgment on themselves as those who contemplate their appearance not as a medley of disjointed facts but as a whole. A woman is not well dressed who has on a sweet hat, an exquisite India shawl, a lovely cambric muslin dress, and the smartest pair of be-buttoned boots with 'simulated' lacings. These things may help to make up a well-furnished wardrobe, but they are not intended to be worn together. The extreme of this style was found in the historical Indian chief who received some officers at his levée attired in Hessian boots, a short tiger-skin petticoat, a shell jacket, and a Scotch cap. Last year, the coming in of extremely high-heeled boots, which this year's taste may or may not confirm as an accepted custom, suggested the use of a cane. Charming little dandy walking-sticks supported the almost tottering steps of fashionable belles in the Continental resorts of fashion, and were really very desirable appendages to the costume of a lady whose figure was thrown alarmingly out of the perpendicular. Then, to improve the figure at the waist, an article of dress was worn under the petticoat to make the bending of the back assume a more graceful line. It is not to be denied that a thoroughly well-got-up demoiselle in this style, at all points quite complete, was a very pretty sight. What was the consequence? People were found to use the cane without the shoes, and the *panier* without either. They had never contemplated themselves as a whole; and a terrible exhibition would be made sometimes when these new things were adopted without the purchase of a new dress or the reform of an old one; or when the train was worn with old loopings-up. We abstain, from pure charity, from describing the consequences. These follies have caused it to be said of our English women that they are ill-dressed. The cases we have given are extreme cases, and of course rare: but the same fault may be seen every day if you look out for them in any part of London frequented by people who *ought* to dress well.

No more becoming costume has been invented in our time than the looped-up velvet dresses with the petticoat showing beneath. Very pretty, very tasteful, very becoming, very convenient, and therefore they have been of very general adoption; but what havoc people have made with their appearance in the matter of petticoats! The velvet surface imperiously demanded the companionship of some refined material. Silk, or soft fine-textured wool of colours that were enriched by the accost of the black velvet were the only things admissible. But have we not seen coarse striped camlet, and scarlet camlet made staring by black braiding, or roughened by frills? It has been difficult to teach people not to choose a petticoat as a petticoat, but as an annexation to the gown. But then the old dread of expense rose up. Silk and satin petticoats! Impossible! These exquisite wools! why they are good enough for dresses themselves. Of course they are; they are for exhibition; with the upper velvet they make a costume. You must take your dress as *a whole*.

The persistence with which English women make mistakes arises unquestionably in a great measure from the rapidity with which they yield to other people's advice and assurances; and because they will not think for themselves.

A perfectly well-dressed gentlewoman in a milliner's room was giving directions for the changing of certain flowers in a bonnet she had been buying. 'Oh, don't change them!' cries a young friend; 'they are so lovely.' 'I can't afford to wear them,' was the unexpected reply. 'It would cost me fifteen pounds. I have not an out-door article in my wardrobe which could be worn with that exquisite shade of mauve.' The lady liked the flowers, but, first of all things, she considered herself.

But the English have lately learnt the beauty and the value of black. France certainly taught that to this country. It tones, unites, and yet gives distinctness. Two or three black dresses of good materials are necessary both for economy, effect, and convenience; a woman may then keep to a few colours as belonging to her style, and always preserve a well-chosen and harmonious exterior.

Last on our list of things that prevent our countrywomen from being well dressed is the dread of being thought *fast*. They will often be guilty of adopting a scrap of a costume, but they shrink from the whole. But 'all or none' is the dictate of common sense, as it is the law of fashion; and to escape the possibility of looking *fast* by the certainty of looking ridiculous is a very bad bargain. No one need be in a hurry to adopt a new thing. Wait. If you are doubtful, always keep quiet, and wait. But if a fashion comes in which appears to suit your life and promises to add to your comfort, study its accessories, and accept it at once. For one thing is certain – if a new fashion is convenient, dismisses a trouble from your life, and adds to your happiness, *it will live*. Short outdoor walking costumes, easily taken off and put on, being worn with bodices, have been acknowledged as a domestic mercy, and will live. The disappearance of covering from the back of the head would not have become so universal but for the uncomfortable crowns of the old-fashioned bonnets, which would not stay on the head, and were receptacles for all the winds that blew in the winter. At last people tied up their heads in an ornamental half-handkerchief, and got rid of them. The present style of bonnets may be carried to an extreme, but no woman old enough to remember the bonnet of the past can say they are uncomfortable; their work may not be much, but they do it honestly; and they, too, will live, though changes may be made in them; the old bonnet which wearied the neck, rubbed the ears, and had to be tied severely tight under the chin to keep it from troubling the shoulders, will scarcely return in our time; its memory among surviving sufferers is too painful.

All good reasons for bad dressing may then be answered generally by two sentences of kind advice. Use your judgment with consideration and courage, and view your appearance as a whole. And now we will say one last word – as important as the proverbial postscript of a lady's letter. Let us bespeak attention, for we shall announce a discovery. There is a reason for English women being ill dressed – there is something that prevents the successful use of reason, and makes a perfect judgment impossible. It is this. That necessity among French women, *the long looking-glass*, is a luxury among English women, and scarcely to be found among house furniture below a certain position in life. How can anybody tell how she looks if she has no means of seeing herself? The important length of dress, and sweep of train, and effect of trimming, is left to – luck! These great things take their chance. Ladies are condemned to see in their looking-glasses their faces only. Is it any wonder that there are a large number of persons whose whole idea of dress is confined to a bonnet? Possibly a generous ambition, if it be winter, has been satisfied by the possession of a sealskin jacket, the most enticing wear that was ever offered to woman; of course, after a gratified survey of a pretty head-dress, and sleeky shoulders, the poor lady goes off happy, dressed, probably, in a palish brown linsey and a green stuff petticoat.

> 'O wad some power the giftie gie us,
> To see oursels as others see us.'

Husbands and fathers, ye are the powers; and the 'giftie,' depend upon it, is a long strip of looking-glass in an honest wooden frame, fastened to the wall of every room in which the ladies' question – '*What shall we wear?*' is finally settled and acted on.

6

E. P. [EMILY PFEIFFER], 'THE TYRANNY OF FASHION.'

The Cornhill Magazine, July 1878, pp. 83–94

THERE is to be found at the heart of modern society a large and increasing minority of women, whose various occupations leave them neither time nor inclination to follow in that fantastic dance of fashion which is instituted for the employment of the inane, and the profit of milliners. It is worthy of inquiry whether some quiet haven, safe from the ceaseless perturbations of this disturbing influence, might not be found for those who are now dragged reluctantly with the current, or for such as, affecting to defy it, are wallowing helplessly in the trough of dowdyism. In the one case, much of energy, in the other, much of practical efficiency, is lost; the unwilling follower, conscious of being always a day too late, is fussy and impatient while suffering from a feeling of self-abasement, and the rebellious sister who has dropped out of the existing system before any other has been organised to receive her, skulks in and out of the feast of life in the disadvantageous position of one who has not on the "wedding garment."

It has long since come to be felt and acted on in the case of men, that these restless shiftings in the fashion of clothes are incompatible with the grave concerns which go to fill up a worthy human career; and for them the evil has practically ceased. That the time must come when relief from the foolish oppression extends to women also, can scarcely be matter of doubt; it remains only to be seen how far the hour is advanced, and in what form the amelioration is likely to appear.

If many-voiced dissatisfaction at the hard work (never ending and leading nowhere) entailed upon women by the gyrations of fashion, may be taken as a sign of the ripeness of the time, then might it seem that any standard of revolt would be likely to attract a large following; but such in effect has not proved to be the case. There have been practical appeals from advanced outposts in the extreme west, and æsthetic appeals nearer home, which have failed to meet adequate response; from which it may be gathered that in order to any large result, the scheme offered must embrace a wider sphere of human aims than has been acknowledged by any of those innovators who have yet proffered arms to the recalcitrants.

Unless the foundations of human society and the relations of the sexes, and not the foundations of society alone, but the very constitution of things, were shaken as they never can be shaken, women, whether busy or idle, earnest or frivolous,

DOI: 10.4324/9781315399980-9

will not cease to be solicitous of the impression their appearance may create. We must accept it as a fact that this solicitude, however attempered by circumstances, can never be generally suppressed; and, therefore, that the disadvantages attending the inert resistance to fashion which results in what has been called "dowdyism," or of the positive resistance whose only watchword is "use," are little likely to find welcome at the hands of any large proportion of even the most occupied of the sex. The harbour of refuge to be provided one day for that cultured *élite* among women who are beginning to feel the tyranny of fashion intolerable, must be one from which beauty is not banished, but where, on the contrary, it finds its securest anchor in use. It would not be difficult to prove that it is through the letting go of this anchor that the whole matter at issue has come at this moment to be so hopelessly adrift. The "coigne of vantage" for which we are on the lookout, must, it may be presumed, be one possessing such ennobling associations in the far past, as would remove it from all competition with the things of to-day, and all contempt of the things of to-morrow; if such a rallying point exist, it will be marked by a monument which genius having eternalised, time can do no more but hallow. It will be obvious to most people in what direction our gaze has turned, and all who are capable of recognising beauty as apart from present fashion, – a far smaller moiety of those even who have the cant of culture on their lips than might be supposed, – will readily admit that from the æsthetic side, our view is wholly advantageous; it is on the point of "fitness" that those doubts will be raised which it is hoped successfully to meet further on. For the present it will be convenient, on behalf of those who have only vaguely formulated to themselves the case against modern female dress, to resume briefly the nature and extent of the evils resulting from the loss of every principle of reason, before advancing further.

To begin with, the price of being beautiful according to the standard of the "mode" is at this particular moment heavy and grievous beyond precedent. The manufacture of the simplest-looking modern gown, closely sheathing two-thirds of the body as it is required to do, has become an affair demanding not only an inordinate degree of skill in the fitter, but a ruinous amount of time, patience, and money on the part of the person fitted. Such a gown has as many pieces as a Chinese puzzle, and the difficulty of putting them together is as unproductive of any valuable result. We live in an age which we are wont to call "busy," and we are resolved to justify its title. We do not leave even to the moth its proper work, but begin with our own hands to "fret" our garments before they are made. Our damasks and brocades are all hacked to death, cut remorselessly through leaves and flowers, and the stalk joined irrelevantly to the heart of the rose, and the mutilated bud to the thorn. Upon this false and complicated foundation comes the even more vile and yet more elaborate worrying of the tissue, which is known under the name of "trimming." If the *cordons blue* of millinery begin by making a hash of their material, they end by making a mince. The rich stuff is chopped into fractional bits, and served up in various devices. How very heavy is the result of all this costly cookery, those only can tell who are condemned to bear it. The carrying about of a gown thus "trimmed," with its burthen of bows – all in the wrong place – and its ironically named puffs, would make a serious item in the day's work of a porter. It would be difficult for a mind untrained in folly, if one can conceive of the existence of such, to arrive at any conclusion as to the object of this laborious effort; the obvious one of enabling the performer to carry the dust and pollutions of the atmosphere about the person, appearing unsatisfactory. As little claim in the light of pure reason might be conceded to the idea that these toilers were tasking themselves in the interest of beauty. That a breathing woman should yield her body to be bound and trussed until it looked as dead as a wooden doll – a thing into which but for its surroundings you would not hesitate to drive nails – would certainly be held by such untaught reason impossible. But assuming that the reason invoked could be made to accept this deformed and stolid mould for the beautiful living frame, it would surely meet the lying tale told further on with indignant denial. For beneath the seeming frankness of modern raiment, there lives not a hint of truth. To the minor make-believe of padding which the senile want of reticence in latter-day dress necessitates, allusion is not here made; we would stigmatise that deeper falsehood which is ever offering to our acceptance the protean monsters of outworn fancy in place of the divine image; which having not long since decreed to the lower half of the person the aspect of a bulbous root, now gives to the wooden doll above the termination of a mermaid below.

But no more; such is the omnipotence of fashion with the majority, it were hopeless at this moment to think of establishing by argument that a single leg may not suffice for beauty; before this truth can be carried home to all minds, we must be content to wait the time when the great arbitrator has decreed again that there shall be no legs at all, or haply that there shall be three. A good illustration of the perverse influence of the tyrant is that an eloquent apology for the teetotum versus the human form was made during the reign of crinoline by a sculptor of eminence to the present writer; and if the whole truth must be told, without dissent from his interlocutor.

In despair therefore of proving that fashionable clothes are ugly, we will return to the charge against them on less fortified ground. Allowing that the effect of the single leg is charming, nobody can pretend that the manner in which it is brought about – the being tied by the two – is pleasant. As hard would it be to maintain that it is agreeable to be sitting on bows of ribbon, on bunches of folds, on keys, or a purse, or on all together; or to be feeling after a "tail" that is painting itself in the mud, with something less than the grace of an antiquated kitten. The strain against the knees of an ordinary travelling dress shortened for action – that dress in which a young woman occasionally rivals the mountaineering feats of her husband or brothers – is such that the endurance she makes proof of should be rated as double. That a woman can look trim about the waist, and at the same time be drawing regular and deep inspirations of breath, like those which minister to the vigour and the sounder health of men, is a pretence that is sometimes made by the disingenuous; but not the less true is it that in this as in all other respects, she consents to be heavily handicapped in that race of life which is becoming daily more strenuous for many of the competitors. To these manifold disadvantages, it may be added, that the vast amount of labour expended on modern clothing is labour of the most disheartening, wearisome, and stultifying kind. The yards – the miles would hardly be a gross exaggeration – of pipings, pleatings, and puffings, which go to make up the life's work of thousands of our fellow-beings, are utterly without ennobling suggestion, as much cut off from the joy and beauty of the universe as they are from its use and service. The man who points a pin has a less unsatisfactory share in the work of the world. His soul is not necessarily subdued to his calling; his hand alone may become the machine, for the fashion of pins is unchanging. But it is in the interests of the wearers and not the workers of our women's clothes, that we are engaged in formulating their demerits. Allowing that to eyes trained in a long course of the grotesque, the dress of the day is wholly delightful; that its lines, if they do not suggest natural form, hint at outlines more pleasing and original; still, its undeniable defects of opposition to the laws of health, and wastefulness of much that is most precious in life, remain, and must alone be held sufficient to justify the desire of reasonable women for the reduction of so inordinate a tax.

It has been said that signs of revolt from the tyranny of fashion are in the air; if it be so it may be hoped that help is near, and if near, that its means may be somewhere within sight. Those who are most cognisant of the special need, are agreed as to what is wanted in one particular, which is shelter from the ceaseless torrent of change. All else as regards this question, is secondary; to the weight the unlikeliest part of the frame will in time become fitted; the organs will learn to keep house in their prison; the legs to forget their liberty; the arms restrict themselves to employment at a low level; but that when all these useful things have been learnt, we should have to unlearn them again; that at the moment of ultimate triumph over these difficulties we should have to turn *volte face,* and envisage new ones with weakened powers; that, worse than all, we should be called upon to build up in the sweat of our own brows the materials of each new claim – this is an overflow of bitterness which it is scarcely conceivable could have been endured so long.

There may be unsympathising outsiders to whom it will appear that no such refuge from the evils of change as that here invoked, is needed; that an attitude of steady resistance to all extremes would be sufficient to protect those desirous of protection from the incursions of folly. It cannot be known to such objectors, if indeed they exist, how constant and wearing is the pressure from without, or how insecure are the foundations upon which resistance has to be offered. A stand made upon any basis of reason might perhaps be maintained against equal pressure; but a position taken up on the sands of an absurdity to which "use and wont" alone have reconciled us for a time, would not fail before long to render firmness ridiculous. The fault of that system of clothing which we see blown about by every breath of fashion, lies deeper than the surface. Whatever the changes wrought upon it, the ground idea of elaborately shaped and tailored garments remains; it is here that it will be found to differ essentially from any standard of dress which right reason could acknowledge, or noble art deign to perpetuate.

In all times and places where the clothing of the body has formed part of a living art, it will be seen on examination to be wrought by the most simple and seemingly artless means. The dress of the Indian ayah, in which a scarf eight yards in length is made to form, without pin or thread, a garment incomparably graceful and convenient, and that of all ranks in ancient Hellas, offer extreme or typical examples of this employment of easy means to admirable and varied ends. Not utterly removed from this noblest ideal, is the quaintly beautiful dress of Japan, and that of the Flowery Land, coloured like an orchid, has a life and permanent character of its own. These, and more or less all peoples of the superior races, who have not been tainted with the Birmingham distemper, enrobe themselves in a manner suited to the dignity of ease and the free play of natural grace; as free, and not slaves to their belongings. How the art of dress came to be corrupted with us, it does not enter into our present scheme to inquire; it is sufficient for our purpose to point out the fact, and invite those whom culture has prepared to admit it, to the conclusion it naturally leads to. And that conclusion is, that those who are in pursuit of stability, convenience, or beauty in this matter of dress, would do well to return to first principles. The writer can imagine the half-amused horror with which this announcement may be greeted in some quarters; the blanket of the Indian will suggest itself; nor has our reference to the dress worn in ancient Greece given rise to more reassuring conclusions. An idea would seem to prevail that not only was the climate of ancient Hellas tempered to the lamb shorn wholly of covering, but that this people was so beloved of its gods that they all – to a woman – died young. With these notions current among us, it might be matter of surprise that clothes, even the most diaphanous, are to be seen on their statues; all the more that they are so often missing from our own. Perhaps when the turn of modern England comes for apotheosis in the clouds of Oceanic fancy, we may be conceived of as having been favoured in like manner. In sober fact, and notwithstanding that the aim of sculpture must ever be the glorification of the human form, the statues of the great age of Pericles are clothed. It is this which may offer ground for some natural surprise until study has taught us to feel how these garments, a-flutter with life and action, are made to surround the forms they veil as with an aura which enlarges the sphere of their vitality. If the old Greek chose by preference youthful shapes for the purpose of decoration, his practice cannot be said to be bettered by our own; the flower of life in the moment of its eclosion will ever be dear to art, and it is a subject for gratulation that in Greek statues and fictile vases so many and needed hints of the reverent treatment of age should have been put on record. The archeologist of the future will, it is to be hoped, look in vain for any sculptural presentment of the modern "cap," whereas the veil which swathes the throat in its charitable folds is a familiar object in ancient work. That two out of the nine figures of the Niobe group have long sleeves, seems in some way to have escaped general observation.

Let us pause, before venturing further, to inquire what might be the typical character of a dress which could be supposed capable of offering that refuge from the tempest of fashion for which we are a-gaze. There can, it is presumed, be no doubt that it should be simple in plan, and that such changes in its lines as the frailty of our nature demand from time to time, should be produced, not by alteration of structure, but by method of adjustment. From the groundwork of such a system, the element of fancy should be excluded; all should proceed on the lines laid down by law in relation to the human frame; that is, the weight should be set where it is least oppressive, the organs left to their free development, the muscles and limbs to their fullest play, and the whole appliance be made and seen to subserve the advantage of the wearer. It would be well that the garments should be put together according to established rule, and so as to receive character and not impose it upon the person. They should be easy to wash where the material admitted of such purification, and should not occupy an undue space either in wearing, keeping, or carrying about. Finally, a dress to suit – we will not say all women for all time, but only a certain number of impatient sufferers for a little breathing space – should be, as we have before observed, removed from vulgar comparison, by association with some great and enduring moment of the past – immortalising associations which would keep the thing reflected on from being either old or new – associations whose revived presence in our midst would be felt as an impulse of higher life throughout the whole sphere of culture.

The fact that a system of clothing – of clothing for both sexes – possessing all the advantages here set forth, was actually worn by the higher class of Britons for a period of nearly 400 years, seems to have passed very generally out of the recollection of those even whose delight in the beauty of classical drapery under classical conditions is the most sincere. That the Romans did, however, wear such a dress, and that this dress, with but slight alteration, was the dress of ancient Greece, is known to all; and that the Romanised Britons, the higher ranks of these Islands, adopted and wore during the period of their stay, and beyond it, the dress of their Roman conquerors, will admit of easy verification by those who are interested in the fact. Since it will hardly be contended that the climate of the northern parts of England included under the name of Cumbria, or of the, at that time, thickly populated highlands of Snowdonia, has undergone radical change, it must be conceded that the garb worn by the chiefs and their household followers was one which could provide adequate protection against the rigours of our skies. It may [i]ndeed be doubted, in view of these several centuries of adoption, if any dress which has been worn among us, borrowers as we have been from every quarter of the earth, and every region of fancy, would, if its normal type did not constitute it universal, have a better claim to be accounted national.

All roads are said to lead to Rome; in affairs of culture it would be a truer word, that all roads lead to Greece. Let us admit at last, frankly and fully, that it is to the sublimated common sense of its young intelligence that we ourselves should point for the cure of the insanities of modern fashion. The bare reading of the prescription for making an oblong piece of stuff, or double shawl, into a Greek tunic or chyton, is enough to affect us as with a breath of health. Receiving into the mind, after the bewildering vagaries of the mode, an idea so fenced in by law, we feel as a patient sickened by dissipation in prospect of a regimen wherein each act of his life is judiciously ordered. But the prescription shall be given to the reader, that he may judge for himself of its efficacy.

The length of the Greek chyton is the height of the wearer, measured from the crown of the head; the width, twice the length, so that the garment forms a square when sewn up – the square, that is, of the person with the arms extended. There is a hem at the bottom, and the trimming, if any, is placed immediately above it. Four loops are now set on the upper edge, back and front, at a distance of rather less than the width of the shoulders apart. A small bunch of pleats is made where each loop is sewn on, and the border of the stuff turned in about two inches. (Observe the excellent engineering; how the pleats and doubling of the stuff strengthen the hold of the loops, while the one gives richness to the folds, the other softness to the upper line of the dress.) The facture of the garment is now complete; before putting it on, a length of firm ribbon is crossed over the back and breast, and fastened securely at the waist. On this – well to the front of each shoulder, just at the point where a milkmaid carries her pails – two ornamental buttons are sewn, and to these the tunic is hung by its four loops. Sleeves to the elbow may be formed by other buttons and loops, if not provided for, as for day wear would be the case, from beneath. The dress being fastened on the shoulders, the zone completes its adjustment, the wearer drawing the garment through it in front, and still more at the sides, until the convenient length is attained. With some knowledge of the hang of classic drapery, no difficulty is found in disposing the folds in a manner to set tailoring at defiance.

Such is the method of producing the garment which may be taken as the type of all that is noblest in dress. Over this tunic it was the practice of Grecian women, as well for purposes of dignity and state as for warmth, to drape shawls and scarfs in an endless variety of arrangement, and it is evident that such additions would facilitate successful effect where awkwardness of figure or clumsiness of hand might otherwise interfere.*

We have then in view a dress, the making of which would be the work of half-an-hour; a dress offering the framework of a system from which it would seem that all we are now in want of might be developed. It is simple, and susceptible of variety otherwise than by practical jokes played upon the human form. It is so much under the control of law, that even the little labour called for in putting it together is regulated, not empirical. There is not a muscle or a limb which it restricts in its action; its seemingly flowing drapery being all upon the person, is never in the way of the wearer or others; and its weight is so disposed that it is

* It should be borne in mind that the garment described is offered only as typical of the simplicity and sincerity of the Greek idea. Of that idea numerous modifications were employed among the ancients, and many more would naturally arise in practice among moderns, which, if they did not retain all the simple grace of the above, might offer a compromise more acceptable to vitiated taste. The blouse form is an example of such a compromise.

practically unfelt. With the power of development inherent in elementary forms, it can be made suitable to every stage of life and variation of climate. It is easy to wash, easier to pack, and its length can be regulated at pleasure. It possesses associations with the greatest moment of culture, and has an ever-present and enduring standard. On its beauty it were needless to insist, since the point must be conceded by persons least capable of feeling it, on the witness of authority such as it is to be feared will never more be equalled in the history of our planet: the sculptors of Attic Greece delighted to reproduce its combinations. Add to this that its beauty, while susceptible of great and legitimate enrichment, is compatible with poor material and an almost total absence of labour, and that it is modest and "womanly" beyond comparison with any fashion to be seen in our day. As set against these unquestionable advantages, and others not less important which have been yet but hinted at, it may be conceived that the adoption of garments so far removed in method of production from our present practice might subject the innovator to invidious remark. To this it is replied that the general outline and "hang" of the shawls or stuffs thus arranged makes so near an approach to that obtained by the cutting and goring, the piecing and ligatures of the present mode, that an eye uninformed of the facility of the means employed would be slow to discover them for itself. The experiment of assembling a number of ladies of all ages in the garb of ancient Greece has lately been tried on a somewhat extensive scale; and notwithstanding that the measures taken were generally successful in securing adherence to the simple type, that is, that shawls, or oblong pieces of stuff, wholly uncut, and with few stitches in them, made all the *frais* of the toilettes, the effect obtained, though admittedly beautiful and becoming, differed so slightly from that to be seen in many artistic circles of the day, that the learned pundits, who had thought to behold animated statues, were disappointed. It was pronounced that with the exception of some half dozen, who might have walked the streets of ancient Athens unchallenged, the remaining ladies could have appeared equally without critical notice in Belgravia or Bloomsbury; a greater freedom of gait, a breath of unwonted life, and a certain ennobling power, being things rather to be felt than commented on.

It has been objected that natural draperies, unhacked and untailored (for of such is Greek dress), are not only inconvenient, but unbecoming to any but the young and comely. Of the first charge our preceding remarks may be held to have disposed, but the second is, alas! in one sense too true; no dress can rejuvenate the aged, or make beautiful the ugly. As to exceptions on the score of convenience, such come strangely from persons who have been victims in turn to every disqualifying folly of the mode, and whose every step is being made at this moment with an effort equal to that of wading through water. As little are the fears expressed in the matter of "becomingness" consistent on the part of those who for the last eighteen months have been victims of a fashion as merciless to defects of person as if invented in cruel irony; and who are now resignedly offering each disgrace of nature or "scorn of time" to the examination of unsympathising spectators. That fashion should compel the display of a shape barren of beauty, wanting in due proportion, or hopelessly run to seed, without a fold to relieve the desolation or attenuate the outline, is proof not alone of its brutal tyranny, but of the obfuscation of the æsthetic sense it has the power to inflict. Apart from this insidious despotism, it could surely not require extraneous proof that an ill-made, over-fat or over-lean female form would offer a pleasanter object for contemplation when made to serve as a point of attachment for draperies whose fall has a beauty of their own. What indeed might have to be admitted as nearer to the truth is, that such draperies have a tendency, not certainly to reduce to a level, but to raise the maltreated something nearer to the eminence enjoyed by the favourites of nature; it might even have to be conceded that where much is obscured or softened which pitifully appeals to such charity, some exceptional beauty might, in accepting the conditions of Greek dress, be debarred that loud proclamation it is permitted now to make of itself. If this were so, indeed, it were a generous sacrifice on the part of the few possessed of this special mark of the favour of the gods, on behalf of the many less richly endowed.

As a protection against the rigours of the weather when abroad, a shawl, square or long, according as it was used as a cloak or a wrap, had with the ancients still to do duty. An inquiry into the various methods of "throwing" this wrap so as to ensure the exact amount of protection needed – methods all graceful, and held to be significant of the status and breeding of the bearer – would lead us into paths where to follow our gracious guides we should need an address and personal initiative such as our habits have tended to suppress. Suffice it to say that there is no necessary reason why any garment, provided its form were simple and honest, should not be worn above a gown whose chief distinction lay in the possession of these characteristics.

That such a dress would cut from the heads of women much of the head-gear which has been seen on them for many a decade past, will scarcely be held to its discredit by those whose advance in the path of "sweetness and light" has brought them to a point from which the inherent grotesque of such objects has become apparent. It is not likely that a matron in the garb of Penelope would be found admonishing her household in a doll's cap. If a doubt can be entertained that the thing we are agreed to call a bonnet would find its most significant adornment in bells, a glance at the bonnet of five years past would prove the point to demonstration. But it is not always easy to obtain such witness; the flimsiness and trumpery of these costly structures consigning them to the rag-bag before a fifth of that time has passed over them. There are signs, however, that hats and bonnets are for a time to be worn on the head; which restoration to an obvious purpose would redeem them from ridicule and incongruity.

It would seem then that if protection from the follies of fashion be among the attainable good things of the future, it will be found in consulting that fine sense of fitness, that idealised common sense, which in its last resort resulted in the creation of the Parthenon. It is not beauty, it is not the saving of money, it is not even the raising of the standard of health, which is felt to be the supreme need in this matter; it is simply the conservation of energy. Certainly at no period of the world's progress has the mind of man or woman been so prepared to rejoice at any easy adjustment of means to ends, as at this present. The hurry of life in our great centres is unparalleled, and for women, with the burthens which are their natural heritage, new paths of labour are opening day by day. Many a working woman who now, from her utter incapacity to afford the time, thought, and money needed for the elaboration of modern dress, bears the stigma of "strong-mindedness," would be able, if the matter were relieved of its difficulty, to carry on her labours unimpeded by the reproach. That the sting of it is often felt where most accepted is certain; for it is inconceivable that women who are turning high gifts to account are wanting as a rule in a love for the beautiful, truer if less devouring than that which actuates the puppet of fashion. That they lay this love, with perhaps many another, down upon the altar of progress, is an item in the sum of sacrifice in which such lives abound. There are women, and such may even constitute a majority, who delight in the fickleness of fashion; and there are some to whom that fickleness gives the sole occupation which fills up their empty days. Let them keep it, in the name of sacred folly; but why should the frivolous many be suffered for ever to impose the sliding scale of a vexatious tax upon the worthier few?

That the adoption by a minority of busy and æsthetically cultured women, of a dress making some approach to ancient simplicity, would seriously tell on the mantua-makers' trade, may be more than doubted. It is not by the custom of such ladies that the exorbitant gains of the magnates of the class are swollen; and if it were it would be hard to say on what ground any appeal to our sympathy on behalf of such persons could be made. These artists (*sic*) stand self-condemned in their own *ateliers,* surrounded not by forms of eternal beauty, but by a headless crowd of deformed phantoms – the blocks which represent their sole ideal of that shape in which all the visible beauty of creation culminates. The culture of this one of the arts of life is left to impudent pretenders, men and women whose ideas of beauty are profoundly vitiated; who are for the most part wholly ignorant of the structure and play of the bodies they denaturalise, and who are constantly exposed to temptations of self-interest, which cause them to invent and set afloat the succession of costly vagaries which are beggaring thousands of lives. The serious concerns and varied aims of the better minds tend more and more to detach them from questions of secondary interest; and thus fashion has become a will-o'-the-wisp, a product of the swampiest flats of human intelligence, and the so-called art of dress relegated to those smug dwellers in low places who fatten upon folly. For its more humble professors, and the whole class of journeywomen, the elevation in the kind of work that would follow upon simplified forms of dress, would be a gain of which it is difficult to estimate the extent. The wasted labour of these poor white slaves is an evil so serious that although it has been touched upon and passed, as beside the immediate question, a word more in this place must be said upon it. Theirs is an industry not only poorly paid and profitless in its result, but one which, spent upon ephemeral forms, partakes of their shiftiness, and reacts injuriously upon the worker. Not alone does it afford no field for the exercise of the higher faculties, but it is made hopeless by the sense of transitoriness. The latest product of the fancy of the man-milliner, heavy with toil, and involved as a bad dream, will have become "old clothes" before the gloss is off the silk. It is contended that labour can only confer dignity on the labourer, when it carries with it a sense of use, or is applied to permanent forms. The shawl or square of stuff which receives enrichment at the hands of the needlewoman is such a form, and offers a legitimate field for beautiful design and careful execution; if its worthier specimens were signed like other masterpieces of art – signed by designer and executant alike when the two were not combined – it would be to the advantage of all concerned.

If little has been advanced as to the costliness in money of modern raiment, it is because its wastefulness in much that is more precious than money makes a graver indictment against it; and, notwithstanding some recent and notorious examples, it would perhaps be difficult to prove that on the whole the item is utterly out of relation to other excesses of a luxurious epoch. There is reason to believe that the dress of ancient Greece was, if not necessarily, still possibly as costly, while it was certainly immeasurably more rich. As little has the question of the injurious effect of pressure upon health been insisted on; and that for the reason that all such insistance has been proved past hope to be vain. A custom that has long found such obstinate adherence must possess a hold in some sentiment of our nature; even as the distorted Chinese foot favours the idea of dependent helplessness which has been widely held to be a charm in woman. In the case of the compressed waist, the motive is not far to seek. Clothes that are fitted to the frame have an inclination to strain and in straining to become thinner over the protuberant curves, while they lie loosely over the receding; from which it follows that in a mode of dress wherein the whole outline is exhibited, there arises a temptation to add to the effect of those diminished curves by binding and pinching. Against this temptation, the physiologist will continue to appeal in vain.

If relief from these manifold oppressions is to be looked for in our day, it may safely be predicted that it either must come shortly or await another turn in the wheel – shall we say the rack – of Fashion? It is the aim of the tyrant at this moment, by her ever-tortuous means, to impart a false air of simplicity to modern raiment, while a modestly (some may think an immodestly) slender claim is made for it upon space above the ground level. One word of advice to the fair Amazons of the period. They would do well, with a view to distant effect, to eschew light pink, and notably flesh-colour in the choice of their "cuirasses." Blue as a tint would be preferable, since the appearance of being dressed only in wode is an advance on being habited in nothing at all. Now this mock simplicity, and this slender claim upon space, might possibly make true simplicity, and the actual size of the human frame, tolerable at the present moment. Let us take the time as we find it. The bodies we see, may be "clothed upon," but when their semblance is changed, and they appear once more as the monsters of some delirious dream, no miracle would get them into the garments of health.

The tyranny of the steel trap in which all the women of the civilised world were caught some few years since was such, that a lady became a beggar without her hoops, and was set upon by the dogs in the street.

Great was Diana of the Ephesians, and great was Pallas Athene; but greater by far is our Goddess of Fashion, whose allies are in the kennel as in the court.

Who shall deliver us from the terror of her frown?

E. P.

7

MRS H. R. HAWEIS, 'IMPORTANCE OF DRESS.'

The Art of Beauty (New York: Harper & Brothers, Publishers, 1878), pp. 11–18

AS in our age and climate the human body is habitually and completely veiled, the veil assumes an artistic importance second only to the forms that are hidden. In nothing are character and perception so insensibly but inevitably displayed, as in dress, and taste in dress. Dress is the second self, a dumb self, yet a most eloquent expositor of the person.

There are garments, as there are faces and natures, which have no 'bar' in them – nothing which stops with a sudden shock your pleasure in them, nothing that dissatisfies or perplexes you. There are colours that are always beautiful because they recall nature, fashions which are beautiful because sensible and fulfilling the aim for which they were invented. In fact, no dress can be beautiful that is not appropriate, and appropriateness consists chiefly in graceful expression and useful purpose.

In modern days – so far removed from those when dress was regarded as a mere covering, and aspired to be no more (although it always admitted of decoration, such as jewellery or needlework) – we no longer look upon a gown as a shield against wintry cold, or a modest veil drawn between ourselves and the outer world. We expect it to be a work of art. Much money, representing much labour, is lavished upon every garment. When the silk-weaver has spent his skill upon the production of even texture, delicate gloss, and rare tints, only half the work is done. We cannot fling and fold the rich piece upon us after the simple fashion of our forefathers. We want it more to express than to hide us. A clever craftswoman must cut it to the approved shape, and sew it into form; it must be clothed upon with other and richer fabrics, which we call 'trimming,' until its original price is doubled. Every form is eagerly borrowed for these trimmings. Patterns old and new are exhausted to form attractive combinations – the Greek frieze, the mediæval missal-border, the whole animal and vegetable kingdoms are laid under contribution – our very discontent with all there is, and our insatiable craving for novelty, is one of the diseases consequent on a certain repletion of variety. Raised work, indented work, tabs, fringes, frills – there is no possible form of ornament

DOI: 10.4324/9781315399980-10

that we have not tried and cast aside. So that a dress now claims to be considered as a work of art.

Now if dress be worth all this elaboration, if it intends to reach, as it evidently aspires to do, the platform of a picture, or a poem, or a fine building, the art it adopts must be either good or bad art. I believe the melancholy truth to be that we can hardly find a modern dress which is not throughout in the worst taste and opposed to the principles of all good art.

Yet at the same time I think that to a certain extent the milliners mean well. I think that the women who spoil themselves with the milliner's devices mean well too. They do want to make the best of themselves, to be 'things of beauty,' and not eyesores. But how to do this they don't know, and they don't think, and they generally refuse to learn. There are some ladies who always look well: they are not necessarily the pretty ones; but they are women gifted with fine natural taste, who instinctively choose right forms, colours, and fabrics, generally without knowing why. These, however, are exceptions.

If everybody who could hold a pencil were suddenly called upon to paint a picture, there would be only a few out of every score at least who would betray any sense of grace, perspective, colour, or design. Would it not be wise for those unpossessed of the sacred fire to receive instruction of some wholesome kind before they wasted time and good material to so little purpose?

But what is true of painting is true also of dress. We need not all paint, but we have all got to dress, and the sooner dress is recognised by our women as an art-product, the better (and probably the more cheaply) they will be able to apparel themselves.

What usually takes place in this country in the matter of dress? Vain persons who are proud of their appearance, and wish to make the most of themselves, spend much time in covering themselves with things that make an artist lift up hands and eyes of regret, astonishment, and pity. Those who are not vain often exclaim, 'Don't ask *me*! I will wear anything that is brought to me!' and both act from ignorance. The vain person wastes time and defeats her own aim; the other is too ignorant to know that there is anything to know worth knowing, and does not sufficiently respect what God has given her, to care how she looks: so there is always a discord between her inner and outer self.

Yet dress and a proper care for it ought not to minister merely to vanity, nor impair in any degree the moral tone. A woman ought to care what she wears for her own sake and for the sake of those about her. It is a fault, not a virtue, to be reckless as to the impression one leaves on the eye, just as it is a fault to be indifferent to the feelings of others; in either case there is a sad absence of those subtle and beautiful perceptions that constitute a delicate and gentle mind.

But how difficult it is for a woman to be really well dressed, under the existing prejudice that everybody must be dressed like everybody else! This notion of a requisite livery is paralysing to anything like development of individual taste, and simply springs from the incapacity of the many to originate, wherefore they are glad to copy others; but this majority have succeeded in suffocating the æsthetic minority, many of whom are now forced to suppress really good taste for fear of being called 'affected.' We shall never have any school of art in England, either in dress or decoration of any kind, until the fundamental principle of good art is recognised, that *people may do as they like* in the matter, and until women cease to be afraid of being laughed at for doing what they feel to be wise and right.

There can be no originality of scheme until individual taste is admitted to be free; and how can there be individuality while all are completely subservient to law, that law usually determined by folk who have neither natural feeling for beauty nor education?

With regard to the milliner, ladies should remember that by trusting to the milliner's 'taste'(?) they are merely playing into the hands of various tradesmen whose interest it is to sell their goods, be they good or bad. The manufacturer's mill must be kept going, *therefore* the fashions must change; the milliner loves her perquisites, *therefore* she encourages every fashion which is of a kind to deceive the eye as to quantity of material. It is to her interest that you should not be able to measure the exact number of yards she has used; it would be to her customer's very considerable interest did the customer calculate and understand more than she usually does, how much stuff is required for flounce, skirt, or sleeve!

It is as absurd to suppose that every variety of short and tall, grave and gay, young and old, must be dressed in one style, as that the same coat must fit every man. How should it be so, whilst nature revels in endless dissimilarity? Why is the woman with taste for colour and form to sacrifice her gift to the others who have it not, and *copy,* when she is capable of originating? Why this deadly fear of being conspicuous? Why is one's individuality, so clear within, to be so confused without?

Alas! perhaps it is a misfortune to be an individual at all. We know the pity, the deep, deep commiseration which satirists say ill-natured women feel for those who are congenitally conspicuous – for *good looks*. Is it a similar commiseration for those who possess the next best thing, *good taste,* which has destroyed the interpretation of a beautiful mind, as it would like to stamp out a beautiful body?

If so, in the name of art and nature both, let us shake off the lethargy which immolates us to a Juggernauth of ignorant opinion, and let us assert our individuality, if we have any, in dress as in other things.

Woman is most beautiful when she is most herself and least conscious of it – in dress as well as in other things: and as I am at present treating chiefly of her looks, which depend in great measure on her dress, I may lay down as a general principle that dress is most beautiful and most becoming when it follows the outlines of the human form.

Dress bears the same relation to the body as speech does to the brain; and therefore dress may be called the speech of the body.

Speech was supposed to be meant for the expression of thought, till a modern cynic told us it was on the contrary for its concealment. Dress once expressed the person, now it disguises it; well, disguise may sometimes be necessary – but when dress carries its anatomical fictions as far as evasion may be carried, as far as falsehood, it ceases not only to be respectable, but beautiful as well.

[. . . .]

Observe further, that plenty of time – too much – is given to the dressmaker. Very little is given to dress itself; no thought is expended on the requirements which the dress is to supply. No Englishwoman considers the meaning of each trimming, or form, or colour. She does not even consider whether it expresses in any degree her character, tastes, or wants.

8

[ANON], STATEMENT AND 'EDITORIAL NOTE', *THE RATIONAL DRESS SOCIETY'S GAZETTE*

The Rational Dress Society's Gazette, January 1889, p. 1

The object of the Rational Dress Society is to promote the adoption, according to individual taste and convenience, of a style of dress based upon considerations of health, comfort, and beauty, and to deprecate constant changes of fashion that cannot be recommended on any of these grounds.

THE Rational Dress Society protests against the introduction of any fashion in dress that either deforms the figure, impedes the movements of the body, or in any way tends to injure the health.

It protests against the wearing of tightly-fitting corsets, of high-heeled or narrow-toed boots and shoes: of heavily-weighted skirts, as rendering healthy exercise almost impossible; and of all tie-down cloaks or other garments impeding the movements of the arms.

It protests against crinolines or crinolettes of any kind as ugly and deforming.

An annual subscription of 3s. 6d. constitutes membership, and includes free delivery of *Gazette* quarterly.

Those interested in the objects of the Society are requested to apply to the Secretary,
MRS. HALL,
At the Society's Depot, 11, SLOANE Street, S.W.

The maximum weight of clothing (without shoes) approved of by the Rational Dress Society, does not exceed seven pounds.

EDITORIAL NOTE.

WE have a great deal to bring before the notice of our readers this month, the most important being the establishment of a new Rational Dress Depôt at 11, Sloane Street, S.W. This depôt is carried out on the ready money system, consequently we are able to offer our customers goods at low prices. Underclothing, rational

DOI: 10.4324/9781315399980-11

corsets and bodices, and divided skirts are among the articles that we provide, and all those interested in rational dress are invited to pay a visit to this establishment.

Two drawing-room meetings have been held by the Society, and a lecture on Rational Dress has been given by special request at the Somerville Club. We hope that these are merely the forerunners of many meetings to be held during the winter. Some work has also been done by Lady Harberton, in an article published in the *Sanitary Record* of Dec. 15th, in answer to Miss Becker's defence of Stays, which appeared on Oct. 15th, in the same paper.

Miss Becker's argument is that only tight-lacing is injurious, not the wearing of stiff corsets, a use which has been firmly established by the experience of ages. "The question we have to consider," she says, "is whether women would do wisely either (1) to discard corsets while retaining in other respects their usual form of dress, or (2) to make such a revolution in their attire as would enable them to dispense with the assistance of stays to support the over-dress. The anti-corset party do not, as a rule, go so far as to recommend the last alternative. They do not venture to suggest that women should wear outer garments adapted to the natural form of the body," &c. Lady Harberton points out that this latter assertion cannot be said to be true. "On the contrary," she says, "the recommendation of a complete alteration is the very keynote of what almost everyone who has lectured or written on the subject of late years has most strongly insisted on." Having thus contradicted Miss Becker's "amazing statement," Lady Harberton proceeds to state the advantages of the dual skirt, and we ecommend our readers to procure the paper which is published by W. H. Allen, 13, Waterloo Place, and to study for themselves the arguments used. In conclusion, we would draw the attention of our readers to the fact that we intend to issue the *Gazette* quarterly for the coming year, and would ask their kind support and subscriptions. At the Annual Meeting of the Society held on the 23rd Nov., it was agreed that the annual subscription to the Society should be raised to 3s. 6d., and should include free delivery of the *Gazette* quarterly to members.

1.2

Outlines; contours; boundaries

DOI: 10.4324/9781315399980-12

1.2.1

Shaping the silhouette

The corset and the crinolette

DOI: 10.4324/9781315399980-13

1.2.1 Shaping the silhouette: the corset and the crinolette

Victorian women's dress has become well-known for its 'essential hourglass' shape[1] that remained constant throughout the latter part of the nineteenth century, despite other changes in style and aesthetics. As Valerie Steele notes, this was created by two elements: 'the long, full, structured skirt and the tailored, boned bodice', which '[intersected] at a narrow and constricted waist'.[2] This, of course, was underpinned by the corset, a mainstay in nineteenth-century women's dress, which was crucial to the creation of the 'hourglass' that was so often regarded as the epitome of femininity. And, while the dimensions and volume of women's skirts dramatically fluctuated during the nineteenth century, ranging from the enormity of the 1860s crinoline to the comparative svelteness of the 1870s silhouette, a small, trim waist remained fashionable throughout the period.[3]

Both the corset and the crinoline experienced a certain notoriety during the Victorian period, Steele describing the corset as 'probably the most controversial garment in the entire history of fashion'.[4] Matters, however, were complex; while the wearing of a corset was not only fashionable but widely expected during the period, a too-tight corset was also stigmatised.[5] One key episode in its Victorian history was dubbed the 'Corset Controversy', which emerged in the late 1860s and took the form of a series of letters, supposedly by readers, published in *The Englishwoman's Domestic Magazine*, concerning the extent to which women 'tight-laced' their corsets.[6] But the crinoline, the hidden steel frame that created the excessively large skirts, also became the focus of media scrutiny, being widely ridiculed by contemporary print media, most notably *Punch*, from the late 1850s onwards.

Correspondingly, both garments have garnered significant scholarly attention, for example, within Steele's seminal study of the corset and in Julia Thomas and Julie Wosk's work on the crinoline, as well as being represented in Rebecca N. Mitchell's anthology of Victorian texts.[7] Accordingly, we do not attempt to replicate this coverage in our volume; rather, we have chosen three extracts that draw out different aspects of Victorian body shaping.

Our first extract is derived from Madame Roxey Caplin, a well-known corsetière of the period who promoted use of the garment for both 'health' and aesthetic reasons.[8] However, our extract from her book *Health and Beauty* focuses upon a lesser known aspect of Victorian corset wear, namely, that geared towards 'gestation' or for use during pregnancy. While this might seem shocking or incredible to the modern reader, it is less so when situated within the context of Victorian culture of gender and sexuality.

While Victorian culture strongly privileged the social role of mother, the 'active sexuality' required to produce children was at odds with the dichotomy of expectation whereby the idealised middle-class woman would be simultaneously maternal yet preternaturally 'and permanently childlike [. . .] even in maturity'.[9] Although a Victorian married woman might expect to spend a considerable length of time in pregnancy,[10] some critics have argued that it was regarded as a taboo or even shameful state, even within the bounds of wedlock. Leigh Summers, for example, claims that 'the pregnant body was considered by polite society to be somewhat repugnant and best kept from view' and that expectant mothers might even be 'ostracized',[11] while Lillian Nayder suggests that pregnancy was '[s]ometimes treated as a condition to be concealed' and, accordingly, 'drove women into varying degrees of retirement'.[12] Indeed, many women chose to continue to tight-lace throughout pregnancy; this arose perhaps from a desire to conceal their condition, as well as from a genuine belief that a corset was necessary for health reasons, as Caplin suggests.

Our extract from Caplin presents a covert solution to both these issues, namely, a corset designed specifically for use within pregnancy. While on the one hand, the reader was reassured that the corset worked in a different way from everyday corsets, being specifically designed to 'support' the pregnant form, they were also subtly reminded that it worked to simultaneously '[preserve] the figure' and, by implication, the small waist that was a constant feature of nineteenth-century female body ideals.[13]

Even in the advent of the twentieth century, the popularity of the corset prevailed. In the advertisement from The London Corset Company of 1900 included here, we are made aware of the need for corsets to fit 'the stout and the slim' alike. The aesthetic ideal of the Grecian form, which promoted flowing, draped fabrics rather than stylised and contoured outfits, is suggested by the naming of the 'La Samothrace' corset, although the garment itself is more indicative of mainstream body ideals of the period. Nonetheless, it is accompanied by an illustration of the Hellenistic 'Winged Victory of Samothrace' that was installed at the Louvre in 1884. The corset's name makes a direct link to the sculptural ideal of 'Nike of Samothrace' and introduces the uninitiated to an illustration of the famous work.[14]

Finally, our third source moves to a different aspect of the female silhouette in the form of the device known as the 'crinolette', seen here in an image from V&A Collections. The crinolette appeared during the late 1860s and presented a kind of transition from the full, round circumference of the 'cage' crinoline, to the more slender outline of the 1870s, by shifting the bulk of the skirt to the back of the dress.[15] While it has attracted comparatively less critical attention than either the corset or crinoline, its significance as an innovation cannot be underestimated, particularly in that it prefigured and facilitated the styles discussed in our next section, namely, the 'Grecian Bend' and the 'Dolly Varden' costumes.

Notes

1 E. Richards, *Darwin and the Making of Sexual Selection* (Chicago and London: The University of Chicago Press, 2017), p. 224.

2 V. Steele, *Fashion and Eroticism: Ideals of Feminine Beauty from the Victorian Era to the Jazz Age* (New York and Oxford: Oxford University Press, 1985), pp. 51–52, 52. See also J. Nunn, *Fashion in Costume 1200–2000*, 2nd edition (London: Herbert Press, 2000 [first published in 1984]), p. 121.

3 Christine Bayles Kortsch discusses the fashionability of the small waist in *Dress Culture in Late Victorian Women's Fiction* (London and New York: Routledge, 2016 [originally published by Ashgate Publishing in 2009]), p. 63.

4 V. Steele, *The Corset: A Cultural History* (New Haven and London: Yale University Press, 2001), p. 1.

5 See, for example, Steele, *The Corset: A Cultural History*, p. 35; Steele, *Fashion and Eroticism*, p. 162; and Kortsch, *Dress Culture*, Chapter 3: 'Fashioning Women: The Victorian Corset', pp. 55–104.

6 As Steele notes, during the late 1860s to early 1870s, *The Englishwoman's Domestic Magazine* published 'more than 150 letters on corsetry', a high proportion dealing with 'tight-lacing to extreme tenuity'. See Steele, *The Corset*, p. 88. Many of the letters reported favourably about corset-wear; Anne Hollander notes that they attested to both the 'unmistakably erotic pleasure as well as a general sense of well-being achieved through extreme tight-lacing'. See A. Hollander, *Feeding the Eye: Essays* (Berkeley and Los Angeles, CA, and London: University of California Press, 1999 [paperback edition published 2000]), p. 126. Some letters also describe, as Steele writes, 'enforced tight-lacing at fashionable boarding schools' (*The Corset*, p. 88), which has led to debates concerning their authenticity, as well as discussions concerning fetishistic elements in these writings. On these letters, see Steele, *The Corset*, pp. 88–93; Summers, *Bound to Please*, pp. 79–80; D. Kunzle, *Fashion and Fetishism: Corsets, Tight-Lacing & Other Forms of Body-Sculpture* (Stroud: Sutton Publishing, 2004), pp. 100–101; and M. Beetham, *A Magazine of Her Own? Domesticity and Desire in the Woman's Magazine, 1800–1914* (London and New York: Routledge, 1996), pp. 81–84.

7 See R. N. Mitchell (ed.), *Fashioning the Victorians: a Critical Sourcebook* (London: Bloomsbury Visual Arts, 2018), specifically Section Three: 'Crinolines and Corsets', pp. 93–122. For further analysis of the corset, see also Steele, *The Corset*; Summers, *Bound to Please*; and Kunzle, *Fashion and Fetishism*. The crinoline is explored in J. Wosk, *Women and the Machine: Representations from the Spinning Wheel to the Electronic Age* (Baltimore and London: Johns Hopkins University Press, 2001), Chapter 2: 'Wired For Fashion: Images of Bustles, Corsets, and Crinolines in the Mechanical Age', pp. 45–67, as well as in Julia Thomas' illuminating chapter 'Crinolineomania: *Punch*'s Female Malady', in *Pictorial Victorians: The Inscription of Values in Word and Image* (Athens, OH: Ohio University Press, 2004), pp. 77–103. See also A. Gernsheim, *Victorian and Edwardian Fashion: A Photographic Survey* (New York: Dover, 1981), pp. 44–48, for further discussion of the crinoline and the ridicule that it prompted.

8 For further discussion of Caplin (including an illustration of her 'Hygienic Gestation Corset'), see Summers, *Bound to Please*, pp. 45–47, and Steele, *The Corset*, pp. 41–42.

9 D. Gorham, *The Victorian Girl and the Feminine Ideal* (London: Croom Helm, 1982), pp. 7, 6.

10 Gorham notes that, during the period 1830–1870, a middle-class wife might expect to bear between five and seven children, although this number decreased as the century progressed (*The Victorian Girl*, p. 15).

11 Summers, *Bound to Please*, p. 37.

12 L. Nayder, *The Other Dickens: A Life of Catherine Hogarth* (Ithaca, NY, and London: Cornell University Press, 2011), p. 70.

13 Caplin, Madame R. A., *Health and Beauty; Or Woman and her Clothing. Considered in Relation to the Physiological Laws of the Human Body* (London: Kent and Co. Paternoster Row, 1864 [3rd edition; first published 1854]), p. 114, and Summers, *Bound to Please,* p. 43.

14 The relationship between women, agalmatophilia, and the sculptural ideal in Victorian literature and culture has been documented by critics. See, for example, P. Pulham, *The Sculptural Body in Victorian Literature and Culture: Encrypted Sexualities* (Edinburgh: Edinburgh University Press, 2020). For the sculptural metaphor in relation to Victorian actresses, see G. Marshall, *Actresses on the Victorian Stage: Feminine Performance and the Galatea Myth* (Cambridge: Cambridge University Press, 1998); for Victorian women writing about sculptures and the corporeal and metaphorical connections, see H. Fraser, 'Women and the Modelling of Victorian Sculptural Discourse', *Visual Resources*, 33(1–2), 2017, pp. 74–93.

15 Nunn describes the crinolette as 'a kind of decadent crinoline [. . .] with hoops at the back only' (*Fashion in Costume*, p. 153). See also L. Johnston (with M. Kite and H. Persson), *Nineteenth-Century Fashion in Detail* (London: V&A Publications, 2005), pp. 132–133, for an image of a crinoline of the late 1868s, which takes a similar form to that described here; it is described as having 'a distinctive flattening at the front and frequently a slight train at the hemline' (p. 132).

9

MADAME ROXEY A. [ANN] CAPLIN, 'ON GESTATION.'

Health and Beauty; or Woman and her Clothing. Considered in Relation to the Physiological Laws of the Human Body. (London: Kent and Co. Paternoster Row, 1864 [3rd edition; first published 1854]), pp. 99–115

"Sweet is the image of the brooding dove,
Holy as heaven a mother's tender love:
The love of many prayers and many tears,
Which changes not with dim declining years –
The only love which, on this teeming earth,
Asks no return for passion's wayward birth."

MRS. NORTON.

"The mother, in her office, holds the key of the soul."

OLD PLAY.

HAVING spoken of the various phases of woman's life up to her maturity in the preceding chapters, we have now to consider one of the most interesting of all the circumstances of her life, at once pleasing and endearing, when she is called upon to give birth to her offspring. In early life the distinction between the sexes was by no means marked: there was the same general outline, the same form and cast of features, the same feeling of isolation – each seemed to live for itself. As the softer passions, however, become developed, the man puts on that robust energy and daring which marks him out as the protector of the other sex; and his manly voice, the deepened tints upon his cheek, and the whole muscular system, show an excess of energy sufficient to qualify him for his position. At this period also a vast change takes place in the woman. The chest is expanded, the eye acquires a brilliancy peculiarly its own, and the frame takes that beautiful undulating form and proportion which gives it its peculiar charm. The province of woman is now to be the preserver of the species, and the several stages of marriage, pregnancy,

DOI: 10.4324/9781315399980-14

and maternity are the destiny which opens before her. It is through these that we have now to acompany her.

In discussing this period of her history, we must entirely set aside fashion and prejudice, and follow without reservation the laws which the Creator, in His beneficence, has stamped upon the frame. The putative mother should feel all the responsibility which attaches itself to the future life and happiness of her child, and ever study the conditions necessary to its healthy and proper development. But unfortunately it too often happens that the mother is as little acquainted with the first principles of physiology as the child, and the consequence is, long suffering and affliction to both parties.

A minute study of the human frame shows us that the form of the female differs from that of the male on purpose that it may be adapted to the necessities of this interesting period. The breadth of the pelvis, the structure of the tissues, and a number of other phenomena, are all modified in her for the purpose of giving life and health to her progeny. Throughout the whole range of animated nature, there are no organisms so perfect and beautiful as those which, in their collected form, are adapted to this purpose; whilst their extreme delicacy renders them sensitive, and predisposes them to inflict severe pain on any who knowingly or otherwise do violence to them.

It is, however, a great mistake to suppose that there is anything dangerous or extremely painful in accomplishing the ends of nature. The natural elasticity which is given to all the organs concerned, the slow and beautiful process by which it proceeds, all prepare for the last and final effort. Immediately that this is effected, another set of organs come into action to supply the offspring with nutrition. The mammary glands begin to secrete a fluid which they have never yielded before, and the organs which have been distended during the previous nine months resume again their normal proportions, and it is to this ebb and flow of the vital force that we have adapted our Gestation Corset.

It will perhaps have occurred to the reader that the conditions which we have to meet in this matter have been neither few nor trifling. The great distension of the abdomen which must necessarily have taken place has severely tried the muscles which form its walls, and this evil is in too many cases aggravated by the use of corsets that, instead of supporting the body, add to the stress already upon it. The ordinary stays have an elastic steel busk, which, on being leaned upon, bends over the stomach and pushes down the contents of the abdomen, causing an additional burden upon a part already weakened. The result of this is a stretching of the whole envelope in such a manner as to endanger the figure for life, and lay the foundation for varicose veins, prolapsus uteri, and other complaints to which ladies are too often subject.

Our Gestation Corset, of which we here present an illustration, is specially adapted to the condition of the body during pregnancy. It will be perceived at once that it is nothing more than a modification of our Hygienic Corset, adapted to the special condition of the body.

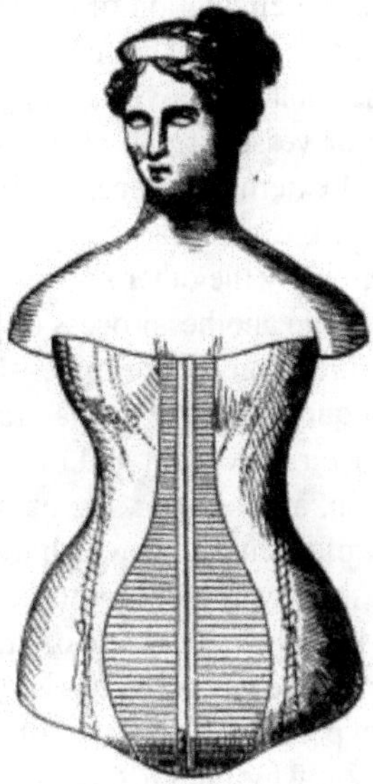

Figure 9.1 Gestation Corset.

Two separate phenomena present themselves in the study of this case. The development of the abdomen is taking place from below, upwards, so that the viscera are pushed out of their normal position, and in consequence of this, the skin and other ligaments yield, in an enormous degree; and to this should be added the fact, that the weight of the body is tending constantly downwards, and hence we have two powers to overcome.

The most casual observer will, by bearing those two considerations in mind, perceive that what is required will be the elasticity of the upper and central portions of the corset, and the contraction of that part which supports the lower abdomen. In accomplishing this we aid Nature in the performance of her operations; when less than this is done, we either labour in vain, or else inflict a positive injury.

The reason why the ordinary stays are so injurious may be demonstrated by tying a piece of thread tightly round the finger. Immediately that this is done, the circulation of the blood is impeded, and the finger becomes blue and painful, and this simply because an unyielding substance is pressing upon it. Now, although the waist is more pliable than the finger, it does not follow that the pressure is less injurious; but, on the contrary, as the organs which are deposited there are of greater importance to the health and strength of the body, so any undue pressure is sure to cause the most grievous injury. This injury is inflicted in consequence of its interference with the circulation of the blood, upon the proper action of which all that concerns our well-being depends.

It is generally known that the circulation of the blood takes place through two sets of vessels – the arteries and veins. The former come from the heart, and are employed in distributing the vital fluid over every part of the system, until they terminate in the capillaries, or vessels small as a hair, which are distributed over the whole of the internal and external surfaces of the body. When its vitality has been exhausted, the colour of the blood is changed from a bright red into a very dark hue, and it is then taken up by the other set of vessels, and carried back again to the heart and lungs, to undergo another process of purification. Any interruption of this circulation by a pressure upon the soft pipes through which the fluid is carried, must, as a natural consequence, lower the natural action of the organs, and by increasing the sensibility, give rise to pain and disease. Hence the headache, the giddiness, dulness, depression, and languor, the numbness of the extremities, the enlarged veins, and other painful sensations which too often accompany gestation; and when all these have passed away with parturition, it too frequently happens that the figure is spoiled for life. Now every one of the evils here spoken of may be avoided. Nature in her beneficence has given to every organ the inherent power to perform its functions without pain; and the organs of reproduction are no exception to this rule. There is no reason why the muscles should become soft, flabby, and relaxed, the pelvis diseased, and the figure spoilt, except it be in the want of adapting the external conditions of the body to the requirements of Nature.

In mentioning the above facts, we desire above all things to impress it upon the mind of the reader that we have exaggerated nothing, as many ladies can unfortunately testify. We have, however, only pointed out the evil for the purpose of suggesting the remedy, which is to have the corsets specially adapted to every occasion in life. Any verbal description, however, would, in a great measure, be inadequate to a proper understanding of the matter: to be fully comprehended the thing must be shown, and it is for this purpose that we have added to our ordinary show-room an anatomical gallery, containing the most perfect and beautiful set of preparations ever exhibited. It is here that we are enabled to demonstrate what the real changes are, which take place in the figure during the whole period of gestation – to point out the particular parts which have to sustain the burden, and the manner in which our external adaptations give support to the internal organs. It is here that we always take the sufferer, that she may see with her own eyes what it is that afflicts her.

From what has been already advanced, it will naturally follow that the manner of constructing the corset must differ with every individual case. A young, slightly-built mother with her first child, will require a very different adaptation from a lady who is the mother of several children, and been subject to painful labour, and has perhaps met with some accident, or is suffering from some disorder or infirmity, in whom the muscular relaxation is great, the bulk heavy, and the abdomen pendulous. It must be obvious, at first sight, that particular adaptations are necessary to meet her case, and that no rule, except that of giving support where support is needed, can be followed here. And this indeed is the principle we adopt, and hence our invariable success.

Hitherto we have considered GESTATION only; it remains now to follow the consequences which result from it. Those ladies who have already passed through the ordeal know by experience what the discomforts are that result from the old routine of bandages; how imperfect, clumsy, heavy, and heating they are; they know the inconvenience of pins; how often they require regulating, and upon the whole, how loose, shifting, and disagreeable they become. But if it was only the discomfort of the moment, it might be easily borne, and would be of little consequence. The ordinary evil that follows is the spreading of the figure, which never should, and indeed never would happen, if proper care had been exercised. What is wanting is a regular and progressive compression, with an even, cool, and smooth surface; and if this be given during the inflammatory process, the muscular fibres will return again to their normal position, and resume their original firmness and solidity. Nor will this process cause the least injury to the particular parts under consideration, nor to the general health of the mother; for the muscles having again attained their state of health, will be prepared to repeat the same process without injury.

Every condition mentioned above has been met by our CONTRACTING BELT, which is a perfect mould for the restoration of the figure. It is smooth, cool, elastic, and accomplishes every end which we had in view. The construction of this article has, perhaps, caused us more thought, care, and anxiety, than any invention which we have ever submitted to the public; but it is a consolation to feel that we have attained the most absolute success. Our belt has now been in extensive use for a long time, and the fact that it has won the patronage of the first medical authorities of the land, and been adopted by the *highest personages of the empire,* is a guarantee of its utility. It is indeed one of those boons for which mothers have long sighed.

The nature of our work, which is designed for THE PUBLIC, compels us to exclude much that is interesting and important to the afflicted mother, as being unsuited

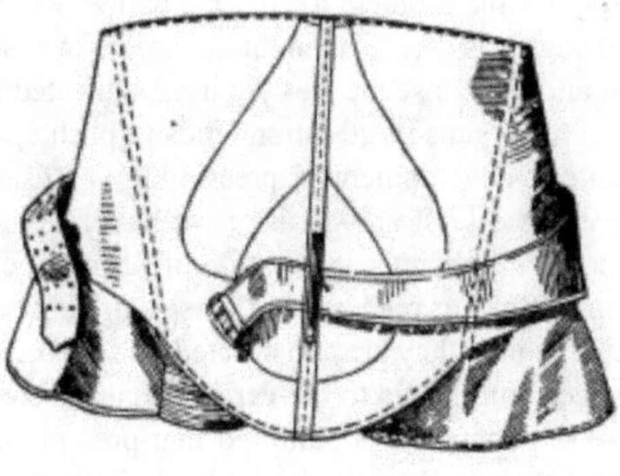

Figure 9.2 Contracting Belt

to our pages. The reader must not, however, suppose that those matters have been neglected by us. We have, indeed, carefully studied every form of uterine disorder and deformity, and have special adaptations for EVERY PERIOD AND FOR EVERY COMPLAINT that woman is peculiarly liable to. The pathology of those stages in her life belongs to the physician; but the special insight into what should give her relief or restore the figure is our business, and where medicine either fails or is useless our work begins.

There is one other matter connected with this subject that we intend to mention, and that is *Abortion* – a thing which may be reckoned amongst the accidents of life, since it generally arises from some external cause. Among the numerous causes, however, of this accident, related in the works dedicated to this special subject, there is one which, although common, is unnoticed – *the tendency of the corset to press downwards!* This fact we will briefly explain. Abortion generally takes place between the eighth and twelfth week, which is the time when the fœtus is increased so as to rise above the edge of the pelvic cavity, and begins to elevate itself in the abdomen, and is then liable to meet with external obstacles created by the corset, which as a consequence compresses the body more closely. The wisdom displayed during these changes is manifest. For as the development progresses there is an extraordinary action by which the increasing bulk goes on, moving in every direction the abdominal organs, which yield under the pressure. The natural weight of the intestines is overcome, the habitual connexion is destroyed, and the locality of the viscera changed; while at the same time the muscles are elongated, and the integuments distended. It is unwise to tamper with, or to attempt to interpose or interrupt these sanatory proceedings; for in the operations of Nature, as well as in the productions of man, there are limits to the special power applied for a given purpose. In the marvellous arrangements of fœtal gestation there is no waste of power, but every process is calculated with unerring certainty, and definite proportions regulate the amount of strength required; therefore any foreign agent which would prevent the abdomen from expanding must be a cause of pain, suffering, and disappointment to the incipient mother; and if she survives the trial, she may be left the remainder of her life permanently injured. It is a very simple problem to comprehend why these results are induced; for if the resisting agent is greater than the organic power supplied by Nature, the latter succumbs, and the consequences we have indicated must follow. The vital power inherent in the organs of gestation tends to push upwards, and if a greater resistance prevents its development by pressing it on all sides, it must distend the parts where there is the least antagonism; we have, therefore, a frequent cause of miscarriage in the injudicious application of ill-fitting corsets! And we would impress on the minds of our readers, that corsets are always injurious during the period of gestation, unless they are constructed on sound scientific principles, and capable of being accommodated to the various changes contemplated.

As a matter of experience it is admitted that pressure on the chest interferes with the great vital processes of respiration and circulation, even under the ordinary states of health. How great then must be the injury sustained during gestation under such circumstances! Whatever affects the mother's health must exert a deleterious influence on her future offspring; and as ill-fitting corsets not only induce these sad consequences, but press on the abdomen and tend to displace its important contents, they cause complex suffering to her whose health and mental calmness are important conditions to the child's future health.

It is very pleasant to point out errors when we have the power to prevent their recurrence, and a long experience, based on an accurate knowledge of the subject, has qualified us for this task. We have had mothers to consult us whose sufferings were very great prior to their doing so, and who have expressed to us, in language of the warmest gratitude, the ease and comfort they have derived from our adaptations. Various have been their exclamations, such as, "There is a magical difference in the ease I now feel. How can I sufficiently thank you, dear madame?" Others have declared that the corset had metamorphosed them completely; for instead of a restlessness and constant discomfort, they had experienced an immunity from all inconvenience. What, then, it may be asked, is the peculiarity of our corset? We answer, that it is made on such accurate scientific *data,* that it fits the body and chest of each individual; that, to quote the words of a medical gentleman when speaking of it – "*Madame, your corset is more like a new layer of muscles than an artificial extraneous article of dress!*" And this is practically the case.

For example, in the instance of the expectant mother, it must be important to give her support without any undue pressure in any part, and at the same time to insure the perfect exercise of the vital organs.

In our corset the wearer can breathe freely, and the pulsation of her heart is not the least interfered with, whilst the various motions of the body can be performed without any extra exertion or fatigue. If she take a walk she derives important support from the closely-fitting corset; and when she reclines the elastic nature of the materials and their accurate adaptation prevent every kind of inconvenience; for at the advanced stages of this interesting period, when it is imperative for the comfort and health of both mother and child that the corset should be enlarged, this is effected by a simple contrivance, by which an increased space can be obtained at the will and pleasure of the wearer, without in any way rendering it less valuable as a support, or less efficient in preserving the figure, whilst a perfectly free action of the whole body is the result. A provision is therefore made for every exigency; so that, under every circumstance, there is effected the great desiderata of perfect ease, freedom, and safety.

It is always gratifying to have one's labour appreciated, and in maturing the corset, so important to the mother, we have had no small share of the public approbation awarded us. It has cost us many years to bring it to its present state of comparative perfection, but we have succeeded at last. To realize this, we had to note many instances of failure in others, evidently the result of ignorance of the structure of the body to which it was to be applied – they were mere "fancy sketches," compared with our more rigid copy from Nature!

10

IMAGE: ADVERTISEMENT, 'THE LONDON CORSET COMPANY'

Hearth and Home, 27 December 1900, p. 317

DOI: 10.4324/9781315399980-15

11

IMAGE: PHOTOGRAPH OF CRINOLETTE, GREAT BRITAIN, CA. 1870 (MADE)

DOI: 10.4324/9781315399980-16

1.2.2

The 'Grecian Bend', 'Little Feet' and the 'Alexandra Limp'

DOI: 10.4324/9781315399980-17

1.2.2 The 'Grecian Bend', 'Little Feet' and the 'Alexandra Limp'

The 'Samothrace' corset of the previous section is a distinctive segue into the selection of sources gathered here, which represent the 1860s' and 1870s' female body as extremely malleable, contoured into the sculptural ideals of previous ages. Our first extract, published in *Sharpe's London Magazine* of 1869, addresses the so-called 'Grecian Bend', a silhouette created by the combination of highly piled hair, thrust-forward chest, tight-laced waist, 'a bunched-up skirt in the *polonaise* style',[1] and (comparatively) high heels.[2] This posture, as David Kunzle notes, was reminiscent of 'the attitude of some figures painted on Attic Greek vases'[3] and was satirised by *Punch* in cartoons, including our selection from 2 October 1869,[4] in which a fashionable young lady's stance is unwittingly mirrored by the old, crouched gentleman in the background. The fashion, as Kunzle also observes, was coincident with the shortening of the skirt, so that the feet – previously fully or partly hidden – were now visible.[5] The article in *Sharpe's*, authored by a writer using the pseudonym 'Uncle Grumbler', assumes a critical tone against the new fashionable wear and deportment of the modern lady. The article begins with a stereotyped and mocking reference to a passing 'Irishman', who is ridiculed for his posture 'carrying a hod of bricks',[6] before making a comparison with this new style in womenswear. Following this, the character of the 'Uncle' engages in lively conversation with his 'pretty niece, Nellie', who believes that the 'Grecian Bend' is nothing but an exaggerated '"sensation" for the papers', only to be proven wrong when her uncle observes that she too favours 'bunchy skirt[s]' and high-heeled boots.[7]

The fashionable interest in the foot is addressed in our next selection, a short story from *London Society* entitled 'The Lady With the Little Feet'. This addresses a far more unusual means of measuring female beauty, inverting the narrative so that the male protagonist becomes the butt of its humour. It focuses upon the small foot, a physical feature that, in Valerie Steele's terms, 'seem[ed] to have erotic connotations', functioning as 'a mark of femininity' as well as holding 'class status'.[8] The story tells the tale of Ranger, a man who holds, as Steele notes, 'an obsessive interest in small feet', becoming infatuated with an unknown woman on the basis of the tiny size of the boots left outside her hotel-room door.[9] While this is eventually revealed to be a misunderstanding, the story reaching a happy conclusion, the narrative nonetheless draws attention to ways in which the 'little' foot, like the tiny waist and delicate hands, powerfully signified contemporary 'feminine' ideals and, in doing so, reinforced gendered iconographies.

Another of our selections, from *The Glasgow* [*Daily*] *Herald* of 1870, details a different boot-based fashion, rather unkindly nicknamed the 'Alexandra Limp'.[10] This fad reputedly prompted women to purchase footwear with differing heel heights to mimic the walk of Alexandra, Princess of Wales, whose gait was rendered uneven following a serious case of rheumatic fever in 1867.[11] Such a fad reveals class as a driver of contemporary fashion, as Alexandra's suffering in the form of her illness is refigured as a desirable signifier of status. Yet, despite the fashion being ridiculed within its nineteenth-century context, we might also interpret the fashion as a forerunner of more inclusive attitudes to the human body now celebrated in modern fashionable culture.

Finally, the satirical journal *Fun* groups together fashionable items and attitudes such as the Grecian Bend, tight-lacing, high heels and the chignon hairstyle, expressing the exasperation of the sensible 'pater-familias', who might feel unable to stop the seemingly-ruthless female march of fashion. In this way, these so-called 'follies' and feminine 'affectations' might persist at the expense of the 'sensible', masculine, head of the family.[12]

Notes

1 J. Ashelford (with Special Photography by Andreas von Einsiedel), *The Art of Dress: Clothes Through History 1500–1914* (London: The National Trust, 1996), p. 229.

2 See D. Kunzle, *Fashion and Fetishism: Corsets, Tight-Lacing & Other Forms of Body-Sculpture* (Stroud: Sutton Publishing, 2004), pp. 102–103, and A. M. David, *Fashion Victims: The Dangers of Dress Past and Present* (London and New York: Bloomsbury Visual Arts, 2015), pp. 9–10. The 'Grecian Bend' is also discussed in C. Breward, *The Culture of Fashion: A New History of Fashionable Dress* (Manchester and New York: Manchester University Press, 1995), pp. 153–155.

3 Kunzle, *Fashion and Fetishism*, p. 102.

4 This image is also reproduced in David, *Fashion Victims*, p. 10.

5 Kunzle, *Fashion and Fetishism*, pp. 102–103. Kunzle reproduces a *Punch* cartoon by Linley Sambourne entitled 'History Repeats Itself', its caption satirically informing the reader that it depicts a '*very* ancient vase' that features the fashionable silhouette of 1870. L. Sambourne, 'History Repeats Itself', *Punch*, 18 June 1870, p. 248. See Kunzle, p. 103. The image is also reproduced in Breward, *The Culture of Fashion*, p. 155.

6 Uncle Grumbler, '"The Grecian Bend"', *Sharpe's London Magazine*, January 1869, pp. 110–111 (p. 110).

7 Uncle Grumbler, '"The Grecian Bend"', p. 111.

8 V. Steele, *Fashion and Eroticism: Ideals of Feminine Beauty from the Victorian Era to the Jazz Age* (New York and Oxford: Oxford University Press, 1985), p. 115.

9 See Steele, *Fashion and Eroticism,* pp. 115–116, for further discussion of this story.

10 [Anon], 'General News.', *The Glasgow* [*Daily*] *Herald*, 25 January 1870, p. 4.

11 See A. Gernsheim, *Victorian and Edwardian Fashion: A Photographic Survey* (New York: Dover, 1981), p. 57; C. Hibbert, *Edward VII: The Last Victorian King* (New York and Houndsmills: Palgrave Macmillan, 2007), pp. 88–89; and 'Alexandra of Denmark, Princess of Wales (1844–1925)', in H. Rappaport, *Queen Victoria: A Biographical Companion* (Santa Barbara, CA, Denver, CO, and Oxford: ABC-CLIO, 2003), pp. 21–26 (p. 24).

12 For further discussion of the social trope or stereotype known as the Victorian 'pater-familias', see D. Roberts, 'The Paterfamilias of the Victorian Governing Classes' in A. S. Wohl (ed.), *The Victorian Family: Structures and Stresses* (London and New York: Routledge, 2016 [first published in 1978 by Croom Helm]), pp. 59–81.

12

UNCLE GRUMBLER, '"THE GRECIAN BEND."'

Sharpe's London Magazine, January 1869, pp. 110–111

"Do you see the 'Grecian bend' yonder?" asked a friend of me, as we walked up the High-street of our town together. An Irishman crossed our path at the moment, bowed underneath a hod of bricks, and I, suspecting a joke, and laughing, asked him if it was the man to whom he referred. "No," said he. "I mean the young lady opposite."

"What – that poor, deformed creature, a pitiable object, though dressed in regal finery? Now, really, my good fellow, I would not have thought you so heartless as to make the unfortunate girl a subject of raillery."

"But she isn't deformed," said my friend, almost convulsed with laughter. "That's the latest style of carriage among belles; you don't know how much trouble and painstaking that young woman has been at, to accomplish that result in her figure."

"You're not in earnest, surely?"

"Indeed I am. You show you were not at the watering-places this season by the ignorance you manifest. It was quite the rage there, I can assure you."

"Impossible," said I, elevating my eye-glass to gaze at the spectacle again.

"It's queer, ain't it," said my friend, after a moment, "how the women all go in flocks after a thing, even to a particular gait or manner. Now these little trivialities of street customs have always been an interesting study to me. They change with the seasons as regularly as the cut of a coat or style of a bonnet. Sometimes it's the way of bowing to an acquaintance; now, every lady will greet you with a low salute, and a great deal of 'empressement;' again, the style will be only a very conservative nod of the head; again, the mannerism will be in the walk. Some two or three years since, it was a certain way of carrying the parasol – a coquetish sticking out of the elbow and grasping the handle high. Every fashionable lady from fifteen to thirty, affected this manner of holding the parasol or umbrella. Finally, I noticed shop-girls and apprentices doing the same, and then the 'ultras' dropped it."

"But do you suppose," said I, "that such a custom as that (pointing to the shape opposite) can become general?"

"Undoubtedly," was the reply. "Why the thing is reduced to a regular science. There's some sort of machinery about it, I don't know what, exactly; you consult the papers, and you'll find out all about it."

DOI: 10.4324/9781315399980-18

So I bought a paper and went home, and sat down to read as follows: –

"The 'Grecian Bend,' is an S-like curvature of the upper figure, caused by thrusting out the chest, bending forward the head, contracting the stomach, and elevating the hips, the latter effect being aided by wearing very high-heeled shoes, and an arrangement upon the hips called a *panier*. The 'Grecian Bend' is quite painful and wearisome, and some girls adopt artificial contrivances to aid them in preserving the posture for several consecutive hours. 'A belt is fastened about the waist, under the skirts. From this belt, down either side the hips, two straps, furnished with buckles, descend, and are attached to strong bands made fast around the lower thighs. As the buckles of the straps are tightened, the hips are drawn up and held in position.' This is a relief, of course, to only one part of the frame. The construction of the upper part has to be preserved with no other aids than the stays, and those often render it the more difficult and tiresome."

I was trying to bring my scattered senses to believe the truth of what I had read, when my pretty niece, Nellie, danced into the room with a new dress on; and after tapping me lightly on the shoulder, tripped up and down the room for the usual inspection, turning herself before the pier-glass, and saying – "How do you like *mes paniers, mon oncle?*"

"My dear," said I, with a tone of severity which made her look sober at once, "I have no longer any patience with these fashionable follies; as long as they were only ridiculous, I could laugh at them. Now they are positively criminal. I must say I am heartily disgusted with them."

"Why, what do you mean? What new foible concerning the ladies, uncle?"

So I gave her the paper indicating the paragraph in question.

"Oh, nonsense," said she, when she had read. "I don't believe it, uncle. It's only a 'sensation' for the papers. I never have seen anything like it."

"Put out your foot," said I. She stuck out a little number two slipper, with a heel full two inches high, terminating in a point no larger than a sixpenny-piece. "Now turn round."

There was the bunchy skirt, or "panier," at her back.

"Those things are rightly named," I said; "they make a donkey of every lady who wears them. And really, my dear, now my attention is called to the subject, I think you present an appearance quite similar to the 'Grecian bend.' Beware, lest unconsciously you fall into the extent of the fashion, which is not only absurd, it is positively wicked. I did think the ladies were growing sensible – now they had put on thick-soled boots, and taken their dresses up out of the mud, but – – – "

"Ay, there's the very trouble," interrupted Nelly; "now you've hit upon the cause of all the folly; these short dresses – they are the occasion for the French heels."

"How so?"

"Why in former days, a lady's feet might be as crooked, flat, and ugly as she pleased, her long skirt hid them, and it was no matter. Now, the feet are so generally exposed they must present a true appearance; and where they are not naturally shapely, why, the bootmaker's art must be called in to effect a remedy. Now the high heels make *instep* whether you will or not. It is impossible for 'the hollow of the foot' to 'make a hole in the ground' when it is lifted two inches from the ground – you see; and that is just how the fashion came about. As for the 'paniers,' it would never do for the ladies to get too sensible; then retired old sages like you would have nothing to scold about. We must have some little weakness, just to prevent us from becoming altogether angelic, spreading our wings and flying away."

"Well, I must say I think you are hurrying yourselves out of this wicked world just as fast as possible. What kind of mothers are these tortured, bent, strapped women going to make, I should like to know?"

"Just such mothers as our grandmothers were before us; those grandmothers whom I have so often heard you laud to the skies."

"They were not drawn out of shape as these women now-a-days."

"I don't know about the straps and buckles, but the high heels they certainly wore. I have a pair of blue satin slippers in which my grandmother walked, or, I suppose you would say 'hobbled,' at sixteen; except that they are somewhat faded, the exact counterparts of a pair which came home from my shoemaker's this very morning. As to the paniers, I refer you to that very common engraving, which one meets with everywhere of Franklin at the court of Versailles. I may not be a judge, but there one may see something which looks marvellously like the 'Grecian' to me."

"But really, uncle, if the grandmothers were, as you have often told me, the type of everything truly excellent, in dress as in everything else, I ought to please you vastly. My hair, fashionably arranged, is an exact copy of the old portrait of my maternal progenitor, which hangs in the garret. My dress is fashioned like hers as nearly as possible, and if I wore such a horrid bonnet and head-dress, I might be made to look as ridiculous as my grandmother."

I had to confess that Nelly rather got the advantage of me on the grandmother's question. We talk with tender memories of those quaint old costumes of our forefathers, but really, we do not realize how very absurd and ridiculous they were until we see them reproduced, and they become again the extravagant follies of the day. Still I cannot believe that any woman, with any true feeling in any age, could lend herself to such horrid monstrosity as this "Grecian bend."

I am, very respectfully,
Uncle Grumbler.

13

S. L. B., 'THE LADY WITH THE LITTLE FEET.'

London Society, June 1869, pp. 494–506

I.

'I WAS always fond of feet, you remember,' said Ranger.

But before I tell you what Ranger said next, I may as well mention who Ranger was, and the occasion of the communication in reference to his partiality for the useful extremities in question.

I can scarcely describe him, however, in the 'Who's Who' sense of the matter. I knew nothing of his family, and had not made his acquaintance through the medium of any common friends. But I had met him from time to time in the course of my travels in most parts of the world, and had found him a well-bred, well-educated gentleman, full of what is called accomplishments, and talents that tell in society – as active as a queen's messenger, and as watchful as a 'special correspondent.'

I met Ranger in different places while I was moving about; but had I stayed in any one place I should have been equally certain to see him; for he was always on the move, and you could no more avoid meeting Ranger than you could avoid meeting the sun. I first came across him travelling in Germany, when he helped me out of a difficulty in which some frontier officials were concerned. His happy English face and pleasant *savoir faire* went a long way, I thought on that occasion, in persuading the hitherto imperturbable Prussians that I was neither a smuggler nor a spy – though by the way he had no reason, beyond my representations, to believe that I was not both. I next met him ascending the great Pyramid in Egypt. We were both being bullied by our guides, and were enabled, by joining our forces, to escape with the payment of no more backsheesh than we had bargained for. Another encounter was at the Crown and Sceptre, Greenwich, where we were both discussing whitebait; and after this we met again on Mont Blanc, during a senseless excursion of mine as far as the Grand Mulets. Among other places where he subsequently turned up was on board a steamer on the Mississippi; and after that I saw no more of him till we met in the Himalaya mountains, one morning when we had both gone out to see the snowy range in the sunrise, mounted upon hill ponies. That was the last I had seen of him until I met him in Paris, where he gave me the reminder recorded above.

 DOI: 10.4324/9781315399980-19

You will suppose, perhaps, that I was as great a wanderer as he. Nothing of the kind. I had done a little travelling in my time, but *he* was always doing it. Wherever he was, he was sure to be going somewhere else, and regarded localities principally from a 'Bradshaw' point of view, as made for arrival and departure; though he certainly managed to make the most of them during his stay.

Nothing could be more natural, therefore, than my meeting him in Paris one day when I went to dine solus at the Moulin Rouge, and found him preparing to dine solus also at the same place. We had a common taste – in summer at any rate – for taking the meal of the day in the open air, and a common taste, too, for not taking it alone if we could avoid it. So we joined our forces, as we had done on the Pyramid, and made as pleasant a party as I dare say could be made by any two men who are likely to meet under such conditions.

It was when dinner was well-nigh disposed of, and we were discussing some Burgundy we both particularly liked – with British reticence in getting to our coffee – that Ranger began to be confidential, and seemed to think that I was bound to know the state of his affections at the period. It was then that he said –

'I was always fond of feet, you remember. Not for vulgar purposes of progression, though I ought to be obliged to them in that particular, for people call me the Wandering Jew. But I need not tell *you* what I mean. I think a woman without a foot – that is to say a good foot, and of course a little foot – is not worth looking at. I like a face as well as most men. A woman can't have too pretty a face for me' – this was a liberal concession at any rate – 'but I insist that she must have a foot. And here, in Paris, at my hotel, I have found some feet that have, so to speak, carried me away with them. I have fallen in love with them, in fact.'

'What a charming chance!' I said, with the sympathy deserved by such a confidence. 'I trust that the face is worthy of the feet, and the lady worthy of both.'

'Well,' he answered, with rather a fall in his enthusiasm, 'that is just what I am unable to tell you. The fact is I have not seen the lady as yet.'

'Then how the deuce have you seen her feet?' I asked, with brutal practicality. Then I added, 'Oh, I see – mysterious muffled lady, all veil – chance glimpse getting into a carriage, and so forth. Well, that is romantic at any rate, and rather creditable to your susceptibilities, considering that you have seen so much of the world.'

'No, not even that,' rejoined Ranger, who was a very good-natured fellow, and did not mind a little jesting at his expense; 'not even that: I have no idea whether the lady is tall or short, stout or thin, young or old. I have not even seen her shadow, and of course have not seen even the feet that have fixed my affections.'

'What have you seen then?' I asked, rather puzzled by this time.

'Well, I have only seen her boots,' he answered, rather sullenly, and disappointed at my want of feeling.

'Oh, I see,' said I; 'case of Cinderella and the Glass Slipper – Prince sees a brodequin in a bootmaker's shop – tree in it very likely – falls in love with it – vows he will never marry any lady whose foot cannot take the place of the tree.

Why this beats the barber in the book who fell in love with the wax lady in the shop window, to say nothing of his prototype, Pygmalion.'

'Now don't be a fool,' said Ranger, losing his patience; 'I said I had seen the boots at my hotel. Of course they were outside one of the doors.'

'Waiting to be cleaned,' I suggested, with a mischievous introduction of the prosaic element.

'Well, and if they were, what then?' asked Ranger almost fiercely. 'The only suggestion which such an arrangement makes to my mind is that the shoeblack ought to be a happy man. But this is the fact. Every night when I pass through the corridor – *au premier* at the Grand Hôtel – on my way to my more elevated chamber, I see these bottines on the mat. Not always the same though. Sometimes they are of plain leather, kid or whatever it may be; sometimes they are of a beautiful bronze; sometimes they are not boots at all, but the sweetest things you ever saw in shoes.'

'You have surely not fallen in love with three ladies at once?' said I, reproachfully.

'No, no; don't, like a good fellow, talk nonsense,' said Ranger. 'Of course they belong to the same person; no other person could wear them. It is a case of the Glass Slipper as far as that fact goes, and I only wish I was in the position of the Prince. As it is I don't know what to do. What would you?'

'Well,' said I, 'if you wish me to take a practical view of the case, I should find out who occupied the room, identify her at the table d'hôte, or wherever you may meet her in the hotel, and then move heaven and earth to make her acquaintance.'

'As if any man, not an idiot, didn't know that!' cried Ranger, impatiently. 'Why I tell you there are two of them.'

He had not told me that, but I took no notice of this little fact.

'But surely,' I further suggested, recurring to the main point, 'you would be in a fair way of finding her out if you watched the ladies at the hotel, and observed if there were any feet going about that seemed likely to fit the bottines! But what do you mean by there being two of them? Do you mean that there are two sets of boots belonging to equally small feet?'

'What I mean is this,' said Ranger. 'I have watched everybody in the hotel, and have seen feet in most of their varieties, but nothing capable of belonging to my bottines. If you were to observe the delicate rise of the instep from the toe, until it melts into the ankle – for of course *my* bottines *are* bottines, and none of your vulgar Wellingtons, Hessians, what do you call them, with tassels – you would agree with me that there is not a foot to be seen in the whole hotel that would fit them. But however, I have progressed beyond the necessity for a general search. When I said there were two, I meant that there are two ladies occupying the same suite of rooms, which has only one entrance from the corridor, and that *my* boots are only one of the two pairs that are always on the doormat.'

'And what are the others like?' I asked.

Ranger answered, in a tone of profound contempt, 'BEETLE-CRUSHERS!'

'Perhaps you take too harsh a view of them,' said I, 'as Heinrich Heine seems to have done with regard to the feet of the ladies of Göttingen. He tells us, as you may remember, that he was earnestly engaged for years in the refutation of the too-prevalent belief that the ladies of Göttingen have *not* enormous feet. For this purpose he not only studied comparative anatomy, and made copious extracts from all works obtainable on the subject, but he also watched for hours the feet of the ladies as they passed him in the street. And in the erudite treatise which was the result of his labours he made separate divisions: – "On Feet in general" – "On the Feet of Antiquity" – "On Elephants' Feet" – "On Feet in connexion with each other" – and so forth. I am not quite sure that he convinced his readers in the case of the ladies of Göttingen, and it may be that you apply the severe epithet of "Beetle-Crushers" without an equally attentive study of the subject.'

Ranger laughed this time.

'At any rate,' said he, 'any ordinary feet would look like Beetle-Crushers beside *my* feet.'

Then returning to the practical point, I argued: 'But surely you have by this time identified the two occupants of the rooms, and after that there should be no difficulty, with a very little amount of the attention bestowed by Heine on a far wider subject, in distinguishing one from the other.'

'So you would think,' said Ranger, cynically, 'and so would all remarkably clever persons. But this is just what I have been trying to do for ten days, without success. There is one fashion in ladies' skirts which has gone out, and another fashion in ladies' skirts which has come in. In neither is any mystery made of the feet; but unfortunately my people will not adopt either one or the other. They neither wear hoops nor short dresses, but clinging drapery trailing on the ground, which defies any investigation, levelling in a common obscurity the "little mice" of the poet and such monstrous things as – Beetle-Crushers.'

Here the waiter seemed to think that coffee was imperative on us, so we went to coffee accordingly, or rather we allowed coffee to come to us, and, spurning the proffered 'Londres,' lit up such Havannas as are pearls beyond all price in Paris.

'And what is to be your next course of action?' I asked, resuming the subject; 'have you made the acquaintance of these ladies?'

'That is the only thing to be done,' replied Ranger; 'but I have not tried as yet. I have been too nervous to take the initiative, and they are not people, evidently, who are likely to talk to stray bachelors without some kind of inducement. Perhaps you might help me in the matter – if you don't mind a table d'hôte dinner. My seat is exactly opposite theirs, and if we could get them to be just civilly conversational, I might, perhaps, establish something like an acquaintance. Not of course that this would necessarily gain me my information, but I should certainly seem nearer to it than now.'

Ever ready in the cause of friendship, I agreed to dine with him at the Grand Hôtel on the following day.

II.

There is no need to apologise for asking a man to dinner at the table d'hôte of the Grand Hôtel unless the objection be to tables d'hôte altogether. So I thought as I entered the gorgeous hall where the repast was served, and received such a sensation of gold ornaments and mirrors, lights, flowers, and silver plate, as was calculated to give an appetite at once by raising expectation – not, I am bound to say, likely to be disappointed – of the *menu*.

Ranger was waiting, and at once conducted me to a seat beside his own near the centre of the room. There were two vacant places opposite.

'Those are *the* places,' whispered Ranger, 'but of course there's a chance that they will not be filled.'

Just, however, as the preliminary oysters were placed on the table, two ladies threaded their way towards the chairs, and took possession of them with continental composure. A glance from Ranger was sufficient to satisfy me of their identity, and I was free to form further impressions for myself.

They were both young, but one was, I should say, several years younger than the other. I would not venture to guess the age of the elder, but that of the younger might be about eighteen. They were both pretty, more than pretty – but their styles were by no means alike. The elder was the darker of the two: her features, not more delicate, were somehow more *piquante*; there was more animation in her mouth, and her black beady eyes conveyed an inevitable impression of suppressed mirth. The younger and lighter, however, had at least equal attractions of her own. Her features were as delicate as those of her companion, and there was a delicious softness about her deep-blue eyes – a softness which indeed pervaded her, and gave the prevailing character to her beauty.

Other things being equal – which they never are – I should think it would be difficult to choose between the two.

Ranger had told me their names and relative positions on the previous night, for he had talked about them all the way from the Moulin Rouge, past the Madeleine, to the very door of the Variétés Theatre, where we finished the evening. The elder lady was a widow named Merridew, and the younger was a cousin of hers, named Pembroke, who lived under her protection. So, at least, Ranger had learned in the hotel, and in hotels a great deal more is known of most persons than their names, after a short residence.

Ranger, by the way, had not informed me of the fact which I now found apparent – that they were both such charming persons in appearance. Absorbed in the important question which he had set himself to solve, he made no observation upon mere matters of detail.

The dinner developed for some time in a highly satisfactory manner as far as the viands were concerned, and we paid a touching attention to widowhood by making considerable acquaintance with Cliquot. But we made no way at all in getting upon speaking terms with our opposite neighbours. But for Ranger's sensibility in regard to them, I should have dashed into an introductory remark – at the risk of a rebuff – which, however, one is not likely to get at a foreign table d'hôte, even from English people. Apart, too, from Ranger's feelings, I was the stranger. He had been sitting opposite to them, at intervals, during ten days, and was plainly the one to take the initiative.

The two ladies in the meantime talked upon indifferent subjects as if we had no existence, though I could not help thinking that Mrs. Merridew looked occasionally at Ranger with an inquiring glance, made the more significant by the twinkle of her irrepressible eye. I fancied she must at least have met him before. Ranger, on the other hand, though acute and observant in most matters, was curiously the contrary where ladies were concerned. I know this failing of old.

Presently an opportunity *did* present itself for joining in their conversation. Mrs. Merridew, in continuation of some previous discussion as to their plans for the season, said to her cousin –

'Yes, if I do not get a letter tomorrow I think we had better go on to Baden-Baden and wait for them there. But it's rather an awkward place for two ladies who are alone. I know it no more than you do, and I am very doubtful as to the hotels. Some of them may be quiet enough, but there is no knowing which, and it would be very weak to trust to the guide-books.'

'If you will allow me, madam,' said I, with a decision which Ranger regarded with looks of dismay, 'I can furnish you with the address of the best and quietest house in the place. It is not exactly an hotel, but the better suited perhaps on that account.'

And I gave her a card which I had in my pocket-book, at the risk, as it afterwards occurred to me, of being taken for a touter engaged by the concern.

I had no need to have any fears as to my reception. Mrs. Merridew was all graciousness, accepted the card, and returned thanks as if for a great favour, assuring me that she would certainly avail herself of my courtesy if she and her cousin – the reference to her cousin was encouraging – should really go to the place. But they were not sure, they expected some friends in Paris – and so forth.

Even Miss Pembroke put in a word or two expressive of pleasure at the reception of so much valuable information; upon which I ventured to say that they were wise not to stay very long in Paris just then, when even the French all ran away on account of the heat.

Both ladies responded pleasantly to this sentiment; and the ice being thus broken, Ranger – what a diffident man he was for such a traveller! – went into the conversation with a plunge. He was quite as well received as myself – rather better, I thought, as far as Mrs. Merridew was concerned. And the result was that before dinner was over we were all upon very friendly travelling terms.

There was only one point in the conversation that need be recorded. Alluding to the many things to be seen in Paris, Mrs. Merridew said –

'We do not, however, see half so much on our way as we might; for we go everywhere in a carriage. I am a very good walker, but my cousin, I am sorry to say, is a very bad one.'

Ranger's face expressed visible satisfaction at this announcement. But he was probably not observed, for the ladies rose immediately afterwards, and we bowed them away from the table – Ranger, by the way, regarding them attentively till they passed out at the door. 'His vulture eye pursued the trip of these small glancing feet' – or would have done so had those objects been in sight.

We of course went on the Boulevards. As Ranger placed his arm in mine preparatory to our saunter among the life of the city, I felt him clutch me with what the French call effusion.

'I am not sure, of course,' said he, 'and would not hazard anything as yet; but I have a strong suspicion that Miss Pembroke's are the Mice and Mrs. Merridew's the Beetle-Crushers!'

III.

Ranger came over to me – he had not to come far, only to the Hôtel des Princes – on the following day, soon after breakfast.

'Congratulate me,' he said; 'I think I have a clue.'

'Clue to what?' said I.

'To the owner of the feet,' he said, exultingly; 'and this is how I have got it. Both of the women – if they will allow me to call them so – appeared this morning at breakfast, and the train of conversation which we commenced yesterday, thanks to you, was continued today, thanks to them, and was made not quite unavailable, I suspect, thanks to me.'

'Well, what's your idea?' said I, bringing him to the point.

'You shall see,' he said. 'Let me tell you what happened. Mrs. Merridew talked quite unreservedly in my presence about their plans – not only prospective, but immediate; not only about Baden-Baden next week, but their little expeditions during the day. And among other things she said to Clara – why the deuce am I calling her Clara? – but that is the name by which she addresses Miss Pembroke. Among other things that she said to Miss Pembroke was this: "We must not forget to call at the bootmaker's." '

'Was that all?' I asked, discouragingly.

'Wait,' returned Ranger. 'In the course of the conversation I actually heard the address of the bootmaker's at which they were to call.'

'Something may come out of that,' said I.

'Something!' cried Ranger, 'everything I should hope. They seem to have boots in preparation. They intend to call at twelve o'clock. *I* mean to call at one – they must surely have left by that time – and it will be hard if I do not find out something. Come with me, like a good fellow.'

So like a good fellow I went with him. It was only into the Rue de la Paix, and the bootmakers were well known. We were there ten minutes before the time, but seeing nobody in the front shop we ventured to enter and open our campaign.

Ranger gave an order for some dress boots, for which he was duly measured, and while this process was being performed he took care to engage the shopman in conversation.

'Do you make ladies' boots?' he asked – the slimy villain, as if the shop was not full of feminine articles.

Yes, without doubt, the Frenchman answered; they made everything of the kind for great ladies of the world.

Were they making many now? was the next question.

Ah, his faith, yes, certainly, for great ladies among the English living at the hotels. They were sending that afternoon to Meurice's, to the Castilione, to the Louvre, to the Grand, and elsewhere.

And the shopman pointed to a number of packets piled on a counter ready for delivering.

Ranger acknowledged the information in a careless manner, and then gave some preposterous order in reference to the making of his own boots, which sent the man away to consult his master.

'Now,' said Ranger, when the shop was clear, 'let us see if we can find out anything like a fact.'

So he overhauled the parcels on the counter with rapid assiduity, and presently raised a cry of satisfaction.

'See,' said he, 'there are two packets for the Grand Hôtel, one directed to Madame Merridew, and the other to Mademoiselle Pembroke.

There were certainly two packets so addressed, and he held them before me triumphantly.

'Look,' said he, 'there seems to be a couple of pairs of boots in each, and one packet is much smaller than the other.'

'There does seem a difference in the size,' I observed; 'and the next question is easy to determine.'

It *was* easy. The larger packet was addressed to Madame Merridew; the smaller one to Miss Pembroke.

Ranger was quite idiotic in his demonstrations at this discovery.

'I told you so,' said he; 'I knew that Clara – that Miss Pembroke – had the small feet. Look, look, here are the Mice, unmistakably; and here – does not the fact proclaim itself? – here are the Beetle-Crushers.'

Appearances were certainly in his favour, and I congratulated him upon the discovery.

'Now,' said I, 'you may make your court without fear of making a mistake.'

He was in ecstasies at the idea, but still seemed to require my help, and insisted that I should dine with him again that night at his hotel. I could not choose but promise.

IV.

At six o'clock – they dine early at tables d'hôte in Paris – I was again among the gilding, the glass, the plate, the flowers, and the damask that distinguish the dinner at the Grand Hôtel beyond all other dinners of its class.

Again we were early; again our opposite neighbours were late; and when they appeared at last they brought with them a companion upon whom we had not counted. It was a hateful being in the form of man.

Not a man that we could object to, however, upon general or particular grounds. He was a gentleman, that was evident, and one who, without any appearance of dictation, took command of the party as if by a natural right. He ordered the wine, and assumed every other function connected with the control of the feast, as if he were in his own house. He was a man, perhaps, of forty years of age – we could not object to that at any rate – a well-looking, well-mannered, conventional style of person, with an air of opulence about him, and a serene way of not seeming to care a straw about anybody, which goes a great way at a table d'hôte, to say nothing of other places.

The new comer engrossed the attention of the ladies during the entire dinner. Beyond a slight salutation at the commencement, and an inane remark about the weather from Mrs. Merridew, they took no notice of us. Their conversation, too, unconstrained as it was, gave us no clue to the relation in which the gentleman stood towards them, or to one of them in particular. He was a cousin, perhaps, or an uncle, or a brother of the elder lady – he was too old, surely, to be a brother of the younger, though he might be a *prétendu* to either of them. The latter idea was not a pleasant one – from Ranger's point of view – for my friend was clearly head over ears in love with the lady who was now inseparably associated in his mind with the little feet. So the dinner passed off in as unsatisfactory a manner as could well be to us both; for apart from my sympathy with poor Ranger in his infatuation, the state of mind in which he was quite spoiled him for purposes of society.

An incident occurred towards the conclusion of dinner, however, which gave him relief. Mrs. Merridew's French maid entered the room, and brought a message from the manager of the hotel, in answer, as it appeared to a previous application. 'Oh yes,' said that young person, 'Mademoiselle could have a chamber adjoining the appartement of Monsieur and Madame; it was quite ready for her reception.'

I thought Ranger was about to express his surprise at this announcement in an audible manner, so visibly impressed was he at the fact disclosed. Mrs Merridew was not a widow, then, after all, and, what was more important, her husband could not be a *prétendu* of Miss Pembroke.

We were in doubt when dinner was over, whether to begin our evening prowl at once, or to look in for a few minutes upon the party in the salon assigned to the residents of the hotel. It was lucky that we decided upon the latter course; for an incident took place immediately on our entering the room, which brought the adventure to a crisis, and was of immense importance – as the event proved – to the future of my friend.

Ranger was looking about him with an object that may be guessed, when an elderly gentleman – whose erect, bold bearing, said 'old soldier,' as unmistakably as his jovial red face, shaded by the whitest of moustache and whisker, said *bon vivant* – tapped him on the shoulder to attract his attention.

Ranger turned round in some surprise, and immediately fell to shaking the elderly gentleman cordially by the hand.

'My dear uncle,' said he, 'I am delighted to see you.'

'And I you, my boy,' returned the uncle, beaming with pleasure. 'It is very seldom that you are caught, thanks – or rather no thanks – to that way of yours of being here, there, and everywhere at once. You are staying at this hotel? So am I. Very fortunate, isn't it, that we should meet?'

Ranger said it was, and evidently meant what he said. He introduced me presently to his jovial relative, who seemed almost as delighted to see a friend of his nephew's as his nephew himself. My new acquaintance proved to be General Holsterley, an old dragoon, who, I afterwards learned, was a very rich bachelor, and had made Ranger his heir.

After a little talk, the General said to Ranger –

'I must leave you for a few minutes. I vote for going somewhere together afterwards, but I must go and speak to some people I see at the end of the room. I promised to meet them here, to do a little Paris with them. But stay, why should I leave you? Come with me, and I will introduce you to a couple of as charming women as you could wish to meet in a day's march – and that's not saying enough for them, by-the-by. And, I tell you what, if you played your cards well, you would have a very great chance with the only one of the two who has a chance left open. Come on, my boy – and your friend too,' he added, seeing that Ranger was doubtful what to do with me.

So we were both marched up to the end of the room, and in another minute the General was exchanging the heartiest of greetings with – our friends of the table d'hôte.

As soon as there was a pause – for they all talked together – Holsterley took an opportunity of presenting his nephew, and then myself, to his friends.

They were all very cordial, and Mrs. Merridew rather demonstrative.

'We were fast becoming acquainted with your friends through meeting them at dinner, though Mr. Ranger was very reserved, and did not seem to trust himself to talk much with strange ladies.'

And she looked at him – what shall I say? well, wickedly if you will – with those beady black eyes of hers which she knew so well how to employ.

Ranger looked a little confused, as a man is apt to look if he thinks he is being ridiculed by a pretty woman; and he told me afterwards that the idea came upon him suddenly that he had seen those eyes somewhere before.

It is sufficient for me to say, however, that we all became very intimate on short notice; that we all went to the theatre together, and had one of the pleasantest evenings possible. It must have been especially so to Ranger, for he had Miss Pembroke nearly all to himself during the entire time; and it was not difficult to see that her deep-blue eyes and soft happy beauty had fairly completed the impression which they had made upon him from the first.

Colonel Merridew – the new comer turned out to be an old comrade of the General's – left us at the door of the theatre, and took the ladies home, while the rest of us went somewhere to supper. The latter arrangement was Holsterley's doing, for Ranger was disposed to make himself as generally disagreeable as persons in a similar condition usually do.

When we in our turn arrived at the hotel the General went off to bed – it was quite time too – and then Ranger, who evidently wanted to talk about himself, insisted upon taking me up to his room. On our way we passed the apartments occupied by our friends, and then Ranger, who dared not speak for fear of being overheard, pointed triumphantly to some objects lying on the door-mats.

At one entrance there were two pairs of boots, belonging to a lady and a gentleman respectively. At the other was a single pair, particularly small, and to an amateur in feet, I should say, justifying all the praise that had been bestowed on them.

I dragged Ranger from the spot, where he seemed absurdly disposed to linger. When we reached his room he became guilty of rapturous conduct to a ridiculous degree, and then asked me, in a lucid interval, if I did not think him the happiest of men.

I declared my very high opinion of his state of bliss, and got away from him as soon as I could.

His must have been pleasant sleep that night – if he slept at all.

V.

I did not see my friend on the following day, but on the day following that he came to me with a message from Mrs. Merridew, asking me to dine with the Colonel and herself, who had a small party in their own apartments.

All was going right, he said, between himself and Miss Pembroke; and he had the advantage, he frankly confessed, of a great deal of backing up from Mrs. Merridew as well as from his uncle. 'I shall propose,' said he, 'the very first opportunity – to-night if I get a chance.' He said nothing about feet this time – I suppose he thought his present relations with Miss Pembroke did not justify such a discussion. But I noticed when we met the ladies that they continued to wear robes so long as to preclude investigation into that particular.

At dinner Ranger was placed as a matter of course beside the blue-eyed beauty, while she of the beaded black divided her attentions very pleasantly between the rest of us – the General and myself being the only other guests.

After dinner we all went to the theatre; and there also Ranger's seat in the box was next to that of Miss Pembroke. He had by this time got so far as to talk to her in whispers.

The box was rather crowded, and the General, the Colonel, and myself, were not sorry to go out for half an hour between the pieces. On our return I noticed that the blue eyes were much cast down, and that their owner was constrained, and evidently indisposed for conversation. The black eyes, on the contrary, were all animation and triumph, and their owner conversational to an unusual degree. I had my suspicions.

Ranger made a remark in the course of the evening which seemed mal-àpropos – I could not tell why at the time. There was a young lady on the stage playing the part of a *soubrette,* with skirts of course which made no mystery of a little foot and a well-turned ankle. Somebody made a remark that she was not quite so pretty as the author of the piece intended her to be.

'No,' said the General, who had a blunt way of expressing his opinion on the 'points' of ladies; 'but her feet are first-rate.'

'I am an immense admirer of pretty feet,' said Ranger to his neighbour, in a voice intended doubtless for a whisper, but which was audible to the whole box.

Miss Pembroke drew herself up, blushed unmistakably, and I thought looked rather indignant. The compliment was perhaps rather too direct.

The General accompanied the Colonel and the ladies home this time. When Ranger and myself were left alone on the boulevard, Ranger clutched me by the shoulder, and said –

'All right, my boy! – congratulate me.'

I did congratulate him, and remarked that he seemed to have managed matters rather cleverly during our absence from the box.

'Well,' said he, 'Mrs. Merridew was very considerate; pushed her chair into a corner and said she had a headache, seemed, in fact, to be asleep; and I popped the question in the quietest manner possible.'

'And received the answer in the same way?'

'Yes, as far as I got any answer at all; and perhaps I am not quite justified in saying that it's all right – she said nothing more than "Tomorrow!" '

And Ranger looked a little nervous at the new idea.

'Oh, I think you are safe if she said that,' replied I, and I congratulated him over again.

We were to meet next day, according to an arrangement made in the course of the evening, to go and see the waters play at Versailles.

VI.

I was at the Grand Hôtel next day soon after noon. I met Ranger in the hall before presenting myself in the Merridews' domain. He was radiant with joy. Miss Pembroke had not appeared at breakfast, but he had sought and obtained an interview with her immediately after, had renewed his suit, and had received the answer which might have been expected after her response of the night before.

'Now,' said Ranger, when he had told me these interesting particulars, 'we will go the Merridews' quarters – the ladies ought to be ready by this time.'

There was nobody in the little salon when we entered; but in a few minutes the two ladies joined us.

A moment's glance at their costume revealed a fact which astonished me, and caused in Ranger nothing less than consternation. I could see what was working within him, though he tried to keep it in control.

Mrs. Merridew and Miss Pembroke were both attired in fashionable costumes which permitted the feet to be visible; and the unaccountable fact became apparent that it was the elder lady who owned what Ranger called the Mice, while to the younger belonged the – I will not use the word which Ranger had ventured upon in his indignation, and the more so as the epithet in its signification as a satire on size was quite unjustified. Miss Pembroke's feet were not remarkably large. They were of very fair average dimensions, strictly proportionate to her figure, which was on a grander scale than that of her cousin. They were very good feet besides, and *chaussé* to perfection. But if diminutiveness were the object in view, no feet could hope to compete with those of Mrs. Merridew. These were on so small a scale that in a statue they would have looked incongruous; but seen in connection with the neat and nicely-clad figure of their present owner, they must have gained admiration from a great many persons besides the Chinese.

I saw Ranger regarding first one lady and then another with looks of wonderment, and I am sorry to add, mortification. Mrs. Merridew, whose beady eyes were merry, I suspect at his expense, seemed to see that something was the matter, and tried to cover his confusion by talking to any extent. Miss Pembroke also seemed to see that something was the matter; but her mode of meeting it took the form of reserve. They were all, I fancy, as much relieved as I was when the General and the Colonel came in and a movement was made for the railway station.

But things were no better when we were in the train. Ranger was moody and embarrassed, even cold in his manner towards the beautiful girl about whom he had been raving little more than an hour before. And Miss Pembroke evidently felt herself slighted. She was seated next to her betrothed, but turned away from him, and addressed her conversation during the short journey almost entirely to me. I could not help thinking, under her charming influence, what a fool my friend was to allow his infatuation to carry him to this extent. Had it been my case – but no matter.

At Versailles we saw all the grand things that were to be seen; but neither the palace nor the gardens had their old attractions for us. A gloom was cast over the party; for none could fail to perceive the breach that was taking place between the lovers, though all could not, I suppose, attribute it to its proper cause.

As we roamed through the rooms and galleries, Ranger walked beside Miss Pembroke, and spoke to her from time to time; but he had lost his power of conversation, and was constrained beyond all attempts at disguise. The lady met his coldness by this time more than half way, and her beauty wore a haughtiness that ill became it – like that of a frozen rose.

In the gardens he offered his arm, but this was decisively refused; and, as if to prevent another demonstration of the kind, Clara – may I call her Clara? – took the arm of Mrs. Merridew.

The elder lady improved the occasion by taking the younger one apart, and holding her for some time in conversation. I watched the pair while Ranger walked on with the two officers. I purposely avoided any colloquy with the former, as I saw that such advice as I had to offer would be ill received.

The effect of Mrs. Merridew's communication upon Clara was far from being mollifying. Indignation was visibly depicted on the young lady's countenance; and as they both rose from the seat where they had taken refuge, and rejoined me, I heard Miss Pembroke say –

'I do not know how to forgive you, Flora. Of course I *do* forgive you, for you meant well; but I consider that I have been the victim of a most humiliating plot.'

We returned to Paris under as unpleasant conditions as ever attended a party of pleasure. When we alighted from the train the ladies entered the open carriage that was in waiting, and Ranger followed them – as I supposed to seek a reconciliation. The rest of us walked. When we arrived at the hotel I excused myself from joining the party at dinner, and took my leave.

Ranger came to me early next morning, and told me that his engagement with Miss Pembroke was broken off.

'Surely,' said I, 'you are not fool enough to quarrel with her for not having Mrs. Merridew's feet! If so—'

'Hear me, man,' said he, sternly. 'I love her more than I ever loved anything upon this earth, and I would marry her if her feet were really the Beetle-Crushers pictured by my depraved imagination. But I seem to have been the victim of a plot in which it is not quite clear that she was not an accomplice; and the joke of the thing is that she makes a similar complaint on her own part.'

'But surely,' I urged, 'this misunderstanding can be accommodated.'

'The difficulty,' said he, 'is now on her side. Look at this letter, which was brought to me with my – with my boots,' he added with a laugh, remembering his absurdities in connection with those articles of costume.

I read the letter. It was a dismissal, couched in sufficiently contemptuous terms, intimating that the writer was not disposed to ally herself with a person whose affection depended upon abstract qualifications.

He would not listen to my persuasions. He was off, he said, somewhere; he had had quite enough of Paris – as if Paris was in fault! – and never wished to see the place again. His intention was to go – well, he did not quite know where. He should either join some foreign service where there was hard fighting, in hopes of being knocked over, or join his friend – – (he mentioned a great name connected with the Geographical Society) in discovering the source of the Nile. He was not sure which.

And so he left me.

Two days after, when I called at the Grand Hôtel, I found that Colonel Merridew and his party had also taken their departure.

VII.

Nearly a year went by, and I saw nothing of Ranger, nor of his friends. But in the autumn succeeding that of our sojourn in Paris I happened to be at Baden-Baden. There, as I came out of the Kursaal one day, I met going in – the entire of our Paris party. Mrs. Merridew, her husband, and the jovial old General, were in front; Clara and Ranger – with their arms in one another this time – brought up the rear.

The meeting was a hearty one, and when it came to my turn to have a quiet confab with Ranger, I could not help saying maliciously –

'Why, I thought you were killed in the Danish war, or held in captivity by that king in Africa who has all the fat wives?'

'Now don't be annoying, my boy,' said he. 'I made it all right, though only six weeks ago by the way, when that lovely girl who has just left my arm, became

Mrs. Charles Ranger, F.R.G.S., and some other distinctions if you did but know them. I thought better of the two alternatives I suggested, and determined to follow the thing up. I did so by letter, and after that by personal appeal, and somehow, after an immense deal of devotion on my part, and no little influence, I suspect on the part of Mrs. Merridew, the lady's scruples were removed. I will tell you all about it after dinner – you will dine with us of course to-day.'

I was delighted to hear what I did, and delighted to dine with them of course; but Mrs. Merridew told me 'all about it' before Ranger had an opportunity. This is what she said, when I gave her my arm, coming away from the Kursaal:

'As Mr. Ranger's friend you ought to know the facts of the case; and indeed I owe it to you, on my own part, that I should explain my share in the proceedings. When I first met Charles at the table d'hôte, I recognized him at once, apart from his name, which I well remembered also, as an old pupil of my father's – my father was a clergyman who took pupils – before he went up to Cambridge. It is a dreadful time ago, but I was a mere girl then, as you may suppose,' – and her beady black eyes here gave a sly glance of inquiry – 'and not grown up. He paid me an awful amount of attention in those days, and was particularly infatuated, as he said, with my feet. He was always raving about my feet, in fact; and as they seemed to be the special objects of his affection, I was less flattered than I should otherwise have been, and merely made fun of him instead of falling in love, which might otherwise have been the case. Indeed his fondness for feet appeared to be of an abstract character, for he took to admiring a housemaid who had gifts in that direction. This was quite enough for me as you may suppose, and after the girl had gone – which I took care should be at an early date after the discovery – I gave him his dismissal also. I was very young then, of course,' – here the beaded eyes again made an appeal for confirmation – 'but even at my age the attentions that he paid were of importance. Well, he went to the University in the natural course of things, and I saw him no more. When I met him at the hotel he did not recognize me. I suppose I am changed.' – Again the beaded eyes looked arch. – 'I was then away from my husband. I thought that had I introduced myself he would be making love to me, and that, of course, would never do. But on the other hand I had a regard for him, and considered that he would make a capital match for my cousin. So I determined to play upon his weakness in a harmless way. I persuaded Clara that the new costumes were indecorous wear for ladies in an hotel by themselves, so we always wore trains. I saw that he was struck with one of us, and guessed that he would find out our rooms, and be bewildered by the boots at the door. I even let him hear the name of the bootmaker, in order that he might prosecute his inquiries there, which he did, as *you* know. When my husband came, I even went so far as to change the boots at the different doors in order to deceive him. All went well, and I almost *drove* him to the proposal at the theatre. It was two days after that that Clara, when we were going to Versailles, suggested that there was no longer any reason for continuing our trains. I had no longer any excuse for opposition, and the result was as you saw. When Charles turned sulky – as you saw also – I had to explain the whole to Clara, who nearly quarrelled with me, and quite threw

Charles off. Nothing but his constant pleadings, for nearly a year, during which time he followed us about with a persistence which left no doubt of his sincerity, and my earnest persuasions directed all the time at Clara, induced her at last to forgive him; and there they are now, man and wife, to the great delight of us all.'

We were a happy party that day at dinner, and for a great many days afterwards. I was the more happy, too, when Ranger told me, in confidence, that he was quite cured of his partiality for feet, and looked upon them in the light of simply useful extremities.

'I would rather be married to Clara,' he added, 'if she had really Beetle-Crushers – which you know she has not – than to anybody else in the world, even though she could step into a glass slipper belonging to Mrs. Merridew.' S. L. B.

14

IMAGE: [ANON], ““THE GRECIAN BEND.””

Punch, 2 October 1869, p. 132

Figure 14.1 “THE GRECIAN BEND.”

DOES NOT TIGHT-LACING AND HIGH HEELS GIVE A CHARMING GRACE AND DIGNITY TO THE FEMALE FIGURE?

DOI: 10.4324/9781315399980-20

15

[ANON], 'GENERAL NEWS.'

The Glasgow [*Daily*] *Herald*, 25 January 1870, p. 4

The last and sweetest thing in fashion is the "Alexandra Limp." Shoemakers in London now offer their fair customers the choice of boots with equally high heels for each foot, or the far more charming variety of a high heel for one boot and a low heel for the other, causing the wearer to halt in a way supposed to be imitative of royalty!

DOI: 10.4324/9781315399980-21

16

[ANON], 'FASHION'S FOLLIES.'

Fun, 2 April 1870, p. 35

THE Grecian bend, the chignon, the Alexandra limp,
The waist pinch'd tight, the hair let down that tongs are made to crimp,
The bonnets of a single rose, the high-heel'd boots; how vext
Does poor Pater-familias in anger ask, "What next?"

DOI: 10.4324/9781315399980-22

1.2.3

The 'Dolly Varden'

A literary fashion

DOI: 10.4324/9781315399980-23

1.2.3 The 'Dolly Varden': a literary fashion

Our next set of selections focuses upon a so-called 'literary fashion', namely, the adoption of the 'Dolly Varden' costume from the late 1860s onwards. This style was inspired by the eponymous Dolly, a character from Charles Dickens' 1841 historical novel *Barnaby Rudge*, who was a young woman of considerable charm and style. Our first extract is formed from the now-iconic description of Dolly from this novel, revealing her winsome appeal, which seems rooted as much in her 'cherry-coloured ribbons' as her physical beauty.[1]

The character of Dolly was illustrated for Dickens' novel by Hablot Knight Browne ('Phiz'), after which she was famously reinterpreted by the artist William Powell Frith in c. 1842.[2] Following Dickens' death in 1870 and the subsequent auction of his possessions, the painting fell into new ownership, prompting, as Taeko Sakai notes, a huge resurgence of interest in its sartorial iconography.[3] As Rebecca N. Mitchell has detailed, the so-called 'Dolly Varden' gown took inspiration from the polonaise of the 1770s and featured 'a tightly bodiced overdress with a decorative overskirt cinched up to reveal an underskirt' that, in its original context of 'court fashion', 'emphasized sumptuous, heavily figured fabric [. . .] the presence of which denoted its owner's wealth'.[4] However, Sakei argues that, by the late 1860s, the fashion was revisioned to incorporate 'outdated printed cotton fabrics', and the fashion became accessible to lower-middle-class women, similar in social status, in fact, to Dolly herself.[5]

Our extracts reflect the growing popularity of this style within fashion and popular culture, which, as critics have explored, included discussions from fashion magazines and even music covers themed around the character.[6] Our extract from *The Englishwoman's Domestic Magazine* of June 1872 deems the costume a 'novelty *par excellence*',[7] while our selected image represents just one of the numerous music covers produced.[8] In a sense, the image also acts as a kind of fashion plate to accompany the music sheet, constructing a synergy between fashionable dress and music that enables the wearer/dancer and music performer to act – perhaps even to inhabit – the 'Dolly Varden' persona. Published in 1872 in Boston, this reflects American interest in the fashion, which is also reinforced by our next selection, an article from *Scribner's Magazine* detailing the popularity of the fashion across the Atlantic. The author praises the character's 'trim, neat and coquettish' style, which seems bound up with her Englishness as well as her 'good, pure, everyday' character, and notes that Dolly's costume also embodies accessibility and the 'domestic [virtue]' of stylish economy.[9] Our final source, however, published in the British periodical *The Ladies' Monthly Magazine*, links the style to its aristocratic French origins while denouncing its interpretation by English women and, we may infer, subtly undermining the efforts of the less economically advantaged wearer.

Notes

1 C. Dickens, *Barnaby Rudge; A Tale of the Riots of 'Eighty* (London: Chapman and Hall, 1841), p. 41.
2 For further discussion, see two essays in M. Bills and V. Knight, *William Powell Frith: Painting the Victorian Age* (New Haven and London: Yale University Press in association with Guildhall Art Gallery, City of London, and The Mercer Art Gallery, Harrogate Museum and Arts, 2006): Chapter 7: E. Ehrman, ‘Frith and Fashion’, pp. 111–129 (pp. 115–116), and Chapter 2: D. Trotter, ‘Dickens and Frith’, pp. 29–39. See also T. Sakai, ‘The “Dolly Varden” Polonaise at the Seaside: A Fashion Revival in the Early 1870s’, *The Dickensian*, 114(506), Winter 2018, pp. 252–261, and R. N. Mitchell, ‘Victorian Faddishness: The Dolly Varden from Dickens to *Patience*’, *Journal of Victorian Culture*, 26(2), 2021, pp. 153–171.
3 Sakai, ‘The “Dolly Varden” Polonaise at the Seaside’. For further, illuminating, consideration of the role of Dickens’ death in the popularising of the Dolly Varden style, see D. M. Dove, ‘Dickens, Death, and the Dolly Varden Dress’, *Victoriographies*, 12(1), (2022), pp. 31–51.
4 Mitchell, ‘Victorian Faddishness’, p. 155.
5 Sakai, ‘The “Dolly Varden” Polonaise at the Seaside’, p. 252. See also Mitchell, ‘Victorian Faddishness’, pp. 160–161.
6 See, for example, Sakai, ‘The “Dolly Varden” Polonaise at the Seaside’, for further discussion of these examples. One ‘song sheet cover’ of G. W. Hunt’s ‘Dolly Varden’ is discussed and reproduced on pp. 254–255, which forms an interesting point of comparison with our music cover selection, also featuring Hunt’s work.
7 The Silkworm, ‘Spinnings in Town’, *The Englishwoman’s Domestic Magazine*, 1 June 1871, pp. 362–367 (p. 362). Also quoted in Sakai, ‘The “Dolly Varden” Polonaise at the Seaside’, p. 254.
8 G. W. Hunt, ‘Dolly Varden’ (music title page) (Boston: Oliver Ditson & Co., 1872).
9 [Anon], ‘Dolly Vardens’, *Scribner’s Monthly*, June 1872, pp. 248, 249.

17

CHARLES DICKENS, *BARNABY RUDGE; A TALE OF THE RIOTS OF 'EIGHTY.*

(London: Chapman and Hall, 1841), pp. 41–42

As to Dolly, there she was again, the very pink and pattern of good looks, in a smart little cherry-coloured mantle, with a hood of the same drawn over her head, and upon the top of that hood, a little straw hat trimmed with cherry-coloured ribbons, and worn the merest trifle on one side – just enough in short to make it the wickedest and most provoking head-dress that ever malicious milliner devised. And not to speak of the manner in which these cherry-coloured decorations brightened her eyes, or vied with her lips, or shed a new bloom on her face, she wore such a cruel little muff, and such a heart-rending pair of shoes, and was so surrounded and hemmed in, as it were, by aggravations of all kinds, that when Mr. Tappertit, holding the horse's head, saw her come out of the house alone, such impulses came over him to decoy her into the chaise and drive off like mad, that he would unquestionably have done it, but for certain uneasy doubts besetting him as to the shortest way to Gretna Green; whether it was up the street or down, or up the right-hand turning or the left; and whether, supposing all the turnpikes to be carried by storm, the blacksmith in the end would marry them on credit; which by reason of his clerical office appeared, even to his excited imagination, so unlikely, that he hesitated.

DOI: 10.4324/9781315399980-24

18

IMAGE: G. W. HUNT, 'DOLLY VARDEN' (MUSIC TITLE PAGE)

(Boston: Oliver Ditson & Co., 1872)

DOI: 10.4324/9781315399980-25

19

THE SILKWORM, 'SPINNINGS IN TOWN.'

The Englishwoman's Domestic Magazine, 1 June 1871, p. 362

In prints, piqués, batistes, and percales I observed some very beautiful designs, and the écru and holland costumes are well worthy of remark; but the novelty *par excellence* is the "Dolly Varden" costume, which is a pretty, coquettish copy of the noted picture of Dolly Varden, which was among Mr. Charles Dickens's collection, and sold at his death. This costume is made in really old-fashioned pattern chintz, and is worn over a cambric skirt of the prevailing colour of the chintz. The "Dolly Varden" is draped over this flounced petticoat, and is most bewitching in blue, rose, and rose and white. I saw it also in gold colour, but did not like the effect. A straw hat should be worn with it, trimmed to correspond.

DOI: 10.4324/9781315399980-26

20

[ANON], 'DOLLY VARDENS.'

Scribner's Monthly, June 1872, pp. 248–249

THERE are circumstances under which curiosity is laudable.

Perhaps we could find it in the Lives of Celebrated Women? Not there. Eminent Christians? Nor there. New England Celebrities? Female Martyrs? Noted Names of Fiction? Our forty-volume Cyclopædia?

Not a line about it in one of them! There was nothing left but to go to the great Library.

Behold us leaning over that classic railing, biographical dictionary in hand, turning the pages end-of-the-alphabet-ward.

At V A R, the urbane attendant, whom we delight to honor, smiled knowingly behind his spectacles.

"You'll not find it there," he said. "It's in *Barnaby Rudge*."

"Ah, thank you! The volume, please."

"Sorry to say, we haven't it."

"What! Not *Barnaby Rudge?* In a great library like this?"

"We have a hundred copies, madame; but they all are out. Everybody is reading up on 'Dolly Varden.' "

The load was lifted. At the mere mention of *Barnaby Rudge,* the locksmith's pretty daughter stood before us. Strange that we could have forgotten her, – the sweet, fresh, jaunty English lass, trim, neat and coquettish, with her bright quilted petticoat, and her gown caught up daintily and pinned at the back. The locksmith's daughter, as we know, was no heroine. She advocated no great public principle, suffered in no noble cause. She was just a good, pure, everyday girl – and that is why we love her. Her name is a character in itself. All Dickens's names are. It means freshness and spring-time and guileless dressiness. And so Dolly Varden is made the presiding genius of the dry-goods world to-day.

She comes in with the spring, as she should, when city folk search the highways for fresh fabrics and millinery as naturally as they would look for arbutus and apple-blossoms in the country. And, truly, it would be hard for forest, meadow or garden to rival the gayly-patterned goods that fill our great shops. Huge nosegays of garden flowers, delicate wild-wood blossoms, birds atilt in branches, birds darting through space, and butterflies dizzy with the nectar of roses. All these have the dress goods, and more: pastoral scenes, a lady under a tree feeding chickens, and

 DOI: 10.4324/9781315399980-27

the ever-youthful shepherdess with her crook! Nay, a cottage has been seen with fence and shrubbery complete, all within a yard of calico. Poor Dolly Varden!

What an innovation upon the plain colors and nunlike simplicity of dress that have been in vogue so long! Why, of late, a lady to be gay had but to display a red bow at the neck of her black gown; to be gorgeous she had but to tie a bright sash over the same somber garment. Now the poor thing is dazed with a prodigality of form and color. At every counter, the clerks shake a whole summer of bloom before her eyes. A little spray, a blossom here and there might do. But this!

At first she wanders in a state of bewilderment among the flower-bedizened silks and calicoes, with a shuddering sense of gay upholstery in her soul. But, after all, everybody must have at least one Dolly Varden costume; and so there is a little crowd and a twitter of excitement around these counters continually. Higher up, to where the great brooding elevators flit and settle, you see cruel effigies, dumb lay-figure Dolly Vardens – "ready-made" things that would have unmade poor, simple, real Dolly at a glance. Only lady-wooers have they, but the coquetry of price keeps up the excitement, and murmurs of "lovely!" fill the air.

Besides the charm of novelty which makes the style attractive, they have also a vague home-like suggestion, – perhaps because they have not yet been adopted as street costumes, – and to see all the world buying home-dresses seems to predict a reign of the domestic virtues. Then, undoubtedly, they gain a borrowed grace from their name, a cheerfulness which does not belong altogether to the painted roses and chickens, but to a certain phase of domestic life as drawn for us by the great novelist. Who does not remember with pleasant emotions the jubilant way in which Dickens drew the scenes of domestic life? Mrs. Crachit sweetened up the apple-sauce, Miss Belinda dusted the hot-plates, Master Bob mashed the potatoes, etc. Or, when Mrs. Whitney tells us how "we girls" made preparations for the party, it was like a merry-go-round, and so much better than the dull vapidities of fashionable calls, that every woman longed for an *art kitchen* and a rolling-pin at once.

The other day, at Stewart's, an old lady, who sat rather insecurely on one of the rotary seats near us, was caressingly fingering some red, red roses – calico ones, on a yellow calico ground – and saying to a matronly woman who accompanied her: "Exactly like the dress I wore the night I danced with the General" – but here the reminiscence was interrupted by the clerk, who said these Dolly Vardens were of the very newest pattern.

"Dolly Vardens and the newest pattern are they? Well, well!" and the old lady nodded her head slowly as if she could give testimony on that subject. But she knew, as we all do, that it wouldn't be worth while, for if Fashion should declare that black was white the world would become color-blind.

What of it? The Dolly Vardens are not a whit the less new and stylish to-day because they were new and stylish in the days of our great-grandmothers.

21

[ANON], 'OBSERVATIONS ON LONDON AND PARISIAN FASHIONS.'

The Ladies' Monthly Magazine, the World of Fashion, July 1872, p. 1

This season has developed a great deal of what the French call the "Pompadour" style; the same which in London has been called the "Dolly Varden." Many pretty Costumes of this style are now being produced by the first Parisian *Artistes des Modes,* and these are really elegant, and could be worn by ladies of the most refined taste; this could hardly be said of some of the Dolly Vardens that we have seen in England.

DOI: 10.4324/9781315399980-28

1.3

Cosmetics

1.3 Cosmetics

Attitudes towards the use of beautifying aids varied hugely during the nineteenth century, often ranging from resigned acceptance to associations with immorality and even prostitution. The topic was unequivocally condemned by the journalist Mrs Eliza Lynn Linton in her 'infamous'[1] 'Girl of the Period' article, published in *The Saturday Review* of March 1868.[2] Decrying the 'false red hair and painted skin'[3] of the contemporary fashionable young woman, the article passionately opposed the use of cosmetics on the grounds that they mimicked the style and tastes of fashionable courtesans and, in doing so, degraded 'respectable' femininity.

It was hardly surprising, then, that Victorian women sought guidance from trusted published sources. Yet, commentators were far from united on this issue. Some writers were cautious, reflecting Linton's reactionary views, while others, such the dress reformer Mrs Haweis, were far more sanguine and permissive.[4] Sarah Lennox notes that while '[s]ome Victorian beauty writers included only the most respectable content in their manuals', such as 'healthy living practices that were thought to naturally beautify the body', in contrast, '[o]thers defied social mores by providing recipes for every type of beautifier, including the most scandalous, that of coloured cosmetics'.[5]

This section addresses the use of cosmetics and skin preparations from the perspective of the contemporary female reader. It aims to capture different aspects of the 'cosmetics debate' and, specifically, how women might have negotiated the ongoing dilemma. Our chosen sources cover both well-discussed and idiosyncratic aspects of the toilette, including the use of various products and preparations. They address the morality of attending to 'beauty', as well as warning against the use of dangerous and adulterated substances. Indeed, cosmetics in the nineteenth century often contained ingredients such as arsenic, mercury and lead, the use of which could cause skin irritation and even death.[6]

Our first source 'Materials for the Toilette', published in *The Saturday Magazine* of 1840,[7] acknowledges both of these perspectives in an article that condemns cosmetics while simultaneously accepting that many women chose to use them. It begins with a notional reminder that lifestyle (including 'simplicity of diet', 'regular exercise' and reliable personal hygiene) is '[d]oubtless' more effective at 'preserving the fresh and healthy appearance of youth', before reluctantly endorsing the use of certain products.[8] It includes a recipe to make a 'cold cream' from natural ingredients, also discussing the use of rice meal for cosmetic purposes, and even for the removal of wrinkles. Then, with a certain sense of trepidation, the writer moves on to consider 'injurious' cosmetics such as rouge and pearl-powder.[9] Rouge, the writer notes, obtains its vibrant colour from the cochineal beetle to create a 'red paint' to be applied to the face, the description implicitly underscoring its artificiality.[10] Another product, pearl powder, is discussed, a substance that created a false 'hue of health' whilst also inflicting 'lasting injury' upon the unfortunate wearer.[11] Issues of class and economy are also raised in the article, in its consideration of the relative cost and quality of different versions of these products.

The safety, as well as the morality, of cosmetics became a significant issue during the Victorian period, as critics including Jessica P. Clark and Laurence Talairach-Vielmas have noted.[12] Accordingly, the authors of our next two sources were keen to reassure the reader of both the safety and effectiveness of the featured products. Our next source, an advertisement for Pears's Rouge & Pears's Pearl Powder, published in *The Ladies' Monthly Magazine* of 1856, described this as containing 'the most innocent ingredients',[13] while the author of our next piece asserted that, unlike its rivals, Rimmel's 'Liquid Rouge' contained no 'mercury or other metallic substances [. . .] liable to cause great injury to the system'.[14]

The following extract, taken from Charles Reade's 1872 novel 'A Simpleton', emphasises the perils of unwittingly applying cosmetics adulterated with dangerous and unwholesome substances, wherein the protagonist, the young and newly married Rosa Staines, is discovered applying face powder containing metal. The conversation also functions as an opportunity to showcase male knowledge over female frippery, as Rosa becomes the recipient of an impromptu lecture from her husband, a physician, who is able to test the substance using scientific equipment. Luckily, Rosa's complexion remains both 'heavenly' and 'admirable', and no further cosmetic tragedy ensues as she reluctantly (yet obediently) follows her husband's directions.[15] Here a wider comparison can be made with Wilkie Collins' 1875 *The Law and the Lady*. In this novel (not excerpted here), the character Sarah Macallan is described as having a 'muddy, blotchy [complexion]' and is suspected of having consumed the 'deadly poison' arsenic in an attempt to redress this.[16] As Aviva Briefel notes, narratives of cosmetic danger 'caution that beautification through artificial means may eradicate the very self that had sought improvement'.[17] Unlike Collins', Reade's novel offers a warning against complete self-effacement through cosmetics.

Our next source, entitled 'The Toilet-Table, and What Should Lie Thereon', published in *The Girl's Own Paper* of 1881, continues in this gendered manner, the author's pseudonym, 'Medicus', presenting an idea of male knowledge and authority to the young female reader. This article, like its predecessor in *The Saturday Magazine* of 1840, again emphasises the importance of lifestyle and self-care in the pursuit of outer '[b]eauty',[18] while permitting the use of certain 'harmless' preparations such as a simple pomade alongside natural rain-water. Yet it simultaneously promotes other gendered rituals, as the reader is actively encouraged to polish and tend to the physical artefacts stored on the eponymous 'Toilet-Table', such as the looking-glass, sponges and hairbrushes. Perhaps this exercise is introduced in an attempt to prepare young girls for their roles as household managers, moving on from the microscopic tending to one's appearance and 'toilet table' to the larger, demanding duties of housekeeping and caring for the family.

By the close of the century, women were well versed in the consequences of toxic substances in cosmetics, our final two sources directing the reader's attention to the use of 'natural' substances. One, an advertorial for rice-powder, appeared in *Myra's Home Journal* in June 1890, and celebrates a product called 'Duvet de Ninon', which is described as 'eminently hygienic'.[19] Yet it is also praised for lending 'a dazzling whiteness' to the skin, which reinforces Lori Anne Loeb's observation that 'a pale complexion' formed part of the '[c]ommercially idealized feminine appearance' of the period.[20] This extract emphasises the narrow and exclusionary nature of Victorian beauty values in terms of race and class, as pale skin was habitually favoured over darker complexions, pallour also reflecting a woman's leisured status and lack of exposure to the sun. Our last selection, which appeared in the same publication seven years later, expounds a different ingredient, the cucumber, and draws upon the work of Dr Anna Kingsford, a medical doctor who campaigned against vivisection and for women's rights. Dr Kingsford's name is used here to endorse wholesome, natural cosmetics, encouraging the reader towards its 'innocent and healthful' vegetable properties.[21]

Notes

1 See K. Tennant, 'The Discerning Eye: Viewing the Mid-Victorian "Modern" Woman', in I. Parkins and E. M. Sheehan (eds.), *Cultures of Femininity in Modern Fashion* (Durham, NH: University of New Hampshire Press, 2011), pp. 103–123 (p. 107).

2 [Anon] [Mrs Eliza Lynn Linton], 'The Girl of the Period', *The Saturday Review*, 14 March 1868, pp. 339–340 (p. 340). Mrs Linton's article is reproduced in R. N. Mitchell (ed.), *Fashioning the Victorians: a Critical Sourcebook* (London: Bloomsbury Visual Arts, 2018), pp. 65–70.

3 [Anon] [Linton], 'The Girl of the Period', p. 340. Also quoted in Tennant, 'The Discerning Eye', p. 107.

4 Haweis takes a more sanguine approach in a section titled 'Sham Delicacy', which appeared in her 1878 work *The Art of Beauty*. See Mrs H. R. [Mary Eliza] Haweis, *The Art of Beauty* (New York: Harper & Brothers, 1878), pp. 195–201. Here she refutes the 'unnecessary amount of contempt' that 'has been cast on cosmetics' (p. 196), instead urging readers to forgive the use of 'a little harmless powder' or 'one tiny touch of white' to obscure blemishes (p. 197). Alison Gernsheim also cites and discusses this aspect of Haweis' work in *Victorian and Edwardian Fashion: A Photographic Survey* (New York: Dover, 1981), p. 66.

5 S. Lennox, 'The Beautified Body: Physiognomy in Victorian Beauty Manuals', *Victorian Review*, 42(1), Spring 2016, pp. 9–14 (p. 10).

6 For some critical discussion of the dangers of cosmetics, see A. M. David, *Fashion Victims: The Dangers of Dress Past and Present* (London and New York: Bloomsbury Visual Arts, 2015), pp. 22–24; J. P. Clark, *The Business of Beauty: Gender and the Body in Victorian London* (London and New York, Bloomsbury, 2020), pp. 78–80; and L. Talairach-Vielmas, *Moulding the Female Body in Victorian Fairy Tales and Sensation*

Novels (London and New York: Routledge, 2016 [first published in 2007 by Ashgate Publishing]), pp. 135–136.

7 [Anon], 'Materials for the Toilette. VIII', *The Saturday Magazine*, 25 January 1840, pp. 27–28.

8 [Anon], 'Materials for the Toilette', p. 27.

9 [Anon], 'Materials for the Toilette', p. 28.

10 [Anon], 'Materials for the Toilette', p. 28.

11 [Anon], 'Materials for the Toilette', p. 28.

12 See Clark, *The Business of Beauty*, pp. 78–80, and Talairach-Vielmas, *Moulding the Female Body*, pp. 135–136. Talairach-Vielmas argues that the contemporary perception was that ladies 'could at all times fall prey to [. . .] enticing [cosmetic] products' and that '[e]tiquette books dealing with female beauty warned against the danger of corrupting the body with such artificial and poisonous products' (p. 135).

13 Advertisement for Pears's Rouge & Pears's Pearl Powder, *The Ladies' Monthly Magazine, The World of Fashion. A Journal of the Courts of London and Paris*, 1 February 1856.

14 'Rouge', *The Englishwoman's Domestic Magazine*, 1 December 1868, p. 317. For further discussion of Eugène Rimmel's cosmetic enterprises, see Clark, *The Business of Beauty*, Chapter 4: 'Professionalising Perfumery: Eugène Rimmel', pp. 109–134.

15 C. Reade, 'A Simpleton. A Story of the Day', *London Society*, December 1872, p. 496.

16 W. Collins, *The Law and the Lady*, ed. with an Introduction and Notes by David Skilton (London: Penguin, 1998 [1875]), p. 124 (p. 170). Collins' novel is discussed in a different context in K. Tennant, 'Female Space, Feminine Grace: Ladies and the Mid-Victorian Railway', in K. Hill (ed.), *Britain and the Narration of Travel in the Nineteenth Century: Texts, Images, Objects* (Farnham: Ashgate, 2016), pp. 53–72 (pp. 68–69).

17 A. Briefel, 'Cosmetic Tragedies: Failed Masquerade in Wilkie Collins's "The Law and the Lady"', *Victorian Literature and Culture*, 37(2), (2009), pp. 463–481 (p. 463).

18 Medicus, 'The Toilet-Table, and What Should Lie Thereon', *The Girl's Own Paper*, 9 April 1881, pp. 443–444.

19 Advertorial for Rice-powder, *Myra's Journal*, 1 June 1890, p. 22. Here, we use the term 'advertorial' rather than 'advertisement', as it appears on the page featuring 'Myra's Answers On Current Topics of Interest' (including readers' correspondence and the magazine's answers). However, in this instance, our selection is located to the bottom left of the page, underneath the main portion of the text, and therefore its status is somewhat ambiguous. For further consideration of the advertorial form within nineteenth-century women's magazines, see M. Beetham and K. Boardman, *Victorian Women's Magazines: An Anthology* (Manchester and New York: Manchester University Press, 2001), p. 157.

20 L. A. Loeb, *Consuming Angels: Advertising and Victorian Women* (New York and Oxford: Oxford University Press, 1994), p. 28. However, in her study of the Victorian corset, Leigh Summers explores the alternative, more 'morbid aesthetic' of the period, which sometimes included a 'pale face'. See L. Summers, *Bound to Please: A History of the Victorian Corset* (Oxford and New York: Berg, 2001), pp. 122–123. This is discussed in detail in Summers, Chapter 5: 'Breathless with Anticipation: Romance, Morbidity and the Corset', pp. 121–142 (pp. 121–124).

21 Dr Anna Kingsford wrote a plethora of works on religion, vivisection and women's rights and maintained a question and answer column in *The Lady's Pictorial* between 1884 and 1886. Subsequently, she published *Health, Beauty and the Toilet. Letters to Ladies from a Lady Doctor* (1886). For a detailed account of Kingsford's life, see A. Pert, *Red Cactus: The Life of Anna Kingsford* (Books & Writers Network, Watsons Bay NSW, Australia, 2007).

22

[ANON], 'MATERIALS FOR THE TOILETTE. VIII.'

The Saturday Magazine, 25 January 1840, pp. 27–28

ON COSMETICS.

THE word Cosmetic is derived from the Greek, and signifies in the original "to adorn:" hence it is applied to the various preparations for refreshing and beautifying the skin.

The advantages and the comfort of retaining that clear and healthy state of the skin, with which we are usually endowed in early years, are sufficiently evident to us all; and it is not, therefore, surprising to find that at the present day, as well as in the time of the ancients, a considerable degree of attention has been given to the best means of attaining so desirable an object. Doubtless it will ever be found that simplicity of diet, and regular exercise, with a proper attention to cleanliness, will do more towards preserving the fresh and healthy appearance of youth, than all the creams, washes, and lotions in the world, for it is not possible by mere external applications to remedy those evils which arise from an unhealthy system, nor will the aid of cosmetics be resorted to with any chance of success, while intemperance, indolence, late hours, or other causes are gradually undermining the constitution, and marking their progress also on the outward frame. Yet, as various perfumed unguents and other articles have been in use for many ages, and are considered by some to possess the most beneficial effects, it becomes necessary to allow them a place in our notice of Materials for the Toilette, and to explain, as far as may be, what they are, how used, and the nature of the benefits ascribed to them [. . . .] Daily ablutions in salt and water, or vinegar and water, succeeded by the friction of a coarse towel, and connected with a due attention to exercise, diet, &c., are nearly certain to keep the skin healthy and free from eruptions, and will be found to produce a far happier effect than the most costly and carefully prepared cosmetics. Since all persons may not, however, be disposed to acquiesce in our opinion, we proceed to name a few of the most approved unguents and washes to be used after a warm bath, or after the daily ablutions just spoken of. The cold cream so much in use amongst us for the cure of chapped hands, &c., is, perhaps, as efficacious for anointing the skin as any substance we can mention. After the

DOI: 10.4324/9781315399980-30

use of it, the skin should be rubbed with a towel till all appearance of greasiness is removed. This cream may be made in the following manner: take three ounces of oil of sweet almonds, and of spermaceti and white wax, each a drachm and a half, melt them together, and beat in while warm eight parts of rose water, and two of orange-flower water, till the oil will absorb no more.

In former times, the meal or flour of beans was a celebrated cosmetic with the ladies, and was thought to possess the power of removing wrinkles. Horseradish scraped and infused in cold milk is likewise considered a safe and excellent wash for the skin.

We might mention other washes and unguents, but it is unnecessary. Where cutaneous diseases prevail, recourse should be had to medical aid, and cosmetics should only be used under proper advice; where the skin is healthy, the less such means of improving its appearance are employed, the better. Before we dismiss the subject, it is requisite to mention an article which still obtains a place in some toilettes, and which may be considered more decidedly injurious to those who make use of it than any other cosmetic; we mean, *rouge*.

Rouge is of various kinds. The best is called *carmine,* and is a powder obtained by the union of a solution of alum, with the colouring matter of a Mexican insect, called the *cochineal* insect. Spanish and oriental wool are also used. Wool is impregnated with a beautiful red colour, and made into small cakes, in which form we receive them. Rouge dishes are also imported covered with a thin layer of colour, but the common rouge is formed by pounding certain substances which yield the desired hue. These are boiled in brandy or vinegar until three-fourths of the liquid have evaporated, and a red paint remains.

By these means an attempt is made to imitate the natural hue of health, and a bright and beautiful colour is obtained, at the expense of lasting injury to the skin. But it is not sufficient that the cheeks are made to suffer; the other parts of the face, as well as the neck and arms, must share the same fate, and means have been found to give them the delicacy of appearance necessary to set off the rouge on the face to the best advantage. A costly article obtained by dissolving real seed pearls in an acid, and then precipitating the powder by an alkali, is used by those who can afford to purchase it, while powders of an inferior description, made from mother-of-pearl, and even from oyster-shell, suffice for the less wealthy aspirants to artificial beauty. There is another powder used to whiten the skin, which very nearly resembles the real pearl powder, but which has the disadvantage of turning black on exposure to the fumes of sulphur.

But we will not dwell longer on the subject of these artifices, degrading as they are to the character of our countrywomen. We would willingly hope that a sense of the important situation they hold in a Christian country, and the influence which their example is allowed to exert on all around them, may lead them to seek for other adornings than those of mere costume or complexion, adornings which will render them lovely and beloved when time has stolen away the brightness of their youthful appearance, and has impressed their features with the peculiar mark of his own hand.

23

ADVERTISEMENT FOR PEARS'S ROUGE & PEARS'S PEARL POWDER

The Ladies' Monthly Magazine, The World of Fashion. A Journal of the Courts of London and Paris, 1 February 1856

Have now been in use by the fashionable world for more than thirty years, and are most essential to all who value personal beauty, as by their use the most beautiful complexion may be obtained, These powders are composed of the most innocent ingredients, and will be found the best preparations ever offered to those whose complexion is impaired by ill health, or the effects of either to much confinement or exposure to the sun, &c.

In Packets 1s. each; or by Post for fourteen postage stamps, directed to

A. F. PEARS,

91, GREAT RUSSELL STREET, BLOOMSBURY

DOI: 10.4324/9781315399980-31

24

'ROUGE.'

The Englishwoman's Domestic Magazine, 1 December 1868, p. 317

ROUGE. – Mons. RIMMEL, of No. 96, Strand, has favoured us with the following: – "A lady, whose letter I inclose, wishes to be informed through your columns if my Liquid Rouge contains any mercury, or any other metallic substance injurious to the skin? Will you kindly allow me to state, for her information and that of others whom it may interest, that the chief ingredients of my Rouge are cochineal and safflower, and of my white compounds an extract of the pearl-oyster, having always carefully avoided the use of mercury and other metallic substances, the absorption of which through the pores of the skin is liable to cause great injury to the system."

DOI: 10.4324/9781315399980-32

25

CHARLES READE, 'A SIMPLETON. A STORY OF THE DAY.'

London Society, December 1872, pp. 495–497

One afternoon Miss Lucas called for Mrs. Staines to drive in the Park, but did not come upstairs; it was an engagement, and she knew Mrs. Staines would be ready, or nearly. Mrs. Staines, not to keep her waiting, came down rather hastily, and, in the very passage, whipped out of her pocket a little glass, and a little powder puff, and puffed her face all over in a trice. She was then going out; but her husband called her into the study. 'Rosa, my dear,' said he, 'you were going out with a dirty face.'

'Oh!' cried she, 'give me a glass.'

'There is no need of that. All you want is a basin and some nice rain-water. I keep a little reservoir of it.'

He then handed her the same with great politeness. She looked in his eye, and saw he was not to be trifled with. She complied like a lamb, and the heavenly colour and velvet gloss that resulted were admirable.

He kissed her, and said, 'Ah! now you are my Rosa again. Oblige me by handing over that powder-puff to me.' She looked vexed, but complied. 'When you come back, I will tell you why.'

'You are a pest,' said Mrs. Staines, and so joined her friend, rosy with rain-water and a rub.

'Dear me, how handsome you look to-day,' was Miss Lucas's first remark.

Rosa never dreamed that rainwater and rub could be the cause of her looking so well.

'It is my tiresome husband,' said she. 'He objects to powder, and he has taken away my puff.'

'And you stood that?'

'Obliged to.'

'Why, you poor-spirited little creature, I should like to see a husband presume to interfere with me in those things. Here, take mine.'

Rosa hesitated a little. 'Well – no – I think not.'

Miss Lucas laughed at her, and quizzed her so on her allowing a man to interfere in such sacred things as dress and cosmetics, that she came back irritated with her husband, and gave him a short answer or two. Then he asked what was the matter.

DOI: 10.4324/9781315399980-33

'You treat me like a child – taking away my very puff.'

'I treat you like a beautiful flower, that no bad gardener shall wither whilst I am here.'

'What nonsense! How could that wither me? It is only violet-powder – what they put on babies.'

'And who are the Herods that put it on babies?'

'Their own mothers, that love them ten times more than the fathers do.'

'And kill a hundred of them for one a man ever kills. Mothers! – the most wholesale homicides in the nation. We will examine your violet powder: bring it down here.'

While she was gone he sent for a breakfast-cupful of flour, and when she came back he had his scales out, and begged her to put a teaspoonful of flour into one scale and of violet powder into another. The flour kicked the beam, as Homer expresses himself.

'Put another spoonful of flour.'

The one spoonful of violet powder outweighed the two of flour.

'Now,' said Staines, 'does not that show you the presence of a mineral in your vegetable powder? I suppose they tell you it is made of white violets dried, and triturated in a diamond mill. Let us find out what metal it is. We need not go very deep into chemistry for that.' He then applied a simple test, and detected the presence of lead in large quantities. Then he lectured her: 'Invisible perspiration is a process of nature necessary to health and to life. The skin is made porous for that purpose. You can kill anybody in an hour or two by closing the pores. A certain infallible ass, called Pope Leo XII., killed a little boy in two hours, by gilding him to adorn the pageant of his first procession as Pope. But what is death to the whole body must be injurious to a part. What madness, then, to clog the pores of so large and important a surface as the face, and check the invisible perspiration: how much more to insert lead into your system every day of your life; a cumulative poison, and one so deadly and so subtle, that the Sheffield file-cutters die in their prime, from merely hammering on a leaden anvil. And what do you gain by this suicidal habit? No plum has a sweeter bloom or more delicious texture than the skin of your young face; but this mineral filth hides that delicate texture, and substitutes a dry, uniform appearance, more like a certain kind of leprosy than health. Nature made your face the rival of peaches, roses, lilies; and you say "No; I know better than my Creator and my God; my face shall be like a dusty miller's." Go into any flour-mill, and there you shall see men with faces exactly like your friend Miss Lucas's. But, before a miller goes to his sweetheart, he always washes his face. You ladies would never get a miller down to your level in brains. It is a miller's *dirty* face our monomaniacs of women imitate, not the face a miller goes a-courting with.'

'La! what a fuss about nothing!'

'About nothing! Is your health nothing? Is your beauty nothing? Well, then, it will cost you nothing to promise me never to put powder on your face again.'

'Very well, I promise. Now what will you do for me?'

'Work for you – write for you – suffer for you – be self-denying for you – and even give myself the pain of disappointing you now and then – looking forward to the time when I shall be able to say "Yes" to everything you ask me. Ah! child, you little know what it costs me to say "No" to *you.*'

Rosa put her arms round him, and acquiesced.

26

MEDICUS, 'THE TOILET-TABLE, AND WHAT SHOULD LIE THEREON'

The Girl's Own Paper, 9 April 1881, pp. 443–444

WITH the toilet-table, as a table, it is not my province to speak, nor to tell you how it should be draped or bedecked; but neatness, tidiness, and perfect cleanliness should reign supreme in a young girl's dressing-room, however splendid and beautiful the fittings thereof may be, or however humble and poor.

Now, under the title I have chosen for this paper, I mean to give you many little hints, and not a few harmless recipes; and if you attend to the former, and make use of the latter, I have no hesitation in saying that improvement in your personal appearance will be the result. Beauty is your birthright, you ought to try to look as well as you can, both for your own personal comfort and for the sake of those around you. By taking pains to improve your looks by natural and simple means while young, you will retain your beauty even when, with the ever-recurring years, youth is slipping slowly away. But nothing in after years can atone for, what I may call, the want of attention to the simple rules of personal hygiene in your younger days. Does, then, attention to these rules lie in the proper use of the adjuncts of the toilet-table, and dressing-room? Not quite. These are mere accessories, indispensable I willingly admit, but accessories nevertheless; and even their constant use has no more effect without something else, which I shall presently name, in retaining true beauty, than an occasional coat of paint to a rotten boat has in keeping it seaworthy. The something else is health – perfect health. And even granting that you have the strongest of constitutions, and the highest of animal spirits, if you do not cultivate habits of temperance and moderation in all your actions and thoughts, take my word for it you are but frittering those precious possessions away.

"Oh!" I think I hear some of my young readers exclaim, "this isn't a medical paper, this is a sermon 'Medicus' is going to preach."

If "Medicus" does preach, depend upon it he will preach common sense, but not one inch will he budge towards the toilet-table, until he has had his say. "As soon," remarks a great authority, "as we begin to live we begin to die." This is true; and even in youth our bodies are but the strongholds behind which we live, and the stouter the ramparts the more likely are they to ward off the shafts of

 DOI: 10.4324/9781315399980-34

disease and death. But these very ramparts themselves have a tendency to crumble away, and we must study to strengthen them; we must look upon them as our foes likely at any time to fall and crush us; in other words, we must conquer self, we must study abnegation in everything, for abnegation leads to temperance, indeed, it is the root and soul thereof, temperance leads to health, and health is the foundation of true personal beauty. Be temperate, therefore, in eating, and temperance in this respect will become a habit, although it may cost you much abnegation to acquire it. But look up, never look down, for in this world, though we may sow in tears, we reap rejoicing in the life which is to come.

Be temperate in your hours of pleasure and sleep. Over indulgence in either produces wrinkles and sallowness of complexion. This is easily accounted for in this way, and I will put it as simply as I can. When the heart is overtired from long hours of wakefulness, or lauguid and weak from over indulgence in sleep, it is unable to receive the blood back sufficiently quick, the tender tissues around the eyes get puffy and swollen, the skin is thus stretched, and when the puffiness goes away it is inclined to lie in folds or wrinkles. The skin, of course, is very resilient and elastic and will regain its former appearance again and again for a time, but a constant drop will wear a stone away, and at last its elasticity is lost and wrinkles are the result. Be temperate in talking and self-abnegating in argument, you will thus preserve your good temper.

Having heard me patiently, I will now advance to the toilet-table, the largest and most conspicuous object on which is the mirror. However big this may be, or however small, let it be a true glass. A few shillings spent on a good mirror is money well laid out. A proper looking-glass certainly will not flatter you, but, on the contrary, it will point out to you in a friendly way all your defects, and if there be means of remedying them it will give you light to do so; but a bad glass is your worst friend, because it not only hides your faults, but gives an imperfect and very far from flattering reflection of your face and figure, and this would be no comfort to you if you were going out anywhere to spend the evening. The looking-glass should be kept perfectly clear and bright; it should be well polished once a week at least, but this must be carefully done. Thus: dust the mirror first with a soft brush to prevent scratching, then take a damp sponge, and sprinkling a little eau de Cologne on it, rub the surface gently over; then dust over with good whiting, and while it is still damp polish with a silk handkerchief. The sponge itself should be perfectly clean, and sponges, whether used for the bath or simply for face ablution, should be invariably soft and clean and pure. When bought new, before you use them, shake out the dust, and then steep them for some hours in soft water several times renewed. Soap spoils sponges. If soap must be used with a sponge, rinse the latter in warm water before you put it away. Press or squeeze a sponge – do not wring it – and if it gets slimy, which it never ought to, soak it in water and soda for some hours. The bath sponge should be a very large one, if you mean to benefit by the use of the bath. The bath itself should be kept spotlessly clean; when spots of rust begin to appear in it, it is time it was repainted, else it will not wear. Iron rust is rather good in the water than otherwise; indeed, I have known much good come from a course of iron baths. The iron bath is a simple tonic one, and should be used every morning for a fortnight or three weeks at a time. It is composed of water one bucketful, sulphate of iron a quarter of an ounce, placed in the bath over night. While taking a course of such baths, a tepid bath with soap should be used twice a week – to thoroughly cleanse the skin – the last thing before going to bed. For young pale girls with weak nerves and languid circulations the iron bath is likely to be of great use, especially if steel drops – ten in a little water thrice daily after food – are taken at the same time.

Meanwhile, I am turning my back on the toilet-table, so I must face round again. Here are a couple of hair-brushes. How beautifully white and clean you keep them! This delights my eye. Of course you wash them occasionally, by dipping them in cold water in which soda has been dissolved – not soap – with gentle friction on the palm of the hand, holding them in such a position that the backs do not get wetted, and afterwards standing them in the wind, but not in the sun, to dry.

Do you ever use the metallic brushes? They are so cooling to the temples on a warm summer's day, but must be kept dry, else they are apt to rust. I sometimes think they stimulate the growth of the hair by their pleasant, cool friction. When you wash your hair do not use soap, unless the very mildest transparent kind, the same as you use for hands and face; but yolk of egg is better, well rinsed out with lukewarm water, then with cold soft or rain water, and, when partially dried by means of soft towels, combed and brushed.

Rain water is a great beautifier of the complexion. Collect it, and keep it in jars, after having it run through a filter. This is a hint worth much fine gold, so lay it to heart and you will look well.

Now, I am not your hairdresser, but I know you want me to tell you of something to increase the strength and beauty of the hair. I am good natured, and can't refuse. Here is a good application, a little of which may be rubbed into the roots of the hair, after moderate friction with the brushes every morning: – Tincture of cantharides, a quarter of an ounce; eau de Cologne, one ounce; bay rum, one ounce; rose water, two ounces. You can make your own bay rum simply enough: get two ounces of fresh bay leaves, and steep them for six days in six ounces of best rum. These are valuable receipts, but they must not be used more than once a day, nor longer than a fortnight at a time, and if they produce the slightest irritation or heat of the skin they must be omitted for a time.

Here is a good and very safe pomade for thinness of the hair: Pure lard four ounces, pure white wax half an ounce, melt, then remove from heat, and add half an ounce of balsam of tolu and twenty drops of oil of rosemary. Equal parts of bay rum, eau de Cologne and castor-oil form a good hair cosmetic.

The most innocent of white powders for face or skin are composed either of oxide of zinc, magnesia starch, or levigated starch. Be on your guard against such as are sold under fancy names. Be on your guard, too, against the dangerous compounds that are advertised by taking titles. Here is a recipe for the best bloom for lips or cheeks: – Early rising, morning tubbing, and plenty of out-door exercise. Soap is a necessity of life, but pray get it pure, non-alkaline, and transparent, and not the dangerously dyed masses of unhealthy curd you see so often exposed for sale.

Toilet vinegar should always find a place on the table. A little in the basin of water you lave your face with is delightfully refreshing.

Does your face often flush – I do not mean simple blushing? If it does you cannot be over strong, you need tonics and more fresh air. No applications will do good, but continuous flushing of the face under the least excitement is very apt to spoil the very best complexion.

Cold cream is one of the most harmless of applications to tender lips or skin.

Here is a lotion for freckles. It is a drachm of the muriate of ammonia dissolved in a pint of soft water, and a dessert-spoonful of eau de Cologne added; apply twice a day. The following is a good wash for sunburning: – fifteen grains of borax, an ounce of limejuice, and a dessert-spoonful of eau de Cologne. Buttermilk applied before going to bed, especially if a little sour, is very cooling after a hot day. Milk of roses (the best) is also a good face application; and here is a very simple one. Dissolve a quarter of an ounce of borax in a pint of elder-flower water, and add an ounce of eau de Cologne. By the way many harmless and delightful preparations can be prepared from flowers, as well as many good but simple perfumes, and if my girl-readers care for it, I feel sure the editor will grant me space for a nice summer article on this subject.

I think, in a former paper, I mentioned tooth-powders. Charcoal is unsightly but very effective, and it can be made more so by rubbing up with an ounce of it as much quinine as will lie on a sixpenny piece; a few drops of otto of roses may be added. Or, make a tooth-powder thus (if you can find a pestle and mortar): Equal parts of burnt crust of bread, white sugar, and Peruvian bark, and a drop or two of otto of roses. If you prefer a paste, add a little honey. Use a soft and a hard tooth-brush, and never omit brushing the teeth inside and out after meals as well as in the morning.

27

ADVERTORIAL FOR RICE-POWDER

Myra's Journal, 1 June 1890, p. 22

One of the most agreeable Cosmetics is Rice-powder, but it needs to be chosen with care, for many face powders are unhealthy or dangerous. The best of all is undoubtedly the DUVET DE NINON – the finest and the most adhesive and impalpable powder known; it is eminently hygienic, and gives the skin a dazzling whiteness. The DUVET DE NINON is supplied by the PARFUMERIE NINON, 31, Rue du Quatre Septembre, Paris.

DOI: 10.4324/9781315399980-35

28

'SAFE COMPLEXION LOTIONS.'

Myra's Journal, 1 September 1897, p. 7

We bring to our readers' notice three exquisite preparations of cucumber for the toilet, originated by one of the highest authorities on the subject, the late Dr. Anna Kingsford, who says: – "Ever since I acquainted myself with the merits of that beneficent fruit the cucumber, I have regarded it as the best basis of all lotions, emulsions, and unguents intended to whiten and cool the skin. 'Cool as a cucumber' is, you know, a proverb, and with good reason. Mr. Mason, of Norwich, has obligingly acted on my counsels in this direction, and has prepared two excellent emulsions of cucumber, thick and thin, which I have not yet seen equalled. To these he has added a *crême froide de concombre,* composed of the best possible ingredients. The formula of this preparation has been placed in my hands, and I am in a position to assure you that it contains only materials of a perfectly innocent and healthful nature. In questions so vitally affecting the hygiene of the skin as the composition of cosmetics designed for daily use, it is well to have the guarantee of a medically qualified judge; so I hope you will not deem my recommendation inopportune[.] You have often asked me what I think of this or that preparation for toilet use, and I have sometimes been obliged to answer unfavourably, or at least doubtingly, not knowing the composition of the cosmetic in question. But Mr. Mason's formulas are in my hands, and both ingredients and proportions have been submitted to me before being made up. Consequently as the responsibility of these formulas rests in a large measure with myself, you may feel sure I should not recommend them unless I had complete confidence in their excellence. On account of this responsibility, it is my habit to submit to Mr. Mason for analysis every cosmetic of which a specimen reaches my hands, and which I think worth special attention." We may add that Mr. Mason will send either of these preparations, post free, to any address for 3*s*. 6*d.*

DOI: 10.4324/9781315399980-36

1.4

Hair

DOI: 10.4324/9781315399980-37

1.4 Hair

The sources gathered here offer a vignette of the complex – and often contradictory – narratives produced by women's hair in the Victorian period. Unsurprisingly, clean, well-kept hair was a visible signifier of a woman's 'character' and moral standing. In addition, Victorian fashion emphasised the importance of grooming hair as an outward expression of a lady's awareness of social etiquette, as hair had to be dressed and restyled for different social occasions and times of day. In this way, hair expressed a variety of meanings and performed a great deal of cultural work.[1] As we shall see in the later parts of this collection, hair was also used in jewellery and in handicraft, locks of hair functioning as tokens of affection, but also as talismans reminding the wearer that the dead were once material, tangible beings. In other sources, women's so-called 'naturalness' and 'authenticity' were celebrated in relation to hair, the previous section on Cosmetics offering a segue into debates surrounding both authenticity and artifice. In Galia Ofek's terms, hair needed to be tamed and 'transform[ed] from a chaotic, wild and natural growth into a well-trimmed, man-made and decorative bower'.[2] Interestingly, the use of artificial aides, such as hair dyes and hair extensions, enabled women to achieve this.

Our first source, a *Punch* cartoon of 1857 entitled 'The Honeymoon', represents a young, newly married couple relaxing in a hotel room. The woman blithely makes a request of her husband, who stands, momentarily startled, in the doorway. The caption makes his consternation clear: his wife, Mary, announces: 'Charles, dear; now we are Married, you know, we should have no Secrets. So do, like a Love, hand me the Bottle of Hair Dye; you will find it in my Dressing-Case'. The shock here seems twofold: firstly, at the revelation of the '[secret]', and secondly, at Mary's ease at imparting this information, as she sits, languid and entirely confident in her request, secure in her new position as wife. The message seems clear: in the role of spouse, Mary no longer needs to conceal her cosmetic efforts from her husband.

In a sense, such cultural episodes might even prefigure and reflect contemporary discourses on biology and evolutionary theory.[3] Two years later, in 1859, Charles Darwin proposed in his *Origin of Species* that many species adapt their characteristics to attract mates, and that aesthetics plays a significant role in adaptation. While it is unclear here whether Mary's cosmetic efforts have secured her marriage, nor does the image direct the viewer's response to this information, we may nonetheless speculate upon how such theories might pervade our selections from M. E. Braddon and Thomas Hardy, as well as informing the gendered stereotypes that they present.

Will Abberley's study on mimicry in Victorian science and culture contends that:

> [p]rotective mimicry was one of a web of theories in the second half of the nineteenth century that framed appearance as a factor in environmental adaptation. Camouflage and mimicry (now known collectively as *crypsis*) could also disguise predators to help them catch prey.[4]

This is aptly illustrated in our second source from Braddon's 1862 'sensation' novel, *Lady Audley's Secret*. In this episode, Lady Audley, a beautiful young woman described by Lyn Pykett as 'bigamous, murderous and possibly insane',[5] sits at her dressing table musing that her maid, the young and colourless Phœbe, might, through a mere 'bottle of hair dye', appear as attractive as her mistress.[6] Here, the 'sensational' trope of female deceit and doubleness is played out through the use of the hair dye, perhaps drawing upon evolutionary ideas about both camouflage and mimicry that reinforce the reductive and threatening ideas about femaleness presented within the novel.

Our next two sources, from *The Dundee Courier* of 1865 and *The Penny Illustrated Paper* of 1869, lament the fashionable hairstyle of the chignon, which, alongside hair dyes and the crinoline, was often seen as a source of folly and ridicule – in one case, even being compared with the practise of applying cosmetics to children. The chignon became extremely fashionable in the 1860s and, as Ofek points out, was popularised to fad levels during the middle of the decade.[7] However, it was much maligned for its size, which was often created by the use of padding and hairpieces.[8] And by 1869, as our source 'Chignons Doomed' informs us, simpler hairstyles, emulating the hairstyles of classical sculptures such as Niobe, were now fashionable. This extract, which draws upon the authority of Paris as an arbiter of fashion, suggests a new trend for natural decorations such as leaves and flowers, rather than extensive use of hairpieces. Here again, we can see an emphasis on dressing and ornamenting women's hair to emulate classical figures, alongside references to nature.

The next two sources deal with hair dyes in their material form. Whereas *Punch* and *Lady Audley's Secret* present this as a misleading medium for deception and even subterfuge, the advertisement in *The Englishwoman's Domestic Magazine*, titled 'L'Eau des Fées', draws on references to Parisian fashion, refinement, and even the fairy world, to promote a product for the transformation of grey hair back to its youthful colour.[9] With a clear awareness of contemporary debates surrounding hair dye and mimicry, the author of this advertisement aims the product at readers who might regard their greying as premature, offering to maintain, rather than falsely appropriate, 'their youth and their beauty'.

Whilst 'L'Eau des Fées' makes imaginative associations with folklore, whimsy and fairyland, our next advertisement, for 'Latreille's Hyperion Hair Restorer', includes engravings that dramatise the product's effects within the everyday world. Pictured are a youthful man and woman, depicted first with grey, and then (having used the 'restorer') with dark hair. With a view to both safety and propriety, readers were simultaneously reassured that the product neither destroyed nor discoloured hair, and was also imperceptible in sunlight, thus evading the danger of 'ridicule'.[10] What is of particular interest is that this advertisement features in Montagu Browne's *Practical Taxidermy* manual of 1884. Its placement within this text is perhaps best explained by Rachel Poliquin's statement that '[t]axidermy wants to stop time. To keep life. To cherish what is no longer as if it were immortally whole'.[11] Indeed, perhaps we may infer that the taxidermist might wish the same for themself, wishing to erase the visible effect of time upon their own body.

Our next source revisits the theme of the newly married couple already seen in the *Punch* illustration. But in this piece, an extract from Thomas Hardy's novel *Jude the Obscure*, the narrator does not satirise the character Arabella's wearing of false hair, but turns it into an episode of grave realisation for Jude, whose selection of a mate will have profound reverberations. We are told that

> [a] little chill over-spread him at her first unrobing. A long tail of hair, which Arabella wore twisted up in an enormous knob at the back of her head, was deliberately unfastened, stroked out, and hung upon the looking glass which he had bought her.[12]

Here, Arabella's use of false hair aligns her with evolutionary mimicry, and is framed as a sign of modernity and class awareness. Arabella associates the false hair with the 'better-class[es]' and '[ladies] of position' of the town,[13] and with her former post as barmaid, all of which horrify the protagonist. Jude's gift of a mirror to Arabella is also symbolic here, as the groom's present to his new bride becomes a place to hang the false hair, rather than retaining its primary function of reflecting nature.

Although the chignon fad had by this point waned, Hardy's heroine of the *fin-de-siècle* shows that the fashion for wearing false hair still held fast.[14] Five years later, at the beginning of the twentieth century, an illustrated advertisement for 'Unwin & Albert Ladies' Ornamental Hair Workers and Expert Wig Makers' features a variety of hairpieces and fringes ostensibly aimed at the 'better class[es]', to draw upon Arabella's term. This illustrated advertisement – alongside the extract from Hardy and the articles on the chignon – also speaks of class tensions, as the provenance of false hair was a much-contested issue in the Victorian period. Largely relying on hair imported from Continental Europe, English ladies would also purchase hairpieces made from domestic hair supplied from convents, prisons, and even hospitals and from those without home or abode. The false hair speaks of exploitation, coercion and illness, and further problematises the relationship between subject and object.[15]

Notes

1 For a discussion of the representation of women's hair in art and literature as powerful and even magic, see E. G. Gitter, 'The Power of Women's Hair in the Victorian Imagination', *PMLA*, 99(5), (October 1984), pp. 936–954.

2 See G. Ofek, *Representations of Hair in Victorian Literature and Culture* (Farnham, Surrey, and Burlington, VT: Ashgate, 2009), p. 35.

3 For a thorough and illuminating consideration of the relationship between Darwin and contemporary women's fashion, see E. Richards, *Darwin and the Making of Sexual*

Selection (Chicago and London: The University of Chicago Press, 2017), Chapter 8: 'Flirting with Fashion', pp. 221–257.

4 W. Abberley, *Mimicry and Display in Victorian Literary Culture: Nature, Science and the Nineteenth-Century Imagination* (Cambridge: Cambridge University Press, 2020), pp. 1–2.

5 L. Pykett, *The 'Improper' Feminine: The Women's Sensation Novel and the New Woman Writing* (London and New York: Routledge, 1992), p. 88. Quoted in K. Tennant, '"Buying in Style": sartorial sensibilities and Victorian popular fiction', in J. Hatter and N. Moody (eds.), *Fashion and Material Culture in Victorian Fiction and Periodicals* (Brighton: Edward Everett Root Publishers, 2019), pp. 87–100 (p. 90).

6 M. E. Braddon, *Lady Audley's Secret*, 2 vols. (Leipzig: Bernhard Tauchnitz, 1862), Vol. I, p. 83. See Tennant, 'Buying in Style', p. 91, for further consideration of this episode. This discussion also draws upon J. Hedgecock, *The Femme Fatale in Victorian Literature: the Danger and the Sexual Threat* (Amherst, NY: Cambria Press, 2008), p. 123; E. L. Steere, '"I thought you was an evil spirit": The Hidden Villain of *Lady Audley's Secret*', *Women's Writing*, 15(3), (2008), pp. 300–319 (p. 312); L. Hart, *Fatal Women: Lesbian Sexuality and the Mark of Aggression* (London: Routledge, 1994), p. 45; and D. Denisoff, *Sexual Visuality from Literature to Film, 1850–1950* (Houndsmill, Basingstoke, Hampshire and New York: Palgrave Macmillan, 2004), p. 41.

7 In her study of Victorian hair, Ofek discusses the chignon as a fashionable fad of the 1860s, noting how it was 'celebrated' as a 'hair craze' by *Punch*'s Almanac of 1866. See Ofek, *Representations of Hair*, p. 212. For further discussion of the significance of Victorian hair and the often exploitative trade in hair, see R. Mahawatte, 'Hair and Fashioned Femininity in Two Nineteenth-Century Novels', in G. Biddle-Perry and S. Cheang (eds.), *Hair: Styling, Culture and Fashion* (Oxford: Berg, 2008), pp. 193–203. See also C. Gere and J. Rudoe, *Jewellery in the Age of Queen Victoria: A Mirror to the World* (London: British Museum Press, 2010), p. 115.

8 See Ofek, *Representations of Hair*, p. 212.

9 [Anon], 'L'EAU DES FEES', *The Englishwoman's Domestic Magazine* [January 1873], p. 50.

10 Advertisement for 'Latreille's Hyperion Hair Restorer' in M. Browne, *Practical Taxidermy: A Manual of Instruction to the Amateur in Collecting, Preserving, and Setting Up Natural History Specimens of All Kinds. To Which is Added a Chapter Upon the Pictorial Arrangement of Museums*, 2nd edition (London: L. Uppcot Gill, 1884).

11 R. Poliquin, *The Breathless Zoo: Taxidermy and the Cultures of Longing* (University Park: PA: The Pennsylvania State University Press, 2012), p. 6.

12 T. Hardy, *Jude the Obscure* (New York and London: Harper and Brothers Publishers, 1896), p. 63.

13 Hardy, *Jude the Obscure*, p. 64.

14 See L. Johnston (with M. Kite and H. Persson), *Nineteenth-Century Fashion in Detail* (London: V&A Publications, 2005), for images of a so-called 'ringlet bunch' or 'set of side curls' fashioned from human hair (pp. 218–219; notes by M. Kite), as well as for a brief discussion of the trade.

15 For further discussion of the false hair trade and issues of class and racial tensions that the hair represented, see J. M. Allan, 'Health and Hygiene: "Monster top-knots and balloon chignons", Purity and Contamination in the False Hair Trade', in S. Heaton (ed.), *A Cultural History of Hair in the Age of Empire*, Volume 5 (London: Bloomsbury Academic, 2019), pp. 83–100.

29

IMAGE: [ANON], 'THE HONEYMOON.'

Punch, 22 August 1857, p. 81

Figure 29.1 THE HONEYMOON.

Source: Mary. "Charles, dear; now we are Married, you know, we should have no Secrets. So do, like a Love, hand me the Bottle of Hair Dye; you will find it in my Dressing-Case."

DOI: 10.4324/9781315399980-38

30

M. E. BRADDON, *LADY AUDLEY'S SECRET.* (Leipzig: Bernhard Tauchniz, 1862), Vol. I, pp. 82–83

Lady Audley was so exhausted when she reached home, that she excused herself from the dinner-table, and retired at once to her dressing-room, attended by her maid, Phœbe Marks.

She was a little capricious in her conduct to this maid; sometimes very confidential, sometimes rather reserved; but she was a liberal mistress, and the girl had every reason to be satisfied with her situation.

This evening, in spite of her fatigue, she was in extremely high spirits, and gave an animated account of the races, and the company present at them.

"I am tired to death, though, Phœbe," she said by and by. "I'm afraid I must look a perfect fright, after a day in the hot sun."

There were lighted candles on each side of the glass before which Lady Audley was standing unfastening her dress. She looked full at her maid as she spoke, her blue eyes clear and bright, and the rosy, childish lips puckered into an arch smile.

"You are a little pale, my lady," answered the girl, "but you look as pretty as ever."

"That's right, Phœbe," she said, flinging herself into a chair and throwing back her curls at the maid, who stood, brush in hand, ready to arrange the luxuriant hair for the night. "Do you know, Phœbe, I have heard some people say you and I are alike?"

"I have heard them say so too, my lady," said the girl quietly, "but they must be very stupid to say it, for your ladyship is a beauty, and I'm a poor plain creature."

"Not at all, Phœbe," said the little lady superbly; "you *are* like me, and your features are very nice; it is only colour that you want. My hair is pale yellow shot with gold, and yours is drab; my eyebrows and eyelashes are dark brown, and yours are almost – I scarcely like to say it, but they're almost white, my dear Phœbe; your complexion is sallow, and mine is pink and rosy. Why, with a bottle of hair dye, such as we see advertised in the papers, and a pot of rouge, you'd be as good-looking as I any day, Phœbe."

 DOI: 10.4324/9781315399980-39

31

[ANON], 'INSANE FEMALE FASHIONS. BUNCHES OF FALSE HAIR BEHIND.'

The Dundee Courier and Argus, 13 November 1865 (attributed to the *Athenæum*)

Is it possible that any woman can be silly enough to paint her children's faces with the pigments that were bought to make her own face "beautiful for ever?" Our eyes seems to report the disgusting fact. What are we coming to? Except in the most debased days of Rome, and those equally vile years when the Grand Monarque ruled France, we do not know that this practice has obtained upon the earth. Whatever a woman may be foolish enough to do with her own countenance in this fashion, she is personally responsible for, and may be willing to bear the ridicule which her folly brings with it. A painted child is nothing less than loathsome. Not many years since it was considered so great a misfortune to have red, or even auburn hair, that all sorts of expedients were adopted to change the unfashionable locks – artists were laughed at for depicting tawny tresses; now many coiffeurs thrive on making dark hair auburn, and even, it is whispered, as the strangest freak of all, in turning that which was auburn to a brighter hue. It is true that the demand for rubious *chignons* far exceeds the supply of Nature, and that one sees very few of those hideous excrescences which go so low in the scale as brown. Was it a French or an English "Anonyma" who set the stupid fashion of wearing ugly bunches of false hair at the back of the head? – a fashion, be it said, which is far more remote from taste than even that of wearing crinoline – now happily so vulgar, and only less irrational than the same, inasmuch as it is tolerably free from danger; nobody need burn herself and others by means of a *chignon*. – *Athenæum*.

DOI: 10.4324/9781315399980-40

32

[ANON], 'CHIGNONS DOOMED.'

The Penny Illustrated Paper, 6 February 1869, p. 91

The *Sport,* a Paris journal, announces that the great ladies of the French capital have determined to abolish chignons. "The character of the headdress," it says, "is to undergo an important reform; the command has gone forth that false hair and wigs must be repudiated." And not only so, but ladies are always to appear as if they dressed their own hair; for, "when the work of a professional is manifest on their heads, prestige ceases. In the day time the hair is to be simply plaited, and confined in a net – in other words, instead of assuming a pyramidal form, it is to have a tendency to fall like that of Niobe. In the evening it will only be necessary to put on the head a crown or a wreath of roses, of ivy, or of some creeping plant." The *Sport* adds: – "All is over with false hair, decked with gilded or metal articles. Henceforth false hair, at best, can only be tolerated as a detail, as a modest auxiliary – it can no longer be the principal or the only ornament of the head."

DOI: 10.4324/9781315399980-41

33

[ANON], 'L'EAU DES FEES.'

The Englishwoman's Domestic Magazine, [January 1873], p. 50

L'EAU DES FEES. – In spite of the sentiment and poetry of the "first white hair" one naturally avoids its appearance, for the second grey hair is by no means as poetical as the first, and means, to our ideas, old age, premature it may be, but still a decline of the vigour and charms of youth. Let us therefore avoid this mark of age by using the celebrated EAU DES FEES of SARAH FELIX (43, Rue Richer, Paris). This magic water transforms the hair gradually to its natural colour, and employed daily prevents the new growth from becoming discoloured. Its efforts are not only innocent of harm but are actually beneficial to the skin of the head, strengthening the roots and preventing greyness. We recommend L'EAU DES FEES to our readers as a method of preserving intact their youth and their beauty.

DOI: 10.4324/9781315399980-42

34

IMAGE: ADVERTISEMENT FOR LATREILLE'S HYPERION HAIR RESTORER IN MONTAGU BROWNE

Practical Taxidermy: A Manual of Instruction to the Amateur in Collecting, Preserving, and Setting Up Natural History Specimens of All Kinds. To Which is Added a Chapter Upon the Pictorial Arrangement of Museums., 2nd edition. (London: L. Uppcot Gill, 1884)

DOI: 10.4324/9781315399980-43

35

THOMAS HARDY, *JUDE THE OBSCURE*

(New York and London: Harper and Brothers Publishers, 1896), pp. 63–64

So to the cottage he took her on the evening of the marriage, giving up his old room at his aunt's – where so much of the hard labour at Greek and Latin had been carried on.

A little chill overspread him at her first unrobing. A long tail of hair, which Arabella wore twisted up in an enormous knob at the back of her head, was deliberately unfastened, stroked out, and hung upon the looking glass which he had bought her.

'What – it wasn't your own?' he said, with a sudden distaste for her.

'O no – it never is nowadays with the better class.'

'Nonsense! Perhaps not in towns. But in the country it is supposed to be different. Besides, you've enough of your own, surely? Why, it's a lot!'

'Yes, enough as country notions go. But in towns the men expect more, and when I was barmaid at Aldbrickham —— '

'Barmaid at Aldbrickham?'

'Well, not exactly barmaid – I used to draw the drink at a public-house there – just for a little time; that was all. Some people put me up to getting this, and I bought it just for a fancy. The more you have the better in Aldbrickham, which is a finer town than all your Christminsters. Every lady of position wears false hair – the barber's assistant told me so.'

Jude thought with a feeling of sickness that though this might be true to some extent, for all that he knew, many unsophisticated girls would and did go to towns and remain there for years without losing their simplicity of life and embellishments. Others, alas, had an instinct towards artificiality in their very blood, and became adepts in counterfeiting at the first glimpse of it. However, perhaps there was no great sin in a woman adding to her hair, and he resolved to think no more of it.

DOI: 10.4324/9781315399980-44

36

IMAGE: ADVERTISEMENT FOR UNWIN & ALBERT, LADIES' ORNAMENTAL HAIR WORKERS AND EXPERT WIG MAKERS.

Hearth and Home, 29 November 1900, p. 130

DOI: 10.4324/9781315399980-45

PART 2

Dressing Up

2.1

Wedding dress and accoutrements

DOI: 10.4324/9781315399980-47

Wedding dress and accoutrements

The sources gathered here focus on the material culture of weddings, from the bridal dress to the trousseau. Our first source is an early Victorian poem titled 'My Wedding Ring' from *Livesey's Moral Reformer,* a monthly periodical published by Joseph Livesey aimed at refining and promoting Christian values to the general reading public.[1] It portrays the wedding ring as a physical representation of the 'joy' inherent in the contract of marriage and also, puzzlingly, as a 'Gordian-knot', connoting a mysterious problem to be solved.[2]

Our next source, a fashion plate published by Elizabeth Henderson and from *The Ladies' Cabinet of Fashion, Music and Romance* of 1847, features a bridal ensemble alongside a public promenade dress. The dresses are characterised by their long, full skirts, stiffened underneath by the rigid petticoat that prefigured the industrial cage crinoline introduced in 1856.[3] But while they are similar in design and silhouette, the right-hand bridal outfit is identifiable by its long veil and additional trimmings and although there is a lack of coherent narrative within the image, this was not unusual within the fashion-plate genre.[4]

As discussed in our Introduction to this volume, the popularity of fashion plates peaked during the mid-Victorian period,[5] and their quality ranged significantly, from the elaborately hand tinted to the less refined.[6] Highly desirable and beautifully rendered French fashion plates often appeared in British publications,[7] and frequently featured two adult women, as in our source, or two adult women and a child, usually female.[8] As Sharon Marcus has aptly noted, such fashion plates were aimed at, and consumed by, women, and the almost-identical faces of the figures 'licensed female viewers to [...] focus their attention and desire on hairstyles and accessories, and on clothes that accentuated breasts, waists, hips, and buttocks'.[9] In this way, '[f]emale consumers seeking information from fashion plates were forced to be fetishists who perceived women as erotic objects'.[10] This perspective offers an interesting layer of interpretation when we look at the woman in the bridal dress as symbolic, yet devoid of the heteronormative marriage union.

Our third selection, from *The Lady's Newspaper* of 1862, entitled 'Letter From Aunt Lydia About Orange-Blossoms', is presented in the epistolary genre of the matronly and knowing aunt providing advice to the bride-to-be. The article navigates the reader through wedding-based etiquette and social conventions, connecting the polite rituals of gift giving and post-nuptial social 'calls' with the material artefacts that punctuate these rites of passage. Interestingly, a question raised is the fate of the wedding dress following the 'one day show' of marriage, with the writer suggesting that it might be usefully adapted by 'chang[ing] its colour through the magic aid of the chemistry of dyeing',[11] thus being transformed for use within the realm of everyday life.[12]

Lucy Johnston notes that '[t]he bride's dress was a focal point of the wedding just as it often is today'.[13] The white wedding dress was popularised after Queen Victoria's marriage to Prince Albert of Saxe-Coburg and Gotha in 1840, and, as Johnston observes, the custom was followed by 'brides of social standing' who 'tended to wear white, ivory or cream', with white holding connotations of 'purity, cleanliness and social refinement'.[14] Yet, the white wedding dress held less social importance to the Victorians than the modern reader might anticipate, and during the nineteenth century it was by no means the only socially acceptable option. Despite the power of its connotations, contemporary writers took pains to point out the unnecessary expense of a white gown, with one article in *Chambers's Journal* of 1878 imploring '[o]f what use is the costly white silk bridal dress, which in all human probability will never in its original state be worn again?' Rather, it will eventually 'be picked to pieces and dyed some serviceable colour'.[15] And, as some of our sources in this section attest, more practical and wearable colours, even black, were also used for wedding dresses.[16]

The expenses of the wedding dress and its accoutrements form the theme of the short story 'My Wedding Bonnet', published in *Le Follet* in 1863. In this tale, a young bride-to-be grapples with social and financial challenges that, somewhat paradoxically, draw uncomfortable attention to her skills in both needlework and household management. In this tale, the central character's moral strength and humility are tested when she loses confidence in her plans to fashion her own bonnet, following a visit by some haughty neighbours. The episode gains wider import, being framed as a challenge to the modest, enterprising spirit of her forthcoming marriage. In doing so, it also hints at anxiety about the middle-class woman undertaking certain kinds of domestic labour.[17]

Amongst the imagined bridal dresses and accoutrements of literature, fashion plates, etiquette manuals and paintings gathered in this section, we include a photograph taken by Julia Margaret Cameron of Annie Chinery in bridal dress.[18] Annie, the daughter of an Isle of Wight doctor, married Cameron's second son, Ewen Wrottesley Hay, in November 1869. On the morning of Annie's wedding, Cameron captured photographs of her future daughter-in-law dressed in bridal finery, as depicted in this photograph, entitled 'Dora as the Bride'.[19] In this image, Annie's facial expression is sombre and discreet, the lines of both her dress and her body obscured by the gauzy, fairy-like veil held by a 'crown' of flowers. But unlike the bride in the fashion plate, whose left hand clasps an item that we may infer to be a prayer book, here Annie's hands are demurely closed into each other. Yet this image simultaneously portrays fashionable femininity, Jill Marie MacLachlan even suggesting that it 'reads like an advertisement in a contemporary bridal periodical, emphasizing the appealing, stylish side of marriage distilled in the image of the fashionably clad Victorian bride'.[20]

Our next source might appear to be a rather incongruous addition to this selection, as it depicts a young widow holding her wedding dress in a watercolour and gouache drawing by Edward Killingworth Johnson. It is included here because the widow's figure, with its almost columnar stance, starkly contrasts with the ornate bridal gown, the weight of which is vividly rendered, perhaps even functioning as a heavy symbol of the unrealised promises of happy matrimony. Indeed, Sophie Gilmartin writes that the painting might initially create an impression 'of pathos and sentimentality' and of 'wasted love and sexuality', an impression reinforced by the visible contrast between the garments.[21] But Gilmartin also points to another interpretation, namely, that the central figure might be considering the future potential for another marriage and 'her chances of wearing [the wedding dress] again'.[22] Thus, the wedding dress' profuse materiality in the drawing creates a *double-entendre* of the expectations and anticipations of the young widow, whilst also drawing attention to itself as a beautifully crafted and expensive costume.

Thoughts of her own impending marriage lilt the speaker in 'May's Wedding Dress', published in the illustrated *Tinsleys' Magazine* of December 1885. This poem describes the making of her own bridal garment, mapping her modest and 'pure' expectations of marriage throughout this process.[23] Here the wedding dress becomes a metonym for the couple, whereby the 'thick, strong silk' represents the groom and the 'clinging lace' the bride, once more observing the cultural dynamic at play between masculine strength and feminine delicacy. However, Queen Victoria's wedding dress, worn some forty-five years earlier, also incorporated lace, a fashion that persisted throughout her reign. Yet, the Queen's specific choice of Honiton lace, as critics have pointed out, extended beyond aesthetics into active support of British lacemakers. In fact, in its recalling of this popular style and its connection to Victoria's deliberate choice of material, we may even infer that the poem's lace speaks as much of supporting national industry and trade as it does of romantic sentiment.[24]

Our next source, 'Modern Weddings', deals with the wedding as a social event, giving attention to such details as '[f]loral decorations' alongside 'bridal dress', jewellery and even the 'travelling' outfit in which the bride departs.[25] This writer takes a rather panoramic view, seeing the material elements as part of the overall 'pretty spectacle of a modern wedding'.[26] In contrast, 'The Wedding Costume', from the 1892 issue of *The Ladies' Treasury*, seems more concerned with understatement. It features a gown that includes all of the traditional elements of the wedding dress, but here the sleeves are somewhat downscaled, being 'less in size than usual', while orange blossoms are 'sparingly used' and the embroidery is comparatively simplified, being rendered in 'silver only' and with 'no pearls'.[27]

Our final sources, a pair of articles from *The Girl's Own Paper* of 1899, deal with the practical preparation of the wedding trousseau as both a social ritual and an economic exercise tolled upon the bride's parents. Taking pains to establish the relevance of the practice within its contemporary context, the author deals with cost, style, practicality and necessity to suggest a range of items applicable to the modern reader, whose needs might range from 'the most moderate' of budgets to more 'expensive' aspirations.[28] Indeed, the layers of clothing itemised in these articles, alongside advice on fabrics, styles, daywear, evening wear, and travelling clothes, all contribute to a sense of 'playing dress-up', although the references to economy and sound advice hint strongly at efficacy in household management.

Notes

1 For further information on Joseph Livesey, see A. Turner-Bishop, 'Livesey, Joseph (1794–1884)', in J. S. Blocker, Jr., D. M. Fahey, and I. R. Tyrrell (eds.), *Alcohol and Temperance in Modern History: an International Encyclopedia* (Vol I A-L) (Santa Barbara, California; Denver, Colorado; and Oxford, England, ABC: Clio: 2003), p. 383.

2 Celata, 'My Wedding Ring', *Livesey's Moral Reformer*, August 1838, p. 152.

3 As James Laver notes, prior to 1856, the bulk of women's skirts was created 'by lining', as well as by the optional inclusion of 'an additional woollen inter-lining added to the upper part of the skirt at the back', adding that '[m]any petticoats were worn' to create 'the tea-cosy effect', which was enhanced by 'the use of a small bustle made of horsehair'. J. Laver, *Costume and Fashion: A Concise History* (4th edition with a concluding chapter by A. de la Haye and A. Tucker) (London: Thames & Hudson World of Art, 2002), p. 174. In 1856, the so-called industrial cage crinoline was brought onto the market, which supported the skirts on a wire frame, as we detail in the Headnotes accompanying our section 'Shaping the silhouette: the corset and the crinolette'. For a detailed analysis of its cultural significance, see C. Breward, *The Culture of Fashion: A New History of Fashionable Dress* (Manchester and New York: Manchester University Press, 1995), pp. 157–161.

4 Valerie Steele describes the fashion plate as an art form 'at one and the same time so obvious and yet so mysterious', in that its composition defies verisimilitude. Steele writes that the figures 'are not intended to represent real people', but '[r]ather, they are mannequins whose function is limited to wearing clothes'. V. Steele, *Paris Fashion: A Cultural History* [2nd edition; revised and updated] (Oxford and New York: Berg, 1998), p. 111. Sharon Marcus also notes that fashion plates most often depicted women wearing 'different dresses' or 'costume[s]' within the same scene. See S. Marcus, 'Reflections on Victorian Fashion Plates', *Differences: a Journal of Feminist Studies*, 14(3), (2003), pp. 4–33 (p. 10).

5 Marcus, for example, describes the period between the 1840s and the 1880s as often deemed 'the golden age of fashion plates' ('Reflections on Victorian Fashion Plates', p. 10). Margaret Beetham also notes that, following the introduction of its 'New Series' in 1860, one of *The Englishwoman's Domestic Magazine*'s major selling points was its inclusion of better quality fashion plates. After this change, each issue of the magazine included two coloured plates, as well as expanded fashion content. See M. Beetham, *A Magazine of Her Own? Domesticity and Desire in the Woman's Magazine, 1800–1914* (London and New York: Routledge, 1996), pp. 72–73. There has, however, been some critical dissent in terms of the heyday of the fashion plate; in his study of the genre, Vyvyan Holland deems the golden age to be the period 1843–1870, declaring himself to be 'in slight disagreement with Doris Langley Moore and James Laver' on the grounds that Moore and Laver both focus upon 'the designs of the costumes', while Holland is 'more interested in the execution of the plates', which he deems to be at 'their highest level' during these years. See V. Holland, *Hand Coloured Fashion Plates 1770–1899* (London: B. T. Batsford, 1988), p. 93. For a seminal and comprehensive text on the fashion plate, see D. L. Moore, *Fashion Through Fashion Plates 1771–1970* (London: Ward Lock, 1971), and, published more recently, A. Calahan, *Fashion Plates: 150 Years of Style* (New Haven, CT: Yale University Press, 2015).

6 See Steele, *Paris Fashion*, pp.111–113, for discussion of the development of the fashion plate as an art-form, and of how, during the later part of the nineteenth century, 'the quality of fashion plates was progressively deteriorating as a result of ever changing methods of reproduction' (p. 113).

7 See Steele, *Paris Fashion*, Chapter 6: 'Art and Fashion', pp. 97–132, for a comprehensive discussion of the fashion plate and of the prominent French fashion-plate artists of the period, including the sisters of the Colin family and Jules David. See also S. Marcus, 'Reflections on Victorian Fashion Plates' (p. 11). As Marcus notes, the Colin sisters were 'better known by their married names: Héloïse Leloir (1820–74), Laure Noël (1827–92), Anaïs Toudouze (1822–99), and her daughter Isabelle Toudouze' (p. 11). For further consideration of the Colin sisters' significance and artistic output, see S. Hiner, 'Feminized Commodities, Female Communities: The Colin Sisters and the Stealthy Work of the Fashion Plate', *French Historical Studies*, 43(2), (2020), pp. 223–252.

8 Steele notes that '[a] typical plate might show two women and a girl' and that, unlike plates produced earlier in the century, in Victorian images, '[s]exual segregation was the rule' (p. 115). See also Marcus, 'Reflections on Victorian Fashion Plates', p. 10.

9 Marcus, 'Reflections on Victorian Fashion Plates', p. 15.

10 Marcus, 'Reflections on Victorian Fashion Plates', p. 15.

11 Aunt Lydia, 'Letter From Aunt Lydia About Orange-Blossoms', *The Lady's Newspaper*, 10 May 1862, pp. 389–390 (p. 389).

12 For a wider consideration of the significance of dye and colour in Victorian women's dress, see C. Nicklas, 'Splendid Hues: Colour, Dyes, Everyday Science and Women's Fashion, 1840–1875', Doctoral thesis, University of Brighton (2009). Available at: https://cris.brighton.ac.uk/ws/portalfiles/portal/318269/C+Nicklas+Thesis+Final.pdf [accessed 13 July 2021]. As Lucy Johnston observes, the notion of adapting the wedding gown following the event was 'acceptable and even desirable'. See L. Johnston (with M. Kite and H. Persson), *Nineteenth-Century Fashion in Detail* (London: V&A Publications, 2005), p. 86.

13 Johnston, *Nineteenth-Century Fashion*, p. 86.

14 Johnston, *Nineteenth-Century Fashion*, p. 86. Here, Chyrs Ingraham concurs, writing that the white wedding dress was much admired, eventually gaining associations with 'purity, virginity, innocence, and promise'. See C. Ingraham, *White Weddings: Romancing Heterosexuality in Popular Culture* (New York and London: Routledge, 2008), p. 27. See also R. N. Mitchell, *Fashioning the Victorians: a Critical Sourcebook* (London: Bloomsbury Visual Arts, 2018), p. 147, and S. Lee, '1840 – Queen Victoria's Wedding Dress'. *Fashion History Timeline*. 28 January 2020. Available at: https://fashionhistory.fitnyc.edu/1840-queen-victorias-wedding-dress/ [accessed 23 September 2021].

15 [Anon], 'Wedding Extravagances', *Chambers's Journal,* 11 May 1878, p. 303. Also cited in J. Phegley, *Courtship and Marriage in Victorian England* (Santa Barbara, CA, Denver, CO, and Oxford, England: Praeger [an imprint of ABC-CLIO, LLC], 2012), pp. 124, 127. See also Lee, '1840 – Queen Victoria's Wedding Dress'.

16 See J. Flanders, *The Victorian House: Domestic Life from Childbirth to Deathbed* (London: HarperCollins, 2003), p. 196. On a similar note, Johnston describes how women who were 'less well off or more practically minded opted for pale blue, dove grey or fawn' (p. 86).

17 The issue of socially acceptable forms of labour is also addressed in our section on Handicraft.

18 See The J. Paul Getty Museum, *In Focus: Julia Margaret Cameron: Photographs from the J. Paul Getty Museum* (Los Angeles: The J. Paul Getty Museum, 1996), p. 76.

19 While this image is entitled 'Dora as the Bride' (with the additional title 'My Ewen's Bride of the 18th of November 1869'), the same photograph is also entitled 'The Bride'

in S. Wolf (with contributions by S. Lipscomb, D. N. Mancoff, and P. Rose), *Julia Margaret Cameron's Women* (Chicago: The Art Institute of Chicago; and New Haven and London: Yale University Press, 1998), p. 70. This text was published in conjunction with the exhibition *Julia Margaret Cameron's Women*, organized by The Art Institute of Chicago. The exhibition was held at The Art Institute of Chicago (19 September 1998–10 January 1999), at The Museum of Modern Art, New York (27 January–4 May 1999), and at San Francisco Museum of Modern Art (27 August–30 November 1999). The image is also reproduced as 'The Bride' in C. Ford, *Julia Margaret Cameron: A Critical Biography* (Los Angeles: The J. Paul Getty Museum, 2003), p. 142.

20 J. M. MacLachlan, '"As if I Had Wings To Fly": The Victorian "Cult of Feminine Beauty" Through the Lens of Julia Margaret Cameron's Pre-Raphaelite Camera', Master of Arts Thesis, Department of English, University of Alberta (1999), p. 42. National Library of Canada. Available at: https://nlc-bnc.ca/obj/s4/f2/dsk2/ftp03/MQ46987.pdf [accessed 13 July 2021].

21 S. Gilmartin, 'The Sati, the Bride, and the Widow: Sacrificial Woman in the Nineteenth Century', *Victorian Literature and Culture,* 25(1), (1997), pp. 141–158 (p. 147).

22 Gilmartin, 'The Sati, the Bride, and the Widow', p. 147. As noted in our Headnotes to the 'Mourning attire' section, see Phegley, *Courtship and Marriage in Victorian England*, p. 158, for a discussion of remarriage. See also K. Heath, *Aging by the Book: The Emergence of Midlife in Victorian Britain* (Albany, NY: State University of New York Press, 2009) for a consideration of nineteenth-century remarriage and also of the complex emotional dynamics specifically applied to widows (pp. 118–120).

23 A. M. Meadows, 'May's Wedding Dress', *Tinsleys' Magazine*, December 1885, p. 523.

24 For details of Queen Victoria's wedding dress and the use of Honiton lace, see K. Staniland and S. M. Levey, 'Queen Victoria's Wedding Dress and Lace', *Costume*, 17(1), (1983), pp. 1–32. See also K. Staniland, *In Royal Fashion: The Clothes of Princess Charlotte of Wales & Queen Victoria 1796–1901* (London: Museum of London, 1997). See also Lee, '1840 – Queen Victoria's Wedding Dress', and Mitchell, *Fashioning the Victorians*, p. 147.

25 For a brief consideration of bridal 'travelling-costume', see K. Tennant, 'Female Space, Feminine Grace: Ladies and the Victorian Railway', in K. Hill (ed.), *Britain and the Narration of Travel in the Nineteenth Century: Texts, Images, Objects* (Farnham: Ashgate, 2016), pp. 53–72 (pp. 66–67).

26 [Anon], 'Modern Weddings', *Le Monde Ēlégant or the World of Fashion,* June 1888, p. 81.

27 [Anon], 'Wedding Costume', *The Ladies' Treasury*, 1 July 1892, p. 426.

28 D. De Blaquière, 'The Trousseau of To-Day. Part II', *The Girl's Own Paper*, 23 December 1899, pp. 177–181 (p. 181).

37

CELATA, 'MY WEDDING RING.'

Livesey's Moral Reformer, August 1838, p. 152

Hail! bright and simple ornament!
  What halcyon days with thee I've spent;
In fond remembrance now I sing,
  And hail with joy my wedding ring!

Sweet token of a husband's love –
  Sweet emblem of the bond above;
Bless'd be the day – the hour, – I sing,
  When first I hail'd my wedding ring!

Sweet jewel, fairest of the fair!
  No gem with thee can I compare;
Thy praises and thy charms I sing,
  And hail with joy my wedding ring!

Sweet pledge of constancy and truth,
  Golden Gordian-knot of youth,
Thy mystic, matchless tie I sing,
  And hail with joy my wedding ring!

Dear valued gift, I prize thee well,
  This truth I hope my life will tell;
The golden chain of love I sing,
  And hail with joy my wedding ring.

CELATA.

DOI: 10.4324/9781315399980-48

38

IMAGE: ELIZABETH HENDERSON, FASHION PLATE, 'PUBLIC PROMENADE AND BRIDAL DRESSES'

The Ladies' Cabinet of Fashion, Music and Romance, May 1847, © National Portrait Gallery, London

DOI: 10.4324/9781315399980-49

39

AUNT LYDIA, 'LETTER FROM AUNT LYDIA ABOUT ORANGE-BLOSSOMS.'

The Lady's Newspaper, 10 May 1862, pp. 289–290

My Dearest Bella, – I take up my pen with the view of completing my last letter, rather than with the idea of commencing a new one; so I will at once resume my subject at the point where I laid it down, and go on with my domestic lecture on the text of "Orange-blossoms."

One of the most important points is neither more nor less than the wedding dress. We must not attempt to specify what this should be, because before the ink were dry upon this paper[.] Fashion may have given a turn to her kaleidoscope, and the whole style be changed. I may, however, say that a rich material will always have the advantage over those which are light and gossamer; besides which, after having made its one day show in robing a bride for her destiny and gone the round of the wedding festivities in good substantial fashion, it may change its colour through the magic aid of the chemistry of dyeing – as mauve, or magenta, violet, brown, or black – until it at last becomes the respectable drudge of the fire-side corner, ladylike to the very end of its protracted existence.

Many of the trinkets of the bride are usually the offerings of the bridegroom, their number and value being regulated by the opulence of his circumstances. Plate, also, is the naturally appropriate gift of relatives and friends; and when these are as confidential as they ought to be, little private committees should be held, so that the purchasing parties may not double or even treble their own gifts. It is provoking for a bride to find that she has half-a-dozen silver teapots and no salver at all; or a dozen fish-slices and not a single tablespoon. Uncles, aunts, and cousins, should compare notes privately, and dot down what each intended to do, so as amongst them to render the appointment as complete as possible; above all, agreeing to make their purchases and to give their orders at the same house of business, so that all the articles may be *en suite*. Odd things may be very good and very useful, but they do not give that stamp of respectability and opulence which always attaches to sets of things. I daresay, my dear Bella, that some of your many relatives will see this *Lady's Newspaper* lying on your boudoir table; and I venture to hint to them that one of the parts of your plate presents should be silver knives for your course of fish, as bread crusts are now quite divorced from

DOI: 10.4324/9781315399980-50

their partnership with silver forks, the use of a silver knife with the fork being the appointed means of discussing the course of fish.

In purchasing your table linen, dear Bella, I must give you a hint, which you may use or not, according to your pleasure. Perhaps a little for pride's sake, but certainly also for taste's sake, let it be made expressly for you, and let your crest be woven in its centre. Some have their coat of arms emblazoned, but I do not recommend that. It might be thought ostentatious, but the simple crest marks it as your own, and gives a sort of stamp of ownership better, as well as of good family style, which lasts to the end of the fabric. In the same way the dinner napkins should also bear similar heraldic honours of ownership.

The bridegroom's presents on these occasions are usually in the shape of some elegant trinket – watch, gold chain, bracelet, inlaid boudoir cabinet, or articles of a similar kind.

The wedding cards. The latest fashion is to have the one which bears the name of the bride before the bridal not with the line drawn through *both,* as was lately the practice, but only through the last. Common sense seems to have rectified this error – as you, my dear child, will still be Bella, whatever name may supersede the one you now bear.

Wedding favours. The wearing of these badges of the grand ceremony used to be confined to bows of white satin ribbon, worn by the servants officiating on the day. Now all the gentlemen of the party are expected to assume them, being formed of silver and white satin ribbon, with a small cluster of orange-blossoms in the centre. The adoption of this favour at once marks the right of the party who wears it to take part in the events of the day. Strange things have been known to happen for want of some such badge; strangers mingling in the festive crowd, unnoticed in the excitement and confusion, sometimes not of the most satisfactory character.

With the wedding cards is one bearing the date of the "At Home," which is of course to take place after the return from the *tour*. The only exception to this rule is when the bridegroom is a clergyman. In this case there is no "At Home," as the selection of those who might be eligible, and those who might be ineligible, would prove very invidious in a parish. Your intended not wearing black cloth, you can choose to whom you will send cards; but I strongly recommend that you should only do this to those with whom you intend to keep up some sort of sociable acquaintance. It is very painful to the feelings of any one, we must all allow, to be invited to some grand reception and then dropped; and you, I am sure, dear Bella, would be the last to inflict one of these cold-hearted injuries.

When the newly-married pair set out on a more prolonged tour, and cannot count with certainty on the time of their return, they send the wedding cards simply with the names, and on their return home despatch the "At Homes."

On receiving these visits the dress of the newly-married lady should be perfectly simple, bearing no mark of the occasion to which it refers. You tell me, my dear Bella, that you shrink from the thought of being overwhelmed with congratulations. Dismiss that idea from your mind altogether. The refinement of modern society never did better service to women than when it abolished those broadsides of hearty good wishes which made their recipients feel so extremely uncomfortable. The style now is scarcely, if at all, to allude to the event which draws the visitors together. If any reference is made it is the slightest and most delicate odour of a wish for the bride's happiness, breathed over the wine just as it reaches the lips, mingling with its aroma; but for set phrases and elaborate speeches, those have gone for ever to the tomb of the Capulets. You will not be expected to talk much; but it would be what I should be tempted to call a sort of indelicate mistake not to speak at all, though I have known some brides who did nothing but bow, and never spoke a single word to any one of their visitors. Of course all these calls are to be returned within a week, or at the most ten days; and as to their order, may I hint, dear Bella, that you should take the list backwards way – that is, that you should begin with the least favoured in worldly affairs, and finish with the most opulent. I am not now referring to your new relations. What strange feelings will come over you when you think of new fathers and mothers, brothers, sisters, uncles, aunts, and cousins! Accept them all, my love, accept them all as if they were really and truly your own. It is the only way to be happy with them, and still more to be happy with him who thus unite you with them in so many new bonds. How often is it fatal to wedded life for the husband and wife to revolt against those family ties which they ought to rejoice in as new blessings from heaven. I know, you know, everybody knows, that jealousies and prejudices run high against these new relationships, and that the effect is to alienate the hearts that have been so solemnly pledged before heaven to each other. I am getting too serious, perhaps, so I will leave this point for you to sleep upon, and dream upon, and think upon; so bidding you once more adieu, I remain,

Ever your own affectionate

AUNT LYDIA.

40

C. SEARS LANCASTER, 'MY WEDDING-BONNET.'

Le Follet, September 1863, pp. 65–69

I

"Of all false axioms, to my mind 'tis plain
The falsest is that 'pride can feel no pain.'"

ANON.

Young Mrs. Wilson was engaged helping (with her accustomed ability and good nature) younger Mary Morrison to make a new dress, when a lady-neighbour was announced.

"For goodness sake," cried the industrious Mary to her married friend, "don't let Mrs. Pleasant see that I'm making my own dress, or she'll tell all the neighbourhood," and she rose to hurriedly conceal the evidence of her industry.

"Sit down again, I insist upon it," said Mrs. Wilson, in a tone of good-humoured authority. "Remember *I* am helping you, so that if you are engaged in employment you are ashamed of, I must share the discredit; and, as you invited me to the task, you acknowledge you have asked me to do something discreditable if you fear to have it known."

"But Mrs. Pleasant is a good neighbour and – – "

"Which do you value most," asked Mrs. Wilson, rising with mock gravity, "a good neighbour or a true friend? Choose between us."

Mary hesitated a moment, kissed her friend, and sat down again to her work. Mrs. Wilson had only time enough to add "the same feeling as yours once cost me fifty guineas, and a heart-ache worth double the money," when the lady entered.

Mrs. Pleasant really *was* a lady, and, after an apology from Mary Morrison, and a little raillery from Mrs. Wilson, responded to an invitation from the latter, by drawing working implements from her pocket, and rendering good service on the spot; thus, not only putting Mary Morrison at her ease for the moment, but assuring her of an immunity of derision, from that quarter at least, for all time to come.

When they were alone again, Mary Morrison, with thanks for her friend's good offices, eagerly demanded a recital of the incident alluded to.

"Ah!" said Mrs. Wilson, "even now, I cannot reflect upon it without my face getting hot, and an uncomfortable sensation in my throat. It was simply this: – I

DOI: 10.4324/9781315399980-51

was engaged in making my wedding-bonnet, aided, as you are just now," she added with assumed vanity, "by the tact and intelligence of an amateur *modiste*. Now, you must know that in my courting days, which were not so very long ago, neither dear George nor I was rolling in riches; for myself, I had simply the small allowance for dress which dear papa made me (quite as much as he could spare out of his pay as a retired officer, I know, but still not too much for, at all events, what one is supposed to require in the station in which we moved), and George had been only three years engaged in a bank, and was not in possession of more than enough to commence housekeeping *quietly*.

"Well, my wedding-dress was a present, so I had no care about that; but I had been so busily engaged in making *other* dresses, and arranging all sorts of etceteras for the coming ceremony, that the day before the intended wedding arrived before I could fairly set to work on my wedding-bonnet (for, you must know, George preferred that to a veil); and so I enlisted the sympathy and, what, for the time, was better still, the assistance of a dear young friend, who, by the way, let out, for the first time, the secret of *her* engagement by pricking her fingers a dozen times and blushing continuously in the first five minutes of her occupation.

"I was particularly desirous to make my own wedding-bonnet, because I had often, amongst my intimate friends, when discussing economy, declared that, whatever might be my prospects *after* marriage – if I were so fortunate (and who, under forty-five, ever thinks she will *not* be?) to obtain a partner, I would carry the notions of home prudence to the very end of my single life, so that I should begin the world free to follow whichever course the compass of the new and good ship Matrimony should point to.

"Let me come to the point. Exactly as we have lately, but agreeably and usefully, been disturbed by the visit of Mrs. Pleasant, so was my seclusion broken in upon by the announcement of Lady Bloomly and her daughter. Lady Bloomly (also, like Mrs. Pleasant, a neighbour) was a universal favourite; and her daughter would have shared the high estimation in which her mother was held but for a certain unsuppressed superciliousness towards all beneath her in position, and an unhidden contempt for every kind of useful occupation in which a woman's fingers could be engaged.

"To be discovered by Lady Bloomly occupied in making a bonnet, and, of all things, a *wedding*-bonnet, would be a discomfort; but for *Miss* Bloomly to make such a discovery would be disastrous. So, having desired the servant to be sure and not say how we were employed, and hastily catching up my nearly-completed bonnet, trimming and all, prepared to run upstairs with it, in order to conceal the evidence of my industry, when voices at the door told me I was too late for exit that way. But when did a woman stumble for want of a resource? I hastily threw the bonnet and materials into an arm-chair, and withdrawing a large anti-macassar from a sofa disposed it over the unconscious source of anxiety so as thoroughly to conceal it. I had only time to sit down, and certainly not to recover my breath, when Lady Bloomly and her daughter entered, finding me with a hastily-opened book before me, having *evidently* been engaged in the respectably-idle occupation of reading aloud to my young friend.

"And to what was I indebted for this unlooked-for visit? *Ostensibly* to the desire of saying good-bye to a worthy neighbour's daughter previous to her marriage; but *actually* to that of crowding as many inquiries as to my arrangements as courtesy would permit and curiosity could crowd into the limits of a 'call.'

"Much of Lady Bloomly's questioning might really have arisen from the ordinary sympathy which our sex feels in such little interesting ceremonies as that in which I was about to take a pleasingly-prominent part; but, after she travelled from what I was going to wear, to where I was going to get it, I felt annoyed, and indeed confused, when the object in question became a bonnet.

"*Was* I going to wear a bonnet? – Oh! yes. Could she see it? – Oh! no. Why not? – The fact was – – Oh! it had not arrived? – Exactly so.

"Thus far I had travelled through the ordeal of cross-examination without committing myself, but more was to follow.

" 'I am quite a connoisseur in bonnets,' continued her ladyship; 'I should like to see yours amazingly.'

" 'So should I,' drawled her daughter, 'much. When do you expect it?'

"I explained that the time was passed by a day, and, indeed (here I was driven to an extremity by a hint of a later visit for the purpose of inspection) I had my fears, more than fears, that I should be disappointed altogether of its arrival that day.

"Lady Bloomly put many questions, apparently offhand, but which piqued me exceedingly, as evidencing some doubt of my word. At last, she point-blank asked me if I was *sure* that the bonnet had not arrived? To which I gave the equally point-blank answer, 'yes;' and a great relief it was, being the first question, by many, to which I could reply without equivocation.

"The daughter, who frequently exchanged glances with her mamma, which I could not at all make out, suddenly put the unexpected question, 'and what, may I ask is the price of the bonnet?'

"Too far committed to recede, I answered boldly – but, with a face like scarlet – 'five guineas.'

"Miss Bloomly looked at her mamma with an expression of triumph, the glance being returned by one something very like mortification.

"Lady Bloomly, who was evidently, for some reason, disconcerted, exclaimed, 'five guineas is a large price, my dear; who has the order?'

"Again driven to my wits' end, I replied, 'yes, but it was to be ordered in Paris; and now I remember that I never wrote my final instructions – how stupid!'

" 'Then you must be disappointed; for there is now obviously no time to communicate with the Continent.'

" 'How unfortunate!" chimed in the daughter; 'and you so far from town. What *will* you do?'

" 'Indeed, indeed! I do not know,' I replied, fairly distressed at the pile of untruths which my first deception had almost necessitated.

" 'If you really desire to repair the omission,' said Lady Bloomly, mistaking my more than vexation; 'I am going to drive to town this evening, and will select a bonnet for you. You may rely upon my taste, and feel certain you need not exceed three or four guineas: will you entrust me with the commission?'

"I made no reply. I could carry on the deception no further; and I determined, no matter how great the humiliation, to acknowledge at once the occupation in which I had been interrupted.

" 'Perhaps you would prefer going yourself,' added Lady Bloomly, observing my hesitation and misinterpreting it; 'and, in case your own milliner should be too busily engaged, I will give you the address of mine.'

" 'Thank you,' said I; 'but – – ' As I spoke, Lady Bloomly rose, and passed to the table on which were writing materials. I forgot to say that she was a remarkably fine woman; indeed, portly; and, before I could finish the sentence that would have put an end to my dilemma, she stamped it inextricably by drawing the arm-chair to the table, and sitting down with the full force of her majestic and remorseless weight, plump upon my wedding-bonnet!

"I could have screamed, but that I was too much horrified. My young companion and fellow-labourer turned as white as if she would have fainted.

"Dejected, humiliated, self-abased, I submitted to my fate without a murmur – accepted Lady Bloomly's offer to make the purchase without a murmur – thanked her for the most miserable visit I had ever received – acknowledged beforehand the worst office I had ever had rendered to me – and witnessed her departure with a relief that brought almost as painful sensations as her presence!

"Neither my friend nor I had the moral courage to survey the work of destruction; so, rushing up to my own room, we threw ourselves upon the bed without a word – cast ourselves into each other's arms – and fairly cried ourselves to sleep!"

II.

"What *must* be – *shall* be!"

SHAKESPEARE.

"And when did we awake? not until a knock at the street door announced that dear George had called to try on the ring!

"Jane (my young friend) and I, looked at each other in mute astonishment and distress. However, there was no time to be lost; so, hastily smoothing our hair, we were down stairs almost by the time that George entered the room. For the first time since our engagement, I felt George's presence not an absolute delight; in fact, I should have been delighted to be relieved from his presence entirely; but countenances *must,* I suppose, if only for the sake of politeness, sometimes tell stories, and so I smiled my best on receiving him, and soon forgot the pain of the past in the pleasure of the present, until by some horribly unlucky chance – men *are* so awkward – the conversation turned upon the wedding-gown, leading, oh! of course, to my wedding-bonnet. Now, the idea of wearing *the* bonnet as it *was* – and it still reposed in its crushed and mutilated state beneath the anti-macassar – was simply impossible, and to commence another at *that* time – for we had lost wretchedly by our long and miserable sleep – was equally so. The result was, a change in my determination: and so, when George asked plainly how I liked my bonnet, I replied that I did not intend to wear one.

"'Not wear a bonnet?' he asked, with more disappointment in his tone than I fancied the matter warranted; 'what then?'

"'Oh! it is obvious,' I replied, 'that if one does *not* wear a bonnet, one *must* wear a veil.'

"'But, you know my preference for a bonnet,' he remarked; 'at least,' he added, mistaking my look of mortification for one that rebelled against dictation; 'at least, I thought you did, but never mind, darling, I dare say you forgot it; of course you did, in the multiplicity of things which you had to think of. I have brought the ring.'

"He appeared disconcerted to a greater extent than I thought was warranted by the mere fact of my preferring a veil to a bonnet, even in opposition to his wish; for the more one blames oneself the less is one prepared to admit the blame of others, so an additional shade came over my features, and there was an uncomfortable pause.

"'The ring, dear,' said Jane, to smooth over the rapidly advancing difficulty.

"I felt very much inclined not to try it on; but, I looked into George's face, and found the shadow that I knew was on my own so clearly reflected from his, that I smiled on the instant, which brought such an immediate return on his part, that I laughed outright, and, with a kiss sealed a truce to the little *gaucherie* that was trying to cast a momentary cloud upon our happiness.

"After an hour of as many pleasant words as it contained moments, and as many charming thoughts as could crowd into the space without making confusion absolutely confounded, George rose to go. At that moment, the maid – awkward creature! – came into the room with a bonnet-box. I had heard a knock a minute before, and the truth at once rushed upon my brain.

"'Put it down,' I said, before she had time to make a remark.

"'But, miss – – ' she persevered.

"'Leave the room!' I cried, authoritatively.

"'Has the young person to wait?' asked the maid, imperturbably. 'She said' – holding out a bill – 'that she was to wait for the money!'

"'Money!' I repeated, abstractedly.

"'Yes, miss – four guineas and a half, for the wedding-bonnet.'

"The words struck me like several bullets from a revolver, all discharged at once. I got to the mantelpiece *some*how, and, taking from one of the ornaments (where I had left it, on purpose to show George), a five-pound note that a dear old godpapa had that day presented me with to purchase a keeper, I mechanically put it into the girl's hand, saying, with unconscious liberality, and as if the complete annihilation of the bank-note would utterly and for ever ignore the incident from my memory, 'Never mind the change!'

" 'Is that for yourself?' asked George, in a tone that sounded like deprecation.

" 'Why not?' I replied, giving interrogatory for interrogatory, in order to gain time to think.

" 'Because I thought you were not going to wear one.'

" 'But you preferred it.'

" 'Undoubtedly – if of your own making.'

" 'Oh!' I exclaimed, with the usual eagerness of the one in the wrong to catch hold of any straw that seems drifting in a safe direction – 'you disapprove of the expense!'

" 'That is hardly a fair remark,' he replied. 'Even assuming that I *did,* how could such a matter affect me *yet?*'

" 'Why, of course,' I returned, arguing his cause instead of my own; 'it is indifferent from whose purse it comes, on the very eve of marriage.'

"I felt that I *had* been guilty of extravagance. I felt, too, that I had been led into it by a folly – indeed, a fault – and was already reaping punishment, in the unhappy feeling of having vexed George; although, at that moment, I hardly acquitted him of being as much to blame as myself.

"George, in some measure, read my thoughts, and, with his usual generous construction, sought to put me at my ease, by asking to look at the hateful bonnet. But I could not bear the sight of it, and so bespoke his patience.

" 'At all events,' I said, 'you will have your wish, George, for you see I am not going to wear a veil.'

" 'Do you know why I preferred a bonnet?' he asked, for he was proverbial for knowing nothing about a lady's dress, beyond admiring the *ensemble.*

" 'No, indeed!'

" 'You will not be angry if I tell you?' he urged, almost timidly.

" 'Oh, no!'

" 'And not give me credit or discredit for parsimony?' he added, with a smile of perfect good-humour that set me again at my ease.

" 'No, believe me.'

" 'Well, then, it was this – On the first occasion of my thoughts turning seriously upon sharing our future together (I had always admired you, recollect, beyond any other woman'), – I acknowledged the compliment, with a blush, – 'you were engaged in trimming a bonnet. I praised it, and asked you whose it was. You said your own; and, on my expressing surprise at your undertaking the labour of such an occupation, you told me that you made your own dresses as well. Your unartificial candour, and the evidence of good-home teaching so usefully carried out, made me, as one who had the world before me, say to myself – what a valuable wife! Of all the circle of my acquaintance, I had not happened to see another young lady similarly engaged. Perhaps I was struck at the difference, in use, of that employment from the eternal crochet; at all events, I thought of you seriously all the way home, and *at* home from that evening onwards. It was not that the little incident *placed* you in my heart, but it set thought to work, and found you there sooner than it might otherwise have done, and, at all events, prevented you from being dethroned. Don't think me mercenary nor vain; (I know *which* of us it is that has drawn the prize). I simply mention the occurrence to account for *why* I wished you to wear a bonnet. It seemed to me (feeling assured that you would exercise your own taste upon it) that it would be like a completion of the cycle of our happy courtship, and a sort of preassurance that our future round of happiness would be unbroken. Darling,' he added, in a tone of serious pain, as he saw by the distress in my features, that he had wounded my feelings, 'pray, pray, don't let my words vex you – and at such a moment. I spoke with my accustomed frankness – not to scold – not even to presume to direct you – but simply to offer an excuse for momentary vexation to-night, and to account for what otherwise appears like dictation in a matter wholly beside my province.'

"As he kissed the tear off my cheek, I felt almost pleased at the *contretemps* that had brought an exhibition of such utter kindliness of heart; and I was about to acknowledge my error, in the full assurance of a full forgiveness, when another arrival was announced in the person of George's mamma. She is a darling woman, as you know, and I was delighted to see her, though I could have dispensed with her company for another half hour.

"'Well, darling,' she said, after an affectionate salutation all round; 'what are you going to buy with the fifty guineas?'

"'What fifty guineas?'

"'That Lady Bloomly presented you with.'

"'When?'

"'To-day!'

"'Why?'

"'For making your own wedding-bonnet, to be sure.'

"An explanation was soon elicited. My dear mother-in-law had called on Lady Bloomly that morning, and, in course of conversation, was extolling her son's good fortune in his intended wife, (that was very good of her, was it not?) and eulogizing me for my good qualities, giving a prominent place amongst them to industry and economy, and proving them both by an acknowledgment that I was actually going to make my own wedding-bonnet. Lady Bloomly, it appeared, joined in the praise, holding me out as a positive paragon, and pattern to my young-lady sisterhood, and making it the text of a sermon on extravagance to her prodigal daughter, who, by the way, affected to point-blank disbelieve the story. Thereupon, Lady Bloomly expressed her determination to present me with fifty guineas (and actually drew a cheque for the amount), to purchase a wedding-present, for my good example, and brought her daughter with her to witness the triumph of 'virtue rewarded,' when I, by my unlucky momentary hesitation, and subsequent untruth, brought the pain and mortification which you can well imagine I had endured, independent of the new source of hearty regret.

"With such bitter tears did I acknowledge and thus half expiate my offence, that dear George and his kind mother were almost broken-hearted in trying to comfort me. And how do you think I occupied myself after they were gone? Why, I spent half the night (with my pretty Jane) in gathering up the fragments and making a new bonnet, while my feet, in revenge, remorselessly crushed its four-guinea-and-a-half rival beneath a capacious footstool. So that, after all, dear George led me to church next morning in a wedding-bonnet of my own making. And now you know how it managed to cost me fifty guineas and a heartache."

As Mrs. Wilson concluded her little narrative, and was receiving the hearty condolence of her hearer, Mary Morrison, the veritable George, her husband, entered, accompanied by a venerable and kindly-looking gentleman, with hair as white as snow, and eyes as bright as glow-worms.

"I'm successful – I'm appointed!" said George, after the greeting and introduction were over.

"To what?" asked his wife, with a flushed face.

"To the post of sub-manager in the new branch of our bank!"

"Indeed!" exclaimed she, hardly realizing the advantage, but delighted because *he* was delighted.

"Yes – and through *you,* too."

"Through *me?* Impossible!"

"Certain; and good Mr. Wilding, our chairman, will explain how."

Thus called upon, Mr. Wilding said: "It was through *your* interest, because I feel interest in *you*. We had to elect one of our clerks to the post in question; and, while I freely acknowledge that your husband deserved it as well, if not better, than others, I should not have given my casting vote (our directors were equally divided) for him more than the other candidate, who was a single man, had I not happened to learn from him, in a conversation on the vexed question of fitting occupation for ladies, a certain little incident connected with your wedding-day. The mortification and loss you had suffered, the deeper pain that your husband and his worthy mother endured at having *cost* you that pain by an accidental discovery, and, above all, for the graceful amends you made to yourself and him by your final work of industry, gave me so high an appreciation of both your characters that I conscientiously gave my casting vote for the new appointment; and heartily say to you both – 'God bless you in its enjoyment!'"

41

IMAGE: PHOTOGRAPH BY JULIA MARGARET CAMERON, 'DORA AS THE BRIDE'

(Sitter Annie Chinery Cameron), albumen print, 1869

 DOI: 10.4324/9781315399980-52

42

IMAGE: EDWARD KILLINGWORTH JOHNSON, DRAWING DEPICTING A YOUNG WIDOW HOLDING HER WEDDING DRESS

Water-colour and gouache on paper, 1877

DOI: 10.4324/9781315399980-53

43

ALICE MAUD MEADOWS, 'MAY'S WEDDING DRESS'

Tinsleys' Magazine, December 1885, p. 523

"I AM making it all myself, dear,
  You would see it? Ah, wait awhile;
You must look at it first in the church, dear,
  As it sweeps up the old stone aisle.
It is white as the fresh fallen snow, dear.
  I pray that our lives may be
As spotless and pure as the dress, dear,
  In which I am wedded to thee.

"You don't know what dreams I have, dear,
  As I work at it, day by day,
How I think of the past and future, dear,
  Years coming and past away;
And I put in such careful work, dear,
  For I would not one stitch should give,
But wear while the dress shall last, dear,
  Like our true love, as long as we live.

"There is lace falling over the silk, dear,
  To make it look fairer still;
It would not look well by itself, dear,
  But over the silk it will.
In the silk and the lace of my dress, dear,
  What emblem d'you think I trace?
Why, you are the thick, strong silk, dear,
  And I am the clinging lace."

ALICE MAUD MEADOWS.

DOI: 10.4324/9781315399980-54

44

[ANON], 'MODERN WEDDINGS.'

Le Monde Ēlégant or the World of Fashion, June 1888, p. 81

A WEDDING is always interesting, especially to the fairer portion of humanity, and preparations for it cause a good deal of pleasant excitement in the families concerned, all being anxious to infuse into the function as much prettiness and novelty as possible.

There are changes of fashion even in the matter of so old a ceremony as marriage; and the ways of our mothers and grandmothers have gradually been altered by the march of new ideas and the discovery of wider resources.

The extension of canonical hours for performing the ceremony has had much to do with these innovations and improvements, and among other changes the Wedding Tea has partially superseded the Wedding Breakfast. This arrangement permits the assembling of a greater number of guests than could be accommodated at a breakfast. In many cases, after the departure of the bride and bridegroom, the guests inspect the wedding presents, unless a special At Home has been previously given for that purpose.

The refreshments provided for a Wedding Tea are very light, and include a plentiful supply of choice fruit. If the happy pair remain for the tea, the bride cuts the cake, which is then handed to the guests.

Floral decorations are a great feature at Wedding Teas. The blossoms are generally of one kind, daffodils, roses, lilies, gardenias, &c., the bride's flower of preference being generally chosen, and a few choice blooms ornament the wedding cake.

If the bride remains for the tea, she wears the wedding dress and veil, changing it for her travelling *toilette* immediately before starting.

Brides have greater choice in the bridal dress than formerly. Very few wedding dresses are now made alike, whereas at one time the regulation white satin was almost compulsory. So many beautiful fabrics are in vogue for bridal dresses, and so many combinations of these materials allowable, that every lady can enjoy a speciality in her wedding gown.

Satin, *moiré, peau-de-soie,* plush, velvet, delicate oriental silks, and gauzes inwoven with gold and silver threads, are all pressed into the gracious service of adorning the bride. Lace plays a prominent part, and the traditional bridal flower is rarely absent from a wedding *toilette*.

DOI: 10.4324/9781315399980-55

The choice of jewellery is decided by individual taste rather than fashion; some brides preferring simplicity, and others the extreme point of adornment in this particular.

The veil no longer covers the face, but is arranged at back of head as for a presentation. Sometimes a small wreath, but more generally a spray, of orange-blossoms is worn in the hair. If jewels are added to the *coiffure,* they vary from the simple pearl arrow or diamond star to the regal-looking tiara of brilliants. When bracelets, brooches, or pendants are worn, they are chosen from the wedding gifts.

If the bride is married in her travelling dress – an increasingly favourite custom – little or no jewellery is worn, and the whole *toilette,* while it may be extremely rich, should be quiet in style and colour.

Bridesmaid's dresses now form the subject of much artistic effort. Harmonious colours and materials are combined with excellent effect, and the fair bevy of bridesmaids form a picturesque setting to that "cynosure of every eye," the bride.

Boy pages, whose duty it is to carry the bride's train, make a pretty feature in the wedding-group, and are usually attired in some quaint and rich costumes of the olden time.

The *toilettes* of wedding guests, especially those of the mothers of bride and bridegroom, can scarcely be too rich. The artistic blending of beautiful lines and gorgeous materials in the dresses, the wave of graceful feathers, the varied colours of flowers in the bonnets, and the glitter of jewels among the wedding guests, add the finishing touches to the pretty spectacle of a modern wedding.

45

IMAGE: [ANON], 'WEDDING COSTUME.'

The Ladies' Treasury, 1 July 1892, p. 426

Figure 45.1 Wedding Costume.

The material is pure white satin, the trimming of silver embroidery only, and no pearls. The sleeves are less in size than usual, the frills of satin on the shoulders being full and wide on the summit. The frontal of pearls set in lace. Orange blossoms are sparingly used. The ample veil of rather a thick tulle.

DOI: 10.4324/9781315399980-56

46

[ANON], 'THE TROUSSEAU OF TO-DAY.'

The Girl's Own Paper, 7 October 1899, pp. 4–6

THE amount allowed for the purchase of a trousseau differs with the circumstances of the family and the number of it, and is governed also a good deal by the kindly generous nature of the parents. In some cases where a marriage is in prospect, which is remarkably good in a worldly point of view, the parents will probably desire to provide more handsomely than they would otherwise do were the prospects less brilliant. The amount of dress needed will be far more considerable in one case than the other; although the number of dresses may be the same, the style of them will be more expensive.

We will take a family of fair position with comfortable means, the daughter marrying an officer in the army or the navy, or a professional man of good position; and here we shall find that the sum set aside for the bride's trousseau will range from £100 to £150, up to £200, the latter being a very usual sum, especially when a girl has no fortune, or very little to take with her to her new home.

The cost of the trousseau of to-day may be rated rather higher, I think, than it was ten years ago; that is, so far as regards the purchasing power of the amount allowed, which is not so great as it was; or rather, perhaps, I should say that we have advanced in our ideas of what is required, and thus dresses cost more than they did formerly. On the other hand we can manage to do with fewer of them; for we unquestionably think it wiser to have less than we did. This rule seems to apply even to the trousseaux of Royal ladies. The number of unmade gowns in them is very large, which shows that the varying moods of fashion are taken into account; and it is evident that there are many materials which can be purchased and laid aside for a time without injury, and also without becoming old-fashioned. But here the common-sense view of the matter steps in, and inquires –

"Why buy them before you need them, if you be not 'a Royalty?' In *their* case we can comprehend the necessity – there are so many people, institutions and nationalities that must be patronised on the occasion of a Royal wedding."

Well, the true answer seems to be, I am sorry to say, in that well-known phrase, "Take it while you can get it" – in short, while people are in the mood for giving. There is also something in the fact of the fixed sum which is laid aside to be spent on the one object. It is best to use it. Perhaps if any of it be laid aside,

DOI: 10.4324/9781315399980-57

circumstances may require it elsewhere. Life is uncertain, and the father and the mother alike know human nature, and as it is their own money, and a kind of last gift to their child, they prefer it to be used as it is intended. To avoid having too many made-up things laid by, which may grow out of date, it seems better to purchase the materials which may be useful in the future, and which are excepted by ever-varying fashions.

Now, serge, blue and black, is one of these materials, and a little consideration will give us others: white dotted muslins and other thin materials, if our steps were likely to be turned to India or any other hot climate; or they would be useful even in England if we continued to have the hot summers of the last three years; and more especially if the heat were to extend into August, we should require quite a stock of clothing.

Perhaps, for the sake of argument, it is well to say that our trousseau allowance consists of £200. Of course there are very many girls who do not get more than half or a quarter of this sum, but still there are certain things that every girl must have and every trousseau must contain, and so one sum is as good as another; for where one girl would be entitled to afford ten guineas for a gown, another would need the same, but would only be entitled to pay five pounds.

Certain fashions obtain in one class which do not in another, it is true; but there are many girls who have to look as well as their richer sisters on half the annual income. This is done at the expense of personal thought and exertion, and of a patient determination which carries all before it. It is done by calculation and attention to the minor details of expenditure, by a knowledge of where to buy, and how to buy in the cheapest market, and also of the exact thing to buy. One girl will look smart and stylish, where another, with far more money, will look dowdy and plain; her gowns will have mysteriously lost their freshness as soon as worn, and nothing will be at its best in her wardrobe.

That mysterious thing which we call style seems to be both a personal attribute and an acquired virtue, as some girls have it by nature, and from their earliest days we know they will look well in whatever they wear – with a touch here, a pull there, and, under the magic touch of their deft fingers, the most untoward garments look well. It is also acquired by many observant girls in a suitable environment, and I think it means that they have the initiative faculty strongly developed. It is a great thing to find out your style and what suits you, and stick to it. Many girls look their best in a coat and skirt, and they appear smart and well set up, while we all know the other girl, who looks and feels untidy and dowdy, and comes unscrewed at her waist. Perhaps really good style consists in an exquisite tidiness, a dainty sweetness and cleanliness which is never forgotten nor omitted: bathing and brushing, and a strictness in mending all the tears, and sewing on all the buttons and strings exactly when they are wanted. All this implies that you possess the highest and best domestic qualities possible to womankind.

The sum we have selected, £200, must be divided into two parts; the first hundred must be apportioned to the dresses of the trousseau, and the second to the underclothing and the numberless other accessories – bonnets and hats, boots and shoes, stockings and gloves, etc. – which go to make up the complete outfit of every woman. So we will begin with what seems to be an ordinary number of gowns for any girl who is in society and expects to have a certain amount of going out in the evening of one kind or another.

In making a list of the gowns we put down the wedding-gown, veil, and wreath, the going-away dress, evening gowns and tailor-mades, as for a wedding at any season these will be needed, and if in the winter, a mantle, jacket, or coat, in addition, and probably some furs. Just at present the wedding-gown is almost always made of ivory satin, with a Court train, this latter being so long and ample that it is nearly another dress. Of course, if the bride intends to be presented on her marriage, this is a very wise arrangement, for it will thus answer two purposes and do for two events. Otherwise, having a Court train strikes me as a clever way of obtaining a second white satin gown, which, if you are to go out much, will be useful. But there is no need of the Court train, and you can have a very handsome wedding-gown without it.

It quite depends on your after use of your wedding-gown how much you spend upon it. Thirty-five guineas, if made of the best satin at about 13s. a yard, would be a handsome sum; but out of your hundred pounds it would be quite excessive. So I should advise you to look carefully at the satins, and if you can get the rightly-coloured ivory – the true hue of old ivory – in the linen-backed kind, do not take a silk one, as the former will wear quite as well and will look very nearly the same. About 7s. or 8s. a yard would be enough to give at a really good shop. If you have any old lace, use it for your wedding-gown, at least, for the neck and sleeves. The tulle veil and wreath together will cost about £2, and after this you will need to consider the shoes and stockings, petticoats and gloves.

What is called the going-away gown is, next to the wedding-gown, of the most importance in a trousseau, for this reason – that it will be for most women the out-of-door *pièce de résistance* for the summer or winter trousseau. A fair sum should be allowed for it, and it should be carefully chosen. I have seen two this season which have pleased me very much. The first was a summer gown of mauve voile, lined with a slightly darker silk, and trimmed with a flat *garniture* of white lace with an edging of narrow black velvet. On the skirt there were two rows of this, and the same was on the bodice, which had a white lace vest and revers, and one of the new lace collars that are quite transparent and stiffened by means of whalebones at the sides, back and front. A hat to match this gown was intended to be worn with it, but I should have preferred a black hat as the wearer was fair, and the contrast would have been effective. A petticoat was made to match of the same silk, which is just now a very usual thing.

The other gown was what is called a tailor-made. It was of the palest grey cloth, the bodice being also simple, with a front of white satin and lace, and revers of the satin, which were braided with black and white. The hat worn with this was one of those gathered ones of chiffon or tulle in the prettiest pale blue. The wearer was dark, with blue eyes. The silk lining of this gown was of a pale blue, with a petticoat of the same. It will be seen that either of these gowns was of a character to be useful afterwards. Perhaps, instead of the blue hat or toque, one might have preferred one of the grey-coloured tulle, or a white one. These two are specimens of what is required in the going-away gown for summer, and the conditions vary but little in winter, for the cloth may be slightly heavier and some fur may be used. But the gown is a smart and dressy one, and, if needful, additional warmth may be procured by means of a cape or mantle; or the gown itself may be cool, and the skirt handsomely fur-trimmed, but suitable for afternoon wear.

As a general rule, three tailor-made gowns would be a fair allowance in such an outfit as this, including, of course, the going-away dress, if that were of cloth, and tailor-made. We must consider the exigencies and requirements of our daily life, and these would demand a knockabout, everyday coat and skirt of tweed, serge, or homespun, and another slightly better and more dressy, but not so dressy as the one I have mentioned. The tailor-made gowns may be classed as good, better, and best, and therefore it is well to look about us and try to find such models for each as we may like. The cost would vary from three guineas, for the everyday one, up to six or even seven, for the best. The tailor you employ would of course make a difference in charge, if extremely fashionable or of a more quiet order.

After the tailor-mades would come the consideration of summer *piqués,* drills, and flannels, with the muslin blouses to wear with them. Most girls have a stock of these already, and there is nothing to prevent them making such additions as will bring them up to the mark. These *piqué* and drill dresses can be purchased at very moderate prices during the sales, and so they need not be considered as expensive. Indeed, most of the girls I know have the skirts and muslin blouses either made at home or done by some "little dressmaker," to whom they supply patterns and materials. A *piqué* skirt, however, it is better to purchase, unless your little dressmaker can manage the strapped seams, for which there is an obligation at present if we would be in the fashion.

As regards the coats of these white gowns, I do not think we, any of us, find them of great value, and we wear out ten skirts to one coat. Frenchwomen wear them sometimes with black or coloured skirts, and I have noticed that they are worn in this way in England; but if you must have a jacket, or do not know what to do with those you have, I should advise you to have something between an Eton and a Bolero made of them. You can purchase a shape to suit you, and have the transformation carried out by any good dressmaker who works by the day, or who will undertake such small renovations and alterations.

The next important question is, I think, the gown for functions or for dinner-parties and small evening reunions; and my experience leads me to say that black satin is the best for these, and that a black satin with three bodices is the most useful. We illustrate two of these made this season for a trousseau. The first had a yoke and sleeves of white lace; the second, an evening bodice with a white lace top; the third bodice was in black, and could be worn out of doors. It was trimmed with sequins and chiffon. A good quality of black satin should be selected, and you must be guided as to price, and whether it should be a silk- or a linen-backed one also, by how much you are likely to require it, as a black satin shows wear rather more than a white one. The less trimming on the skirt the better, as trimmings so often mark the date of a gown, and you will be anxious that your trousseau gowns should render you as long service as possible. So you must be careful only to select designs that are not of an extreme character; and both materials and patterns should be fashionable, but not too "loud." In this you will need wisdom, and if you patronise a good shop, they would help you. The extreme of style one year will often become the special fashion of that which follows.

The next gown is one which, while suitable for a dinner at an hotel or restaurant, could also be made suitable for a *very* smart garden-party. It is of white silk and chiffon, with white lace over it. The bodice was a square with transparent lace sleeves. These lace gowns were much worn this year, and I have always thought them perfect epitomes of smartness and beauty. The gown illustrated cost about ten guineas, I believe; but this expense could be lessened in various ways, as the shop was a very fashionable one, and nothing was grudged in its construction as to the material.

The other gown which was prepared for the trousseau, was a white, satin-faced foulard, with a tiny mauve design on it of leaves and spots. This was an afternoon visiting and concert gown, and was not very costly, only about six guineas. It was made with a pointed double skirt, and the trimming was tiny gathered ruchings of white silk. In the winter the place of it would be taken by a handsome, tailor-made gown of cloth. I think that, taking into consideration the garden-parties of summer, the trousseau of the winter would probably be less expensive. But still, if you were wise, something would be laid aside, or some preparation made for the summer gaieties that are sure to follow.

The next thing that I must dwell upon here is the hats and bonnets. The fashions of this present season seem to require a hat or a bonnet for every costume: but, on the other hand, we never had such a year for black hats, and they were quite correct for any costume, so the law was abrogated in its original sternness, which spelt ruin for some moderate allowances. Still, the going-away hat or bonnet looks better when not black: and it seems more suitable, too, that it should either match the dress or contrast with it. This year the drawn chiffon hats were so much in vogue that they were often chosen. Otherwise, a white hat is the prettiest possible choice for a youthful bride. The tailor-made travelling gown must be considered in the choice of a hat or bonnet, which would be of a quieter style, and one that would be afterwards the ordinary walking headgear. The bonnet and hats for this trousseau would cost from seven to eight pounds.

In the matter of gloves we are very fortunate, for it seems to be the fashion now to wear white for every toilette. I see some black worn, however, as well as grey and lavender, and for the evening Swede are still used. White are to be obtained as low as 1s. 11½d. a pair, and if you go to a well-known shop, they are very good, and can be cleaned two or three times, but they must be kept mended and the buttons sewn on. Of course, your evening gloves cost more, but with care they can be made to last. Of gloves you would need – one kind and another – perhaps two dozen; and you should select a supply of all those suitable for the various purposes as you may need – riding, driving, cycling, ordinary walking in the country, best, second best and evening, and when you have got them, please remember that you must see to their preservation and keeping, and find a suitable basket or box and a dry place to keep it in.

Veils, parasols, waterproof, *en tout cas,* umbrella, pocket-handkerchiefs, neck-ties, feather boa, and endless small lace additions to dress – all of them cost money. In fact, one of my recent brides, on going over these last things, declared that her trousseau consisted of sundries; and that, when she added the boots and shoes and stockings, she might as well have £25 at once. This was the girl I have always admired for her straightforward consideration of the subject, as she said that it was the only time in her life she was sure to have all she wanted – a regular outfit – and she meant to have it.

"If I were only one of the boys!" she said. "They are always having outfits for somewhere; if not Ashanti, it is India. And just see what they want. Bullock-trunks and theodolites; and if the War Office changes a button or a tag, there is a new uniform at once. Oh, *you* don't know about boys! Their millinery is *so* expensive!"

And after this outburst the boys assured me with groans that it *was* really dreadful.

(*To be concluded.*)

47

DORA DE BLAQUIÈRE, 'THE TROUSSEAU OF TO-DAY. PART II.'

The Girl's Own Paper, 23 December 1899, pp. 177–181

PART II.

So great a diversity of opinion exists as regards underclothing that I look upon this as the most difficult portion of my subject, for out of the half-dozen women to whom I have spoken on the subject, no two of them wore exactly the same things, and no two of them had been influenced quite in the same way. But there were points on which they *all* agreed. Indeed, if you consider the number of things which women do, you will see at once that there *must be* a diversity of opinion as well as a great difference as to necessities. The woman who travels or lives in the country will need a different selection from that of the woman who lives in London, goes into Society more or less, and at any rate has plenty of smart occasions where she likes to look like her neighbours. A lady who was noted for her epigrammatic sayings once remarked that women were divided into two classes, "those who wore clothes, and those who were dressed," a difference involving much experience and a great deal of money.

"Oh, she is quite a coat and skirt girl!" was a phrase used to me this year, which was explained as meaning that the person mentioned wore a coat and skirt every day and all days until she got into her evening dress for dinner at night. The intermediate part of the day, when people wore frivolous day-gowns, did not exist for her. In a kind of dialogue story which appeared in a recent magazine I found another definition. A girl is talking about her lover, and as he is poor, she says she supposes "she shall have to give up silk petticoats and her lovely lace and muslin flounced ones and take to plain white and those awful striped things if she marries him." Fortunately in the end that kind fate that presides over story-books steps in. An aged uncle dies, and the lover succeeds to a title and some thousands a year, and so the petticoat question is happily disposed of.

The lesson derived from these two episodes is that there is a certain kind of dress to which you must not aspire unless your dress allowance be very large, at least running into hundreds a year, and happy is the girl who is sensible enough to see and be guided by the fact in selecting her trousseau.

 DOI: 10.4324/9781315399980-58

In this century we have to chronicle numbers of inventions and improvements and a general advancement in knowledge, but we women have learned perhaps more than our brothers by the teachings of science as regards our clothing. We have been earnest listeners to the many writers and teachers who have spoken to us of the distribution of the weight of our clothes and the necessity for lightening it as far as possible, and that the same equal distribution must exist where their thickness is concerned, so that the body might be kept warm evenly; and we have learned the respective advantages of cotton, wool, and linen. Though the rage for woollen garments has, in a measure, passed off, we have learned from it more of our real requirements than we should have otherwise learned. A great good has followed, namely, that the subject of underclothing has come to be dealt with personally by each wearer, and hence the diversity of opinion which I mentioned above at the beginning of my article, for everyone seems to have certain requirements which she must meet. So we have every kind of mixture in the way of garments.

Years ago the underlinen formed the largest portion of the trousseau. It was prepared by dozens, and a small trousseau would have from a dozen to a dozen and a half of each article. In Germany the numbers seemed fabulous that were thought needful, and included the houselinen as well. Even in England I have known women who, after thirty years of wedded life, still possessed remains of their trousseau, marked with their maiden names. Even those immense outfits for India are greatly pruned down, to the saving of our purses and the amount of our luggage.

The reason for much of this reduction may be found in the universal adoption of woven undergarments of wool, silk, cotton, and thread, or any two of them mixed together. Their popularity seems unbounded, and the origin lay, in some degree, in the Jaeger craze; but certainly in hot countries and in others where the heat of the summer is great, the wearing of these woven silk, cotton, and thread vests was found far more satisfactory than cotton chemises next the skin. And so we find them used everywhere as well as in England, where, united with the knickerbockers, in either coloured cotton, alpaca, or serge, they seem to form the chief apparel. There is a diversity of opinion about the drawers of cotton and nainsook, but if the woven combinations be worn, they are very generally omitted, as not being at all needful.

The flannel petticoat is another garment about which there is some discussion, but not much, for it is very generally dismissed from all our wardrobes, as we do not in the least degree require its added weight, when we wear combinations of any kind; and it was the one inequality in our clothing, to avoid which we wear the drawers or combinations which certainly supply its place completely. It was the source of much over-heating when it was worn, especially to girls and children. Now, for the summer, we do better without it, and in the winter its place is occupied, where petticoats are concerned, by a silk, alpaca, or moirette skirt, lined with flannel, flannelette, or alpaca, the latter an excellent material for a lining. Otherwise, we use the ever-useful knickers, which can be purchased in any material, from cotton, drill, alpaca, and Oxford shirting, to serge, tweed, silk and satin. Galatea is a favourite material with many ladies for both knickers and combinations.

The subject of petticoat bodices, and indeed of all forms of stay and neck coverings, and other kindred garments, is a very large one, and as, to my mind, it is closely connected with the comfort of dress, I intend to give the fullest consideration to it, for they are very needful articles, even if you do wear combinations high to the neck. Many girls have left them off for this reason, judging that they were not wanted. The old-fashioned petticoat or slip-bodice, made of cotton, high to the neck, with a little edging at the neck, seems to have been succeeded by a woven stockingette bodice of much the same shape, in either cotton or silk, and these seem worn. There are also several forms of low necked bodices [. . .] which are popular, but I fear many girls do not wear anything, if they use, as I have said, the combination high to the neck. Of course, where the muslin or cambric blouse has a slip-bodice, it is not needed; but otherwise, nothing can exceed the ugliness of the appearance, and the untidiness also. The very best thing for ordinary wear is a tiny kind of Bolero jacket [. . .] made of muslin and lace, which meets with a button or ties in front over the chest, and is long enough to cover the stays to the waist at the back. Fine nainsook for ordinary day-wear, and a good strong muslin for best, with a Valenciennes edging round it, and an insertion too, if you like to go to the trouble and expense it will incur. With this little addition you will look quite presentable when you go to your dressmaker's. No one knows what some women look like when they go to be "tried on" at their long-suffering couturière's. The French call them *cache-corsets,* a far better name than ours, and much more descriptive.

[. . .] In silk, some of these are really beautiful, being made of pink, pale blue, or white, with insertions of lace, and trimmings of pink baby-ribbon. This, however, is also to be seen as an additional ornament to the fine *batiste* and cambric ones. In fact, there is no extent of luxury to which you cannot go, in the extravagance of your linen, and I must not omit in this article to illustrate and to tell you all about these beautiful things.

The underlinen of plain cotton, trimmed with embroidery, seems to be considered entirely English, while that made of nainsook is called in our London shops, French, and is invariably trimmed with edgings and insertions of more or less good imitation Valenciennes. Most trousseaux contain several sets of it, as well as of white or coloured silk; both of them are, naturally, more expensive and as lasting, and of course they suffer in the hands of our rather incompetent washerwomen. But they are fashionable, and so we must consider them in our trousseau [. . . .]

That great leaning towards over-trimming that makes dressing so expensive, is quite visible in this under-clothing, and every year makes it greater. To many a girl the trousseau is the one time in her life when her aspirations after the pretty and charming are satisfied, and if she have not a fair stock at her marriage of really best things, she will find it well-nigh impossible to get them afterwards.

Next to the petticoats of muslin come those of silk and others of a warmer kind. The silk ones can, I think, be made more cheaply at home; at least, I have seen a lovely accordion-pleated pink silk one, the flounce being deep and full, and the whole handsomely made at home for 28s., when it could not have been purchased for, at least, £2 10s. or perhaps more. The accordion-pleating was sent out to be done, and a good pattern was purchased, and those were the chief expenses beside the actual making.

The part of our underwear that shows least change, is, perhaps, the night-gown, which has altered little, save in the direction of increased luxury in material and trimming [. . . .]

A large proportion of our newest night-gowns of superior quality show a tendency to this style, and are either half-high or low; and in several instances I have seen short sleeves, with a sailor collar, opened in a pointed shape. The third model here is of white silk, with frills of silk, embroidered, and edged with real lace [. . . .]

A very general practice prevails, however, of making them of white satin, of a very large size, and edging them with deep lace. In England these ideal sachets have become a favourite wedding-present for those young ladies to make who are clever with their fingers, and do not desire to enter into any great expense [. . . .]

The dressing-gown may be bought so very cheaply that I should advise its being purchased[.] This opens the whole question of purchased or home-made, in connection with the trousseau; at least, as respects the underclothing part. In these days of out-of-door sports, of tennis and bicycling, and golf, every woman seems to have enough to do; and I hear it constantly stated that both useful and fancy work are no longer done by anyone. I am afraid it is a question which must be decided for themselves by each household, and so it must be left.

I have to conclude drawn up a list of the ordinary articles needed in a trousseau, which may be added to, or taken from, as you may choose. Since I concluded my first article, I have found, on inquiry, that some of the best West-End firms give estimates for trousseaux, and lists of items. One of the very leading houses has an estimate for a trousseau for fifty pounds, including the wedding-gown, wreath and veil, which are, I hear, put down at the cost of fifteen guineas. If I were getting a trousseau, I should write for an estimate for a price below what I wished, and then proceed to build my own edifice upon it.

The following would represent the ordinary requirements: –

Dust or driving-coat, smart cape, going-away gown, afternoon silk, or voile, tailor-made tweed, tailor-made cloth, tailor-made serge, one black satin, with three bodices, one cream satin wedding-gown, two evening-gowns (one lace), four pairs of evening shoes to match, four silk blouses, eight muslin and cotton shirts, four washing dresses, or skirts, two waistcoats, one bonnet, two best hats, one sailor hat, one felt hat, one waterproof, one golf cape, one *entout cas,* one umbrella, one parasol, one riding habit, etc., four pairs of house shoes, two pairs of walking shoes, two pairs of boots, one pair of riding boots, one opera cloak, two tea-gowns, six dressing jackets and wrappers, one dressing gown, handkerchiefs *ad lib.*, *Suède* and kid gloves, white and coloured, evening, driving, chamois, and dog-skin, four knickers, silk, satin, alpaca, or serge, four silk petticoats, four long-cloth petticoats, four muslin petticoats, two ordinary petticoats, six merino combinations, six woven silk, or cotton, twelve chemises, silk, cotton, or nainsook, twelve pairs of drawers, silk, cotton, or nainsook, four pairs of corsets, eight under-bodices, twelve pairs of stockings, black or tan thread, six pairs of cashmere or cotton stockings, two pairs of silk stockings, six cotton night-gowns, four best silk or nainsook night-gowns, four flannelette night-gowns.

This list would be a guide for the most moderate, as well as for an expensive trousseau.

2.2

Mourning attire

DOI: 10.4324/9781315399980-59

Mourning attire

This section focuses on the materiality and objects of Victorian mourning, and particularly its dress conventions, which even in the present day are well-known for their complexity and rigidity. Sonia A. Bedikian notes the period's 'prescribed set of stringent rules for mourning wear',[1] which amounted, in Lou Taylor's terms, to 'a cult that hardly anyone dared defy'.[2] But these rules were something of a paradox; as Judith Flanders writes, they were 'detailed, complex, and constantly changing',[3] as we also observe through our selection of sources, which are drawn from periodicals, literature and manuals. Indeed, despite their prescriptive nature, in practice, these sartorial codes were 'impossibly complicated',[4] sometimes even forming, as Rebecca N. Mitchell contends, 'a tangle of worrisome (and sometimes conflicting) social edicts'.[5]

These rules were also, according to Pat Jalland, 'applied most rigorously to widows', whose mourning costumes were the most complex, and the process the longest lasting.[6] In contrast to widowers, who, as Taylor observes, 'were able to remarry as soon as they pleased',[7] widows were bound by stricter conventions, as well as by changing fashions. Female mourning was a particularly complex and protracted process. In her detailed study of Victorian death culture, Jalland recounts how widows 'were required to wear full black mourning for two years [. . .] followed by nine months of dullish black silk, heavily trimmed with crape, and then three months when crape was discarded'.[8] Following this, '[w]idows were allowed to change into the colours of half-mourning, such as grey and lavender, black and white, for the final six months'.[9]

To complement this, our first two sources turn to hair jewellery, deemed 'one of the commonest ornaments of woman's wear'[10] by the narrator of Wilkie Collins' 1854 novel, *Hide and Seek*. And, when woven into bracelets, earrings, brooches, rings and necklaces, these locks of hair represented, as Deborah Lutz intimates, 'the most cherished of secular relics in nineteenth-century Britain'.[11] Our first selection is authored by a woman signing herself as 'Helen' in an 1846 issue of *The World of Fashion*, and presents an ambivalence at giving up an outward sign of remembering the dead. As a second-wife-to-be, the speaker contemplates her remarriage with the sad acceptance that she must cease wearing a locket containing a piece of her first husband's hair.[12] It is notable that this poem was published in a fashion journal, where bridal wear and trousseaux might be advertised in the same pages as mourning wear, confronting the reader with a polarity of life's events. It is also striking for the choice of author's pseudonym, which recalls one of the most famous women of antiquity, Helen of Troy, and her supposed lack of scruples in abandoning her living husband, Menelaus, for the sake of Paris. In our poem, the woman's ambivalence at figuratively 'giving up the ghost' of her former spouse (in favour of his living successor) is dramatised through the commemorative jewellery that she wears close to her heart.

Alongside its sentimental import, hair jewellery also became very fashionable, and intricate hair-work patterns were presented in both catalogues and books of patterns.[13] The simplest jewellery was usually formed of a lock of hair either contained within a locket or protected under the glass of a brooch, but hair was also worked into intricate plaited arrangements, or even landscapes or figures, as the selection of brooches held in the Wellcome Collection indicates. In this way, as Victoria Sherrow notes, such items were 'meant to serve both as a memento of the loved one and as a reminder that death is inevitable'.[14] However, the intimate nature of such designs also gave rise to anxiety about the commodification, and even 'industrialization', of such deeply personal and sentimentally affective materials, as both Ofek and Schaffer have argued.[15] As we also see in our selection on hair jewellery in our Handicraft section, women were encouraged to learn how to work hair into jewellery for themselves to avoid the '[risk of] its being lost, and the hair of some other person being substituted for it'.[16]

As Mitchell points out, while mourning was intended as an outward representation of the tumultuous inner emotions of the grieving process,[17] it also held considerable economic import, forming a significant part of the clothing market during the nineteenth century.[18] This was both encouraged and facilitated by establishments specifically geared towards mourning wear, most famously Jay's Mourning Emporium of Regent Street, London, founded in 1841.[19] Our next pair of sources focus on the commercial realisation of mourning in both the North of England and London. The extract from Elizabeth Gaskell's 1848 novel *Mary Barton* dramatises the relationships between social convention, mourning etiquette, financial resources and the dynamics between seamstress and mourner, while throwing into relief debates surrounding the expense of mourning, the outward signs of sorrow, and the notion that mourning preparations enabled those grieving to return to 'everyday' dynamics. In this extract, the dressmaker Mary Barton observes that funeral mourners 'cheered up wonderful while [she] was there, and [she] asked 'em for more directions than usual, that they might have something to talk over and fix about', adding that she 'left 'em [her] fashion-book (though it were two months' old) just a purpose'.[20] Here, Mary's talk illuminates the perceived importance of mourning as it facilitates the continuation of daily life, while also emphasising the ephemerality of fashion; even in this moment, she notes that the 'fashion-book' is already 'two months' old'.[21]

An example of the commercial realisation of mourning – perhaps as a resistance to the permanence of death and grief – is included here and derived from *The Lady's Newspaper* of 1850. Describing outfits available from another 'Mourning Warehouse', namely, that of a Mr Turner in Ludgate-hill, this article sets out an array of clothing suitable for mourning wear that is both socially appropriate and aligned with the latest fashions.

If the woman in mourning uses her clothing to perform an inflection of her identity, then etiquette columns might offer her the prompts to inhabit other emotional and intellectual roles that might be far from easy to master. Our next extract is taken from *The Ladies' Treasury*'s 'Conduct and Carriage' series, and sees the gentle and unassuming Gertrude Vernon being guided by her mother, following the unexpected death of her fiancé's brother.[22] Yet, Gertrude's natural wish to console is tempered by propriety: because they are yet to be married, her mother reminds her that she is 'in the eyes of the world neither a relative nor connection',[23] and it would therefore be deemed inappropriate to assume overfamiliarity. This is borne out in the discussions that follow, as Gertrude agonises not only about the words she writes to her fiancé, the nobly named Launcelot, but about details including the border of the writing paper upon which she notes her condolences.[24]

However, the calibration of adhering to social etiquettes, and even the enjoyment of displaying outward signs of mourning, informs both satirical and fashion writing of the time. Our next source, a short column from *Punch* of 1864, returns to the issue of so-called 'fashionable mourning' with characteristic cynicism. Yet while this concept might initially seem crass or insensitive, the social context for Victorian mourning meant that, in reality, many women would end up 'in mourning' for protracted periods of time. In this way, as Bedikian points out, '[s]tarting from the beginning of the nineteenth century, mourning wear became a regular part of a woman's wardrobe'.[25] Women were also encouraged to sport 'fashionable' versions of mourning dress, with ladies' magazines regularly featuring fashion plates depicting mourning 'versions' of contemporary clothing. The result, as Taylor notes, was that '[m]ourning clothes were made up in every nuance of style' throughout the period.[26] But while concessions were sometimes made towards a plainer iteration of modish dress following prescribed conventions, other costumes were far more 'ostentatious'; to use Mitchell's words, these included 'fancy mourning accessories and fashions of the very latest *mode*' such as 'jewelry and other baubles of bereavement'.[27] These sentiments are dramatically realised in our next selection from M. E. Braddon's 1864 novel *The Doctor's Wife*. In this extract, the jaded, Byronic-style poet Roland Lansdell returns home after the death of his mother and is inflamed with indignant fury to discover his aristocratic fiancée, his cousin Lady Gwendoline Pomphrey, entertaining friends wearing 'deep mourning; all a-glitter with bracelets and necklaces of shining jet'.[28]

For our next two sources, we return to hair jewellery and the stunning patterns contained within William Halford and Charles Young's *The Jewellers' Book of Patterns in Hairwork* (1864). Deborah Lutz aptly observes that, '[t]he relic makes apparent the terrible poignancy of the body becoming object',[29] drawing attention to the desire of the living to cling to materiality and, by implication, to what has been lost. This is rendered here in brooch and bracelet, items that invite the wearer 'to dwell in and with the moment of loss itself'.[30] Indeed, Marcia Pointon has read hair jewellery as 'a material figure for memory',[31] also arguing that 'the individual mourning jewel functions as a museum in miniature'.[32] Through intricate hair-work patterns, we might experience the craftsmanship and wearability of subjects-turned-objects, engendering a desire to both enliven and to remember. In this case, this is conveyed through ornamentation and the closeness of such material objects on a living, moving body.

We next move on to photography, a practise that has been extensively linked with, and theorised in relation to, death.[33] Our next chosen source is a photograph taken by Julia Margaret Cameron and described in the Wellcome Collection as '[a] young woman in mourning dress'. It is included here as an example of fashionable, jet-trimmed mourning wear, as well as of the photograph as a material object. To evoke Roland Barthes, the image captures the moment of 'a subject who feels he is becoming an object', and in doing so 'experience[s] a micro-version of death'.[34]

Our next two extracts address a mourning-related anxiety that also pervades our previous extract from Gaskell's *Mary Barton*, which concerns the significant financial outlay demanded by the social ritual of bereavement. This is reflected in our extract taken from *The Englishwoman's Domestic Magazine*, which outlines the expectations levied upon widows in particular, who might find themselves overwhelmed by a 'grief doubled by the burden of poverty and the miseries of a crippled income'.[35] The article extensively discusses the use of the fabric known as crape in mourning wear. The material could prove very cumbersome in hot weather, and to this end, the writer mentions the 'Albert Crape' as an honourable alternative. Our next extract, taken from the 1876 guidebook *How To Dress Well on A Shilling a Day* by the author known only as 'Sylvia', also outlines the expectations placed upon female mourners during this period, although it is sensitive to individual budgets and circumstances.[36] However, the following selection 'Mourning as a Fashion', taken from the *London Reader* of 1877, challenges the notion that mourning dress was required, drawing attention to issues of class and financial inequality.

A similar sentiment is expressed in our next selection, an extract from a short story published in *The Argosy* of 1885, in which a young servant's elegant restraint in mourning contrasts visibly with that of her more affluent employer. Indeed, it seems that refinement through education and personal taste have turned the lady's maid into a model for emulation. The orphaned maid's dress is described as 'rigorously plain' and 'of some soft black stuff that clung closely to her figure with the narrowest rim of white at throat and wrists'.[37] This style is also evoked in Edward Killingworth Johnson's drawing (included in our section on Wedding dress and accoutrements) and points at an understated profundity of mourning, which requires neither jet trimmings nor ornaments. Nonetheless, the protagonist finds herself amidst a narrative of theft and suspicion, her ladylike appearance both reinforcing and undermining her integrity. In this way, while mourning wear functions as a supposedly clear visual signifier, it also presents significant challenges of reading and interpretation.

Our penultimate source, an illustration of summer mourning dresses from an 1899 issue of *Hearth and Home*, offers suggestions for mourning in lighter fabrics. While the designs are still accentuated with crape trimmings and jet buttons, the alternative fabric, namely, the 'thin Henrietta cloth',[38] seems to gesture towards both practicality and ease for the wearer. Our final article, published in *Bow Bells* of 1894 and titled 'Fashion in Mourning', illustrates shifts in mourning fashions that enabled wearers to feel comfortable in their 'garb of grief'.[39] In this article, the writer observes that mourning customs had been changing for the past twenty years, again noting the move towards less weighty material. Nonetheless, they conclude with a concession to tradition, reminding readers that crape might still 'announce to friends and acquaintances and others that our loss is so recent and our grief so acute that we must be excused from ordinary conversation or bearing our part as usual in the social or business world'.[40]

Notes

1 S. A. Bedikian, 'The Death of Mourning: From Victorian Crepe to the Little Black Dress', *Omega*, 57(1), (2008), pp. 35–52 (p. 38).

2 L. Taylor, *Mourning Dress: A Costume and Social History* (Abingdon and New York: Routledge, 2009 [originally published in 1983 by George Allen & Unwin, Ltd]), p. 122.

3 J. Flanders, *The Victorian House: Domestic Life from Childbirth to Deathbed* (London: HarperCollins, 2003), p. 343.

4 Taylor, *Mourning Dress*, p. 133.

5 R. N. Mitchell (ed.), *Fashioning the Victorians: a Critical Sourcebook* (London: Bloomsbury Visual Arts, 2018), p. 147. As previously noted, Mitchell's anthology contains invaluable discussion of, and sources reflecting upon, Victorian mourning culture. See *Fashioning the Victorians*, pp. 145–150, and pp. 163–165. See also R. N. Mitchell, 'Death Becomes Her: On the Progressive Potential of Victorian Mourning', *Victorian Literature and Culture*, 41, (2013), pp. 595–620 (p. 598).

6 P. Jalland, *Death in the Victorian Family* (Oxford: Oxford University Press, 1996), p. 300. Here Jalland refers to mourning conventions of both the eighteenth and nineteenth centuries.

7 Taylor, *Mourning Dress*, p. 133.

8 Jalland, *Death in the Victorian Family*, p. 300. Crape (also spelled 'crepe') was a term that referred to a fabric specifically developed for mourning, which, according to Taylor, became 'a social necessity' for the Victorians and 'epitomises the middle-class Victorian widow' (*Mourning Dress*, pp. 223, 203). Taylor describes crape as 'a lightweight, semi-transparent, black silk fabric, crimped into three-dimensional patterns' that went through 'an elaborate process' to lend it 'an extraordinarily lugubrious and hard finish' (*Mourning Dress*, pp. 203–204). See Taylor, *Mourning Dress*, pp. 203–223, for a full account of its history, production and significance.

9 Jalland, *Death in the Victorian Family*, p. 300.

10 Cited in H. Hind, '"Pondering on that little circle of plaited hair": Hairwork, Materiality, and Identity in Wilkie Collins's Hide and Seek (1854)', *Wilkie Collins Journal*,

17, September 2019. Available at: https://wilkiecollinssociety.org/pondering-on-that-little-circle-of-plaited-hair-hairwork-materiality-and-identity-in-wilkie-collinss-hide-and-seek-1854/ [accessed 14 July 2021]. This article gives a full and illuminating discussion of hair jewellery in the novel; in this instance, the novel's narrator refers specifically to the 'Hair Bracelet'.

11 D. Lutz, *Relics of Death in Victorian Literature and Culture* (Cambridge: Cambridge University Press, 2015), p. 130. For further consideration of mourning jewellery, see C. Gere and J. Rudoe, *Jewellery in the Age of Queen Victoria: A Mirror to the World* (London: British Museum Press, 2010), pp. 119–127, and for the 'cult of hair work', pp. 162–167.

12 Helen, 'Lines on Giving Up Wearing a Locket of Hair', *The World of Fashion*, 1 February 1846, p. 33. Gere and Rudoe discuss the significance of the locket within Victorian culture; see *Jewellery in the Age of Queen Victoria*, pp. 162–164. They describe it as 'the epitome of "Victorian" jewellery types', noting that lockets habitually '[marked] great occasions both happy and sad' (p. 162). On the mixed emotions of remarriage, see J. Phegley, *Courtship and Marriage in Victorian England* (Santa Barbara, CA, Denver, CO, and Oxford, England: Praeger [an imprint of ABC-CLIO, LLC], 2012), p. 157. Jalland points out that remarriage was statistically more likely for widowers, and that widows' prospects were dependent upon youth and beauty (*Death in the Victorian Family*, pp. 253–255). See also K. Heath, *Aging by the Book: The Emergence of Midlife in Victorian Britain* (Albany, NY: State University of New York Press, 2009) for a consideration of nineteenth-century remarriage and also of the complex emotional dynamics specifically applied to widows (pp. 118–120).

13 For hair work as a commodity, a fad and a profession for women, see S. Yan, 'The Art of Working in Hair: Hair Jewellery and Ornamental Handiwork in Victorian Britain', *The Journal of Modern Craft*, 12(2), (2019), pp. 123–139. See also Jalland, *Death in the Victorian Family*, pp. 298–299.

14 V. Sherrow, *Encyclopedia of Hair: A Cultural History* (Westport, CT, and London: Greenwood Press, 2006), p. 260.

15 See G. Ofek, *Representations of Hair in Victorian Literature and Culture* (Farnham, Surrey, and Burlington, VT: Ashgate, 2009), p. 46; and T. Schaffer, *Novel Craft: Victorian Domestic Handicraft and Nineteenth-Century Fiction* (Oxford: Oxford University Press, 2011), pp. 148–149.

16 [Anon], *Elegant Arts for Ladies* (London: Ward and Lock, 1856), pp. 3–4.

17 Mitchell points out that '[m]ourning attire externalized grief, obviating the need to articulate what one was feeling' (*Fashioning the Victorians*, p. 147).

18 See Mitchell, *Fashioning the Victorians*, p. 147.

19 See Taylor, *Mourning Dress*, p. 191, and Mitchell, *Fashioning the Victorians*, p. 147.

20 [E. Gaskell], *Mary Barton: A Tale of Manchester Life*, 2 vols, 2nd edition (London: Chapman and Hall, 1848), Vol. I, p. 69.

21 Gaskell, *Mary Barton*, p. 69.

22 [Anon], 'Conduct and Carriage; Or, Rules to Guide a Young Lady on Points of Etiquette and Good Breeding in her Intercourse with the World', *The Ladies' Treasury* [November 1857], pp. 270–272. As we have noted, while the young woman in this extract is named Gertrude, there was some inconsistency within this series; in other instalments, she is called Geraldine.

23 [Anon], 'Conduct and Carriage', p. 270.

24 See Jalland, *Death in the Victorian Family*, pp. 307–317, for a discussion of the etiquette and social codes of the 'condolence letter'.

25 Bedikian, 'The Death of Mourning', p. 39.

26 Taylor, *Mourning Dress*, p. 149.

27 Mitchell, 'Death Becomes Her', p. 611.

28 [M. E. Braddon], *The Doctor's Wife*, 3 vols. (London: John Maxwell and Company, 1864), Vol. II, p. 16. Jet was widely worn within mourning during this period, particularly the material known as 'Whitby Jet', which is discussed in *The Englishwoman's Domestic Magazine* of 1868. See The Silkworm, 'Spinnings Out of Town', *The Englishwoman's Domestic Magazine*, April 1868, pp. 209–211. See also Taylor, *Mourning Dress*, pp. 233–237, and L. M. de Carvalho, F. M. Fernandes, M. de Fátima Nunes and J. Brigola, 'Whitby Jet Jewels in the Victorian Age', *Harvard Papers in Botany*, 18(2), 2013, pp. 133–136.

29 D. Lutz, 'The Dead Still Among Us: Victorian Secular Relics, Hair Jewelry, and Death Culture', *Victorian Literature and Culture*, 39, (2011), pp. 127–142 (p. 135).

30 Lutz, 'The Dead Still Among us', p. 128.

31 M. Pointon, 'Materializing Mourning: Hair, Jewellery and the Body', in M. Kwint, C. Breward and J. Aynsley (eds.), *Material Memories* (Oxford and New York: Berg, 1999), pp. 39–57 (p. 45). Quoted in Lutz, 'The Dead Still Among Us', p. 135. For further discussion of the emotional and cultural significance of mourning jewellery, see also M. Pointon, 'Wearing Memory: Mourning, Jewellery, and the Body' in G. Ecker (ed.), *Trauer Trager – Trauer Zeigen: Inszenierungen der Geschlecter* (Munich: Fink, 1999), pp. 65–81.

32 Pointon, 'Materializing Mourning', p. 42.

33 Although not included within our selections, another characteristically Victorian practise of the material culture of death was that of post-mortem photography. Photographic portraits of the dead, or group photographs with living relatives, were objects treasured by the bereaved. Nicola Bown has argued that 'the materiality of the post-mortem photograph [. . .] is central to its ability to console'. Focusing particularly on the photographs of deceased children, Bown argues that 'photographs themselves, as objects, invite touch, and become miniature substitutes for the dead child'. See N. Bown, 'Empty Hands and Precious Pictures: Post-mortem Portrait Photographs of Children', *Australasian Journal of Victorian Studies*, 14(2), (2009), pp. 8–24 (p. 9). For a wider discussion of post-mortem photography, see B. Bell, 'Taken from life: the unsettling art of death photography'. *BBC News*, 4 June 2016. Available at: https://www.bbc.co.uk/news/uk-england-36389581 [accessed 21 July 2021].

34 R. Barthes, *Camera Lucida: Reflections on Photography* (trans. by Richard Howard) (New York: Hill and Wang: 1980), p. 14.

35 The Silkworm, 'Spinnings in Town', *The Englishwoman's Domestic Magazine*, [November 1871], pp. 298–303 (p. 298).

36 Sylvia, 'Widow's Mourning', in *How To Dress Well on A Shilling a Day: A Lady's Guide to Home Dressmaking and Millinery* (London: Ward, Lock, & Tyler, 1876), pp. 87–93.

37 E. M. Davy, 'A Glove's Evidence', *The Argosy*, February 1885, pp. 154–163 (p. 156).

38 [Anon], 'Some Summer Dresses For Mourning Wear', *Hearth and Home,* 8 June 1899, p. 169.

39 [Anon], 'Fashion in Mourning', *Bow Bells*, 30 November 1894, pp. 545–546 (p. 545).

40 [Anon], 'Fashion in Mourning', p. 546.

48

HELEN, 'LINES ON GIVING UP WEARING A LOCKET OF HAIR.'

The World of Fashion, 1 February 1846, p. 33

Go forth, thou last memento, go,
  Of one still dear to this sad heart;
Long hast thou been its shield from woe,
  And bitter 'tis from thee to part.

Go forth, go forth – no more repose
  Where once I fondly hoped that thou
Would stay until life's latest close –
  Go – it were wrong to wear thee now.

Adieu! then fondly cherish'd guest,
  Another's bride must keep thee not;
But tho' thou art absent from my breast,
  Thy donor ne'er can be forgot.

HELEN.

DOI: 10.4324/9781315399980-60

49

IMAGE: MOURNING BROOCHES CONTAINING THE HAIR OF A DECEASED RELATIVE

 DOI: 10.4324/9781315399980-61

50

[ELIZABETH GASKELL], *MARY BARTON: A TALE OF MANCHESTER LIFE.*

2 vols., 2nd edition (London: Chapman and Hall, 1848), Vol. I, pp. 66–70.

Mary hurried home one evening, just as daylight was fading, from Miss Simmonds', with her shawl held up to her mouth, and her head bent as if in deprecation of the meeting wind. So she did not perceive Margaret till she was close upon her at the very turning into the court.

"Bless me, Margaret! is that you? Where are you bound to?"

"To nowhere but your own house (that is, if you'll take me in). I've a job of work to finish to-night; mourning, as must be in time for the funeral to-morrow; and grandfather has been out moss-hunting, and will not be home till late."

"Oh, how charming it will be. I'll help you if you're backward. Have you much to do?"

"Yes, I only got the order yesterday at noon; and there's three girls beside the mother; and what with trying on and matching the stuff (for there was not enough in the piece they chose first), I'm above a bit behindhand. I've the skirts all to make; I kept that work till candlelight; and the sleeves, to say nothing of little bits to the bodies; for the missis is very particular, and I could scarce keep from smiling while they were crying so, really taking on sadly I'm sure, to hear first one and then t'other clear up to notice the sit of her gown. They weren't to be misfits I promise you, though they were in such trouble."

"Well, Margaret, you're right welcome, as you know, and I'll sit down and help you with pleasure, though I was tired enough of sewing to-night at Miss Simmonds'."

By this time Mary had broken up the raking coal, and lighted her candle; and Margaret settled herself to her work on one side of the table, while her friend hurried over her tea at the other. The things were then lifted *en masse* to the dresser; and dusting her side of the table with the apron she always wore at home, Mary took up some breadths and began to run them together."

"Who's it all for, for if you told me I've forgotten?"

DOI: 10.4324/9781315399980-62

"Why for Mrs. Ogden as keeps the greengrocer's shop in Oxford Road. Her husband drank himself to death, and though she cried over him and his ways all the time he was alive, she's fretted sadly for him now he's dead."

"Has he left her much to go upon?" asked Mary, examining the texture of the dress. "This is beautifully fine soft bombazine."

"No, I'm much afeard there's but little, and there's several young children, besides the three Miss Ogdens."

"I should have thought girls like them would ha' made their own gowns," observed Mary.

"So I dare say they do, many a one, but now they seem all so busy getting ready for the funeral; for it's to be quite a grand affair, well-nigh twenty people to breakfast, as one of the little ones told me; the little thing seemed to like the fuss, and I do believe it comforted poor Mrs. Ogden to make all the piece o' work. Such a smell of ham boiling and fowls roasting while I waited in the kitchen; it seemed more like a wedding nor* a funeral. They said she'd spend a matter o' sixty pound on th' burial."

"I thought you said she was but badly off," said Mary.

"Ay, I know she's asked for credit at several places, saying her husband laid hands on every farthing he could get for drink. But th' undertakers urge her on you see, and tell her this thing's usual, and that thing's only a common mark of respect, and that every body has t'other thing, till the poor woman has no will o' her own. I dare say, too, her heart strikes her (it always does when a person's gone) for many a word and many a slighting deed to him, who's stiff and cold; and she thinks to make up matters, as it were, by a grand funeral though she and all her children, too, may have to pinch many a year to pay the expenses, if ever they pay them at all."

"This mourning, too, will cost a pretty penny," said Mary. "I often wonder why folks wear mourning; it's not pretty or becoming; and it costs a deal of money just when people can spare it least; and if what the Bible tells us be true, we ought not to be sorry when a friend, who's been good, goes to his rest; and as for a bad man, one's glad enough to get shut* on him. I cannot see what good comes out o' wearing mourning."

"I'll tell you what I think th' fancy was sent for (Old Alice calls every thing 'sent for,' and I believe she's right). It does do good, thought not as much as it costs, that I do believe, in setting people (as is cast down by sorrow and feels themselves unable to settle to any thing but crying) something to do. Why now I told you how they were grieving; for, perhaps, he was a kind husband and father, in his thoughtless way, when he wasn't in liquor. But they cheered up wonderful while I was there, and I asked 'em for more directions than usual, that they might have something to talk over and fix about; and I left 'em my fashion-book (though it were two months' old) just a purpose."

"I don't think every one would grieve a that way. Old Alice wouldn't."

"Old Alice is one in a thousand. I doubt, too, if she would fret much, however sorry she might be. She would say it were sent, and fall to trying to find out what good it were to do. Every sorrow in her mind is sent for good. Did I ever tell you, Mary, what she said one day when she found me taking on about something?"

"No, do tell me. What were you fretting about, first place?"

"I can't tell you just now; perhaps I may sometime."

"When?"

"Perhaps this very evening, if it rises in my heart; perhaps never. It's a fear that sometimes I can't abide to think about, and sometimes I don't like to think on any thing else. Well, I was fretting about this fear, and Alice comes in for something, and finds me crying. I would not tell her no more than I would you, Mary; so she says, 'Well, dear, you must mind this, when you're going to fret and be low about any thing. 'An anxious mind is never a holy mind.' Oh, Mary, I have so often checked my grumbling sin' she said that."

The weary sound of stitching was the only sound heard for a little while, till Mary inquired, "Do you expect to get paid for this mourning?"

"Why I do not much think I shall. I've thought it over once or twice, and I mean to bring myself to think I shan't, and to like to do it as my bit towards comforting them. I don't think they can pay, and yet they're just the sort of folk to have their minds easier for wearing mourning. There's only one thing I dislike making black for, it does so hurt the eyes."

* "Nor," generally used in Lancashire for "than."
"They had lever sleep *nor* be in laundery." — *Dunbar*.

* "Shut," quit.

51

[ANON], 'THE PARIS AND LONDON FASHIONS.'

The Lady's Newspaper,
9 November 1850, p. 260

Figure 51.1

DOI: 10.4324/9781315399980-63

Figure 51.2 Promenade Costume.

DESCRIPTION OF THE ENGRAVINGS.

Figure 51.1. *Mourning Costume for the Carriage or Promenade,* furnished from Mr. Turner's Mourning Warehouse, 16 and 17, Ludgate-hill. – The cloak shown in this figure is one of the novelties of the present season. It is composed of fine black cloth, and the cape, the skirt of the cloak, and ends of the sleeves, are edged with the new vicugna trimming of a beautiful black, above which there is a row of Parisian figured braid, of a very elegant pattern. The dress worn with this cloak is composed of a newly-introduced material called Utrecht, a most successful imitation of the celebrated Utrecht velvet, formerly so much in favour. The ground of this new material is grey alpaca, and the pattern, consisting of wreaths of flowers and foliage in a material resembling velvet, is woven in. The bonnet shown in our figure is of black therry velvet, having on one side a bow of the same material, and on the other side a long craped feather. Under-trimming white lisse and black bead flowers. Black kid gloves, and white book-muslin under-sleeves, consisting of a single puff of moderate size.

Figure 51.2. *Promenade Costume.* – Dress of black satin turque, the front ornamented with soutache, in a rich arabesque pattern. The corsage is high to the throat, close in front, where it is ornamented with soutache. The sleeves are open at the ends, and trimmed in corresponding style. White muslin under-sleeves, gathered at the wrists on bands of needlework. Mantelet of dark blue velvet, edged with braid of the same colour, set on in a lozenge pattern. Bonnet composed of folds of black satin and rows of black lace disposed alternately. Under-trimming white tulle and small pink flowers.

GENERAL OBSERVATIONS ON FASHION AND DRESS.

To families wearing mourning we feel that we are rendering no unimportant act of service by directing their attention to Mr. Robert Turner's warehouse, of which the address is given above (see description of Figure 51.1). A recent inspection of some of the principal articles of mourning costume in this well-arranged establishment enables us to bear testimony to the taste and variety of the selections, as well as the very reasonable rate of prices. We may here briefly mention a few of the articles which particularly attracted our attention.

In addition to a vast variety of cloaks in black silk and cloth, suited to deep mourning, we observed some elegant novelties adapted to a lighter style of mourning costume. These were cloaks of grey and lavender-coloured cloth, in a variety of shades, all exquisitely ornamented with borderings of black braid in rich and fanciful arabesque designs. On some, the braid is of the same colour as the cloth itself, thus producing a more quiet though less showy effect. They are lined with quilted silk of the colour of the cloth.

Among the bonnets suited to slight mourning we remarked one of grey satin, covered with black stamped velvet. On one side a small rosette of grey satin and stamped velvet, and on the other a blackcock's plume. The under-trimming of this elegant bonnet consisted of white lisse and black bead flowers, and the strings were of a beautiful figured ribbon, grey, edged with black.

In Mr. Turner's show-rooms there will likewise be found a tasteful selection of mourning jewellery, consisting of jet brooches, bracelets, buckles, &c., in all the newest designs.

The subjoined observations relate only to coloured costume. – The newest bonnets are very fully trimmed; the trimmings consisting for the most part of ruches of lace, velvet foliage, bows of ribbon and velvet, or feathers. A pretty style of inside trimming consists of bows of ribbon of different shades of one colour; for example, if green ribbon be selected, the bows pass in gradation from a dark to a pale tint; or, if lilac ribbon be employed, the tint graduates from deep violet to pale lilac. Bows of ribbon made up with a small white or pink rosebud in the centre, or intermingled with white tulle or black lace, are not unfrequently used as inside trimmings. Foliage interspersed with loops of ribbon may be named as another variety. Many new velvet bonnets have appeared since our last. Among those most conspicuous for novelty and elegance we may notice one of garnet-coloured velvet, trimmed with black lace, the cap being of white tulle, ornamented with variegated heartsease. Another is a drawn bonnet of green velvet, the runnings wide, and the under-trimming tulle and flowers. Satin bonnets of dark hues are lined with white, or with satin of some bright tint, as pink, blue, &c. They may be trimmed with velvet foliage of the same colour as the bonnet, or with bows of ribbon and velvet in tints harmonizing with the colour of the bonnet. We have seen a green satin bonnet ornamented with a water lily, the foliage being intermingled with long, narrow leaves, made of velvet of different shades of green. The effect of this variety of colour in the flower is very pretty. The inside trimming of this bonnet consisted of light green velvet foliage, intermingled with quillings of white and green tulle. The new felt bonnets are among the novelties suited to plain outdoor dress. Owing to improvements in the manufacture of felt, bonnets of that material are made in a variety of colours, and they have a gloss resembling silk or velvet. We have observed some of dark blue, green, and other colours, trimmed with velvet the colour of the felt. A black bonnet of this description intended for mourning has been trimmed with a black cassowary feather and black velvet ribbon.

Isly green is a favourite colour in Paris for dresses as well as for bonnets. One of the dresses recently made by a fashionable Parisian milliner, to be included in a bridal trousseau, is composed of moire antique. The colour is Isly green, broché green and white. The corsage is low, in the Louis Quinze style, and the dress is trimmed with lace.

52

[ANON], 'CONDUCT AND CARRIAGE; OR, RULES TO GUIDE A YOUNG LADY ON POINTS OF ETIQUETTE AND GOOD BREEDING IN HER INTERCOURSE WITH THE WORLD.'

The Ladies' Treasury [November 1857], p. 270

SCENE. – *"The Elms," near Windsor.* GERTRUDE *at her desk.* MRS. VERNON *at work. Both looking very sorrowful.*

GER. Oh, mamma, I did not think a letter of condolence was so hard to write. I do not know what to say to dear Launcelot – he so loved his brother! and every word with which I wish to comfort him, seems to me so likely to renew his grief.

MRS. V. Yes, that is too often the case with letters, miscalled letters of condolence. People often, to show their own eloquence or faith, harrow up the feelings of the bereaved, and dwell on the sufferings or virtues of the dear departed, until what was professedly meant to console, rouses grief to anguish and heightens regret into despair!

GER. How *shall* I write to him? – perhaps I had better not write at all just yet.

MRS. V. That would *not* be like his own warm-hearted, sympathising Gertrude, his bride elect; the woman who, but for this sudden and terrible misfortune, would now be the wife of his bosom. You would have comforted him *then;* surely you would not be silent now that he is doubly bereaved?

GER. No, mamma; but I fear if I write all I feel I shall say more than I ought. If I *were* Launcelot's wife, I could not say too much.

MRS. V. Write from the depths of your own pure, affectionate heart, my love. It would be as impossible for the moon to scorch the night-blowing Cereus, as for you to say one word that maiden dignity could disown.

GER. Then I shall say all I think and feel, mamma; and above all, how much I regret that I have not as yet the blessed privilege of sharing his grief – wiping away his tears, and wearing outwardly that mourning which my heart and spirit must wear while *he* mourns so deeply.

DOI: 10.4324/9781315399980-64

MRS. V. Right, my love. If I mistake not, it is in dwelling on your love, and showing him what he has left, you will comfort him most efficiently for what he has lost.

GER. Would it be wrong to beg him to come and stay with us as soon as he can, mamma?

MRS. V. It would be rather inconsiderate, my dear, while his mother and sisters are in the first helpless agony of bereavement. As your marriage must now be for some time postponed, it would be better and kinder, when Lady and the Misses Lisburn are a little recovered, for you to visit them. But that suggestion must not come from us, dearest. All you can do now is to say, that if there is anything you can do, in any way, to comfort Launcelot, or his mother and sisters, you would find the best solace to your own sorrow in doing it.

GER. Would it be wrong for me to write on black-edged paper, mamma? There is plenty in your desk, very deep.

MRS. V. It is not customary – since, though nearer to Launcelot's heart than any one else, you are in the eyes of the world neither a relative nor connection. I have known engaged women, on the death of their intended, go into widow's weeds; but it was always thought romantic, affected, and even indelicate.

GER. Old Mrs. Brown did, mamma. When she was Miss Skipworth she was engaged to a Mr. Hieover (a hunting farmer); he was thrown on his head, and killed; and she went into the deepest widow's weeds. Indeed, it was in her garb of woe she made a conquest of Mr. Brown, who, being a widower, wished to marry a widow, and tried to break it off (Bertha says) when he found his mistake; but her mother threatened him with an action for breach of promise.

MRS. V. No wonder Bertha is what she is, brought up by a woman who seems, not like many others,

"To know the right, and yet the wrong pursue,"

but not to have, or ever to have had, the least idea of what is right or proper.

GER. Ah! mamma, had Bertha been blest, as I am, with a mother so thoroughly at once the Christian and the lady, she would not be constantly offending the man she loves, and running the risk of a separation in a vain attempt to realise her mother's schemes for managing and ruling him.

MRS. V. As I have said before, my darling Gertrude, the three graces of life are – good taste, good feeling, and good temper; and if woman is adorned by them, she is sure to please, and rule, as much as it is wise or right for her to rule.

GER. But how can she insure the attendance of those three graces, mamma?

MRS. V. Any woman who "searches the Scriptures," and takes them and their precepts as her rule and guide, will become all that is loveliest in a

Christian woman, nay, a Christian lady. How dignified, sweet, and admirable a wife would that woman be who formed herself merely by the inspired teaching of the great apostle of the Gentiles; but I interrupt you, my love. Write your letter, and then we will talk a little more.

GER. Yes, dearest mamma. I have several questions to put to you from Bertha, and some things I want to know myself.

MRS. V. *continues her work.*

GER. (*after writing for some time*) There, dear mamma, now I have done. That letter has cost me many tears; but I hope it will dry up some of Launcelot's. Surely I may seal it with black. It goes so much against my feelings to send to that house of deep mourning a letter looking like those I wrote when hope and joy were dwellers there.

MRS. V. Well, my love, I think you may indulge your sympathy and affection so far. Your using black wax implies that you mourn, but not (as deeply as black-edged paper would do) that you mourn as if you *were* the near relation you would be were you Launcelot's wife, and which it would be like forestalling a privilege to affect at present.

GER. But even Sir Thomas Lawrence, mamma, as we read in that interesting memoir of the modern Vandyck, in Cassell's "Art Treasures," after the death of Miss Siddons (to whom he was engaged), always used black wax, and even wore black; and he was not merely a well-bred man, but a perfect courtier; and if Launcelot should come home, or I should go to visit his mother at the Priory, I cannot wear white or bright colours, mamma, when he and his family are in the deepest mourning.

MRS. V. Nor should I wish you to do so, my love. It would be in worse taste than your going into mourning too. There is in all things a happy medium, a golden mean. Black silk, dark purple, sober gray, and lavender; from these you should choose what is commonly called "complimentary mourning." You remember that coxcomb at "Crocodile's," in —— Street, who showed us up into "The Mitigated Affliction Department?" Well, there were dresses there exactly suited, not to your feelings, which, I know, are deeply affected by Launcelot's grief, but to the position – the delicate position in which you are placed with regard to the family of your intended.

53

[ANON], 'FANCY BLACK.'

Punch, 30 April 1864, p. 175

ADVERTISED in a contemporary, amidst a lot of other melancholy millinery, we find, "Articles de Fantaisie Pour Deuil."

Only fancy articles of fancy for mourning! Fancy-mourning; fancy-weeds: how fanciful! And what are they? – "Chemisettes, Tulle Sleeves, Berthes, Canzons, Jupons, Robes de Chambres, Garnitures des Robes," &c. What sadly sweet things in mourning! Elegance in sables! The idea of fancy mourning dress suggests that of a fancy mourning dress ball. There is a "Lord Lovel Quadrille," which might be danced on such an occasion, for one thing, and some dance-musical genius might compose a "Coffin Quadrille" for another; also a "Shroud Waltz," a "Knell Polka," and a Cotillon, which might be called "The Cemetery." To descend from the fashionable sphere of dancing to the plebeian, the more vivacious of the gay and festive mourners, attired in *articles de fantaisie pour deuil,* might trip it on the light fantastic toe to an "Undertaker's Hornpipe" or a "Mute's Jig." Fancy mourning, perhaps, is meant to denote the grief of the heirs of rich old gentlemen and ladies.

DOI: 10.4324/9781315399980-65

54

[M. E. BRADDON], 'OH, MY COUSIN, SHALLOW HEARTED!'

The Doctor's Wife, 3 vols. (London: John Maxwell and Company, 1864), Vol. II, pp. 16–17

At the end of his second session Roland went abroad with his dying mother. He came back alone, six weeks after his mother's death, and went straight to Gwendoline for consolation. He found her in deep mourning; all a-glitter with bracelets and necklaces of shining jet; looking very fair and stately in her trailing black robes; but he found her drawing-room filled with callers, and he left her wounded and angry. He thought her so much a part of himself, that he had expected to find her grief equal to his own. He went to her again, in a passionate outbreak of grief and anger; told her that she was cold-hearted and ungrateful, and that she had never loved the aunt who had been almost a mother to her. Lady Gwendoline was the last woman in the world to submit to any such reproof. She was astounded by her lover's temerity.

"I loved my aunt very dearly, Mr. Lansdell," she said; "so dearly that I could endure a great deal for her sake; but I can *not* endure the insolence of her son."

And then the Earl of Ruysdale's daughter swept out of the room, leaving her cousin standing alone in a sunlit window, with the spring breezes blowing in upon him, and the shrill voice of a woman crying primroses sounding in the street below.

DOI: 10.4324/9781315399980-66

55

IMAGE: WILLIAM HALFORD & CHARLES YOUNG, MANUFACTURING JEWELLERS, *THE JEWELLERS' BOOK OF PATTERNS IN HAIR WORK: CONTAINING A GREAT VARIETY OF COPPER-PLATE ENGRAVINGS OF DEVICES AND PATTERNS IN HAIR; SUITABLE FOR MOURNING JEWELLERY, BROOCHES, RINGS, GUARDS, ALBERTS, NECKLETS, LOCKETS, BRACELETS, MINIATURES, STUDS, LINKS, EARRINGS, &C., &C., &C.*

(London: 1864), pp. 28, 39

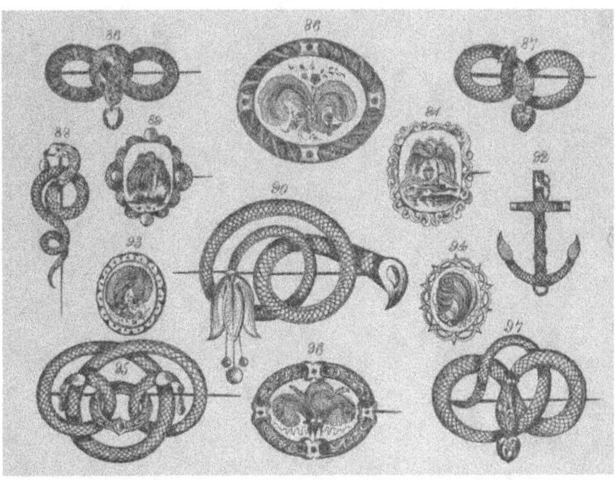

DOI: 10.4324/9781315399980-67

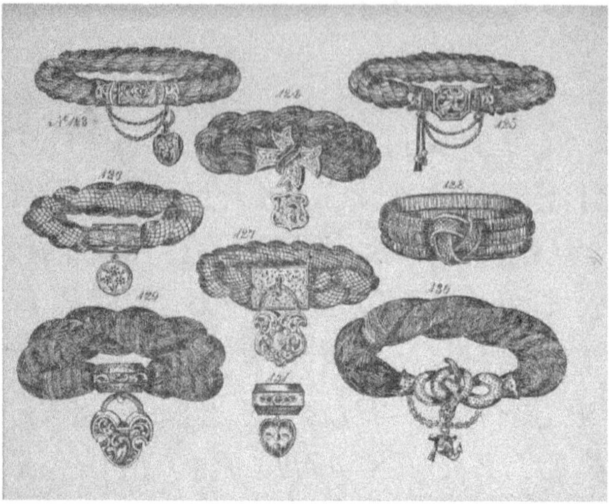

56

IMAGE: PHOTOGRAPH BY JULIA MARGARET CAMERON, 'A YOUNG WOMAN IN MOURNING DRESS', 1868/1872

Credit: Wellcome Collection.
Public Domain Mark

DOI: 10.4324/9781315399980-68

57

THE SILKWORM, 'SPINNINGS IN TOWN.'

The Englishwoman's Domestic Magazine, [November 1871], pp. 298–299

"O very gloomy is the house of woe,
  When tears are falling while the bell is knelling,
With all the dark solemnities that show
  That Death is in the dwelling.

"O, very, very dreary is the room
  When love, domestic love, no longer nestles,
But, smitten by the common stroke of doom,
  The corpse lies on the trestles!"

HOOD's *Haunted House*.

[. . . .]

Crape – the name alone is saddening; it is associated with darkened rooms, with suppressed sobs, with whispered questions, and with all

"The dark solemnities that show
That Death is in the dwelling."

Crape, too, is very costly, and by a refinement of cruelty, the goddess Fashion demands that her most-to-be-pitied victim should appear, after the saddest of all losses, smothered in this garb of woe. Few women have the courage to resist the words "it is usual for widows," and rather than show "disrespect" to the departed, will bear, through burning July suns, the intense heat of paramatta covered with double crape. Again, there are circumstances when this "depth" of mourning is rendered as overwhelming, on the score of economy, as ever July sun can make it, and many a night's rest is spoiled by anxious thoughts of the "mourning bill."

It is sad indeed when the heaviest of losses is still further embittered by pecuniary embarrassments, when the widow and the fatherless cannot even mourn for their dead without incurring heavy debt, and when day after day drags its

DOI: 10.4324/9781315399980-69

slow length along, and there is still no prospect of freedom from the harassing cares of debt, and from the miseries consequent upon having too little of the precious metal.

> "Vulgar cares,
> That belong to common household affairs,
> Nocturnal annoyances such as theirs,
> Who lie with a shrewd surmising,
> That while they are couchant (a bitter cup),
> Their bread and butter, on getting up,
> And the coals, confound them, are rising."

Truly Hood wrote from bitter experience of the griefs and sorrows of the poor – of sorrow enhanced and of grief doubled by the burden of poverty and the miseries of a crippled income. It is to those who are not at liberty to spend a great deal upon their mourning that I would recommend the use of the Albert crape, which is sold at less than half the price of ordinary crape, and which exactly resembles that desideratum of deep mourning. Albert crape is of deep rich black, with the exact "pattern" of crape, forming regular and handsome "crinkles," and producing precisely the effect of *rich, handsome crape*. Now, of course we all welcome any material which looks precisely the same when made up as does a fabric more than double its cost; but how about the *wearing qualities?* for we all know that no economy is effected unless a material wears at least as well as the fabric it replaces. As I mentioned some months ago, I have made trial of this crape, although in a different manner to that test to which I intended subjecting the Albert crape. Four months' hard wear has been given to this crape; it has been worn in and out of the house, on the edge of a dress (always a trying position for crape), on the bodice, mantle, and bonnet in daily wear of two intimate friends; but the coquettish little apron which I designed to wear myself, and thus personally try the Albert crape, remains in pristine crispness; for, to confess the truth, my boys like pretty colours and lace trimmings on "mamma's aprons," and the crape was vetoed at once; so I must plead apologies for non-performance, and murmur *mea culpa,* from behind the curly heads that are always pretty close to the apron aforesaid. But, nevertheless, I can fully confirm the excellence of the wear of this crape, for I have constantly remarked its freshness, and believe it wears even better than the finer kinds of ordinary crape, and equally as well as coarse crape. The Albert crape trims admirably, and whether for folds, tucks, or fancy trimming, is perfectly satisfactory in all respects. The Albert crape is of so deep a blue-black, that, contrasted with other crapes, it makes the very best among them look brown. The Albert crape, therefore, exactly *matches* mourning materials, paramatta, merino, &c. It is impossible to over-estimate the importance of matching the crape with the dress fabric, as brown-tinted dresses not only turn rusty after a few weeks' wear, but cause the dress to look blue instead of black, a most undesirable effect in deep mourning.

The period of mourning varies with situation and circumstances. For a parent, the usual period of mourning is eighteen months, twelve of which are passed in deep crape and six in lighter mourning. A widow should mourn in crape for eighteen months, and for six months longer in black without crape. For brother or sister we mourn one year; for uncle and aunt, six months; for other relatives or complimentary mourning, six weeks; for children six months and twelve months, according to their age. Widowers mourn eighteen months only, being six months less than widows' mourning.

Mourning materials are crape, paramatta, lustreless silk, grenadine, cashmere, cloth, tweed, alpacas, lustres, merino, lisse, crêpe de chine, net, muslin, linen, jet, ivory, furs; astracan is the only mourning fur, but seal and otter fur may be worn.

58

SYLVIA, 'ON THE ETIQUETTE OF MOURNING.'

How To Dress Well On A Shilling a Day: A Ladies' Guide to Home Dressmaking and Millinery (London: Ward, Lock, & Tyler, 1876), pp. 87–93

It is of course impossible to draw up any set of rules on this subject that shall be absolutely applicable to all cases; for instance, it is quite possible to live on terms of such intimacy with a cousin that the customary period of mourning would be quite inadequate to symbolize the grief experienced for the loss. I can, therefore, only speak generally, and indicate the terms and degrees of mourning which are sanctioned by custom as being usual and sufficient, leaving individuals to adapt them to their own circumstances as they may think best. Also, although I shall of course indicate the amount of crape usually worn, I would be by no means understood as laying down an arbitrary and incontrovertible law. In many households mourning is a very serious expense, and while wishing to indicate to those desirous of following strict etiquette the depth of mourning considered correct by society, I am equally anxious to avoid leading those to whom economy is an object into needless expense. It was well observed in a letter to one of the newspapers on the subject of the "Mourning Reform Association," that "the expense of mourning is much exaggerated, and is very far from being necessarily so great as those who dislike it would fain have the world believe; but it would surely be more sensible if those who cannot afford it would give up the notion which seems to prevail that in mourning, though at no other time, must they wear the magnificent attire suitable to the very rich, and were to use their common sense and discretion as they would about ordinary clothes; a plain black dress is by no means inordinately costly." An article in the *World* on the same subject, entitled "Mitigated Mourning," published in June, 1875, is also well worthy of perusal, as it treats the matter in an extremely sensible light.

The first degree of mourning is of course that of a widow; the dress is always of paramatta entirely covered with crape to within an inch or two of the waist, the crape being in one piece, not in separate tucks, for the first nine months. If after this period it requires renewing, it may be put on in two deep tucks, with about

DOI: 10.4324/9781315399980-70

an inch space between them, but must come up as high on the skirt as before. The sleeves are tight to the arm, the body entirely covered with crape, and deep lawn cuffs and collar are worn. The cap was formerly constructed so as almost entirely to conceal the hair and to fasten under the chin; but this severe style is now considerably mitigated, and many different shapes are worn, the Marie Stuart, so familiar to us in the portraits of her Majesty, being the most general. It must be worn for a year and a day. The outdoor dress has a jacket or mantle of paramatta very heavily trimmed with crape; neither fur nor velvet can be worn. The bonnet is entirely crape, with a widow's cap tacked inside it, and with a crape veil with a deep hem. This constitutes the dress for the first twelve months. After that time has expired, silk, heavily trimmed with crape, may be worn for six months, after which the crape can be considerably lessened, and jet trimmings used to brighten the toilette. After nine months, plain black, with jet ornaments, is permissible; and after two years mourning may be laid aside, though it is in much better taste to wear half-mourning for at least six months more. Many widows never put on colours again. Of course during the first year of mourning a widow can neither accept invitations nor frequent places of public amusement; a widow's cap in such scenes has a most incongruous appearance. After the year has elapsed she may, if so inclined, gradually return to society.

The next degree of mourning is that of a child for a parent or a parent for a child, which are, of course, identical in degree. The period of mourning is twelve months, and for the first three paramatta, heavily trimmed with crape, and with lawn collars and cuffs, is worn. Of course with crape no jewellery of any kind is admissible. Earrings, brooch, and watch-chain must all be of jet. A crape bonnet with jet ornament or a black feather. No fur can be worn excepting sealskin, and even that is best avoided for the first three months. After that time silk may be worn with rather less crape, but the same collars and cuffs of lawn. After six months, crape is laid aside, and plain black, still with black ornaments and black gloves, worn for two months, after which plain gold or silver, diamonds, pearls, and grey gloves, sewn with black, are correct. After nine months, half-mourning is permissible. Society must be entirely relinquished for at least two months, and may then be gradually resumed; but it is better taste to abstain from balls while crape, the symbol of really deep mourning, is compulsory.

A wife wears mourning for her husband's parents, or any of his other relatives, precisely as she would for her own. Husband and wife are one, therefore the same mourning in every particular would be worn for a husband's sister as for the sister herself. The orthodox period of mourning for brother or sister is six months, of which three must be in crape, two in black, and one in half-mourning; for grandparents nine months – three in crape, three in black, three in half-mourning. Three months for an uncle or aunt, nephew or niece. No crape is requisite, but invitations should be declined until after the funeral. Two months are sufficient for a great uncle or aunt. For first cousins the period is six weeks, three of which may be slight, and three weeks are sufficient for a second cousin, though, indeed, mourning is very frequently omitted altogether for so distant a relation, unless there has been considerable personal intimacy. These cases, I think, exhaust the list of absolute relationship. There are, however, some cases where complimentary mourning is usual. Such is the case of a mother whose married son or daughter loses his or her father or mother-in-law, when the mother should wear the complimentary mourning of black, without crape, for six weeks, and slight mourning for six more. It is also customary, when a man has married a second time, for the second wife to wear slight mourning for three months on the death of either of the parents of the first wife. This is not compulsory, but it is usual, more especially if the first wife has left any children. The second wife is not expected to mourn for any other member of her predecessor's family.

It is a fact which should never be lost sight of that mourning is not only the outward sign of our own grief for the loss of relatives, but also a tribute of respectful sympathy with the sorrow of those nearer and dearer to them than we ourselves may chance to be. The thought of this would often check the murmur so frequently heard at "that tiresome mourning," and the reflection that the premature abandonment of the outward signs of woe may be regarded by the children or other near relatives of the deceased as an act of disrespect to their memory, and may consequently wound them bitterly, would surely enable any one not absolutely heartless or frivolous to endure with equanimity the orthodox period of abstinence from colours.

It is graceful, although by no means obligatory, to pay the first visit to a house of mourning, even of those to whom we are not related, in slight mourning, or, at any rate, in raiment of subdued colouring. This, however, is entirely a matter of taste, not of etiquette. Cards returning thanks for kind inquiries are sent to all those who have left cards, as soon as the mourners feel equal to receiving the visits of their friends. In the case of a widow they should never be sent before six months have elapsed, and are very frequently not sent for a year. Notes of condolence should always be written on paper with a slight black edge, and neither surprise nor annoyance should be felt if they are left unanswered; it is often an unbearable trial to write answers.

It is the fashion to abuse mourning, to shorten by every pretence the period of wearing it, and more especially to complain of crape, in the words of the "Mourning Reform Association," as expensive and ostentatious." The latter adjective is certainly most inappropriate. The use of crape has a distinct and recognized meaning, explaining even to those least initiated in the minutiæ of etiquette that the wearer's mourning is for some really near relative, and by this means saving an inquiry painful to answer supposing that the questioner has not heard of the loss.

If persons would but exercise their common sense, and only purchase mourning suited to their means, there is really no reason why it should be so inordinately costly as its opponents love to represent it. I would draw the attention of these objectors to a fact, often quoted, but worthy nevertheless of reiteration, that one of the marked signs of the times prior to the Great Revolution was the display of the heartlessness of the French aristocracy, who first curtailed the orthodox period of mourning for their nearest relatives, and then discarded the outward signs of woe altogether.

To judge from indications that have appeared on the same subject in our own country during the last year or two, many members of the English upper classes are drifting slowly in the same direction, but as long as the English people retain the national characteristic of honest home affections, there is little fear that the custom of wearing mourning garments for the dead will cease to be observed, notwithstanding the efforts of a small, though perhaps influential, minority.

59

[ANON], 'MOURNING AS A FASHION.'

The London Reader, 17 February 1877, p. 376

THE habit of expressing the grief of a bereavement by outward signs, such as the colour of a dress, is one that we cannot find fault with. We think it is not only harmless, but appropriate. It tells to observers that there has been a death in the family without asking, and forbids the levity of conversation that might otherwise be indulged in with the bereaved.

Besides, the habit of mourning is universal among nations and peoples, and it would, probably, be impossible to abolish a custom that has its origin in some deep-seated instinct of human nature. But when mourning becomes a mere fashion, when the heart's grief comes to be measured by so many inches of black border to the veil to be worn before the world for a certain length of time, then the matter has degenerared into a wicked and flippant trilling with sorrow.

A bruised heart needs no sable weeds to express its anguish. The soul that really and deeply feels its loss when a beloved one that was its pride, its joy or support, has been snatched away, does not require sombre folds of crape and funereal stuff to make a decent and proper proclamation of its grief. There lies a shadow on the hearth, a mournful vacancy in the seats and places once occupied by the lost one, that does the work more thoroughly than all the devices and arts of the fashionable milliner and dressmaker. It matters little to the bereaved whether she be clad in a black suit of the latest fashion, or in her usual garments.

Respect for the world's opinion makes it advisable, perhaps, that a mourning habit be adopted, but the genuine grief will rest on the heart and glisten in the eye, and express itself in the bowed and humble form, whatever may be the cut or colour of the dress. The poor cannot always wear mourning, yet the poor feel their losses and mourn them no less than the rich.

Respect for the memory of the dead is a holy and pure feeling, always to be encouraged; but a conventional mourning, that varies with every whim of fashion, is a weak and wicked vanity.

DOI: 10.4324/9781315399980-71

60

E. M. DAVY, 'A GLOVE'S EVIDENCE.'

The Argosy, February 1885, pp. 156–157

The new maid, however, had not been many days in Lady Jakes's service before it became painfully evident to the latter that there was more of the lady about Margaret Johnson than about Lady Jakes herself. This knowledge gave rise to an uncomfortable feeling which her ladyship in vain tried to dispel. At first she resented the fact, but ultimately determined to turn it to account. It is true the country brewer's daughter had received a fair enough education at a large school, but it was somewhat humiliating to find that the daily companionship of a refined girl like Margaret Johnson opened out a new branch of learning. It showed her her own deficiencies. She knew herself to be loud, abrupt in speech, quick and gauche in manner. Her maid, on the other hand, spoke slowly, softly, with few words; but those she used were spoken in a low, sweet, melodious voice. Her movements were the embodiment of grace. Her dresses – rigorously plain – were of some soft black stuff that clung closely to her figure, with the narrowest rim of white at throat and wrists. She was in mourning for her father, who had died a few months back, she said; but on all matters referring to herself or her antecedents the girl was reticent in the extreme.

Lady Jakes loved to have her hair brushed. She was a vivacious little woman, and excitable; perhaps the action soothed her. She would sit by the hour before her toilet glass in an elaborately-trimmed peignoir, while Margaret stood brushing with slow monotony the thick, rather coarse, light hair, which afterwards had to be plaited and curled and frizzed.

One day, little more than a month after Margaret's arrival, mistress and maid were thus engaged, when the former said abruptly:

"You wear no ornaments, Johnson."

"No, my lady."

"Many mistresses forbid their servants to wear jewellery, but that can't be your reason for wearing none. What is it?"

"I do not think jewellery suitable with deep mourning, my lady."

"But I am in the deepest mourning, and I wear these." And Lady Jakes, holding up both her little white hands, smiled as she saw the diamonds flash.

"It is a matter of feeling, I suppose, my lady."

"Do you think it bad taste – in plain English, *vulgar* to wear these splendid rings?"

 DOI: 10.4324/9781315399980-72

"If I am bound to answer, I think it is scarcely in *good* taste, my lady."

The lady laughed a little scoffingly. Her ruddy cheeks grew ruddier. She bit her under lip.

"You're a strange girl, Johnson," she remarked presently, "and you know a good deal more than I would credit most maids with knowing, who haven't been out before. How you got your ideas of refinement puzzles me, but you *have* got them. I've a good mind to put down my jewellery till I begin my second mourning. And – I like those plain black gowns you wear. There is certainly a style about them, and the way you do your hair."

"I wish I could catch a little of that girl's manner," she thought as she watched her in the glass. "I wish I were as tall and slim as she is! What pretty hands she has – as white almost as mine – but they are not so small. . . . No. I am quite sure her hands are not so small as mine . . ."

From that day Lady Jakes laid by her rings, her thick gold chain. She ceased to friz and curl her hair. The small white lisse arrangement rested securely on her head without the aid of diamond pins. She lowered her voice in speaking – when she could recollect. She moved about more slowly – when she had time. To her servants it was no secret that Lady Jakes was copying her maid. They looked on as at an amusing comedy, and smiled.

61

IMAGE: [ANON], 'SOME SUMMER DRESSES FOR MOURNING WEAR.'

Hearth and Home, 8 June 1899, p. 169

Figure 61.1 SOME SUMMER DRESSES FOR MOURNING WEAR.

THE gown on the left for deep mourning is composed of a thin Henrietta cloth, with yoke and bands of crape. The Princess bodice is fastened with dull jet buttons. The centre dress is of black silk spotted voile with tucks and insertions of black guipure silk. The third dress is of crêpe de chine, or one of the many varieties of Henrietta cloth, trimmed with a yoke of embroidered lisse and cross-cut rolls of dull black silk.

DOI: 10.4324/9781315399980-73

62

[ANON], 'FASHION IN MOURNING.'

Bow Bells, 30 November 1894, pp. 545–546

AT first sight fashion would seem to have as little to do with mourning as it has with grief, but as those who wear the garb of woe are not invariably mourners in the strict sense of the term, fashion influences this form of dress very appreciably. Of late years the periods for wearing it have been very much abbreviated, and many other changes have taken place in what may be called, for want of a better word, the etiquette of mourning.

It used, for instance, to be a strictly observed rule that no member of the family who had just sustained a bereavement should put on deep mourning until a week after the death. The reason of this was that doing so would imply that the dresses had been prepared in advance in expectation of a death which might, after all, not have taken place. This would be a cold-blooded course of conduct which very few would be likely to adopt; but now this old-fashioned prohibition is extinct.

The making of mourning dresses is now conducted with such speed, as compared with the deliberate and leisurely mode of procedure of long ago, and money is so much more freely spent now-a-days than it was in the thriftier times of our grandparents, that such a rule is now naturally obsolete.

The great houses that make a speciality of mourning costumes have every detail so well in hand that a few hours suffice to provide all that can be needed at the moment for the complete equipment of the mourners. Besides, black dresses are so very much worn in ordinary circumstances just now that there is generally some available compromise in the wardrobe. In the old days, when the above-mentioned rule held good, very few people wore black gowns unless they were in mourning, or were widows well on in years.

All deep mourning dresses are in woollen materials, many of which are manufactured with a view to making them resemble the texture of crape as nearly as possible. The severity of outline that once characterized deep mourning dress is now replaced by a degree of elegance that would once have been considered inconsistent with the garb of grief.

An idea of ultra smartness is conveyed by new mourning, even that worn by widows in the first twelvemonth of their widowhood. Their dresses are made in the very height of the reigning fashion, and the widow's caps of to-day are but the

DOI: 10.4324/9781315399980-74

light and airy descendants of the uncompromisingly large and heavily built ones of thirty years ago.

In those days a long black shawl was indispensable in the first days of deep mourning, and is even now used during the first weeks of bereavement by those who cling to old customs; but among the more advanced in the century-end ideas, it is replaced by smartly-cut capes or coats heavily trimmed with crape. In fact, so very fashionable and elegant is modern mourning that the lavish use of crape in its initial stages is an absolute necessity in order to distinguish it from an ordinary black costume, such as may be seen by the score in an hour's turn in the park on a summer morning.

The head-gear remains distinctive, but far less so than it used to be when bonnets were crowded over with loops and quillings of crape and sprays of flowers made of the same material, with occasionally a floral interlude, if so it may be called, of black grapes composed apparently of blow-glass in its most fragile form.

It used to be an article of faith that widows should wear black woollen gloves during the whole of the first year after the husband's death; but that was in the days when suéde gloves had not been invented. The gloss of French kid would have been considered incompatible with the dull blacks that custom laid down as indispensable. Now suédes and silk gloves are permitted, and in a couple of months are succeeded by French kid.

It is only within the last twenty years that it has been permitted to widows to lighten the intensity of their weeds by the addition of collar and cuffs of white batiste. Formerly folds of black crape were the only wear at the neck and wrists, embroidered with jet after the first few weeks, and not allowed to give place to linen collars and cuffs until six months had elapsed.

It is now by no means unusual to see widows wearing linen collars a month after their bereavement. It is an age of unconventionality in many ways, and when old customs begin to be modified or rejected there are always those who take advantage of transition periods, and commit flagrant errors in taste. Not long ago a widow in deepest weeds was present at a wedding, contravening all the laws of good manners by so doing.

These rules may seem trivial to many, but they are a crystallization in externals of kind-heartedness and those good manners that are "the fruit of noble minds," and are worthy of consideration. It is the bridegroom who might feel aggrieved at the association of ideas caused by the presence of a widow in weeds at his marriage. There are thousands of men who can view the prospect of death with serenity and calm, but there are few who on their wedding morning care to contemplate their bride in the character of a widow and themselves as inhabiting an early tomb.

In the periods of duration of mourning there have of late been radical changes. Widow's weeds used to be worn for a year and six months. It was then reduced to a year and a month, the vulgar reading of which was a year and a day.

During the last few years deep crape and distinctive headgear have been dropped at the end of six months, the period known technically as "black silk" then setting in, this lasting for six months instead of three, as used to be the case when the very deep weeds were worn for a year. It is followed by three months of half-mourning, the changes in which are quite as radical as those of previous periods.

In old days only gray, white, lavender, and a certain shade of violet were permissible, but now the introduction of mixed tints so numerous, and possessing such subtle affinities with each other, has led to a state of things when practically almost any colour, save green, blue, and brown, may be worn with a black gown. Things seem tending towards the gradual elimination of what has always been called half-mourning, so closely has it approached of late to the character of the second period of Court mourning, regulated by the Queen, in which coloured ribbons, fans, flowers, and feathers are admissible with black dresses.

Another change perceptible of late is in the type of dress worn by widows on their re-marriage. In England, white used to be forbidden to them, as it has been for time immemorial among the bourgeoisie of France, brides of higher rank in that country wearing on re-marriage a simply-made white dress with a long black lace veil falling over the face and covering the greater part of the back of the dress. An English widow of position, who recently re-married, wore white satin hemmed with sable, and a white velvet bonnet trimmed with the same fur.

A mourning dress worn by a very great lady for the late Czar is in black crape cloth, the bodice composed of folds of black crape over white silk, and the skirt trimmed with three rows of wide woollen braid. The introduction of white silk, almost hidden though it be under close folds of crape, is a new departure, but it is in this instance strictly in accordance with etiquette, Russian mourning being a mixture of black and white.

There are those who advocate the abandonment of crape in deep mourning, pointing, as an example, to a royal lady, who refused to wear it when suffering bereavement some time ago. This is no valid argument so far as the general public are concerned. The use of crape is to announce to friends and acquaintances and others that our loss is so recent and our grief so acute that we must be excused from ordinary conversation or bearing our part as usual in the social or business world. It is the accepted sign of mourning, and its absence exposes the true mourner to inquiries and remarks that probe the heart to its very depths.

In the case of the royal lady in question, every soul in the kingdom knew of her loss, and felt deepest sympathy with her. Humbler mothers feel grief as deep, though only a few of their immediate circle may be acquainted with the circumstance, and for them the wearing of crape is a necessary protection when they begin to go forth into the world again after a short period of necessary seclusion.

2.3

Adornments

DOI: 10.4324/9781315399980-75

2.3.1

Chatelaines

DOI: 10.4324/9781315399980-76

Chatelaines

The addition of a circumflex accent, as Jessica Rose Harpley observes, is what differentiates the châtelaine, the Medieval mistress, who carried on her person the jingling keys of her castle, and the similarly-spelled chatelaine, a term coined by the Victorians to describe an ornament made of silver chains hung from the waist.[1] This item was used by eighteenth-century 'ladies of standing' to attach their watch, along with other charms and trinkets, to their belts, and it became a fashionable item in the nineteenth century. Yet, an article in *The World of Fashion* of 1839 was ambivalent as to the returning fashion, the writer observing that,

> those large, heavy, chased gold hooks and chains which our great-great-grandmothers used to fasten their massive watches to their waists are not revived, not only in their antique form, but even in their antique rust, if we may so express it, the more fashionable they are. The watch, the smelling-bottle, and eye-glass suspended from the chatelaine, are all of elegant workmanship, which forms a contrast ridiculous enough [. . . .][2]

Like many fashionable trends, the chatelaine, the author suggests here, is a fashion of recovering great-grandmothers' accessories, but perhaps it is taken a step too far when even the patina of old was evoked.

While the chatelaine might seem like a 'cumbersome' ornament of days long past,[3] it became sufficiently popular to be satirised in John Leech's engraving entitled 'The Chatelaine; A Really Useful Present', which appeared in *Punch* in January 1849. Interestingly, this was not the item's only reference in this publication,[4] and is reproduced here in order to showcase the chatelaine's ambiguous status between a 'utility' and a 'fashionable' item. In this engraving, a delicate young lady, whose small waist supports the massive chatelaine, is showing off a new gift to her mother, while the giver, who we infer to be her husband or suitor, stands proudly behind. The chatelaine itself is humorously and disproportionally adorned with domestic household appliances including brushes, pans and fire fenders. Whilst her mother looks up from her book to inspect the gift, the daughter stoops over its weight of domestic objects, marvelling at the chatelaine's beauty, and by extension, her husband's affections. Here objects adorning the chatelaine merge together the domestic utensils of the servant and items a 'lady' might use, and in doing so, the cartoon parodies the metonymic link between the lady of the castle holding the keys, and the housekeeper.[5]

While, as Charlotte Gere and Judy Rudoe note, chatelaines widely appeared in advertising and modish images, 'the extent to which they were actually worn is harder to establish'.[6] Indeed, the chatelaine seemed to dip in and out of fashion before the middle of the century, but with the advent of the crinoline, it began to steadily gain popularity, maintaining its appeal even when skirts became narrower in the later Victorian period.[7] To this end, an advertisement in the 1889 issue of *Le Follet* showcases delicate chatelaines made from sterling silver and in antique designs, a trend that enjoyed some popularity. We might notice that the chatelaines in these advertisements have fewer chains and are smaller in size, being cast in silver, while larger, more extravagant chatelaines were made from cut-steel.[8] An example of one such cut-steel chatelaine is held in the Victoria and Albert Museum, a photograph of which is included in our selections. Cut-steel chatelaines were more affordable for the middle-class consumer, and as we see from this item, the chains could be adorned with a variety of useful and decorative ornaments that problematised the relationship between utility and miniaturised novelty. Holding scissors, scent bottles, magnifying glasses, tiny pencils and notepads, thimbles and even tiny purses,[9] chatelaines functioned as visible markers of the accoutrements deemed essential to a lady, but in their miniature form, might also evoke dolls'-house ornaments. Indeed, the tactility of the chatelaine might frame it as a fashionable plaything for its owner and even, as Harpley suggests, as 'an aid to flirtation'.[10]

As bags and purses became more widely used at the end of the nineteenth century, the engraving titled 'Parisian Toilette' in *Myra's Journal* of 1895 presents a chatelaine that is much simpler in design. Made of silk ribbon, this chatelaine is in also lighter and not augmented with trinkets and trifles. However, as the 1900 article 'The Return of the Chatelaine' suggests, the heavier, antique chatelaines of old were still popular, sporting both beautiful and useful adornments, even if their jingling irritated those of sensitive nerves and acute hearing.[11]

Notes

1 See J. R. Harpley, 'Glittering Baubles: An Examination of Chatelaines in Britain, 1839–1900', *The Journal of Dress History*, 4(3), (Autumn 2020), pp. 45–71, for an exploration of the Victorian chatelaine in Victorian literature and culture, and p. 48, for a discussion of the 'distinction between chatelaine the object, and *châtelaine*, the medieval lady'. Claire Wilcox also notes that '[*c*]*hâtelaine* translated from the French means "lady of the castle", or the lady of the house'. C. Wilcox, *Bags* (London: V&A Publications, 1999), p. 63. For further consideration of the chatelaine in relation to class, see L. Young, *Middle Class Culture in the Nineteenth Century: America, Australia and Britain* (Houndmills and New York: Palgrave Macmilan, 2003), pp. 171–172.

2 The editors have made every effort to retrieve the original article, which is quoted in G. B. Hughes, 'Georgian and Victorian Chatelaines', *Country Life*, 4 October 1956, pp. 727–731 (p. 731). Hughes provides a comprehensive account of eighteenth- and nineteenth-century chatelaines and their methods of production. See also G. E. Cummins and N. D. Taunton, *Chatelaines: Utility to Glorious Extravagance* (Woodbridge: Antique Collectors' Club, 1994); Harpley, 'Glittering Baubles', p. 46; and K. Ledbetter, *Victorian Needlework* ([Victorian Life and Times series] Santa Barbara, CA, Denver, CO, and Oxford, England: Praeger [an imprint of ABC-CLIO, LLC], 2012), p. 103.

3 Harpley, 'Glittering Baubles', p. 46.

4 See, for example, SENEX, 'The Chatelaine of the Haunted House. A Tale of Fashion', *Punch*, [13 January 1849], p. 22, in which the writer describes a humorous misunderstanding concerning this fashionable item. This article is also discussed in Harpley, 'Glittering Baubles', pp. 57–58. For 'The Chatelaine; A Really Useful Present', see Young, *Middle Class Culture in the Nineteenth Century*, p. 172.

5 For a discussion of this illustration and the use of the chatelaine as a pocket substitute, see C. T. Matthews, 'Form and deformity: the trouble with Victorian pockets', *Victorian Studies*, 52(4), (Summer 2010), pp. 561–590. Matthews is also cited in Harpley, 'Glittering Baubles', p. 46.

6 C. Gere and J. Rudoe, *Jewellery in the Age of Queen Victoria: A Mirror to the World* (London: British Museum Press, 2010), p. 115.

7 See Wilcox, *Bags*, p. 63.

8 Referring to another Victorian style influence, Gere and Rudoe describe how the American jeweller Tiffany produced 'silver ornaments in the Japanese taste', including 'chatelaines with [. . .] overlapping forms'. See Gere and Rudoe, *Jewellery in the Age of Queen Victoria*, p. 313. See also our Headnotes on Jewellery for further discussion of Japanese influence upon Victorian style.

9 See Harpley, 'Glittering Baubles', p. 47, and Ledbetter, *Victorian Needlework*, p. 103.

10 See Harpley, 'Glittering Baubles', p. 60.

11 See Harpley, 'Glittering Baubles', pp. 57–58, for discussion of the noise created by this accessory.

63

IMAGE: [JOHN LEECH], 'THE CHATELAINE; A REALLY USEFUL PRESENT.'

Punch, [13 January 1849], p. 16

Figure 63.1 *LAURA*. "OH! LOOK, MA'DEAR; SEE WHAT A *LOVE* OF A CHATELAINE EDWARD HAS GIVEN ME."

DOI: 10.4324/9781315399980-77

64

IMAGE: CUT-STEEL CHATELAINE WITH ATTACHMENTS, ENGLAND, CA. 1863–1885

DOI: 10.4324/9781315399980-78

65

IMAGE: 'NOVELTIES IN JEWELLERY.'

Le Follet, 1 July 1889

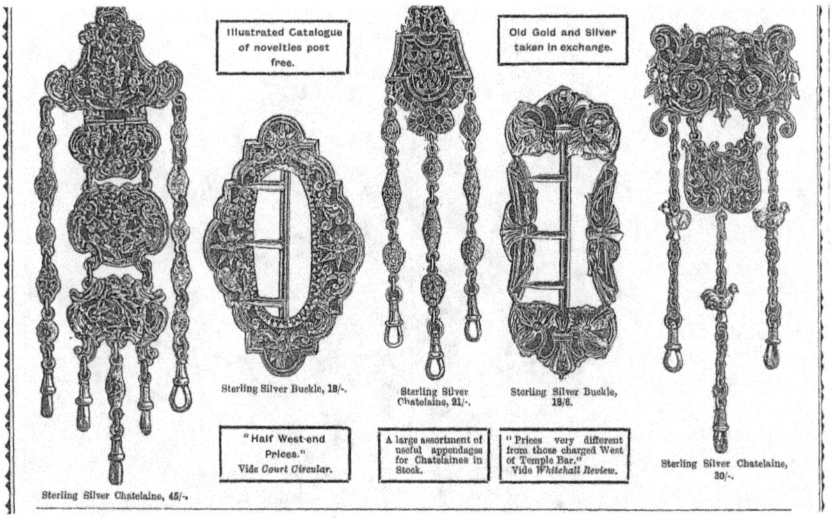

DOI: 10.4324/9781315399980-79

66

[ANON], 'A PARISIAN TOILETTE.'

Myra's Journal, 1 July 1895, p. 3

Figure 66.1 A Parisian Toilette.

DOI: 10.4324/9781315399980-80

Very full skirt of shot pink and grey silk open in front over an underskirt of pink Liberty satin trimmed on the hem with a narrow band o[f] antique guipure headed by tucks. Jacket of the silk with open rounded fronts showing a plain vest of the pink satin and black satin belt. The back and side pieces form a plain bodice. Antique buttons, and black satin ribbon chatelaine. Fichu of two flounces of accordion-pleated black silk muslin forming a deep collar at the back, and two flounces covering the upper part of the silk sleeve. Pink straw Lamballe hat trimmed with moss green ribbon, white lace, and black feathers. Quantity of silk required, 15 yards.

Prices of Flat Patterns, Skirt, 6½d., Bodice, 6½d., of MADAME MYRA, 95, *Regent Street, W.*

67

[ANON], 'THE RETURN OF THE CHATELAINE' IN 'OUR HOME CIRCLE. NOTES AND HINTS BY A LADY.'

The Newcastle Weekly Courant, 27 January 1900, p. 5

When there are no important changes in the world of fashion we set about evolving something that will serve to give a little variety to our dresses. Now we we'come the return of the chatelaine, always a pretty addition to a gown, and a useful detail, too. So many of the little attachments are constantly needed by the wearer – thimble, scissors, tablets, knife, stiletto, scent bottle, etc. Ornamental as it is, a chatelaine is something more than a mere ornament. Very beautiful are the Norwegian belts and chatelaines made of old silver; they are most artistic, and the agreeable jangle reminds one of silver bells, quite different from the clatter made by steel chains and pendants, but if one cannot afford the more costly metal a good steel chatelaine is not to be despised. Then, if one's nerves are irritable, the leather-covered chatelaines can be worn; these, in red or green leather, are a pretty finish to a morning dress. Just a word of advice on this subject – if your figure is short and round, see that the chains of the chatelaine are a good length, and hook it on to the waistband rather near the point of the bodice. Short and bunchy chatelaines prove unbecoming to all but the slenderest figures.

DOI: 10.4324/9781315399980-81

2.3.2

Jewellery

DOI: 10.4324/9781315399980-82

Jewellery

In the last two sections, we observed some of the multifaceted emotional and practical work facilitated by personal ornaments. From sentimental hair jewellery to the decorative and functional chatelaine, jewellery performed nuanced cultural work during the Victorian period. To this end, in this section we offer a small taste of the jewellery worn in the latter part of the nineteenth century.[1]

Jewellery was no longer the sole product of individual craftsmanship, and alongside handcrafted ornaments, advances in mechanisation meant that pieces could be produced *en masse* and in a variety of materials and styles. In addition, the distinct geographical provenance of jewellery was often difficult to trace, as the exchange of ideas in international exhibitions – and through the press and photography – meant that regional and national styles were often amalgamated in jewellery design. However, jewellery – whether made for the Queen or for the middle-class lady – also spoke of the pillages of imperialism and the disembowelling of the earth for precious stones and minerals. Furthermore, as Adelene Buckland aptly illustrates in the *Raw Materials* volume of this series, the extraction of gold and diamonds was bloody, messy and destructive. Although not included here, Wilkie Collins' *The Moonstone*, published in 1868, is one such example, whereby the theft of a precious stone unfolds a story of plundering and blasphemy, alongside racial and class tensions.

Yet jewellery was, as Jean Arnold notes, 'ubiquitous as an object of desire'[2] during the period and functioned as a signifier of status. Nonetheless, women were cautioned against the ostentatious display of wealth (either inherited or earned) through the purchase and display of expensive gemstones. One writer for *The Englishwoman's Domestic Magazine* of 1853 warned readers that, '[l]adies of good taste seldom wear jewellery in the morning; and when they do, confine themselves to trinkets of gold, or those in which opaque stones only are introduced', avoiding those of 'brilliant' appearance.[3] Thus, alongside the etiquette for correct dress, a corresponding etiquette for correct ornamentation was also in place.[4]

The Victorian fascination with the past (marked by archaeological excavations taking place in Europe and Egypt), alongside interest in natural history, also found its way into jewellery design. As we shall see in the following section, 'curiosity jewellery' made from birds and insects became popular in the 1870s. Here, our first two selections offer examples of the influence of both antiquity and natural history upon fashionable jewellery.[5] 'A Word About Cameos', from *Cassell's Household Guide*, provides information to potential purchasers on the quality and originality of cameos, an item that represented a high-end product speaking of travels to Italy, of collecting as a leisure activity, and the cameo's status as 'middle-class curio'.[6] Arnold reads contemporary interest in cameos as a celebration of 'domestic space', which 'project[ed] carved images to women within everyday life' and which 'resides within [the] Victorian fashion framework containing clothing, commodities, and jewelry'.[7] However, Lauren Miskin posits 'that the Victorian taste for cameos offers insight into Britain's process of fashioning an imperial identity, particularly Britain's widespread cultural efforts to align its rapidly expanding empire with that of imperial Rome'.[8]

Our next extract features jewellery made from coral, described by Katharine Anderson as 'ambiguous organisms, straddling the boundaries of plant and animal life', which enjoyed its British 'heyday' as a fashionable material during the 1850s.[9] Nonetheless, our extract, published in *The Morning Post* of the early 1870s, attests to a resurgence of interest, realised in an exhibition by Messrs. Phillips Brothers and Son. Comprising 'the finest known specimens both of mounted and unmounted coral' and containing 'several necklaces of simple round beads', the exhibition, the writer proudly declares, represented 'the most remarkable show of coral ever publicly exhibited'.[10] For our next source, we turn to George Eliot's novel *Middlemarch*, published in 1871–1872 (but set some forty years earlier), in which jewellery becomes a significant trope of both femininity and capital. In this episode, the protagonist, Dorothea, has to choose cameos for her sister, although she herself is disinterested in these particular ornaments. Despite her efforts to select them, she is doubtful about her powers of discernment, finally owning, 'frankly, I don't think them a great object in life'.[11]

Yet Dorothea's attitude to the cameo was far from universal, as it enjoyed 'cult' status in Victorian fashionable life,[12] and, to borrow Charlotte Gere and Judy Rudoe's terms, 'occupied a special place in Victorian culture'.[13] More widely, jewellery often featured in the pages of women's magazines and was also discussed in newspapers, which included extended descriptions of the jewellery worn by royalty at public events. Indeed, such pieces rapidly became both popular and covetable. An 1881 advertisement for 'The Beatrice Silver & Gold Jewellery' focuses on items designed for, and 'supplied to', Queen Victoria's daughter, H. R. H. Princess Beatrice. This was published during a period of economic depression experienced by Birmingham jewellery makers in the late 1870s and early 1880s (lasting until 1886) and here publicly coincides with Princess Beatrice's patronage.[14] Fashioned from more affordable silver, the bracelet was therefore made available to a wider range of consumers.[15] The advertisement also notes that the artefact could be posted to buyers, enabling aspirational readers to emulate the fashionable dictums of royalty.

In the same advertisement, a fan brooch is also presented. While the inspiration is not specified, the bamboo handle and the bird design echo the late nineteenth-century appropriation of Japanese culture and its artefacts, 'packaged' for the middle-class Victorian consumer.[16] Here we might draw upon Anne Anlin Cheng's poignant discussion of 'ornamentalism, with its almost homophonic echo of Orientalism' and the ways in which 'the oriental, the feminine, and the decorative' might form 'critically conjoined presences',[17] notions that seem to be conveyed in this small silver brooch.[18] Additionally, this brooch and bracelet might offer their wearers a sense of commodified connection with royalty and of traveling to distant places, realising these within the tangible form of each jewellery item.

Our next selection, 'Jewels and How to Wear Them', focuses on the relationship between precious stones and the wearer's physical appearance, including 'complexion' and eye colour.[19] It is included here for the way in which it exemplifies the perseverance of association between women and their 'things'. It also functions as an example of how the Aesthetic movement was becoming realised in fashionable dress, making reference to the 'Liberty' prints that became so iconic of the style.[20] In doing so, it aligns this style with an array of semi-precious stones. But even within this context, the female wearer is presented as a canvas, as a work of art requiring aesthetic consonance between body parts, eye pigmentation, and decorative objects.

Unfortunately, the rendition of the intricate craftsmanship of jewellery was not always successfully conveyed in the periodicals of the time. Our final source, published in *Hearth & Home* of 1897, features 'the latest ideas in jewellery', including buckles, ornamental hair combs, lockets and fine chains.[21] These, we are told, are depicted as 'seen at Swan and Edgar's', the department store located at Piccadilly and Regent Street, London. The department store jewellery section also marks an era of affordability and democracy in jewellery.

Notes

1 For a comprehensive study of Victorian jewellery, see C. Gere and J. Rudoe, *Jewellery in the Age of Queen Victoria: A Mirror to the World* (London: British Museum Press, 2010). Margaret Flower's *Victorian Jewellery* also remains both informative and useful. See M. Flower (with a foreword by M. J. Biggs and a chapter on collecting by D. L. Moore [revised ed.]), (London: Cassell, 1967).

2 J. Arnold, *Victorian Jewelry, Identity, and the Novel: Prisms of Culture* (Farnham, Surrey and Burlington, VT: Ashgate, 2011), p. 5. See also Chapter 1: 'Introduction: Jewels and the Formation of Identity in Victorian Literature and Culture', pp. 1–32.

3 [Anon], 'The Toilet', *The Englishwoman's Domestic Magazine*, June 1853, p. 62.

4 See Gere and Rudoe, *Jewellery in the Age of Queen Victoria*, pp. 101–103, for consideration of '[j]ewels and etiquette', and specifically of the contemporary disapproval of any inappropriate 'display of excessive finery' (p. 102).

5 For a discussion of the influence of the classical world on Victorian jewellery design, see C. Gere and J. Rudoe, 'Jewellery at the 1862 Exhibition', *The Journal of the Decorative Arts Society 1850 to the Present*, 38, 2014, pp. 82–105.

6 L. Miskin, 'The Victorian "Cameo Craze": Cameos, Femininity, and the Fashioning of Britain's Imperial Identity', *Victorian Review,* 42(1), (Spring 2016), pp. 167–184 (p. 180). See also Gere and Rudoe, 'Victorian Cameos', in *Jewellery in the Age of Queen Victoria*, pp. 464–481.

7 Arnold, *Victorian Jewelry*, pp. 113, 106.

8 Miskin, 'The Victorian "Cameo Craze"', p. 168.

9 K. Anderson, 'Coral Jewellery', *Victorian Review*, 34(1), (Spring 2008), pp. 47–52 (pp. 49, 47).

10 [Anon], 'Coral jewellery and peasant ornaments', *The Morning Post*, 27 May 1872, p. 2.

11 G. Eliot, *Middlemarch: A Study of Provincial Life* (Edinburgh and London: William Blackwood and Sons, 1871), Vol. I, p. 398. For further discussion of the novel and the significance of cameos, see Arnold, *Victorian Jewelry*, Chapter 5: 'Cameo Appearances: Aesthetics, and Gender in *Middlemarch*', pp. 101–126. Yet despite her indifference to cameos, Dorothea keenly (and rather guiltily) feels the allure of the fine jewels inherited from her late mother, deeming them 'very beautiful' and 'like fragments of heaven' (Eliot, *Middlemarch*, p. 13). For further discussion of this episode, see C. Hughes, *Dressed in Fiction* (Oxford and New York: Berg, 2006), pp. 93–94, and D. Wynne, *Women and Personal Property in the Victorian Novel* (Farnham, Surrey, and Burlington, VT: Ashgate, 2010), pp. 107–108.

12 Gere and Rudoe, *Jewellery in the Age of Queen Victoria*, p. 467.

13 Gere and Rudoe, *Jewellery in the Age of Queen Victoria*, p. 467.

14 See L. de Propris and L. Lazzeretti, 'Measuring the Decline of a Marshallian Industrial District: The Birmingham Jewellery Quarter', *Regional Studies*, 43(09), (2009), pp. 1135–1154.

15 See also Gere and Rudoe, *Jewellery in the Age of Queen Victoria*, pp. 194–195, for a brief discussion of the burgeoning cheaper end of the market (however, in this context, specific attention is devoted to so-called 'imitation' jewellery).

16 See M. Yoshihara, *Embracing the East: White Women and American Orientalism* (Oxford and New York, Oxford University Press, 2003), p. 26, for discussion of the use of bamboo and birds as design elements in other nineteenth-century Japanese-inspired artefacts. For further discussion of the influence of Japan (as well as China) upon Victorian jewellery design, see Gere and Rudoe, *Jewellery in the Age of Queen Victoria*, pp. 310–315. Additional consideration of the Victorian fascination with Japan is given by Anna Jackson, who points to the taste for '[c]ircular' and 'natural motifs', which often included '[f]lowers, birds and even insects'. A. Jackson (with M. Hinton), *The V&A Guide to Period Styles* (London: V&A Publications, 2002), p. 142, and G. E. Lavery, *Quaint, Exquisite: Victorian Aesthetics and the Idea of Japan* (Princeton, NJ, and Oxford: Princeton University Press, 2019). For a brief account of the movement from an art history perspective, see C. Ives, 'Japonisme' [Essay; Heilbrunn Timeline of Art History], MET Museum, October 2004. Available at: https://metmuseum.org/toah/hd/jpon/hd_jpon.htm [accessed 8 July 2021]. For the assimilation of Japanese aesthetics into the literature and culture of the late nineteenth century, see Y. Chiba, 'Japonisme: East-West Renaissance in the Late 19th Century', *Mosaic: a Journal for the Interdisciplinary Study of Literature*, 31(2), (1998), pp. 1–20.

17 A. A. Cheng, 'Ornamentalism: A Feminist Theory for the Yellow Woman', *Critical Enquiry*, 44(3), (Spring 2018), pp. 415–446 (p. 429).

18 In her study of 'Aesthetic Orientalism' in American artefact design, Yoshihara discusses the case of the Rhode Island–based Gorham Manufacturing Company, which was, she notes, 'one of the two leading silver manufacturing companies in America along with Tiffany & Co.' Yoshihara describes the company's 1870s'–1880s' 'Japanesque' design of household and decorative products that featured motifs such as 'bamboo [. . .] and birds' (Yoshihara, *Embracing the East*, p. 26). While this study focuses upon the American market as opposed to the contemporary British one, the design features and their cultural significance seem to be comparable within this context. See also Gere and Rudoe, *Jewellery in the Age of Queen Victoria*, pp. 313–315.

19 [Anon], 'Jewels, and How to Wear Them', *The Belfast News-Letter*, 27 December 1894, p. 7. See also Gere and Rudoe, *Jewellery in the Age of Queen Victoria*, pp. 117–118, for a discussion of the use of gemstones.

20 For further consideration of the Aesthetic movement in fashion, see V. Steele, *Fashion and Eroticism: Ideals of Feminine Beauty from the Victorian Era to the Jazz Age* (New York and Oxford: Oxford University Press, 1985), pp. 151–158 (see p. 156 for the 'deluxe Liberty "picturesque" dresses'). The discussion appears within the chapter 'The Revolt Against Fashion: Dress Reform and Aesthetic Costume', pp. 145–158. See also C. B. Kortsch, *Dress Culture in Late Victorian Women's Fiction: Literacy, Textiles, and Activism* (London and New York: Routledge, 2016 [originally published by Ashgate Publishing in 2009]), pp. 81–84, for further discussion of later Victorian 'anti-fashion', including so-called 'artistic garments' (p. 83). Kortsch also considers the significance of Liberty dresses, noting that the 'artistic' style of the later century – which was distinct from the previous, supposedly 'antiquated Pre-Raphaelite style' – produced 'beautiful, historic, individualized garments that allowed for freedom of movement', of which Liberty was considered an exemplar (p. 84). For an example of a Liberty dress from c. 1894, the year in which our selected article was published, see 'Dress: ca. 1894 (made)'. V&A Collections. Available at: https://collections.vam.ac.uk/item/O15543/dress-liberty – co/ [accessed 10 July 2021].

21 [Anon], 'The Latest Ideas in Jewellery Seen at Swan and Edgar's, Piccadilly and Regent Street', *Hearth & Home*, 4 November 1897, p. 1029.

68

[ANON], 'A WORD OR TWO ABOUT CAMEOS.'

Cassell's Household Guide: Being A Complete Encyclopædia of Domestic and Social Economy, and Forming A Guide to Every Department of Practical Life (London: Cassell, Petter, and Galpin, [1869]),Vol. I, p. 123

THE term *cameo* is popularly applied to precious stones and shells, the surfaces of which are covered with raised figures, mostly of a different colour from the ground, and mounted as brooches, bracelets, pins, ear-rings, finger-rings, and other personal ornaments. What are called stone cameos are most valuable and durable; but the actual cost varies greatly, owing to differences of material and workmanship. Very often fraud is practised by unprincipled artists, who cut out the figures separately and attach them by cement to the flat surface of stones prepared for them. Many cheap imitations of cameos are formed in moulds and fastened to glass or some other common material. A splendid Roman cameo for a brooch may cost fifteen or twenty pounds, while one of the same size and inferior work in shell will cost but a few shillings. We gather the following from an interesting essay on this subject: – "There are antiques, to produce which the chemical skill of the artist had to be exercised. A species of enamel was made, and with this cornelians of the required grain and density were covered by the application of fluxes and intense heat, thus forming, artificially, the much-desired layer of clear hard substance, out of which to cut the wished-for design. Many works which rank amongst the stone or true cameos, although of comparatively simple design, moderate size, and not antique specialities, are worth £50 and upwards; whilst *shell cameos,* well executed, and representing precisely the same subjects, may be bought for £2 10s. or £3. The reason for this immense difference in value lies, first, in the intrinsic worth of the material operated on; next, in the great facilities afforded to the artist, who works on the soft and yielding shell with instruments and appliances of ordinary power; and lastly, in the almost indestructible qualities of the stone cameos when finished." Cameos in onyx, agate, cornelian, and some others are particularly beautiful when the colours of the layers of the stone or veins are strongly contrasted. The oriental onyx is black and white; the cornelian,

DOI: 10.4324/9781315399980-83

brown and white; the agates vary. Shell cameos are chiefly of two sorts, some having a reddish ground, others a brownish ground, both with white or whitish figures. Those with a vivid reddish-tinted ground and pure white figures are best. There are antique cameos which are very expensive. Many modern pieces with classical subjects are also costly, though, when of inferior materials and finish, they are often cheap. The settings, of course, are of all kinds, and should correspond in material and value with the cameos they display.

69

[ANON], 'CORAL JEWELLERY AND PEASANT ORNAMENTS.'

The Morning Post, 27 May 1872, p. 2

THE INTERNATIONAL EXHIBITION.

CORAL JEWELLERY AND PEASANT ORNAMENTS.

A case just completed in the jewellery court has attracted and will continue to attract a large measure of admiration, for of its kind it is unique and worthy of being placed amongst those exhibits which cannot be too highly commended. This is the exhibition of coral by Messrs. Phillips Brothers and Son, of Cockspur-street, a firm not only of high repute in the metropolis, but one which is well known throughout Europe as having largely developed this interesting and important branch of commerce. The object sought, and certainly attained, by this firm is that of placing before the public a collection of the finest known specimens both of mounted and unmounted coral. Here are ranged many of the finest specimens of these beautiful treasures of the sea; the gradation of colour extends from the palest and most delicate pink to the deepest red; a circumstance which, taken in conjunction with the fact that several of the specimens are of an extraordinary size, justifies the remark that Messrs. Phillips have produced the most remarkable show of coral ever publicly exhibited. Without going into unnecessary detail, it may be said that the collection includes several necklaces of simple round beads, the value of which ranges from £100 to £350; and that the adaptability of this beautiful material to various branches of the goldsmith's art is exemplified by its employment in connection with cameos and other graceful sculptured forms. Several of Messrs. Phillips's exhibits are of the most recent pattern, and have been manufactured for their wholesale market. Nothing in the department is prettier or more artistic in design and workmanship than are these specimens of coral jewellery.

DOI: 10.4324/9781315399980-84

70

GEORGE ELIOT, *MIDDLEMARCH: A STUDY OF PROVINCIAL LIFE*

(Edinburgh and London: William Blackwood and Sons, 1871), Vol. I, pp. 397–398

Dorothea, who had not been made aware that her former reception of Will had displeased her husband, had no hesitation about seeing him, especially as he might be come to pay a farewell visit. When he entered she was looking at some cameos which she had been buying for Celia. She greeted Will as if his visit were quite a matter of course, and said at once, having a cameo bracelet in her hand,

"I am so glad you are come. Perhaps you understand all about cameos, and can tell me if these are really good. I wished to have you with us in choosing them, but Mr Casaubon objected: he thought there was not time. He will finish his work to-morrow, and we shall go away in three days. I have been uneasy about these cameos. Pray sit down and look at them."

"I am not particularly knowing, but there can be no great mistake about these little Homeric bits: they are exquisitely neat. And the colour is fine: it will just suit you."

"O, they are for my sister, who has quite a different complexion. You saw her with me at Lowick: she is light-haired and very pretty – at least I think so. We were never so long away from each other in our lives before. She is a great pet, and never was naughty in her life. I found out before I came away that she wanted me to buy her some cameos, and I should be sorry for them not to be good – after their kind." Dorothea added the last words with a smile.

"You seem not to care about cameos," said Will, seating himself at some distance from her, and observing her while she closed the cases.

"No, frankly, I don't think them a great object in life," said Dorothea.

DOI: 10.4324/9781315399980-85

71

IMAGE: ADVERTISEMENT, 'THE "BEATRICE" SILVER AND GOLD JEWELLERY.'

Le Follet, 1 October 1881, n.pag.

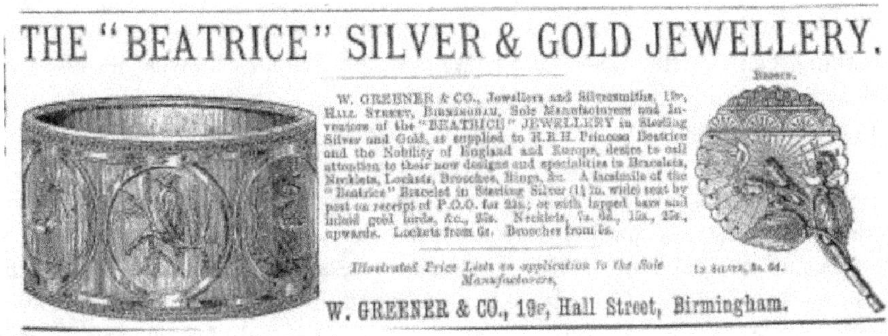

DOI: 10.4324/9781315399980-86

72

[ANON], 'JEWELS, AND HOW TO WEAR THEM.'

The Belfast News-Letter, 27 December 1894, p. 7

FIRST of all, jewels should relate to spots of colour, and these spots are chiefly to be found in the eyes. The woman who knows the secret of making the most of herself will dress to show these off. Opaque stones are best for day wear, and sparkling gems by night; so that a hazel-eyed girl, who, if she wear jewellery at all, will frequently choose small diamond earrings, would look far better with larger stones repeating the colour of her eyes. Such ornaments are not so difficult to find. Hazel eyes have generally in the iris rays of different hue, and any of these – yellows, greens, or browns – may be chosen. Labradorite – an iridescent stone, somewhat resembling the opal, but less fiery, and of varied shades of grey, brown, and greenish brown – though inexpensive, is artistic, and harmonises with eyes of changing hue. Cats'-eyes, too, are beautiful stones for day ware, especially the yellow Oriental cat's-eye, though the green and grey quartz cat's-eye are not without beauty. According to one's natural colouring, antique turquoises, topazes, cairngorms (because they are yellow enough to do without gas, and yet are not pitched in too high a key), cornelians, cameos, and lapis lazuli may be recommended for day wear. A brown-eyed woman, with dark hair and sallow skin, if she have no true artistic feeling for dress, will probably go to a ball attired in conventional black satin and diamonds, and pass unnoticed. The same person, arrayed in an evening dress of soft, transparent, brown, accordion-pleated chiffon over brown silk, fastened with lacings of cairn-gorms, and caught by a girdle of the same, ropes of cairn-gorms in her dusky hair, will look radiant, and be admired by all. Crocidolite – at one time rare, but now common – is of a golden brown colour, and might well be utilised for personal adornment. A fair woman with dark blue eyes, brown hair, with reddish or yellow lights, and a clear complexion, will find the sapphire to be her stone *par excellence*, while the topaz, the cairn-gorm, and deep-hued amber, avoiding the lighter shades, will also suit her. Cameos, too, she will find becoming, and an ideal costume to set off her good points would be a gown of Liberty silk or velvet, the exact shade of the background of a cameo, draperies caught by cameo brooches, and a cameo necklet encircling the throat – From *The Paris Mode* for December.

DOI: 10.4324/9781315399980-87

73

IMAGE: [ANON], 'THE LATEST IDEAS IN JEWELLERY SEEN AT SWAN AND EDGAR'S, PICCADILLY AND REGENT STREET.'

Hearth & Home, 4 November 1897, p. 1029

Figure 73.1 THE LATEST IDEAS IN JEWELLERY SEEN AT SWAN AND EDGAR'S, PICCADILLY AND REGENT STREET.

DOI: 10.4324/9781315399980-88

PART 3

Animal and Insect Accessories; Home Decoration

3.1

Animals and insects as adornments and home decorations

DOI: 10.4324/9781315399980-90

Animals and insects as adornments and home decorations

Rachel Poliquin's conundrum on taxidermy, '[a]nimal or object? Animal and object?'[1] aptly captures this group of sources, which collectively deal with the materiality of animals' and insects' bodies when turned into fashionable adornments and commodities. Our selections draw out the complex and somewhat uncanny relationship between Victorian fashionable ladies and animals as (both living and dead) accessories, including jewellery, hats, furs, muffs, gloves, pets and home decorations.[2] From the keeping of birds as a quintessentially 'feminine' hobby, to feathers in hats and dress trimmings; and from affordable fur to insect jewellery, our sources provide examples of animals' 'diverse afterlives as dead things'.[3]

Questions of authenticity, and the appropriateness of the use of particular animals, are raised in our first source, entitled 'The Best French Kid Gloves', which appeared in the middle-class periodical *The Ladies' Cabinet* of 1857. In this article, unsuspecting readers are led to believe that they will read where to purchase, or how to distinguish, gloves of the costly and covetable material known as 'kid'. Traditionally used for glove-making and made from young goatskin, kid had the ability to contour one's hands to appear smaller, whilst (as Ariel Beaujot notes) creating an illusion of the 'tapered' fingers so desirable during this period.[4] Despite the cost, middle-class women were expected to own several pairs of clean, neat gloves, thus denoting both respectability and leisured status.[5]

Meeting this need, the mechanization of glove production in the mid-nineteenth century meant that gloves became readily made and more affordable.[6] By 1850, England was a large importer of French gloves, and their popularity continued into the 1860s. Yet, the truth of this *Ladies' Cabinet* story is both unwelcome and macabre, as the narrator titillates the reader with a great, uncontainable secret that merges fashion, affordability and the grotesque. For these gloves (which we may infer were also imported to Britain) are revealed to be made not of the much-desired soft kid leather, but from rat skins, hunted and captured by the article's protagonists. We might alternately recoil and laugh as the tone is subversively humorous, tapping into wider Victorian anxieties about authenticity. But it also serves another function, showcasing an important aspect of animal use in fashion. If, to use Sarah Amato's syllogism, an animal's 'material origins are disembodied, abstracted, and recalled through the mental effort of associating' (in this example of the rat with the glove),[7] then perhaps the Victorian lady ought to be more alert to the possibility of herself falling prey to the allure of the affordable, yet inauthentic, accessory.

From the animal morphed into a fashionable item, we move on to a different 'flight of fancy', namely, the objects surrounding the fashionable hobby of bird-keeping. Imaginative links between women, bird cages and bird-keeping in the Victorian period are plentiful and have been examined by a number of critics.[8] Our selection here derives from the publisher, author, ornithologist and aviary enthusiast, William Kidd. Published in *The National Magazine* of 1857, the article describes the beauty of 'The

Fairy Bird-Cage', an artefact made of pure crystal and promoted as an item of luxury. Here Kidd advises '[y]oung ladies' to take up cleaning and polishing this birdcage, work usually relegated to domestic servants, as evidence of the relationship between domestic labour and the labour of love. Kidd concludes with a conflation of the birds as both feeling subjects whose importance is felt and '[*known*]', and their status as objects of admiration situated within luxurious environs.[9]

From the birdcage, we move on to the use of feathers in fashion, as the calibration of refinement and fashionability is played out in our next source. Taken from Ellen Wood's (Mrs Henry Wood's) 1861–1862 sensation novel *East Lynne*, this episode suggests intruiging tensions between fashionable middle-class women and bird feathers. As we discuss in our Introduction to this volume, sensation novels often acted as vehicles for the dissemination of fashionability, as well as being fashionable – if hotly debated – reading material. The scene features Barbara Hare, a middle-class provincial character, the narrative charting her changing perception that the pink feather decorating her hat has turned, in the space of a morning, from fashionable adornment to a shameful signifier of gaudiness. This is made all the more acute in comparison with the elegant Isabel Vane, whose simplicity of dress reveals the true 'aristocracy' of her nature.[10]

Our next source, a fashion plate from the French *Journal des Demoiselles* of 1864, features women's and girls' clothes alongside another 'fad' artefact, the aquarium. Becoming popular and commercialised in the 1850s, the aquarium, similar to the birdcage, was a mirror of its owner's social and financial status, also functioning as a means of imparting knowledge to the residents of the fashionable home. As Valerie Steele has noted, animals and birds often populate fashion plates, seemingly emphasising the female figures' nurturing capacity.[11] In this particular fashion plate, the marine life contained by the glass and bronze structure attracts the attention of one of the ladies, whilst the little girl's curiosity is also piqued, vying for her mother's gaze and pointing to the tank's inhabitants.[12] Although the fashion plate's emphasis is ostensibly on the garments, the aquarium is figured not just as mere ornament but as a coveted, desirable and curiosity-inducing item. In this way, the image illustrates Steele's assertion that the fashion-plate not only depicted dress, but 'the circumstances for which the clothes were designed', including modish surroundings and background features.[13]

Seven years after the publication of *East Lynne*, we see that the fashion of wearing feathers on bonnets still holds. This becomes apparent in an article on 'The Fashions' in *The Englishwoman's Domestic Magazine*, which describes both modish headgear and the use of feathers. It also introduces a fashion that gathered even more force in the 1870s and 1880s: the use of insects as adornments in jewellery. On this subject, Michelle Tolini notes that:

> [t]he trend had taken hold as early as 1872, when a London exhibition featured South American hummingbird and beetle jewelry created by

> two English firms, Ward & Co. and A. Bouchard. These pieces, described as fashionable, were praised for their outstanding color.[14]

Partly worn by women for their iridescent and delicate beauty, partly for novelty, and partly because they acted as indexes of the wearer's interest in natural history, these fashionable adornments might be seen as material embodiments of the rhetoric of learning about the natural world.[15]

'Art-Inroads on Natural History' also showcases the relationship between science, art and commodity in its descriptions of how insects were subjected to the imagination of the jeweller. The article details the items on display at the London Exhibition and tells of a history of colonialism, pillaging and transportation, as well as the transformation of insects and birds into jewellery. The Victoria and Albert Museum notes that the adornment of clothes with beetles' wings became fashionable in the 1820s and 1830s, and that subsequently, 'by the 1860s, beetle wings were being imported to Britain in volumes of 25,000 per consignment'.[16] In our selections from *The Ladies' Treasury* of 1874, the colonial transportation of beetles' wings, whose iridescence will soon adorn British fashionable dress, speaks of an appropriation of the use of emerald green beetle's wing decoration, turning 'a symbol of high status during the Mughal period (1526–1756)', into an item of novelty.[17]

Our next pair of sources offer a satirical response to the use of animals' and insects' bodies as they are turned into adornments. Both sources display a certain caustic tone towards the female wearers of such items. In 'The Strange Story of a Sealskin: A Tale of Metempsychosis', published in *Judy* magazine in 1875, a fur muff has retained the consciousness of its previous body, that of a baby seal, as it narrates its sad biography and afterlife. Drawing on the eighteenth-century popular genre of 'it-narratives', in which an object is able to offer its own perspective as a once-living, entity-turned-thing, the sealskin muff's tale is one of various stages of transmutation, from animal to muff, and from ownership by the first 'gracious Mistress and the High Life' in her company, to the sad ending of cannibalism during a visit to the Brighton aquarium with the new mistress, a golden-haired 'Lady of the *Corps de Ballet*'.[18] The article evinces particular criticism against the use and abuse of seals for clothing, and for the fashionable ladies' desire for such items, irrespective of their class status.[19]

The human self-consciousness displayed by the seal poses an ambiguity in the distinction between animal and object. This is also evident in the next source on live adornments. Tolini propounds that '[i]n a bizarre inversion of the nature/artifice shift, some women actually wore live insects as adornment. The insects traversed the boundary of inanimate ornament, yet their life was preserved'.[20] This is farcically illustrated in the poem 'Living Jewellery', published in the comic, heavily illustrated *Funny Folks*. This source satirises the trend for insect jewellery and adornments by referencing the animal-turned-object as a living thing which crawls down the back of its young lady wearer, who '[wriggles]' and '[writhes]' whilst being asked for her hand in marriage.

Our next selections turn our attention to the art and craft of taxidermy. *Practical Taxidermy*, one of the most influential guides to the amateur taxidermist, shows how objects usually designated for a museum of natural history can now be turned into a jeweller's art. And, as we shall see in the following section on Handicraft, this practise appropriated a traditionally 'masculine' area of knowledge into fashionable feminine adornment. Here, one of our selections is an advertisement printed in the last pages of the manual, which also gives information on where to purchase all relevant material for home taxidermy and display.[21] As Poliquin eloquently puts it,

> [a]ll taxidermy is driven to capture animal beauty. It is always a spectacle whose meaning depends in part on the particularity of the animal being displayed. It is motivated by the desire to tell ourselves stories about who we are and about our journey within the larger social and natural world.[22]

This might also invite us to consider taxidermy as a means of performative storytelling, and as one way of understanding the use of birds and feathers in hats, bonnets and as hair adornments.

This fashion, however, was heavily criticised by Mrs Haweis, who, as we have discussed, was well-known as an exponent of fashion and art. The graphically titled article 'Smashed Birds,' published in the middle-class and aspirational *Belgravia*, animates a variety of discourses on imported fashion, this time from North America.[23] In this piece, Mrs Haweis critiques the aesthetic value of animal-based fashionable commodities and the impact of killing birds upon the environment. In doing so, she crudely evokes a bird-wearing racial stereotype that she terms the 'Wild Indian', alongside a reference to a dingy lower-class girl who, she suggests, might capture, kill and decorate a sparrow to display on her 'unkempt head'.[24] What is also of interest in this article is the way in which Haweis criticises the merging of popular culture and high fashion as 'vulgar', whereby the taste in particular fashion items seems to homogenise, rather than distinguish, between social classes. Yet somewhat surprisingly, taxidermy was also perceived as a fashionable hobby for women, who might subsequently decorate their homes with stuffed small animals. To this end, the December 1892 issue of *Le Follet* advises its female reader on the purchase of small, taxidermied ornaments as gifts for Christmas and the New Year.

Our next source is on the wearing of fur, which became especially fashionable during the Victorian period and, as Elizabeth Ewing notes, was heavily showcased at the 1851 Great Exhibition.[25] Indeed, by the 1880s, 'most British stores had their fur departments',[26] and the 1896 article from *Myra's Journal of Dress and Fashion* gives an account of the new styles in fur. It also advises readers on how to fashion old fur items into the 'Figaro' style, which required much less material, as well as dispensing advice on the use of affordable, plush rabbit fur to imitate the more costly sealskin and chinchilla. Thus the article, aimed at the fashionable middle-class lady, reassures the reader that her refinement can be gained not by mere crude mimicry of aristocratic tastes, but through materials that are more durable, but equally pretty as, the more luxurious item.

Our last source, 'Victims of Vanity' from *The English Illustrated Magazine,* is infused with undertones of Western civility and misogyny, as it is women who return to these 'barbaric' practices of adornment.[27] Here the 'woman' and the 'wild animal' are associated in a popular *fin-de-siècle* rhetoric.[28] The article provides an overview of the various plumes used in fashionable headgear, criticising the practice and the maltreatment of animals, and offering estimates on the number of birds killed for the sake of producing feathered accessories. These fashionable items participate in the blurring of boundaries between natural and artifice alongside human, animal and adornment. They were also, as we see in our last few selections, criticised as awareness of outsourcing and the near-extinction of particular species grew; and through the pervasive fashionability of animal adornments, a counternarrative developed.

Notes

1 R. Poliquin, *The Breathless Zoo: Taxidermy and the Cultures of Longing* (University Park: PA: The Pennsylvania State University Press, 2012), p. 5.

2 See L. Johnston (with M. Kite and H. Persson), *Nineteenth-Century Fashion in Detail* (London: V&A Publications, 2005), for visual depictions and discussions of various animal and bird-derived fashions, including a feather-trimmed fan decorated with a 'stuffed hummingbird' (p. 108; notes by Persson), a 'mantle of white down' deemed 'luxurious' (p. 210; notes by Persson), and a 'dramatic cape' adorned with '[b]lack and green cock feathers' (pp. 112–113; notes by Persson). Indeed, Persson notes that '[d]uring the last three decades of the nineteenth century, there was a passion for using parts of dead animals as ornaments, both for the person and the home', adding that '[t]he more exotic the natural history specimen the better' (p. 108). For specific discussion of the use of animals, insects and natural material in jewellery and accessories such as the fan, see section on 'Nature Imitating Nature: Jewellery and Natural Products' in C. Gere and J. Rudoe, *Jewellery in the Age of Queen Victoria: A Mirror to the World* (London: British Museum Press, 2010), pp. 225–234.

3 S. Amato, *Beastly Possessions: Animals in Victorian Consumer Culture* (Toronto, Buffalo and London: University of Toronto Press, 2015), p. 183.

4 A. Beaujot, V*ictorian Fashion Accessories* (London and New York: Berg, 2012), pp. 43–44, 47, 41. For a full discussion of ladies' gloves, see Chapter 1: '"The Beauty of Her Hands": The Glove and the Making of Middle-Class Womanhood', pp. 31–61. For a wider consideration of gloves and their history, see M. Redwood, *Gloves and Glove-Making* (Oxford: Shire Publications, 2016), and specifically the chapter 'Gloves in Fashion', pp. 45–56.

5 Beaujot, *Victorian Fashion Accessories*, p. 43.

6 See Beaujot, *Victorian Fashion Accessories*, pp. 46–47.

7 Amato, *Beastly Possessions*, p. 190.

8 See, for example, T. Logan, *The Victorian Parlour: A Cultural Study* (Cambridge: Cambridge University Press, 2001), pp. 148–150; J. Flanders, *The Victorian House: Domestic*

Life from Childbirth to Deathbed (London: HarperCollins, 2003), pp. 210–211; and M. A. Danahay, 'Nature Red in Hoof and Paw: Domestic Animals and Violence in Victorian Art', in D. D. Morse and M. A. Danahay (eds.), *Victorian Animal Dreams: Representations of Animals in Victorian Literature and Culture* (London and New York: Routledge, 2017 [first published in 2007 by Ashgate Publishing]), pp. 97–119 (pp. 109–110).

9 W. Kidd, 'The Fairy Bird-Cage', *The National Magazine*, February 1857, p. 240.

10 For further discussion of these examples, see K. Tennant, 'The Discerning Eye: Viewing the Mid-Victorian "Modern" Woman', in I. Parkins and E. M. Sheehan (eds.), *Cultures of Femininity in Modern Fashion* (Durham, NH: University of New Hampshire Press, 2011), pp. 103–123 (pp. 116–117).

11 V. Steele, *Paris Fashion: A Cultural History* [2nd edition; revised and updated] (Oxford and New York: Berg, 1998), p. 119.

12 For an extensive analysis of the cultural function of the aquarium, see S. Granata, *The Victorian Aquarium: Literary discussions on nature, culture, and science* (Manchester: Manchester University Press, 2021), as well as S. Granata, 'The Dark Side of the Tank: The Marine Aquarium in the Victorian Home', in H. Kingstone and K. Lister (eds.), *Paraphernalia! Victorian Objects* (New York and Abingdon: Routledge/Taylor & Francis, 2018), pp. 81–98.

13 Steele, *Paris Fashion*, p. 118.

14 M. Tolini, '"Beetle Abominations" and Birds on Bonnets: Zoological Fantasy in Late-Nineteenth-Century Dress', *Nineteenth-Century Art Worldwide*, 1(1), (Spring 2002). Available at: http://19thc-artworldwide.org/spring02/206-qbeetle-abominationsq-and-birds-on-bonnets-zoological-fantasy-in-late-nineteenth-century-dress [accessed 23 June 2021]. Here Tolini cites S. Bury, *Jewellery, 1789-1910: The International Era* (Woodbridge, Suffolk: Antique Collectors' Club), 1991, p. 372.

15 C. Schmitt, 'Victorian Beetlemania', in D. D. Morse and M. A. Danahay (eds.), *Victorian Animal Dreams: Representations of Animals in Victorian Literature and Culture* (London and New York: Routledge, 2017 [first published in 2007 by Ashgate Publishing]), pp. 35–51. For further discussion of the use of beetle-wings in jewellery, see Gere and Rudoe, *Jewellery in the Age of Queen Victoria*, pp. 230–232.

16 'Dress (1868–9)', V&A Collections. Available at: https://collections.vam.ac.uk/item/O1387342/dress/ (accessed 21 June 2021). For further information on the use of beetles in Victorian women's clothes and their provenance, see The Victoria and Albert Museum, 'Fashioned from the animal kingdom' [from *Fashioned from Nature* exhibition, 21 April 2018–27 January 2019]. Available at: https://vam.ac.uk/articles/fashioned-from-animals [accessed 23 June 2021]. The Victoria and Albert Museum currently holds a dress on display embroidered with beetle wings.

17 Victoria and Albert Museum, 'Dress (1868–9)'.

18 [Anon], 'The Strange Story of a Sealskin. A Tale of Metempsychosis', *Judy, Or The London Serio-Comic Journal*, 24 November 1875, p. 52. For 'it-narratives', see C. Lupton, 'The Knowing Book: Authors, It-Narratives, and Objectification in the Eighteenth Century', *NOVEL: A Forum on Fiction*, 39(3), Summer 2006, pp. 402–420. For a discussion of the short story in terms of the Victorians' fascination with seal fur, see J. Miller, 'Fiction, Fashion, and the Victorian Seal Fur Hunt', in K. L. Edwards, D. Ryan, and J. Spencer (eds.), *Reading Literary Animals: Medieval to Modern* (London: Routledge, 2019), pp. 212–226.

19 For further contemporary discussion of Victorian sealskin and its animal origin, see [Anon], 'Sealskin Coats, Alive and Dead', *Chambers's Journal*, 27 November 1886, pp. 753–756.

20 Tolini, '"Beetle Abominations"'. See also J. Long, 'Portable Pets: Live and Apparently Live Animals in Fashion, 1880–1925', *Costume*, 43, (2009), pp. 109–126 (pp. 112–113), for a discussion of the 'integrating [of] live animals into dress' (p. 112).

21 Indeed, somewhat surprisingly, the Victorians did not seem to consider taxidermy as inherently unfeminine, with scholars pointing to sources aimed at women. See Long, 'Portable Pets', p. 117, and T. Logan, *The Victorian Parlour: A Cultural Study* (Cambridge: Cambridge University Press, 2001), p. 147.

22 R. Poliquin, *The Breathless Zoo*, p. 7.

23 See also A. M. David, *Fashion Victims: The Dangers of Dress Past and Present* (London and New York: Bloomsbury Visual Arts, 2015), pp. 92–94.

24 [Mrs] M. E. [Mary Eliza] Haweis, 'Smashed Birds', *Belgravia*, May 1887, pp. 336–344 (pp. 338, 339). In this article, Haweis lauds the work of both the (American) Audubon Society, and the (British) Selborne Society, organisations dedicated to conservation and wildlife protection.

25 E. Ewing, *Fur in Dress* (London: Batsford, 1981), p. 102. The 'raw materiality' of fur is presented in Adelene Buckland's section on 'Fur' in the *Raw Materials* volume of this series.

26 Ewing, *Fur in Dress*, p. 106.

27 C. W. Gedney, 'Victims of Vanity', *The English Illustrated Magazine*, August 1899, pp. 417–426, (p. 417).

28 N. Gauld, 'Victorian Bodies: The wild animal as adornment', *The British Art Journal*, 6(1), (Spring/Summer 2005), pp. 37–42.

74

[ANON], 'THE BEST FRENCH KID GLOVES.'

The Ladies' Cabinet, January 1857, pp. 32–33

Ladies, I have a horrible secret to tell you. I feel I should retain it, but I *cannot;* I ought to bury it in the inmost recesses of my mind; I ought to strive to forget it; but I can neither forget nor bury it, so I must divulge it. Do you know of what those soft, easy-fitting, lady-like, lovely-coloured French kid gloves are made? No, you don't. I shall thrill you with horror – they are made of *rat's* skins!

I learnt the terrible fact only some days back, and I have been struggling with myself till now to keep it *to* myself, but I have told you, and this is *how* I came to learn it: When I am in Paris I take my breakfast at a little crêmerie, kept by a couple of Bretonnes. Mdlle. Rosalie, who sits and beams behind a trim counter, who chatters and artfully arranges bouquets, is the younger. Let me introduce you to them, ladies, – Mdlle. Rosalie, Mdlle. Rosalie's sister. I don't know the elder sister's name: I only know her as the grand Rosalie's sister. Once I was inclined to be angry with Rosalie, for sitting there comfortably, and letting her sister do all the cooking, and all the marketing, and all the polishing and scrubbing; but I have changed my opinion some time, ever since I told Rosalie's sister that I didn't like Rosalie's conduct, when I asertained that Rosalie was worthy of my pity rather than my blame (so said the sister), for Rosalie had no *dot,* and Rosalie couldn't cook; Rosalie could do nothing, alas! except chatter, so Rosalie would never find a husband, which misfortune was quite enough to warrant Rosalie's sister in putting up with all Rosalie's ill humour – and Rosalie the brilliant *could* be ill-tempered. Rosalie's sister (not knowing whose name makes me tautological) had *dot,* could cook, and what was more, was going to be married as soon as ever a certain amount of francs – thousands of francs – could be got together; so I learnt to pity Rosalie in the French manner.

I am now going to speak of that frightful morning, when I learnt – you know what.

I go to my crêmerie, and what do I see? – anarchy, chaos, revolution, topsy-turveyness. Every chair and table, every stool and every thing are piled in one heap in the centre of the shop. Rosalie's grand counter has also met with a shock, and stands zig zag; the bouquet is stowed away on a shelf. What *is* this? Are Rosalie and Rosalie's sister rehearsing a barricading? Mdlle. Rosalie, herself, has her clothes tucked about her ancles, and that young female wields a broom, that I can

 DOI: 10.4324/9781315399980-91

only compare to an English carpet-broom well ironed; Mdlle. Rosalie's face is of the reddest; Mdlle. Rosalie's sister flies about madly with a stick; I stand aghast. What does it all mean? I ask what it all means.

"*Des rats,*" says R's sister, and plunges into a dark corner, and seems to contend with something.

"A rat," say I, little thinking there is more than one; "dear me, for I don't like rats."

"*Les miserables!*" says Rosalie, and dashes into the corner too.

Then I comprehend. Rosalie and sister are hunting. I stand by, and look on. I am invited to hunt too. I refuse mildly; so I look on again. A moment, and out they come from that corner in a screaming tail. One, two, three, four, as I live. They are in as straight a line as though they had been ruled. I shut my eyes. I pass over the horrid recital. I know the enemy are slain, that the tables and chairs are shot back with marvellous rapidity, as though the shooters were accustomed to the business, and then I sit down to breakfast – with what appetite I may. But I cannot help asking questions about rats – I think it so wonderful that young French-women can be so courageous as to beat their lives out with sticks; why! ladies in my clime would fly to chairs, tables, &c., and scream for help. I feel I must ask questions; and I learn somewhat. I hear that Rosalie and her sister are continually at it; that they get up in the dead of the night, and are at it: at a moment's notice they are prepared to hunt, and hunt successfully. They have destroyed as many as ten of those *mechants* in a single night. Rosalie's sister shows me wood, thick wood, that has been gnawed through by rats. I believe her; she then shows me corroded iron as the work of rats. I don't believe her, though I daresay she believes it herself – well may she believe anything of rats. We talk of nothing but rats all breakfast time, and I am told that if I walk the streets of Paris after midnight I shall learn something of rats.

I wait till midnight, and I then begin prowling about. I havn't prowled one minute when I come upon a rubbish heap, as there are thousands of such heaps every night in Paris, and from it radiate in every direction a perfect flock of rats; I go on to another heap – it is ratless; I come to a third – pewgh! more rats than ever. I interrogate a chiffonnier, who, I see, hates rats, and is dexterous in killing them: he tells me millions are killed every year. "Why?" I ask. He cannot say – for some purpose.

Now I have a mission – I must go about asking why millions of rats are killed in Paris every year. I ask everybody I meet, and at last I get the answer – leather for gloves.

So I came to learn the secret; and now I have no trouble to tell how every little grizette can be supplied with a pair of light-coloured French kid-gloves.

Have I made you sufficiently uncomfortable, ladies? Well, well – *all* French kid-gloves are not made of rat-skin, I suppose.

75

WILLIAM KIDD, 'THE FAIRY BIRD-CAGE.'

The National Magazine, February 1857, p. 240

KEEPING in view the object of "The Home" department of this Magazine, I have been zealously studying how to introduce (with the new year) a novelty more than ordinarily attractive and useful for the drawing-room, the study, and the fireside. If somewhat costly, it is, at all events, unique.

The novelty is now perfected and patented. It is a showy BIRD-CAGE of pure CRYSTAL GLASS (a material now used for the first time), altogether dispensing with wire and other disfigurements, and allowing a bird's plumage to be viewed to the best advantage. In praise of the workman, it must be observed, those only who know the nature of glass will comprehend the obstacles that have had to be surmounted in making it thus obedient to the human will.

In the production of this domestic cage, – whose figure and proportions may be regarded as a correct model for all cages, – there has been a double motive; for not only is the beauty of the inmate shown off to unusual advantage by the reflecting and refracting powers of the crystal palace in which he resides, but the palace itself is so constructed as to render it a matter of necessity as well as delight for the wives and daughters of home *to keep it brilliant* by their own individual exertions. The glass and all its *minutiæ* must be daily polished. A soft cloth and a delicate wash-leather are the only requisites.

Young ladies have hitherto been in the habit of too frequently trusting their pets to the care of servants to save themselves trouble. I now propose to set this habit on one side, while putting in a plea for "the poetry" of bird-keeping. No person can dispute the fact, that personal attention adds greatly to the sympathy existing between man and animals; nor will any person deny that these sympathies are very delightful. It is because they are so seldom courted that they are so little understood.

The "Fairy Bird-cage" – so named because of its lightness and extreme brilliance – is of very simple construction. All the bars are of solid transparent glass, compacted together so as to unite in a strong body. The form of the cage is an oval. It is mounted on a sexagon base, and supported by six lapidary-cut crystal knobs, beautifully prismatic. The six panels in front are of fine-grained satin-wood. On each of the six corners rises a brilliant pyramid of the purest (cut) crystal glass.

DOI: 10.4324/9781315399980-92

Immediately above the panels and between each bar of glass is introduced a *movable* length of polished ornamental glass, richly cut. Of these lengths, or pieces, there are no fewer than thirty-two. To secure them at their bases (they are made to fit close between the bars), there runs all round the cage an ornamental gilt metallic band. When adjusted, no joins are observable. We see only a polished surface of radiating gems.

These fringes (as they may be termed), when fixed, serve a twofold purpose. They prevent the seed being scattered over the table or carpet; and when exposed to the rays of the sun, or the reflection of a fire or candle, they shine with a lustre that is worthy of fairy-land. Their prismatic colours are really beautiful. These fringes are easily removable and readily cleansed; but, as before hinted, it requires the light gentle hand of a fair maiden to prevent accidents. After two or three experiments, she will enter *con spirito* upon her pleasing daily duties, and never care to relinquish them to a stranger. The interior of the cage is so constructed as effectually to exclude all vermin, and so as to afford unusual opportunities for extreme cleanliness. The seed and water, too, are quite removed from contact with any impurities. Both are supplied in miniature cut-glass barrels, which are fixed in glass galleries, projecting one on either side of the cage externally. Each of these galleries revolves on a pivot, so that fresh seed and water can be readily given to the bird. They are so contrived as to admit of a bath being supplied, in summer, at the same opening. The cage-door is formed (invisibly) by two bars of glass. These may be removed or replaced at will.

The perches (square) are made of Bohemian ruby-glass. There is also a swing-perch of crystal and malachite. These colours add greatly to the beauty of the inhabitant. The top of the dome is of richly-cut crystal glass, powerfully refractive; and above it is a strong metal ring, by which the cage is to be suspended. It hardly need be added, that when raised above the head, it is seen to the greatest advantage, though it is ornamental any where. To prevent the bird being subjected to draughts when standing on a table, a movable screen, made of strong tinted cardboard and mounted on hinges, may be placed round one side of his cage. The screen, if painted, would be a neat ornament.

With a view to secure the uniformity and elegance of the exterior of the cage, the tray (or drawer) is *not* introduced in the usual manner. *The bottom of the cage forms the drawer*. This is removed by turning a screw, fastened (externally) in its centre. On its removal, a tripod is in readiness to take its place. On this flat surface, adapted to the size of the opening, the cage is quickly placed while the drawer is being cleaned and sanded. Once more lifting the cage with the left hand, the drawer is adroitly supplied with the right, and the screw turned from below. All is then complete. Two minutes or less suffice for the change.

The happiness and the whimsical conceit of birds living in these "fairy bird-cages" – particularly Love-Birds, Australian Paroquets, Canaries, Bullfinches, and Goldfinches – can be but faintly conceived. They *feel* their importance, and they *know* they are objects of admiration. It is perhaps difficult to say which is the happier, the bird or his mistress.

WILLIAM KIDD.

76

MRS. HENRY [ELLEN] WOOD, *EAST LYNNE.*

3 vols., 2nd edition (London: Richard Bentley, 1862), Vol. I, pp. 91–94

East Lynne had changed owners, and was now the property of Mr. Carlyle. He had bought it as it stood, furniture and all; but the transfer had been conducted with secrecy, and was suspected by none. Whether Lord Mount Severn thought it might prevent any one getting on the scent, or whether he wished to take farewell of a place he had formerly been fond of, certain it is that he desired to visit it for a week or two. Mr. Carlyle most readily and graciously acquiesced; and the earl, his daughter, and retinue had arrived the previous day.

West Lynne was in ecstasies. It called itself an aristocratic place, and it indulged hopes that the earl might be intending to confer upon it permanently the light of his presence, by taking up his residence again at East Lynne. The toilettes prepared to greet his admiring eyes were prodigious, and pretty Barbara Hare was not the only young lady who had thereby to encounter the paternal storm.

Miss Carlyle completed her dinner preparations, all she did not choose to trust to Joyce, and was ready for church at the usual time, plainly but well-dressed. As she and Archibald were leaving their house, they saw something looming up the street, flashing and gleaming in the sun. A pink parasol came first, a pink bonnet and feather came behind it, a grey brocaded dress, and white gloves.

"The little vain idiot!" ejaculated Miss Carlyle. But Barbara sailed up the street towards them, unconscious of the apostrophe.

"Well done, Barbara!" was the salutation of Miss Carlyle. "The justice might well call out! you are finer than a sunbeam."

"Not half so fine as many another in the church will be to-day," responded Barbara, as she lifted her shy blue eyes and blushing face to answer the greeting of Mr. Carlyle. "West Lynne seems bent on out-dressing the Lady Isabel. You should have been in at the milliner's yesterday morning, Miss Carlyle."

"Is all the finery coming out to-day?" gravely inquired Mr. Carlyle, as Barbara turned with them towards the church and he walked by her side and his sister's, for he had an objection, almost as invincible as a Frenchman's, to give his arm to two ladies.

"Of course," replied Barbara. "The earl and his daughter will be coming to church."

DOI: 10.4324/9781315399980-93

"Suppose she should not be in peacock's plumes," cried Miss Carlyle, with an imperturbable face.

"Oh, but she's sure to be – if you mean richly dressed," cried Barbara, hastily.

"Or, suppose they should not come to church?" laughed Mr. Carlyle. "What a disappointment to the bonnets and feathers!"

"After all, Barbara, what are they to us, or we to them?" resumed Miss Carlyle. "We may never meet. We insignificant West Lynne gentry shall not intrude ourselves into East Lynne. It would scarcely be fitting: or be deemed so by the earl and Lady Isabel."

"That's just what papa said," grumbled Barbara. "He caught sight of this bonnet yesterday, and when, by way of excuse, I said I had it to call on them, he asked whether I thought the obscure West Lynne families would venture to thrust their calls on Lord Mount Severn, as though they were of the county aristocracy. It was the feather put him out."

"Is is a very long one," remarked Miss Carlyle, grimly surveying it.

Barbara was to sit in the Carlyle pew that day, for she thought the farther she was off the justice the better: there was no knowing but he might take a sly revengeful cut at the feather in the middle of service, and so dock its beauty. Scarcely were they seated, when some strangers came quietly up the aisle; a gentleman who limped as he walked, with a furrowed brow and grey hair; and a young lady. Barbara looked round with eagerness, but looked away again: they could not be the expected strangers, the young lady's dress was too plain. A clear muslin dress with small lilac sprigs upon it, and a straw bonnet: Miss Corny might have worn it herself on a week day, and not have found herself too smart; but it was a pleasant dress for a hot summer's day. But the old beadle, in his many-caped coat, was walking before them sideways with his marshalling baton, and he marshalled them into the East Lynne pew, unoccupied for so many years.

"Who in the world can they be?" whispered Barbara to Miss Carlyle.

"The earl and Lady Isabel."

The colour flushed into Barbara's face, and she stared at Miss Corny. "Why – she has no silks, and no feathers, and no anything!" cried Barbara. "She's plainer than anybody in the church!"

"Plainer than any of the fine ones – than you, for instance. The earl is much altered, but I should have known them both anywhere. I should have known her from her likeness to her poor mother; just the same eyes, and sweet expression."

Ay, those brown eyes, so full of sweetness and melancholy: few, who had once seen, could mistake or forget them, and Barbara Hare, forgetting where she was, looked at them much that day. "She is very lovely," thought Barbara, "and her dress is certainly that of a lady. I wish I had not had this streaming pink feather. What fine jackdaws she must deem us all!"

77

IMAGE: UNTITLED FASHION PLATE

Journal des Demoiselles, August 1864

DOI: 10.4324/9781315399980-94

78

[ANON], 'THE FASHIONS.'

The Englishwoman's Domestic Magazine, June 1868, pp. 312–314

WE have anticipated so much upon the fashions for the summer in our descriptions this last month or two, that we have now scarcely anything new to mention in the way of dress.

With one exception, however – bonnets are still and for ever changing in shape and appearance, although their size remains as diminutive as ever.

The newest whim of fashion is to have the bonnet very high in front, the trimming forming a sort of coronet or diadem.

The *last sweet thing* in bonnets is the *chapeau Cocodette;* it is composed of three bouillons of tulle, edged and divided by satin rouleaux; this forms a puff, which is posed just on the top of the head above the chignon, and does not come down at all upon the ears. In front there is a coronet of flowers, and upon the bonnet a feather, which droops down over this coronet.

[....]

The present tendency of the bonnet is [. . .] to rise higher and higher above the forehead. It is a mere bandeau, coronet, or diadem, which leaves the head and ears completely uncovered. The strings are as often as not tied under the chignon, and the question of streaming ends at the back is also left to choice.

Whatever flowers are chosen for the diadem the leaves are metallic, more frequently of a golden brown colour than green. Feather flowers are also very fashionable.

Thus a diadem of feather field flowers looks remarkably well. Poppies are especially well copied from nature. Wheatears, blue cornflowers, wild violets, and large white daisies are added to them.

Then we see a perfect collection of insects, especially flies, bluebottles, bees, and beetles, swarmed once more within the domain of fashion, and sporting upon the flowers which adorn our bonnets and coiffures. Butterflies have become rare; but I saw at my *modiste's* quite a museum of flies and beetles. These are no imitations; they are the real insects – dried, prepared, painted, and varnished, so no wonder they look so natural. No art could imitate the wonderful delicacy of the thread-like legs and feelers.

This strange fashion occasioned a curious mistake the other day. A young lady dressed according to the very last decrees of *La Mode* was paying a visit to an old and respectable friend of ours unacquainted with all the changeful whims of

DOI: 10.4324/9781315399980-95

fashion. Suddenly the old lady gets up, quietly takes off the small bit of tulle and lace which served as an apology for a bonnet upon the head of her fair visitor, and begins to shake it out of the window.

"My dear," says she to the young demoiselle, who was looking on in amazement, "I would not frighten you by screaming out, as I felt very much inclined to do; but you have a horrible cockroach upon your bonnet. It no doubt fell from some tree as you walked up the Avenue. The garden is full of them this spring."

It was with great difficulty the young lady succeeded in persuading her friend that the disagreeable-looking creature was placed upon the tiny bonnet by way of ornament.

The fact is, I should shrink even from naming half the horrible creatures that now form part of the most elegant parures. But one need not carry this eccentricity so far, and there are some blue and green flies as dazzlingly bright as sapphires or emeralds, which really look very pretty, and make the exquisitely-copied flowers look still more natural.

79

P. L. SIMMONDS, 'ART-INROADS ON NATURAL HISTORY.'

The Art-Journal, November 1872, pp. 271–273

BY P. L. SIMMONDS

CIVILISATION and commerce are increasing the demands for Art-productions and artistic materials; hence the latter have to be sought over a wider range of supply, and the substances at command must be amplified and extended. Not very many years ago mineral substances were the chief stay of the jeweller, and vegetable products of the Art-manufacturer.

The sea and the air, the fields and the forests, have, it is true, always been the grand sources of inspiration for the painter; while the elegant palms, beautiful shells, and birds and animals, formed objects for the modeller and sculptor: but in this practically utilitarian age, larger inroads continue to be made on animated nature for artistic purposes and personal decoration. A note or two on these recent and extensive innovations may not be out of place in the *Art-Journal*. Some of these, such as shells, furs, feathers, mother-of-pearl, ivory, tortoise-shell, and coral, are special branches of trade which, in their commerce and various applications, are of sufficient importance to deserve separate notice hereafter. In this paper I shall therefore merely group together some of the miscellaneous animal and vegetable products which are now frequently applied to ornamental and decorative purposes.

Of coral, which resembles the lips, and pearls the teeth, of the fair wearers, we can all recognise appropriateness and elegance for ornaments; but it is far otherwise with some of those substances and ornaments frequently worn now. In an examination of the Indian, Queensland, the jewellery, and other courts of the annual London Exhibition, now closed, the feature to which I have thus drawn attention developed itself somewhat largely.

Dr. Birdwood, for instance, in the Indian Court, arranged a very instructive case of the fruits, seeds, seed-vessels, and other natural objects from which the Indian jewellers have taken their designs for ornaments and other artistic purposes. Although these were not scientifically named, there was no difficulty in identifying the common castor-oil seeds and seed-vessels, the coral seeds

DOI: 10.4324/9781315399980-96

of *Adenanthera pavonina,* the little red seeds with a black spot of the wild liquorice plant (*Abrus precatorius*), the seeds of the cashew-nut (*Anacardium occidentale*), and of the marking-nut (*Semecarpus Anacardium*), the capsules of the ochro (*Hibiscus esculentus*), the leguminous pods of the *Acacia* and *Mimosa* tribe, the red bean-seeds of other legumes, some undetermined horn-shaped seed-vessels, Job's tears, the seeds of *Coix Lacryma* and the seed of a less common *Coix* – for there appear to be several of this stony graminaceous seed, which is so commonly used for rosaries. One rare species, probably of *Coix Koenigii,* was shown at the London Exhibition, 1–62, in the petticoat of a Laos female, tastefully ornamented with it; this was sent home by the late Sir Robert Schomburgh from Siam. The vegetable-ivory nut is occasionally turned into ornamental necklets, hair-pins, and brooches, but with no very satisfactory result, for it soon darkens, and, even when stained mauve, is by no means an attractive article. In the Madras jewellery shown in the Indian Court, there were bracelets of the small corrugated seeds of *Elæocarpus ganitrus,* better known as Brahmin's beads; also other red, drab, and brown seeds, set and strung into necklaces and bracelets.

Elaborately carved (so-called) peach-stones of Chinese workmanship were also shown, set as bracelets. The minute carving of these is something wonderful. The native peach-stones of Australia, called quandung-nuts, the corrugated seeds of the *Fusanus acuminatus,* are also shown, set and mounted in gold as bracelets and scarf-pins. They much resemble in appearance the Brahmin's beads of India.

With the exception of coral, the mollusca, reptilia, and marine animals generally have not contributed much to the purposes of Art-decoration. Futile attempts have been made to bring the large scales of some fishes into use; but fish-scale ornaments appeared and soon passed away, novel though the application was. Shagreen made from the tuberculated skin of some species of ray, which was at one time largely employed for spectacle-cases, snuff-boxes, and other small fancy articles, is now scarcely ever seen. The Japanese, however, still prepare it in a beautiful manner for their sword-hilts, as it gives an excellent grip for the hand, and has a very ornamental appearance.

In the jewellery from Bombay, besides rosettes of the money cowry-shell, there was a native necklace of rough pieces of the chank, a large porcelaneous shell extensively used in the Madras Presidency and other localities, for cutting solid sections from, to form armlets and bangles for the legs; these are richly painted, adorned, and gilded.

Shells were some years ago much more used for artistic purposes and decoration than they are at present. The imitation flowers of shells, shell-boxes, and other made-up devices were, for the most part, hideous; evincing little or no skill or taste in the arrangement or the colouring of the shells to imitate nature. Some of the work in natural shells from the Bahamas was, perhaps, an exception to this general censure; and the polished Venetian shells have still a certain degree of popularity for necklets, bracelets, hair-pins, and such like. Shells in the aggregate have not been very tastefully used in an artistic point of view, large as the commerce is in them for various purposes. There were a few applications of shells to jewellery in the Exhibition, among which may be cited, in the Queensland Court, a small species of olive-shell, tastefully set in gold as an ear-ring, and ear-pendants and *solitaires* of shell and gold from Victoria. In the Queensland Court, as well as in the Jewellery Gallery, there was a new application of the polished *operculum* of some shell, set as bracelets, necklets, and *solitaires,* which were showy. A pair of small *Murices* are also set as ear-pendants, not a very sightly object, nor, we should think, pleasant to wear. A polished white limpet-shell, mounted as a brooch, was another instance of bad taste. To compensate for these incongruities, we may allude to four fine specimens of Roman shell, – cameos by Francati and Santamaria: a Madonna, priced at £25; a head of Flora, £30; and two 'Ecce Homo,' cut respectively on the red shell, and on a black ground, priced at £20 and £25 each. The shells used by the cameo-cutter are the bull's mouth (*Cassis rufa*), which has a sardonyx ground, and the black helmet (*C. Madagascerensis*), which has an onyx ground. Shell cameo-brooches, ear-rings, and pins have gone much out of fashion in this country, but still sell on the Continent and in America. There is a very highly ornamented application of the *Turbinella pyrum* among the musical instruments of India, in the form of a trumpet, a use to which certain shells are frequently put. The metal mounting and chasing is in good taste, and elaborate.

Ladies who would shudder or scream at the sight of a black-beetle or humble-bee can yet tolerate other insects on their person, and glory in a host of entomological spoils, in the shape of beetle ear-rings and necklets, and tiny insects attached to the artificial flowers they wear. Indeed, they are as savagely bedecked with the spoils of the animal kingdom as any aboriginal American *belle,* save that theirs are more richly set and strung, and involve more labour and outlay on the manufacture. A lady may almost be clothed and decorated from head to foot with products of the animal kingdom. The insect tribes will furnish her silk robes and hose, the gauzy tissues she wears can be embroidered with dazzling beetle-wings. She may indulge in necklets of beetles, and ear-rings and brooches of the same. Her coronal or tiara may be of the brilliant breasts and heads of the humming-bird, or other most costly nodding plumes.

For submarine spoils she may indulge in elaborately carved coral, cameos, or other shell jewellery, with pearl rings for her dainty fingers. Her gloves and her shoes will be of kid. Her fan, of ivory, of tortoiseshell, of pearl, or with feather trimmings, may have much ornamentation from the hand of the carver, or delicate flower-painter. Her opera-glass may be of ivory, of mother-of-pearl, or of tortoiseshell setting. Indeed, there is no limit to the obligation she will be under to the animal kingdom, as subsequent remarks will show. And first, I will enumerate some of the brilliant insects now laid under extensive contribution.

Among the green beetles at present employed for ornament are the large, long *Sternocera chrysis* of India, and the *S. cochinchinensis, Chiloloba acuta* of India, *Chrysochroa variabilis* of Malacca, the *Callospistra callypyga* of Malaysia, the *Lampetis orientalis* of India and the *Calosonia Francia,* both green with a bronzish tinge. The green and bronze *Cetonia aurata* of Europe, and the small *Chrysomela* and *Phaneus Damon* of Mexico; the small green *Atichira concina* of Mexico; the dark green *Onthophagus chevrolatii* of Mexico; the wasp-looking *Tetracha Mexicana;* the tiny *Cryptocephalus militaris* of Mexico; the brown and black marked *Chelymorpha biannularis* of Mexico, and a species of *Cyphis,* with black stripes on blue. The little blue *Hoplia farinosa* of Europe is very commonly fixed on flowers now by artificial florists.

Mr. A. Boucard showed a case of bird and insect jewellery, consisting of a coronet, brooch, and ear-rings, made with humming-bird feathers, and several sets of brooches and ear-rings made of *Buprestidæ, Cetonidæ,* and other insects with brilliant *elytra,* or wing-coverts.

Even the flimsy moths are turned to ornamental use, for we have the blue Cyprus butterfly mounted on a pin as a hair-ornament. Nature's animated kingdom is, of a truth, being ransacked now for ladies' ornaments.

The feet of birds and animals are also utilised for other ornamental purposes. Thus among the numerous applications of natural history objects for the nobility made by Mr. Edwin Ward, of Wigmore Street, I have noticed the lower skin casing of the foot of the elephant mounted as receptacles for various articles; the feet of the flamingo for whip-handles, fox-pad scent-bottles and match-holders; the feet of the little mouse deer of the Indian islands made into crochet-needle handles and pen-holders, &c. While in order to propagate natural history information, this zealous naturalist makes silver boxes for holding snuff, or scent or other things, the exact model of the brain of the royal Bengal tiger; and further utilises the skull for ornamenting the smoking or billiard-room, the eye-sockets being made to hold lights, and the other cavities, cigars, snuff, and whatever else may be required; while skull letter-boxes are another natural history application.

Claw-jewellery is a comparatively recent innovation; and the endeavour now is how to convert the unsightly objects of tusks and claws of animals into ornaments for the person. Tiger's claws and leopard's claws can be had set as ear-rings, brooches, or pins, from thirty shillings up to as many pounds. There was a good specimen of elaborate ornamentation of this kind from India in a brooch or pendant of a pair of tiger's claws tipped and cased with gold, suspended from a delicate gold chain, and having a square gold ornament attached, set round with rubies, emeralds, &c., priced at £25; a tiger-claw necklet with gold-setting and suspended locket was shown by Lady Garlies.

The combination of two claws into a lyre shape, with appropriate gold-setting, is not an unsightly ornament; another pattern is in the form of a snake-brooch, with a silver arrow passing through it. They are also made into *solitaire* studs, and taper-holders for the pocket. I have also seen the long claws of the great South American ant-eater mounted as a desk seal handle. Then small teeth and tusks are utilised to form paper-knife handles; rhinoceros teeth from the Gaboon for ear-rings, a back comb for ladies' hair made of wild boar's tusks, the canine tooth of the musk-deer mounted as a brooch, badger's teeth charms, a thimble made from the tooth of the crocodile, coat-links of teeth, a support for fruit-dishes on the dessert-table made of wild-boar's tusks, and the clavicle or collar bone of the tiger made into tooth-picks and tobacco-stoppers. Who after this can say that every part of animals is not utilised? A mere enumeration, without descriptive figures of the style and setting, conveys, however, but little idea of the adaptation and curiosity of many of these trinkets and ornaments.

The so-called bird-jewellery now consists of brooches, necklets, and pendants, as well as tiaras. The ruby and topaz, the garnet, emerald, violet-crested, and Clorassa humming-birds are those chiefly utilised; the head and beak being set in gold mountings of different kinds. How long these novelties will continue fashionable remains to be seen. Then we have even the foot of the ptarmigan and grouse set as a brooch. What these singularities portend we cannot say, or whether there is any fancied special charm in wearing them as amulets.

One of the most choice specimens of bird-jewellery is the head of the king humming-bird for a centre, surrounded with the crests and breasts of the ruby and topaz humming-birds. Nothing can compete with this for brilliancy and play of colour.

There was a head-dress or tiara shown made of the breasts of several kinds of humming-birds, and a variety of brilliant-coloured beetles: while, for those who like to match their jewellery, a brooch of the blue warbler can be had, or a roseate circular brooch of the head and breast of the garnet humming-bird.

In former times the entire body and plumage of the rare bird of paradise was, with the exception of stray feathers, the chief coveted ornament of the ladies; now that fashion has stamped its *imprimatur* on this style of personal decoration, all the gorgeous-plumaged birds are in large request for hat-plumes, necklets, and other ornamental uses.

Before science had taught the art of dyeing all kinds of feathers with artificial colours, the natural feathers of the bright-plumed birds were eagerly sought after for making feather-flowers and other ornaments, and the choice handiwork of the nuns of the convents of Madeira and Brazil possessed considerable value. The best were those of a purple, copper, and crimson colour, from the breasts and heads of humming-birds; one of these feather-flower wreaths has a beautiful effect, reflecting different coloured light. The wing-cases of brilliant beetles were also used, and glittered like precious stones. Even savage rulers and chieftains prided themselves on the rarity of their feathered ornaments. Hence plumes, garlands, and mantles made of one or two choice feathers from scarce birds came to have a fabulous value, as in the state-cloak of the Sandwich Island monarch, which is made of the feathers of a rare bird (*Melithriptes pacifica*), only one yellow feather under each wing being obtainable; so that the garment, which has been in course of manufacture during several reigns, is valued at a million of dollars.

Science has thus helped on even the use of feathers, for these can now be tinged to any colour, and a method has been discovered of turning black feathers into grey, so that they may take bright colours. Feathers of natural colours are, however, still preferred where they can be obtained. Thus in Brazil the cocks of the rock, white herons, roseate spoon-bills, golden jacamars, metallic trogons, and exquisite little seven-coloured tanagers (*Calospiza tatao*), with many grey parrots and other beautiful birds, offer an assortment of colours capable of producing the most exquisite effects, as is frequently seen in the fancy work applied to the border or fringes of their hammocks.

A pair of Chinese ear-rings of gold and feather-work, was exhibited by Miss Francis Redgrave, and a pair of a similar class of Japanese origin by Miss R. Cole.

But bird-skins are now turned to other ornamental purposes by artificially and artistically disposing them into articles of furniture, for fire, hand, and lamp-screens. The male giant Argus pheasant, the horned Argus pheasant, the Impeyan pheasant, and other showy-plumaged birds are thus arranged: the head and neck are made the centre of ornamentation, and the feathers of the breast, body, wings, and tail are disposed around. The capercailzie and other native game-birds have been thus formed into ornamental fire-screens. Mr. E. Ward, of Wigmore Street, has brought this style of ornament very largely into use.

But it is not the plumage alone of which we despoil the feathered tribes for artistic purposes and decorations. The eggs of some of the larger birds, especially the ostrich and the emu, are now handsomely mounted and set as drinking-vessels, goblets, sugar-holders, &c. A fine mounted specimen of the ostrich egg was shown in the French Court, and was one of the most chaste in its setting that I remember to have seen. Of the dark olive-green emu egg, many specimens were shown in the Queensland Court. The silver mountings and settings of some were in very good taste, and contrasted well with the dark colour of the shells. A few of these were shown in the "Illustrated Catalogue" published with the August number of this Journal.

Ornaments made of human hair have almost gone out of date, and we seldom see now hair-chains or rings. But novelties of this kind appear to be still in request. If we do not, like the Japanese, make strong cables of human hair, our ladies appreciate things that are rare; hence the few stiff bristly hairs on the tail of the elephant are thought worth setting in gold filigree-work for a bracelet. The Australian aborigines wear a twist of opossum hair for necklets, and the Indians of Canada pluck and dye the hair of the moose deer, with which they embroider their mocassins and fancy baskets; whilst in India the spiny quills of the porcupine are formed into many ornamental articles for the table.

These few stray notes will serve to show how ruthlessly we attack animated nature for the purposes of commerce in the first instance, and artistic applications in the second. There is ample room, however, for the development of more taste and artistic skill in the arrangement of some of the objects and materials thus attempted to be brought into general use.

80

[ANON], 'BEETLE-WINGS.' ('ENQUIRIES.'; ENQUIRY FROM 'ELSIE') [A] AND [ANON], 'BEETLE-WINGS (ELSIE).' ('ANSWERS TO ENQUIRIES.'; RESPONSE TO 'ELSIE') [B]

The Treasury of Literature and The Ladies' Treasury, 1 September 1874, p. 168 [a], and 1 October 1874, p. 224 [b]

ENQUIRIES

[....]

BEETLE-WINGS. – I have a box of the beautiful green beetle-wings sent to me from India. What use can I make of them? – ELSIE.

ANSWERS TO ENQUIRIES

[....]

BEETLE-WINGS (ELSIE). – Send them to a florist's to be mounted in diadem form for the hair. They also make pretty trimming for ball dresses, arranged alternately like myrtle leaves.

DOI: 10.4324/9781315399980-97

81

[ANON], 'THE STRANGE STORY OF A SEALSKIN. A TALE OF METEMPSYCHOSIS.'

Judy, Or The London Serio-Comic Journal, 24 November 1875, p. 52

ONCE upon a time I was – ALIVE.

ONCE upon a time, not very many years ago, I was a living, breathing, believing, plump, and happy little Seal.

Now I am only a Muff – a sealskin one, battered, worn, and cynical; for I have had a hardish time of it, I can tell you – have passed through many strange adventures – known many strange folks.

We were the last of our race, my little brother BOB and I; we were twins, and loved each other dearly. Papa and mamma, uncles and aunts, brothers and sisters, cousins, and all the rest of our happy family had been cruelly slaughtered to satisfy the wicked desire of a set of wretches called Young Ladies, who had them brutally murdered, and their bleeding, palpitating skins made into Coats, Muffs, Hats, Purses, and other articles of selfish luxury, which administered to their inordinate vanity and thoughtless gratification.

At last *our* time came. Whilst gambolling in innocent playfulness on the beach one fine morning, we were attacked by the hired emissaries of our natural foes – the Young Ladies, who, I have since learnt, form part of, and as such are tolerated as a necessary evil by the useful members of the species known as Human Beings.

Our innocent young heads were both stunned by the same cruel instrument. One crushing blow was quite enough for me – I was always considered the delicate one of the family – and I gave up the ghost. In my last agony I heard my brother's voice bidding me a plaintive "Farewell!" and my glazing eyes saw him taken up – not unkindly, it seemed – in the arms of another emissary just as my murderer was about to deal him another blow.

"What," I murmured sorrowfully, before quite losing all consciousness, – "what though dear BOB's life is spared for the present, what, oh! what, will be his future fate?"

DOI: 10.4324/9781315399980-98

Little did I then imagine that I, in the spirit, should see him once again, after long years, in the flesh!

* * * * *

I will not dwell upon the painful details of the period of my metempsychosis; let it suffice that, when that most uncomfortable performance was completed, I became an extremely handsome – SEALSKIN MUFF.

In my lamentably altered state, however, the doctrine of metempsychosis proved itself no false creed; I still retained my seal soul, and my heart beat as warmly as ever for my poor little twin brother. One dreadful thought agonized me.

"For," I asked myself, with a throb of conscious pain, "supposing dear BOB *is* still alive, and supposing, by some extraordinary chance, I should meet with him, would *he* know – recognize *me* in my present guise?"

* * * * * * *

But I will not unfold the tale of my Life and Adventures as a Muff. I will refrain from giving you glowing descriptions of my first gracious Mistress and the High Life I saw in her company. At last she tired of me – a way gracious mistresses have, I'm told – and made me over to her maid, who sold me in bondage to her Uncle, a long-nosed gentleman of the Hebrew persuasion. In this abiding-place was I subjected to the degradation of the Spout, and witnessed many strange sights.

Exposed for sale, as an "unredeemed pledge," in the window, I soon found a purchaser. But I will not reveal the identity of the pretty Young Lady with the golden hair who thus rescued me, only to drag me into a vortex of dissipation, and prematurely ruin my constitution by long nights passed in gas-lit, heated "dressing-rooms" – for my golden-haired Mistress was what is called a Lady of the *Corps de ballet* – in unlimited "half-and-half," lobster suppers, and late omnibuses.

One Sunday morning my Mistress, with another Young Lady from her theatre, took a cheap return ticket to Brighton, to visit a place called "the Aquarium."

To me this "Aquarium" was full of interest, containing, as it did, many denizens of my former and native element; but my Mistress and her friend seemed to find the ham-sandwiches and bitter ale of the Refreshment Department more in *their* line. As we were on the point of coming away, the friend said suddenly, –

"Why, gracious me! POLLY, we've never been to see the best part of it – the Seals, you know."

I nearly fell off my Mistress's hands with surprise. What was that? – *Seals!* My heart throbbed loudly; my breath came quickly.

"This way," the Young Lady said, and we went it.

In a couple of minutes we were looking over a low rail into a little pond, prettily arranged with rockwork.

Behind a large boulder in this pond a round shiny head appeared, and a pair of bright eyes regarded me steadfastly.

Merciful heavens! As I gazed my memory went back through many long years, through the strange life of my present form, to one bright morning on a quiet sunlit beach, and two small seal brothers gambolling in fraternal affection – to the sudden attack of cruel assassins – to the Oblivion of Death – to the awakening in a new state of existence – to loving thoughts and cherished memories of the missing brother – and *now* – – !

For that sleek head, though developed to twice its then size, those eyes, that gazed at me so unconsciously, belonged – *to my brother* Bob!

Yes, I had at last found my long-lost twin, and now – *now he didn't know me!*

It was more than I could bear. The cruel blow stabbed me to the heart. I started involuntarily, and fell forward into the pool.

The next moment I felt two rows of sharp teeth seize me in their grip. *My twin brother had takes me for something good to eat!*

And yet there *are* friends, other Muffs like myself, who wonder at my bitter tongue, and dub me Cynic!

82

[ANON], 'LIVING JEWELLERY.'

Funny Folks, 8 March 1879, p. 77

["Living jewellery" – beetles and so forth – is likely to become fashionable.]

An anxious look was in her eye –
   She wriggled in her seat –
Nor seemed to heed the well-born youth
   Who pleaded at her feet.

"Be mine! he sighed; "believe me, love,
   On you I set such store" —
She did not sweetly ask him "Why?"
   But wriggled more and more.

"You hear me, don't you, ownest own?
   Say, when shall we be wed?"
She rose, and writhing as she stood,
   "It tickles so!" she said.

"Good heavens! darling, what's amiss?
   Do pains my poppet rack?"
"*My living locket,*" she replied,
   "*Is crawling down my back!*"

DOI: 10.4324/9781315399980-99

83

MONTAGU BROWNE, *PRACTICAL TAXIDERMY: A MANUAL OF INSTRUCTION TO THE AMATEUR IN COLLECTING, PRESERVING, AND SETTING UP NATURAL HISTORY SPECIMENS OF ALL KINDS. TO WHICH IS ADDED A CHAPTER UPON THE PICTORIAL ARRANGEMENT OF MUSEUMS.*

(London: L. Uppcot Gill, 1884), p. 261 and advertisement

JEWELLERY. – Following the example of the ladies who indirectly send expeditions to "frosty Caucasus or glowing Ind" to take tithe of animals for the sake of their skins, of birds for their plumes, and of insects for their silk, to be used in adornment, society demands that objects of natural history should not be all relegated to the forgotten shelves of dusty museums, but live as "things of beauty and joys for ever." Hence the new alliance between the goldsmith and the taxidermist, resulting in a thousand ingenious combinations of nature and art – a list of a few of which may not be unacceptable as hints.

For earrings, two leopard's claws are mounted as miniature Robin Hood bugles, the mouth and bell of each being of gold, attached to which is a chain depending by its centre from the ear-wire. Two tiger's claws placed base to base, their hooks pointing inwards, are strung and clasped with gold, thus forming the lyre of the Tragic Muse, as a brooch or ornament for the breast. Beetles, usually of the genus chrysochroa, also, are set as earrings. Humming birds' heads, their throats surrounded with a fillet of gold, form also handsome brooches. The feet of the various species of grouse and owls are capped with silver or gold (in which is set a cairngorm), the toes tipped, or the tarsus banded with silver or gold, to form clasps or brooches.

 DOI: 10.4324/9781315399980-100

84

[MRS] M. E. HAWEIS, 'SMASHED BIRDS.'

Belgravia, May 1887, pp. 336–340, 342–344

A CORPSE is never a really pleasant ornament: most people with a real feeling for beauty will agree with me. Holbein painted one with terrible truth to nature. Other old masters, equally great, painted many corpses: but they were all painted with a motive – to startle, not to tickle, the pulses. All the ideas awakened by such an image are *charnelle,* not joyous; and the primary object of all decoration is to give joy and pleasure, to appeal through the eye to the happiest emotions: which a corpse does not do – even when it has glass eyes. I think Nero (though a man of taste for the arts, it is said) was wrong in lighting the arena at night with corpses. I do not believe it gave anyone pleasure, even those robuster visitors with a contempt for death and pain, and great lack of sympathy for the individuals who blazed.

Neither did I ever enjoy the monks in the ossuarium at the Cappucini, Rome, though they were fairly well set up, and stuffed out, and meant, I suppose, originally, to renew happy and grateful associations in those who had known and loved the good fathers when alive, and came to see them dead. 'Ah! happy morning,' one pious visitant may have exclaimed, 'that I spent with Padre So-and-So, only three years ago; it is nice to see his kind face again, though somewhat crushed by the weight of yonder holy soil!' 'Benedicite!' another humble soul would add, 'is it possible that three years have passed since the kind father laughed, talked, walked with me? how it reminds me of pleasant days to see him now on his feet again, rest his soul, holy saint as he is!'

No doubt this was the mood meant to be excited in visitors, with a soft undercurrent of warning, 'As he is, thou shalt be' – and a comfortable gush beneath that, 'But, hurrah! I'm not yet.'

But nineteenth century visitors do not feel the same for these poor corpses. They do not like the corpses at all, and I must repeat, I do not think glass eyes would mend matters.

Why do we not like human corpses? Because the living human frame is so familiar to us, so full of interest and meaning in its motion and activity, that the mere casing, when deprived of that life and movement on which its whole meaning hangs, startles us as inappropriate. The stillness chills us and vexes the heart. The

DOI: 10.4324/9781315399980-101

attitudes are unfamiliar, and vex the eye. Well and scientifically stuffed, the corpse even of our dearest friend would be objectionable, I fear; and badly stuffed, with all the muscles and joints misunderstood, it would be horribly disagreeable. And given the normal frame undisturbed – why, the fervidest dissector would hardly recommend a 'dem unpleasant body' to decorate the drawing-room, bed-room, dining-room – no, nor the kitchen, nor even the garden. Nowhere, I think, would the corpse be in place: and BECAUSE – because we are too familiar with the living body to be able to endure it dead; because *all* our pleasant associations are with life, and only unpleasant ones remain with the image of the Cessation of Life.

Now, why do people, and especially small children, like stuffed animals? because they are not sufficiently familiar with the living body of the animal to feel any shock on seeing the dead one. They miss no familiar action, they are ignorant of the proper curves, and they think the glass eyes look so harmlessly 'alive again.' But that is a fault in training.

They think them beautiful; they do not see that the colours are dull, faded, or ridiculously renovated with dye. Such is their ignorance that they feel as the peasants felt when they saw the good father who had christened the child, or calmed the sick, standing up in a nice frock, looking as good as new. Oh, crass stupor of the senses! bluntness of feeling for the reality of association! it is not the frock which makes the monk, it is not the fur which makes the squirrel, nor the wing nor the glass eye which brings back the song and the rustling of trees, and the darting flight in the sunshine. Nothing but being unaccustomed to the form and action of the creature living, makes that creature pleasant to us when it is no longer alive. This becomes obvious when we replace the foreign bird with an English puppy or kitten, or some creature we are used to see about us. Is a bird more suitable than these to carry on the head? is it, for instance, a greater respecter of places than a white mouse? Does it weigh less?

I once visited the stuffed birds departments of the old British Museum with an accomplished ornithologist. He was very unhappy at all he saw, and pointed out to me the ill-shapen breasts, over-stuffed or crooked crops, damaged heads, crazy and paralysed legs. Stuffing is better done now, but it is ever an art more fitly relegated to scientific museums than used for home decoration, because decoration implies beauty, and beauty means pleasure; and death, *to those familiar with life,* is not a pleasurable idea. Even the admirably mounted birds *au naturel* in the new departments at South Kensington are far better there than they would be anywhere else, and the most elegant bird's nest is mistakenly placed on a hat.

When I was in America two years ago, in many ways the pleasantest tour I ever made, I found a fashion rife which had not yet submerged England, the fashion of wearing huge birds, mostly in a rather smashed state, on the head gear. When I went into a car of a morning, I could not help immediately counting half a dozen smashed birds; I changed to a second, nine smashed birds met my gaze; went into a third, sixteen smashed birds. Along the street, every other woman had a smashed bird on her head, every bonnet-shop was full, and at Boston, where, the weather being rainy, black waterproofs were commonly worn by all classes, this gay-coloured smashed bird peering from the macintosh hood, ever and aye, struck me as quite comic. I have seen a grey parrot put to this use, and I constantly saw gulls towering two feet from the face. Once a whole car was set laughing by a 'funny man,' who asked a lady passenger 'if it pecked?' She had a large bird of prey spatchcocked on her. In England we are unaccustomed to a livery as universal as this. I am sorry to say I once rashly made a small remark about this everlasting smashed-bird-and-macintosh, which of course got into the papers, and several peoples' feelings got damaged, for which I was, and still am, very sorry, because I spoke inadvertently and without malice.

Since then the disease has reached England. We too spatchcock on us, back or front, monstrosities which set some of us wondering whether they are most heartless or most hideous. The raggedest girl can clap a smashed bird on her smashed bonnet, and she does it. If she cannot afford to buy one, she can trap a young sparrow, tread on it, and pin it to her unkempt head. The richest leader of fashion is radical enough to keep her in countenance, for in England equality of woman is a *furor*; and there no longer exists the prejudice that 'what everybody does' is 'vulgar' – indeed, vulgarity is a *culte* in more ways than one, by reaction. From America comes our levelling tendency; from America, our smashed bird. Let us take from America now the example set by her most cultivated ranks, and discourage the indiscriminate slaughter of creatures, so useful and beautiful in their proper places, in order to put them to an unnatural use in pursuit of – it sounds ironical to say beauty and joy – so we must say ugliness and pain. America's Audubon Society did not actually precede our Selborne Society; but it is fifty times as active, and therefore fifty times as useful.

Now, the reason I did not like these smashed birds was (1) because I am acquainted with live birds, and the agonised attitudes vexed my eye. The poor impaled beasts seemed to cry aloud from the hat, 'Help me! I am in torture.' They seldom had their limbs in the right places; generally the head down, one wing up, the other – well, occasionally on the contrary side of a bow – and the legs splayed out like horns. Miserable it was, to an art-student. (2) A big bird, even when properly placed, legs below, head up, and a wild hilarity in its eye, is a considerable weight, and such a burden is out of place at the edge or front of a hat. A living bird could not stand there; the head could not bear the weight. A live pigeon weighs 1 lb., a gull from 2¼ lbs. to 5 lbs.; and therefore its being there in effigy contradicted the canons of good taste.

Every way this Wild Indian fashion struck me as in the worst taste, partly because the stuffed birds recalled death so much more than a fur trimming, or a fine ostrich plume—just as a hare sent up *au naturel* is sickening, whilst hashed hare is not; and partly because the size and angularities of the wings and legs firing out detracted from the delicate curves and colours of the face below, and many faces were quite obliterated under them.

Then I began to hear of the harm done in the rural districts by such wholesale destruction of feathered creatures, because insects multiplied when their enemies were massacred, and the crops up country suffered as much as our eyes in the streets.

Visiting North Devonshire not long ago, Lee and Morthoe, I noticed that never a bird's song struck the ear; one never saw a bird. I was told the wise and intelligent natives had long waged war on all small birds; and what was the result? Why, that hardly a single walk could be taken in the woods for the mass of slugs that lay all over the rich grass everywhere, sometimes in uncounted numbers, only four or five feet apart – slugs so huge that they reminded one of snakes, only that a snake is less disgusting, and has better manners; at least it will politely remove itself when it sees you coming. The brutal slug is like the slimy lounger, heavy with drink or selfishness, who will bar your way without apology, when there is no road but past a public house.

Pretty Lee was a purgatory to me thus; whichever green glade I sought to penetrate, Fafner barred my progress, and stretched and yawned in his vile content at being too horrible to crush. Why were these disgraceful slugs fattening all over Devon? because the birds were writhing on hats, or hanging in tatters on barn doors. And snails, earwigs, all the grubs and beetles one can think of, avenged the birds on the farmers' crops and the gentry's pleasaunces. The 'caterpillars innumerable' eat more than the birds did. In vain the indignant farmers wail! God is 'on the side of the big battalions,' even when the army is of slugs, and it is of no use praying for good harvests whilst we make them impossible. Much of the failure of crops and the fall in the value of land and home produce is directly traceable to our interference with the proper balance of nature in her creatures.

However, were the fashion of wearing mangled birds and beasts on the head really pretty and pleasant to the educated eye, no consideration for farmer or innocent pedestrian could be expected to touch the thoughtless votaries of *la mode*. Still less can they be touched on the sentimental side – have not some leathern girls danced at balls with a trimming of robin redbreasts on their half-clad forms? – and questions of cruelty are certainly best discussed distinct from questions of beauty. I have never been unphilosophic enough to argue the question of dress from the moral side, though I may nurse a private opinion that a moral side exists and has a most deep influence, because dress is an index to character. And it is only because so many pretty faces on both sides the Atlantic have been spoilt by this smashed-bird excrescence of sick Fancy, that I venture to allude to the farmer as above; who deserves scant pity, no doubt, whilst himself remains the worst naturalist.

I only wish to intimate that whilst a properly-stuffed beast (only of small size) as an article of dress may be allowed to be a matter of opinion, a contorted rag of one, with wrenched muscles, or bits of him mixed up with bows of ribbon, can be nothing but an insult to both Art and Nature.

But of this I am convinced: it is only because the actions and attitudes of birds are unfamiliar to the common eye – because natural history is almost never studied except from prints and dead specimens – that women (otherwise of taste) can tolerate such objects, intended for the most important part of the frame, the head, as everybody sees at her milliner's.

English knowledge of wild creatures in their natural habitats is disgracefully neglected. There is hardly an English painter who can draw a bird; whilst the poor Japanese draughtsman can sketch in three strokes not only the outward bird, or fish, or fly, but the whole vivid life and habits of the creature. His drawing is excellent in its grace and freedom – but his knowledge of natural history behind it gives us a solid satisfaction which leaves the European artist very far out in the cold. Take any sixpenny Japanese fan, you can almost hear the finches chitter and polish their beaks – the wood-pigeon coo to his resting mate with head turned over her back – the flip of the water as the red fin cleaves it in search of the whirring prey!

[. . . .]

Those of my readers to whom the names of the Audubon and Selborne Societies aforementioned are as unfamiliar as the anatomy of birds, may be glad to know that when rural property and rural pleasure in America, were seen to be in danger through thoughtless shooting by boys and indiscriminate trapping by milliners' envoys, when entire species were disappearing from the groves and fens, the lovely humming-bird exterminated in several places, the innocent bobolink[1] and others becoming extinct, the American Ornithologists' Union got an Act passed for the Protection of Birds other than game birds, and their nests and eggs. (The game birds were already under protection.) The Audubon Society set itself to create a public sentiment in support of the law. The active members endeavoured to enlighten the crass ignorance of the common people by instructing them in the important functions performed by birds in planting seeds, fertilising virgin and poor soil, devouring young grubs, chrysalids, and flies on the wing, and many more ways. They popularised 'dry' scientific reports on natural history of all kinds, and taught those classes whose liberty was restrained by the prohibitive Acts, *why* legislation was vital, and what would be the consequences of indifference. The society rapidly grew to immense proportions, and one of the first effects was the reduction of the odious fashion of wearing smashed birds.

The Selborne Society in England, named after the place made famous by the fervent naturalist Gilbert White, is doing much the same work, and the members include the names of most of our best artists and scholars, and many men and women of the highest rank, headed by the Princess Christian.

The Selborne Society does not confine its interest to birds, of course; it also strives to protect places where wild flowers grow, from destruction by the mischievous root-sellers, who dig up annually thousands of bulbs (to sell part and waste part) and often injure what they leave behind. Near Wolverhampton many spots once the haunt of primrose and bluebell are now entirely denuded, and this in the Black Country is especially deplored.

But the Society markedly includes a Plumage Section, to which belong those ladies who forswear smashed birds. They do not forbid themselves ostrich plumes, than which nothing is more beautiful, an occasional eagle's or peacock's feather, or a blackcock's tail, nor other feather trimmings obtained from birds carefully farmed, or killed for food; but they try to discourage the wholesale destruction of

1 Innocent in the Northern States. Many birds are harmless in one district, as rooks and starlings in Wilts and Gloucester, and mischievous in another, as the same birds in Kent.

insect-eating and song birds in every district indiscriminately, for the mere purpose of disfiguring hats, muffs, and screens.

Over 30,000,000 birds of bright plumage, it has been calculated, are killed *annually* for the above purpose alone! and this does not include victims by accident, wanton lads just promoted to a gun, and the loss of deserted eggs. This shocking and disgusting fact can be only gradually realised; but worse particulars can be obtained from the Secretary, Mr. George A. Musgrave, F.R.G.S., 45 Holland Park.

It is much hoped that clergymen, employers of labour, heads of colleges, and those connected with classes of workwomen and workmen, seeing the advantage of at least an elementary knowledge of natural history, will do all they can to bring this useful little Society into notice in every town and village, beat up new members, and send up new subscriptions: though children and the poorer sort can join it as *free members*. Classes and village magazines should be started to encourage such notes and queries as we thank Gilbert White for to-day – *not* to grub up rare plants and kill rare birds and butterflies to stock museums, but to observe the *living* habits and character: or if there must be some destruction, at least to spare young broods and eggs, and to replace seeds where the blossom has given pleasure.

Landed gentry are asked to check their keepers in destroying owls, kestrels, and other mice-eating birds, and reminded that rats and mice like pheasants' eggs for breakfast. Farmers, to observe *which* birds do the mischief – and *where* – before they kill off every insectivorous songster. Mothers and fathers, to teach humanity to their boys and girls, and not selfish greed. Women . . . not to make themselves mere walking Death's-heads!

However, tenderness for innocent creatures must not trench on the primary question of what is becoming in dress; and if death can minister to beauty and joy, death will do so. Leigh Hunt, a man of heart before a man of stomach, would not eat larks, because 'it was like eating a hymn.' Some object to *pâté de foie gras* because it is prepared by frightful cruelties. But others are of robuster fibre, like those who watched Nero's Christians blaze in pitch to light an evening *fête*; and my own humble opinion, which is distinctly against the skeleton at the feast, cannot be imposed on others consistently with my well-known principle that in dress, if dress is properly an index of character, *everyone must do as she likes*.

Still, likes and dislikes can be regulated, and I am not without hope that with improved education, new sensitiveness will develop itself in the armies of the obtuse; that a fashion rooted in want of feeling will be scouted as a solecism, because want of feeling is another word for want of taste; and that Englishwomen, following the lead of better-bred sisters across the Atlantic, seeing that heart and character betray themselves even in a bonnet, will come to 'like' their costume to mirror only good qualities. And with the 'sweet reasonableness' of the New York women, let them confess that what their good sense cannot sanction their heads must not flaunt. It is better to have a heart in one's body than to wear it 'on one's sleeve' for every daw – and that smashed – to peck rebuke at, especially when one gains nothing in good looks.

M. E. HAWEIS.

85

[ANON], 'CHRISTMAS & NEW YEAR GIFTS.'

Le Follet, December 1892, p. 10

Our readers know – and, doubtless, many of them share – our thorough admiration of Mr. Rowland Ward's wonderful skill in the preservation of wild and tame animals, and of birds.

To speak of any animals from his studio as "stuffed" would class them with the mis-shapen bolsters, or bundles of straw covered with skins, that are sometimes shown as specimens of taxidermy in the shops, and that is out of the question.

Mr. Rowland Ward is an artist, as Landseer was, and his animals are as natural in their pose and their expression as any Sir Edwin ever painted; indeed, being a sportsman – and of great fame, too – he has studied wild animals under circumstances Landseer never was in. The general expression of wild animals is that of ferocity, or of greed, or simply sleepy contentment; but some of those in the collection at 166, Piccadilly, have been made to express anything Mr. Ward chooses, without in the least losing their natural character. A delightful instance of this is shown in two tiger cubs, which are utilized as dumb waiters, standing on their hind legs holding card trays in their fore paws. These new "page-boys" are in different rooms, but it is impossible not to be startled with the wonderful contrast in their expressions. One has a nervous, timid look, as if "this was his first place," and he knew he was not up to the work, but was very anxious to please. The other cub was equally desirous of giving satisfaction, but evidently felt he "was a very good boy indeed."

Either of these would make an admirable Christmas present to a man fond of sport. For those who like eccentricities we should counsel the purchase of a Crocodile, with his head and fore paws on the ground, his body erect against the wall, his hind paws spread out, and part of his back utilised as a receptacle for umbrellas and similar things. A large sofa with high back, covered with Zebra skin, would be a welcome addition to any hunting lodge.

For ladies, also, there are many unique and most artistic and attractive things at this studio. Among them are some exquisite cases of birds – not the stiff wooden and wire birds perched on twigs, that the words "stuffed birds" bring to our minds. The birds here are all in natural and most varied positions. One case that specially charmed us represented a piece of broken stone wall, over which trailed a branch of blackberry foliage. On this were two little common sparrows – the whole thing

DOI: 10.4324/9781315399980-102

so natural, so artistic, it was worth all the glass cases of gorgeous hued tropical birds ever seen.

A large tortoise, brilliantly polished, was fitted up as a work-box, disclosing, on the lifting of his back, all the necessary implements for needlework in a turquoise-blue satin case. This was made for Lady Brooke. Another tortoise contained a musical box.

At the Burlington Gallery – 27, Old Bond-street – are some very attractive screens – hunting, racing, and coaching subjects, framed as screens, in all sizes, from those to stand on tables to any height or number of panels desired. Two we specially admired would make very acceptable presents to most men, and handsome additions to any room to which their subjects would be suitable.

One screen, about three feet high, had the four panels representing phases of otter hunting, painted in very artistic and most spirited manner by Mr. Alfred Davies. The other – four feet six – had two large folds, in which were twelve coaching scenes, some of modern, others of olden, coaching times, all most admirably painted, and a source of never-failing interest.

The table screens have beautifully-executed photographs of sporting subjects, copies of paintings from the same Gallery.

86

J. H., 'NEW STYLES IN FURS'

Myra's Journal, 1 November 1896, p. 32

QUITE the latest thing in furs is the Figaro. It should be made up in some close fur like seal, beaver, caracul, or astrakan, so that the figure is not needlessly disguised. Anyone with an old-fashioned cape of such a fur should have it re-made into a Figaro, like Figures 86.1 and 86.2.

This model does not take much fur, though it has a smart little epaulet, fluted in the latest style, and the fashionable *évasé* collar. The collar, as illustrated, is lined with chinchilla, but the same fur could be used throughout, for collar-lining and Figaro. To prevent the little coat from being too heavy its silk lining is very slightly wadded.

The large buttons are purely for ornament, the Figaro hooking down the front if required to be closed.

Figures 86.1 and 86.2 are an entirely extra wrap, quite apart and independent of any *vêtement* which may be worn with it. But if your quantity of fur is limited, you could have a sacque coat trimming made in the Figaro form, which is very new and stylish.

Smart jackets and long full capes will be worn, made of seal or astrakan. What do my readers say to a long seal cape for three or four guineas? This seems an impossible price, but it is not impossible with the new electric seal.

This fur, equal in appearance to any seal short of the very best, is really the coat of the tame rabbit (wild rabbits will not do) judiciously pruned and dyed by the aid, I believe, of that all-potent factor, electricity. It is a wonderfully effective fur. How it wears it is too early as yet to say.

Figure 86.3 shows a good way of using up broad bands of white Thibet lamb – bands which formerly edged a long opera cloak. The fur, lined with satin, is mounted in the new flutes upon a green velvet yoke cut in one with an *évasé* collar. The collar is lined with lamb, the yoke with wadded green satin. Points of jewelled lace decorate the yoke and collar. The small muff (figure 86.4) can be made out of the same band of fur.

Figure 86.5 is a new style of pèlerine specially adapted for seal, sable, or beaver. It is a great collar, forming flutes in front before it tapers into fichu points which are tipped with bows.

DOI: 10.4324/9781315399980-103

Figure 86.6 is another charming method of modelling a Thibet lamb wrap. It is a cape for evening or dressy wear, and is made on the same principle as figure 86.3, but the yoke and collar are of the lamb, like the fluted edge and the collar lining. This lovely wrap should be lined with quilted white satin.

Figure 86.7 is the latest edition of the sable *vêtement* tipped with tails. The cape is not very full and has a very moderate collar. It is new, stylish, and really elegant. Without the tails it is a good model for electric seal. The small sable muff (figure 86.9) completes the set.

Figures 86.1 to 86.14 New Styles in Furs.

Those ladies with fewer specimens of the sable's glossy coat at their disposal would be able to muster enough, perhaps, for the elegant *vêtement,* figure 86.8, which is a deep shoulder cape finished with long square fichu ends, tipped, like the cape, with tails. Figure 86.10 is yet a third example of the fichu pèlerine so fashionable this winter. The fur is deeply fluted on the shoulders. Sable tails and heads finish the collar and the waist. Tails tip the fichu ends. The sable muff, figure 86.11, is of the well-known bag shape, trimmed with a head and tail.

For ordinary cloth coats there is no fur decoration preferable to the broad collar and revers (figure 86.12), which is carried out in all furs this year. Caracul, chinchilla and sable furs are perhaps the favourites for the purpose.

Figure 86.13 is a beautiful cape of a type very prevalent. The yoke and *évasé* collar are of caracul. The fluted edge or added cape is of black Thibet lamb. The good remnants of two sets of furs can be utilized for this model.

The comfortable and stylish little *vêtement,* figure 86.14, is of sealskin, the big collar and revers being lined with chinchilla. Four large and handsome buttons trim the front.

The fur which is being more "imitated" than all other furs but seal this season is chinchilla. Like seal we have the natural, the real chinchilla; we have it in a false fur (chinchilla is very successfully imitated by manipulating the skins of certain rabbits); we have it in a silk plush. Seal has been imitated in plush for some time with excellent results; but now for the first time is chinchilla plush really satisfactory. The manufacturers (like the dyers of "electric" seal) found great difficulty in producing the lights in chinchilla fur (the source of its beauty), to say nothing of its exquisite softness and thickness combined. The analogy of chinchilla plush with seal plush goes further. Both are more durable than the real fur. Although sealskin is so expensive, it loses its perfect bloom much sooner than seal plush does; it is more injured by a thorough wetting and the unavoidable "rubbing" which wear entails. The same with chinchilla plush, which lasts much longer in good condition than the most evanescent of furs; chinchilla is sadly liable to moth, and it soon looks frowzy and worn. Yet it is very expensive when really handsome.

J. H.

87

C. W. GEDNEY, 'VICTIMS OF VANITY.'

The English Illustrated Magazine, August 1899, pp. 417–426

IT is somewhat remarkable that the most civilised nations should be those whose womenfolk delight to deck themselves with the plumes of birds. There can be no doubt that this is the survival of a fashion which dates back to the days of our barbaric state, and it tends to confirm the popular theory that women are strongly conservative. Several years ago an association of earnest and good ladies was formed in London for the protection of birds. These bird-lovers – with Sir John Lubbock as their President – have waged war against the wearing of birds or feathers for personal adornment. A very large section of the English Press supported this movement. But public opinion is one thing and fashion is another, and when feathers and birds are the "correct thing," our womenfolk will wear them in spite of all the newspapers in the country. Thus we find that the importation of rare skins and plumage, for millinery purposes, is greater than ever at the present time. For several seasons past there has been a run on the nuptial plumes of the scarce herons and cranes, and the other birds have, as a consequence, been in less demand. But the vagaries of fashion are so great that the garden-hats of to-day may presently give place to something much smaller and quite different in style. The unwritten laws of fashion are inexorable, and however courageous a woman may be in other matters, there are very few of the sex who would wear an unfashionable head-dress and run the risk of being called "dowdy." The ladies of Switzerland have formed a very strong league, in which some thousands of them have signed a pledge not to wear any bird or feather (except ostrich plumes) for a period of ten years.

Paris is credited with the responsibility for the present fashion in hats and bonnets, and the prodigal display of birds and their plumage by way of adornment. If such be really the case, it is curious that our anti-plume wearers have not attacked the French ladies of the Gay City, and induced them to follow the example of their Swiss neighbours. As a matter of fact, some such efforts are being made, or were proposed to be made, at the last annual meeting of the English Society for the Protection of Birds. Meanwhile the trade in skins and feathers goes on apace, and our well-dressed womenfolk carry their borrowed plumes with the consciousness that these adornments are both costly and *chic*. Writers and speakers who argue against the cruelty and waste of rare bird-life which such fashion entails, are usually accused of doing injury to the cause they advocate by excessive zeal. I hope

DOI: 10.4324/9781315399980-104

to escape such adverse criticism by appealing to facts and figures rather than to sentiment, and I have been careful rather to under than over-state the case.

Amongst many other attempts made to educate public opinion against the killing of birds for their plumage, the American "notion" of a "bird-day" appears likely to bear good results in the future. If you want to convert a woman, you must catch her young; and our cousins across the water have decided to start on the schoolchildren. The study of ornithology and the protection of birds has been added to the curriculum of nearly all the schools in the States. The natural savagery of the boy, however, is a factor to be taken into account in this connection. He may not have the slightest idea that he is guilty of wanton destruction; but it comes naturally to him to rob nests alike of their eggs and callow young, regardless of their rarity. But we must hope for some changes of fashion, some developments of public opinion, and the passing of legal enactments, if those who are to succeed us are to see living specimens of brilliant-plumaged birds. At the present rate of destruction, the end is not far off; and future generations will assuredly anathematise us for impoverishing the earth of its most beautiful birds.

EGRETS AND OSPREY PLUMES

Much has been written and spoken, both from Press and pulpit, about the killing of these birds when actually feeding their young, for the sake of those nuptial plumes which are erroneously called "ospreys" in the trade. An osprey is a fish-hawk, which produces no feathers for millinery purposes. The birds which supply those costly plumes which are now so fashionable are egrets, which belong to the heron or crane family. There are several members of these waders, although it is chiefly from the Eastern and Western Hemispheres that we derive our supply of egret feathers. Tropical America furnishes the bulk of the white plumes, which are the most valuable, while China, Rangoon, and other Eastern countries contribute their shares, especially of the coloured varieties. West Africa produces some beautiful slaty egrets (*Aodea gularis*), whose plumes are almost as valuable as the white ones. These birds are all fish-eaters, who build rough platform-nests of sticks on branches which overhang water. They congregate in big colonies at such times, and lose much of their shyness, so that the hunters can make a clean sweep of the whole settlement by shooting the parent birds on their nests. At other times these birds are so exceptionally shy and wary that it is difficult to get a shot at one. Their plumes get soiled and frayed in the process of feeding and rearing their young, and such feathers are of small value in the trade compared with those obtained in the earlier stages of nesting. The hunters only pull out the plumes, and leave the dead birds on the ground.

Until quite recently – less than a year ago – the officers of our Royal Horse Artillery, Hussars, King's Royal Rifles, and the Rifle Brigade wore aigrettes of these rare feathers in their head gear. Thanks to the efforts of Sir John Lubbock in the House of Commons, the War Office has abolished the use of these plumes in the Army.

According to Mr. Witmere Stone, Chairman of the American Ornithological Society, the dry season of 1898 enabled the egret-killers to penetrate the swampy Everglades, and thus collect an exceptionally heavy crop of feathers.

It is impossible to obtain complete figures as to the trade done in egret plumes in London alone, but we can measure its extent approximately by the City auction sales. These by no means represent the total consignments, because only the large importers send their feathers to the hammer. The small dealers dispose of their goods direct to middlemen and milliners. For the purposes of this article, I omit altogether those who form the outer fringe of the trade, and deal only with the four large importers whose goods were sold at the London Commercial Sale-Rooms last year. The names of these four firms of importers are: Messrs. Lewis and Peat, Messrs. Hale and Son, Messrs. S. Figgis and Co., and Messrs. Eastwood and Holt. These four firms alone sent, between Feb. 15, 1897, and Dec. 13, 1898, the following bird-skins to auction in our City sale-rooms: birds-of-paradise, 34,960; packages of osprey plumes, 2209; and cases of various bird-skins, 2140. Osprey plumes are sold by the ounce, and the "packages" vary in size considerably, but taking the smallest as a basis of calculation, there were 50,000 ounces of white egret feathers sold by auction in London last year. These plumes are exceedingly light in weight, and it requires the nuptial feathers of six egrets to make up an ounce of "shorts," as the best plumes are termed in the trade. They have varied in prices, according to the supply, from £10 to 70s. per ounce. Taking 50,000 ounces as the total weight (which it was not) of the egret feathers sold in London last year, and allowing six parent birds for each ounce of plume, this represents the slaughter of 300,000 adult egrets, to say nothing of their nestlings. It is well within the mark to quadruple these figures in order to arrive at the total annual destruction of these birds for dress ornamentation. American women are as keen on osprey plumes as their European sisters. The various States have prohibited the killing of egrets, but the law is an utter farce, as there is no one to enforce it, and the possession of such feathers is no offence.

As may be imagined, there are tricks in the trade of making up feathers into ornaments, as in every other money-making industry. By a little skill and ingenuity a single long plume can be made to do duty for two "shorts," which are the most valuable. This is "good business" with feathers which may have cost between £5 and £10 an ounce. The plume is cut in half, and manipulated in such a manner as to conceal the operation. All attempts to manufacture artificial "ospreys" have failed – more's the pity. Some fashionable milliners, however, have had to allay the misgivings of customers by assuring them that their plumes were artificial. But these are only fictions, used in defence of trade interests against those people who make an outcry about the cruelty of the egret feather trade.

CROWNED PIGEONS

From Australia and New Guinea we obtain these, the largest of the pigeon tribe, and their crowns are utilised, in the same manner as egret plumes, for the adornment of women's head-dress. In size, these graceful birds are equal to a domestic fowl, and their towering crests make them appear even larger. To kill such scarce and beautiful birds for the sake of a few feathers from its crown can only be described as wanton slaughter. Fortunately, they can be bred in confinement, even in this country, under favourable conditions, and I am told that the plucking of crest feathers from the living specimens is a regular industry. The delicate French-grey tint of these plumes is a very fashionable colour, and they do not lose their pristine beauty so quickly as the pure white osprey plumes obtained from the egret. I don't think there is any risk of the crowned pigeon being actually exterminated.

The head, with short piece of neck, is the only portion of this king of the pigeon family which possesses any market value for dress purposes. From what I gathered among dealers, the supply of these bird-skins had dwindled down to very small numbers in the London market. There were not more than 500 altogether came under the hammer last year in our city, and the price realised did not exceed 5s. per head.

SOME AMERICAN TRIBUTES TO THE GODDESS OF FASHION

The scarlet tanegar (*Phyranga rubea*) is an American songster which is in great request among the skin-collectors who supply the market with birds for hats. The tanegar is very showy, his brilliant red breast and body being well set off by dense glossy black wings and tail. Measuring only some seven inches long, this bird is in great demand, and some twenty years ago I used to see many cases containing one thousand skins each in the hands of East-End dealers. But such consignments are no longer made, and the spring migrations into the Northern States are now as limited as are the nightingales in our own country. The female tanegar is quite unlike her resplendent mate, her body-colour being an olive-green, merging to yellow on the abdomen, while the wings and tail are rusty brown, tinged with green. Like most of the very brilliantly plumaged foreign birds, the tanegar moults twice a year, assuming a rusty, shabby coat in winter, and donning his showy wedding garments with the return of spring. It is surprising that our American cousins have not adopted some repressive legislation to save these pretty songsters from destruction, especially as America is not particularly rich in song-birds. Not that I would say for one moment that, in point of numbers, we can compare with America for birds that warble rather than sing.

Another of the American songsters whose handsome plumage is fast leading to the destruction of his race is the Virginian nightingale, or crimson cardinal (*Fringilla cardinalis*). In addition to the wholesale slaughter which goes on to supply the demand for decorative purposes, many thousands of these cardinals are annually imported into Europe as cage pets. In size they are equal to a thrush, being eight inches long, and the cock is a vivid crimson throughout, save his face, which is covered, as by a black mask. He has a crest of red feathers, which he can erect or depress at pleasure, which makes him a very strikingly handsome bird. Both male and female sing the true nightingale song, the "jug-jug" and water-bubble notes being very strong, though lacking the sweetness of our English spring prima donna of the bird world. These birds are caught in the snow, with nets, the same as larks are netted in this country; and it is a pitiful waste of bird-life to slaughter these songsters by the thousand for the gratification of a craze in dress. There are several kindred varieties of the Virginian nightingale being decimated in the same manner – namely, the various gros-beaks and the grey cardinals, with crimson heads and crests, which form a striking contrast to their sober body-colour. Nor must I omit from the American songsters that are being killed off the face of the earth for dress ornamentation, the indigo bird, the bobolink, purple finch, and painted nonpareil. Apart from mere song and sentiment, the orioles perform a very useful part in the economy of nature, for they are snake-killers, and, by ridding the country of tree-climbing, poisonous snakes, these birds are doing service to man. The Baltimore oriole, in his brilliant livery of orange-yellow body with black extremities, makes a very showy ornament to a lady's hat; as does his next-of-kin, the chocolate and black. But no one who has known these lovely birds either in a wild state or as cage pets can see them used as headgear without a feeling of repugnance. The orioles are very domesticated birds in the States, choosing orchards by preference for their breeding-places; arriving in the spring and departing with the first signs of winter. They build a pouch-like nest, suspended by grass fibre, beneath the fork of a high branch, and these nests swing to and fro in the wind. And woe betide the black snake which is caught in the attempt to poach either eggs or young from such nests. The poacher is inevitably blinded by the fierce attacks of the orioles, whose slender, needle-pointed beaks peck out the eyes of the intruder. There is some lumping together of American small-bird skins in the sale catalogues; but of scarlet tanegars and blue robins alone there were sold in our City last year 120,000 specimens.

HUMMING-BIRDS

These exquisite little gems of the bird world were for many years much in request among the élite as ornaments both for bonnets and hats, high prices being paid for the more brilliant specimens. The inevitable results followed, in accordance with the law of supply and demand; and, as a consequence, Florida is now the only country in which the humming-birds are found, except as rarities. A small bird that will realise a dollar in the skin – firsthand – for a woman's hat-ornament is not likely to survive long, and those which do are for the most part only the commoner and less brilliant of the varieties. I may mention that the very rarest specimen known to naturalists was bought in a Paris bonnet-shop, distorted out of shape, as an ornament for a woman's hat! Mere words cannot describe the varying brilliancy and vivid contrasts of these wee creatures' feathers. When darting about in the sunshine sipping honey from flowers, they flash like burnished gems, now ruby, now emerald, then flashing gold and turquoise-blue. They are essentially exotic little creatures of the sunshine, flitting from flower to flower, like bees and butterflies, and extracting with their long tongues the nectar upon which they, for the most part, subsist. Their nests, suspended at the extremities of slender branches – over water by preference – are exquisitely finished specimens of nest-making art. They are cup-shaped, but being tossed about by every breath of air, the top rim of the cup is curved inwards to prevent the eggs rolling out. In this, as in everything else, the humming-birds show that mere size does not count, either with regard to intelligence or courage, for they are the most fearless and aggressive little creatures imaginable, and fight like game-cocks among themselves. There are a great many varieties of these birds, varying in size from that of a swallow to tiny little mites half the size of an English wren. Although they vary greatly in form – some fork-tailed, others crested, and some with elongated centre tail-feathers – yet they all possess the same glittering class of plumage. Asked as to the average number of these bird-skins which came under the hammer in London, a well-known dealer in both fur and feathers replied by turning up some old catalogues. Quoting from these, he said that from 80,000 to 100,000 skins would be well within the mark, the brighter-coloured varieties predominating. And be it remembered that there are at least three or four other capitals wherein quite as many humming-birds are annually sold as dress ornaments.

BIRDS-OF-PARADISE

Of all the gorgeous birds that are killed for the adornment of women, those referred to in the above headline are the most beautiful, as they are also the scarcest and most expensive. In bulk of body the largest is not much larger than an English blackbird, but its resplendent appendages make it appear a much bigger bird. The commonest variety, which one usually sees in ladies' hats, is the emerald, and this has a rich chestnut brown body, with a yellow head, and a throat of vivid green; but it is the glorious tail which forms the striking part of this superb plumage. [. . . .] New Guinea is the home of the three or four varieties of birds classified as *Paradisea,* but they are all so utterly unlike each other in size, shape, and plumage that there appears to be nothing in common between them. For a long time the capture of birds-of-paradise was confined to the natives, but the demand for skins, as articles of dress, tempted white men into the trade, and in the near future these gorgeous creatures will be as extinct as the dodo.

Last year proved an exceptionally bad one for the few surviving birds-of-paradise, no less than 25,000 skins being sold in the London auction-rooms. But there was a "slump" in the market for these birds, fashion favouring the upright aigrettes of the herons and crane family. In one auction sale of 6174 skins last October, I find that the top prices for birds-of-paradise were from 23s. to 10s. apiece, while some of the smaller varieties – including kings – sold from 1s. to 2s. 6d. each. It is said that some of these skins were old stock, held back for a rise from previous seasons' importations. A well-informed dealer assured me recently that the larger birds-of-paradise were almost exterminated. According to Professor Alfred Newton's figures, there were offered for sale in London auction-rooms alone last year 34,960 birds-of-paradise.

GOLDFINCHES

Although our English birds are the most famous songsters of the whole of the feathered tribe, they are too sober in their colouring to find favour as dress-ornaments. The goldfinch is one of the exceptions, and, as a consequence, these charming finches are becoming – indeed, they have become – exceedingly scarce. Within the recollection of those of us who call ourselves middle-aged, the southern and western counties of England produce great numbers of these "thistlefinches." Such is no longer the case; the netters have practically exterminated them. They are "protected" during the nesting season by Act of Parliament, but our Legislature, in its wisdom, left them to the mercy of the trappers in the autumn, when they most needed protection. At this period of the year they congregate together, and migrate in flocks, lingering for weeks upon our coasts. This is the harvest of the clap-net bird-catchers. Goldfinches have an inordinate love of thistle seeds, and they are, therefore, among the most useful of birds to those who cultivate the soil. But a row of thistle-heads, set up between folding nets, with call-birds in small cages, has tempted this race of beautiful finches to what amounts, practically, to extermination. A certain proportion of the youngsters so captured survive, and end their miserable lives in cages about the size of a cigar-box in some city slum. The adult goldfinches, however, will not stand captivity, and they go to deck the headgear of those rustic beauties whose resources do not admit of mounting egret plumes. There are not wanting apologists for the bird-trappers, who thus rob us of our most beautiful songsters; and these good people tell us that the decrease of thistles accounts for the disappearance of goldfinches! Unfortunately those of us who live in the country know, to our cost, that – thanks to derelict farms – there never were so many thistles and dandelions and so much groundsel as there are at the present time. It is not a question of food supply. We have simply allowed a horde of bird-catchers to overrun the country and sweep into their nets these charming finches, year after year, until the race has now become almost extinct. It is pitiful that birds so exquisitely brilliant and beautiful as the English goldfinches – and such skilful songsters, too – should be sacrificed to deck the hats of womenkind, or perish miserably in reeking alleys.

THE TOUCAN

In the building up of "combination" feather ornaments, the plumage of these gorgeously coloured birds is largely used. They are natives of Guiana, Mexico, Columbia, Cayenne, the Upper Amazon, and tropical South America. Naturalists classify the toucan as being a near relation of the cuckoo, but it requires some effort of the imagination to trace any likeness between the two. It is difficult to understand what purpose the toucan's huge beak was designed to serve in the economy of nature. These birds are for the most part fruit-eaters, but they will snap up a mouse or a small finch if they get the chance of doing so. It is the breast plumage of the toucan which possesses a market value for dress decorative purposes. These pads of vivid colouring are chiefly in favour as ornaments to winter toques, surmounted by some other feathers rising out of this brilliant foundation. But for the ponderous and apparently unwieldy trunk of the toucan, he would be a graceful bird. His huge beak, however, is as light as a strip of cork; and it is astonishing with what ease and delicacy the bird can manipulate his serrated mandibles. One of the peculiar uses to which this big beak is put is the trimming up of the primary tail-feathers. These are cut round by the toucan's bill as clean as if they had been shorn off with a pair of scissors.

OWLS

Women are not alone responsible for the killing of rare birds, and I therefore venture to say a few words against the crass folly of those men who shoot owls. The average keeper cannot resist the temptation to kill anything at all out of the common, and I am afraid that Velveteens is not the only sinner in this respect. In those large English forests which are left to us a few owls still survive, but in sadly diminished numbers, and the village church towers, which were formerly their havens of rest, know them no more. Their skins, however, possess a market value, but it is difficult to understand the bad taste which prompts a woman to wear an owl's face in her hat! These nocturnal birds sleep through the day and feed at night, sweeping by you on their soft and silent wings, and ridding the land of innumerable mice, which destroy the corn crops.

According to official catalogues, I find that the sale of hawks' and owls' skins for dress ornamentation is larger than would be imagined. There were sold of these birds' skins no less than 22,000 in our metropolis last year. Of jays and kingfishers 100,000 came under the hammer, and the bulk of these went to the salmon-fly dressers. The blue chatterer, which used to furnish the "cheek" feathers of modern salmon-flies, has been practically exterminated, and the flymakers have now to fall back on the turquoise feathers of the kingfisher.

COMBINATIONS

Under this heading must be classified some of those wonderful productions of the milliner's art which one sees in churches and other places where the sex do congregate. Into these composite plumes all kinds of wings, body, plumage, and feathers are included. For the higher class goods, the Impean pheasant and peacock's body skins are used as "foundations," with fearfully and wonderfully inappropriate things springing out of them, in the shape of wings and feathers. It is to these made-up ornaments that most of those plumes go which are classified as "various" in the plume trade catalogues. Peewits, turtle-doves, greenfinches, shrikes, little grebes, sea-swallows or terns, hawfinches, house-martins, swallows, jays, and magpies – these are all among the "real" English birds and feathers so employed. With the use of dyed feathers I am not concerned in this article, but it is worthy of note, in passing, that the gaudy productions of the dyer's art fail to find favour with the élite. They will have the real thing, and cheerfully pay their guineas for such ornaments. There is no means of arriving accurately at the numbers of British birds thus sacrificed to fashion, because the sale catalogues only give the number of parcels and packages, without stating their contents. Then there is a large trade in wings, etc., done by trappers, gamekeepers, and others, with milliners in country towns and villages; and the extent of this cannot be arrived at even approximately.

PART 4

Handicraft

This selection of sources offers some examples of the variety of objects women produced at home. Within this context, middle-class women were strongly advised against undertaking so-called 'plain' needlework or the mending of clothing (especially in company), and were instead encouraged to pursue recreational activities such as crochet, embroidery, scrapbooking and paper craft, alongside trinket and picture-making from natural materials including leaves, shells and seaweed.[1] These 'home handicrafts' were intended either for personal use or for gifts, and signified a woman's skillfulness, imaginativeness, household management, thriftiness, and crucially, her access to leisure time. And, as the Victorian period unfolded, boundaries between the production of domestic objects and commodities became porous, and ladies moved beyond amateur creativity into professional artistry. Here, however, we focus on the material culture women produced, both in and for the home, as decorations and adornments.[2]

Our first source is a pamphlet on the craft named 'potichomania' (also known as 'potichomanie') and instructs the reader in how to emulate costly and highly fashionable porcelain artefacts using affordable materials such as cut-out paper pasted on painted glass.[3] Indeed, these 'imitative arts' such as 'potichomanie' and 'diaphanie' (a source on which is also included in this section) bore testament to the refinement and manual dexterity of the craftswoman, as well as to the enjoyment she derived from producing such illusion-causing objects. As Talia Schaffer points out, when observing so-called 'imitative art [. . .] [t]he viewer had to be momentarily tricked into believing the illusion, while knowing at a deeper level that it was fictional and puzzling out the method that produced it'.[4] In a similar vein, our second source is an extract from Mrs [Rebekah] Skill's book on modelling wax flowers. Wax flower models were used for the study of botany from the later part of the eighteenth century, and the craft became a favourite activity for women of social standing (or aspirations of such) during the 1840s and 1850s. Moving, as Ann B. Shteir writes, 'beyond most writers of wax flower manuals', Skill invites her readers to closely study flowers and attain knowledge of botany in order to achieve truly remarkable results in their own work.[5]

The author of 'Curiosities of Industry Among the Ladies', published in *Chambers's Journal* of 1855, adopts the persona of a 'solitary bachelor' who has become 'deluged' with handmade gifts from his young relatives.[6] Interestingly, the author draws direct comparisons between the material culture of amateur craft and modish clothing, observing that domestic handiwork is 'as much the subject of fashion as the dress of the fair operatives, and has undergone almost as many mutations and revolutions as feminine costume itself'.[7] Offering a dizzying array of the various crafts that young ladies produced in the period, this article's very title draws attention to the relationship between handicraft, leisure time and gender. Yet in spite of the inconvenient (and sometimes bizarre) nature of the items created, the writer concludes that rather than stifling 'the natural instinct' of producing an artefact, this might be redirected to a more 'lofty and efficient purpose'.[8]

The next source is excerpted from *Elegant Arts for Ladies,* a manual which includes a section on etiquette for various social occasions, as well as guidelines for making (and illustrations of) a variety of home decorations and ornaments. The extracts we have chosen concentrate on hair work, deemed 'as truly feminine an occupation as the finest crochet or richest embroidery'.[9] As we have seen in our earlier section on Mourning attire, hair jewellery was a popular means of commemorating the dead. In this spirit, the author of *Elegant Arts* suggests that women's delicacy and their affections for their lost loved ones can produce meaningful commemorative pieces. In another section reproduced here, beadwork is revealed to be a useful and economical pastime by which women could decorate their own clothes with beaded fringes and buttons of their own making, thus avoiding the costlier shop-bought ornaments. Indeed, Schaffer observes that 'handicraft was closely associated with fashion: both appeared in lavish illustrations in women's magazines, both used elaborate textiles, both involved patterns, and both were offered in new sets every month'.[10] Here, echoing the sentiments of the *Chambers's* writer, the reader was reminded that fashionability extended beyond sartorial dress into the production of objects following the season's trends.

The following extracts include selections from middle-class periodicals such as *The Ladies' Treasury*, *The Lady's Newspaper,* and *Bow Bells,* which offered patterns and advice on beadwork, imitation coral, and crafts using both seashells and seaweed. Emphasis was placed upon the imitation of both natural and artificially-made substances, as we see in the crafts imitating 'white coral'.[11] Here, natural materials such as seashells and seaweed are also used to produce trinkets and albums. In doing so, they bear testament to the appropriation of natural history – an area traditionally dominated by men – to women's handicraft.

As we have seen in our sources on potichomanie, fancy beadwork and natural history, both class and cultural appropriation are prominent themes within this section. Ariel Beaujot points out that 'middle-class adjustments to aristocratic style were not seen as shams or imitation, but as modifications that allowed the middle class to see itself as a class apart, distinct from the aristocracy while still appropriating its symbols of refinement'.[12] The extract from *Cassell's Household Guide* (which included a variety of advice from calisthenics to children's medicine) focuses on diaphanie, guiding the reader in achieving the effect of stained glass with paint, thus making aristocratic and artistic trends affordable to middle-class women.[13]

Our next source, the didactic short story 'A Fair Hand', published in *Our Young Folk's Weekly Budget*, negotiates the tension between desire for, and pretensions of, social standing through the theme of handicraft. Although aimed at a younger audience, the magazine also included material aimed at young people, and specifically girls. In this tale, the working-class protagonist Agnes Mason is anxious not to spoil the appearance of her hands, fearing that they might become swollen by the everyday household tasks of washing and ironing. But while she is skilled at making pretty wax flowers, her aspirations for leisure are already compromised as she utilises her talents out of necessity, namely, by offering lessons to ladies who wish to learn the craft. There are various issues at play here, and, as Agnes' employment enterprise proves a failure, she is left in charge of the household following the death of her overburdened mother. Predictably, Agnes can only be 'rewarded' by the eventual outcome of marriage when she has learned to become adept in household management. Ultimately, it seems, handicraft should only become the domain of those who can afford it.

Dora Hope's fictional narrative 'How to Preserve Leaves and Flowers', was published in the so-called 'Holiday Number' of *The Girl's Own Paper*, a weekly magazine that included a variety of articles on issues relevant to the lives of girls and young women. In contrast with 'A Fair Hand', this tells the tale of a ladylike governess of reduced circumstances, who nonetheless maintains her social standing and who creates beautiful pressed flower arrangements in her modest, but tasteful, dwellings. Likewise, the article 'Uses for Shells and Sea-Weeds' concentrates upon moral, educational and even sentimental reasons for collecting items from the natural world, presenting the reader with ideas of how to create 'a pleasing memento' of their outdoor experiences.[14] But these 'pretty' and 'delicate' trinkets only tell part of the story,[15] as the process of cleaning shells involved a highly corrosive substance called muriatic acid, now known for its health risks.[16] Yet this did not deter the Victorian female crafter. The 'Answers to Correspondents' instruct readers on how to apply this liquid, which, they are told, 'will remove the rough quality on the outside of shells', and simultaneously warns them of its corrosive properties.[17]

Handicraft could also function as emotional currency, and our next source is taken from John Strange Winter's (pseudonym of Henrietta Eliza Vaughan Stannard's) 1886 novel *Mignon's Secret*,[18] which, as Terence Cave documents, formed part of a literary fad that emerged in the wake of Goethe's 1796 novel *Wilhelm Meisters Lehrjahre*.[19] The extract charts a minor episode within Winter's novel, but one which reveals the pervasiveness of craft as a means of covert expression of attachment or 'devotion'. This incident focuses on the antimacassar, a decorative item created as a means of protecting furniture from damage caused by men's Macassar hair oil, which became popular from the 1830s.[20] Yet, this item was notorious in its status as an unwanted gift, and was often daunting to male visitors, being particularly notable for uncontrollably sliding off chair backs 'directly you touch it'.[21] In our extract, which appears early in Winter's novel, a ten-year-old girl uses craft as a method of thanking Captain Lucy, a Scarlet Lancers officer who, as Cave explains, 'rescues her from mistreatment at the hands of her stepmother'.[22] In response, the child, nicknamed 'Jack', plots to make Captain Lucy an antimacassar, seemingly undaunted by her lack of skill in this area. The episode culminates when Jack regards the result of her labour, an ill-made and dirty example of handiwork, with evident satisfaction, oblivious to its technical defects and, by implication, to certain conventions of polite femininity.

Finally, the extract from the satirical periodical *Pick-Me-Up* distils discourses of sentimental value, leisure time, curiosity and handicraft, representing them as self-referential of women's aptitudes. When nothing else is left to crochet, imitate or adorn, ladies of standing turn to tattooing their own skin. In doing, they move beyond the premise that handicraft is an extension of a woman's selfhood, or a performance of gendered and class expectations and aspirations, into handicraft as a literally embodied female activity.

Notes

1 See S. Hyde, *Exhibiting Gender* (Manchester and New York: Manchester University Press, 1997), p. 93. This discussion focuses upon the popularity of embroidery, and specifically the style known as 'Berlin woolwork'.

2 For the transition from domestic creative labour to professional production, see K. Hadjiafxendi and P. Zakreski (eds.), *Crafting the Woman Professional in the Long Nineteenth Century: Artistry and Industry in Britain* (Farnham, Surrey and Burlington, VT: Ashgate, 2013), and specifically K. Hadjiafxendi and P. Zakreski, 'Introduction: Artistry and Industry – the Process of Female Professionalisation', pp. 1–22.

3 This source refers to the imitation of porcelain in styles as diverse as 'Indian, Etruscan, Sèvres, and Japanese China', but pays little attention to the differences between them, merely directing the reader to choose between 'the Chinese, Etruscan, Sèvres, Egyptian, or Japanese pattern, as [their] taste may direct'. See [Anon], *Potichomania; Or, the Art of Imitating Porcelain* (London: Hutton & Co., [1850]), (n.pag.). This attitude does not seem anomalous; another article on 'Potichomanie', published in *The Englishwoman's Domestic Magazine,* makes general reference to 'such quaint-looking articles as come from China and Japan', here giving no attention to the design or cultural inspiration for these items. See [Anon], 'Potichomanie', *The Englishwoman's Domestic Magazine* [n.d.; Vol. 3, 1855?], p. 303. This would reflect Anne Anlin Cheng's wider observation that 'there is no room in the Orientalist imagination for national, ethnic, or historical specificities'. See A. A. Cheng, 'Ornamentalism: A Feminist Theory for the Yellow Woman', *Critical Enquiry*, 44(3), (Spring 2018), pp. 415–446 (p. 425).

4 T. Schaffer, *Novel Craft: Victorian Domestic Handicraft and Nineteenth-Century Fiction* (Oxford: Oxford University Press, 2011), p. 38. For a discussion of the popularity of imitative arts and, briefly, of potichomanie, see pp. 38–41.

5 A. B. Shteir, '"Fac-similes of Nature": Victorian Wax Flower Modelling', *Victorian Literature and Culture*, 35, 2007, pp. 649–661 (p. 654).

6 [Anon], 'Curiosities of Industry Among the Ladies', *Chambers's Journal*, 7 April 1855, pp. 209–212 (pp. 209, 211).

7 [Anon], 'Curiosities of Industry', p. 209.

8 [Anon], 'Curiosities of Industry', p. 212.

9 [Anon.], *Elegant Arts for Ladies* (London: Ward and Lock, 1856), 'Weaving or Plaiting Hair Ornaments', p. 4.

10 Schaffer, *Novel Craft*, p. 48.

11 See also Schaffer, *Novel Craft*, for an illuminating and engaging reflection upon the Victorians' interest in the imitation of coral using wax. See 'Introduction: How To Read Wax Coral, and Why', pp. 3–26.

12 A. Beaujot, *Victorian Fashion Accessories* (London and New York: Berg, 2012), pp. 4–5.

13 For a discussion of stained glass, see volume VI of this series on *Victorian Arts*.
14 [Anon], 'Uses for Shells and Sea-Weeds', *The Girl's Own Paper*, 13 November 1880, pp. 99–100 (p. 100).
15 [Anon], 'Uses for Shells and Sea-Weeds', p. 100.
16 The dangers of muriatic acid, also known as hydrochloric acid, are outlined in a report published by Public Health England in 2019 (updated version). Specific to dermal exposure, these include 'pain, blistering, [and] ulceration' (p. 1). Public Health England, *Hydrogen Chloride/Hydrochloric Acid: Incident Management*, August 2019 [first published June 2016; full document updated August 2019]. Available at: https://assets.publishing.service.gov.uk/government/uploads/system/uploads/attachment_data/file/825230/Hydrogen_Chloride_incident_management_PHE_2019.pdf [accessed 15 July 2021]. The hazards and inconveniences of shell-cleaning are also discussed in [Anon], 'Curiosities of Industry', where the author recounts how this practice caused 'ladies' to '[burn] the skin off their fingers and [create] holes in their dresses' (p. 210).
17 [Anon.], 'Answers to Correspondents' (Response to 'G. R.' and 'P.'), *The Girl's Own Paper*, 2 January 1886, pp. 223–224 (p. 224).
18 J. S. Winter, [pseud. Henrietta Eliza Vaughan Stannard], *Mignon's Secret* (New York: George Munro, 1886 [Seaside Library Pocket Edition]).
19 T. Cave, *Mignon's Afterlives: Crossing Cultures from Goethe to the Twenty-First Century* (Oxford: Oxford University Press, 2011), p. 1.
20 See A. McEwan, 'The antimacassar in fact and fiction: how textual resources reveal a domestic textile', in M. Hayward and E. Kramer (eds.), *Textiles and Text: Re-establishing the Links between Archival and Object-based Research: Postprints* [AHRC Research Centre for Textile Conservation and Textile Studies: Third Annual Conference 11–13 July 2006] (London: Archetype Publications, 2007), pp. 164–172 (p. 164).
21 Quoted from a retrospective account by Laurence Housman in an article reflecting upon the fashions of the Victorian period. The article, 'Petticoat Government', appeared in *The Contemporary Review*, November 1913, pp. 663–672. Reproduced in L. Delap, M. DiCenzo, and L. Ryan (eds.), *Feminism and the Periodical Press, 1900–1918*, Vol. II (London and New York: Routledge, n.d. [first published by Abingdon: Routledge, 2006]). See also Eliza Kerr's novel *The Mystery of Grange Drayton*, in which a minister 'timidly' sits down on a chair adorned with an unfastened antimacassar, which ends up in 'a little crushed heap behind his back' and 'did not add to his comfort'. See E. Kerr, *The Mystery of Grange Drayton* (Ludgate Circus Bldgs., E.C.: Wesleyan Methodist Sunday-School Union, 1884), p. 25.
22 Cave, *Mignon's Afterlives*, p. 156.

88

[ANON], *POTICHOMANIA; OR, THE ART OF IMITATING PORCELAIN.*

(London: Hutton & Co., [1850])

Introduction

Potichomania, the interesting amusement of Decorating Glass to give it the appearance of Indian, Etruscan, Sèvres, and Japanese China, has been recently occupying the Parisians; and as its introduction into England has claimed the attention of English ladies, we have taken means to ascertain the most correct mode by which perfection in the art may be achieved. The instructions contained in one of the following pages, whilst ample for all requirements, will be found simple and easy of operation.

Although apparently of a mechanical nature, it will be found that the occupation will call into exercise the judicious blending of colours and considerable skill, and will moreover lead to the development of an amount of taste and artistic talent that will render it charming to the lovers of the fine arts.

We may further add, that whilst with a few shillings all the needful articles may be obtained; with a few hours of easy labour, accompanied by skill and taste, the amateur will witness the transformation of a glass vessel into an elegant Porcelain Vase, or such other ornamental construction as may have been chosen.

An inexhaustible variety of articles may be produced, suitable to the interchange of friendships, and worthy of a place amongst other articles of *vertu.*

HUTTON & CO.

Articles for Potichomania

1. A Sheet of Coloured Designs, representing either the Chinese, Etruscan, Sèvres, Egyptian, or Japanese Pattern, as your taste may direct.
2. A Glass Vase.
3. One straight and one curved Hog Hair Brush, and one of Camel Hair, for applying the Gum.
4. A Bottle of inalterable Varnish.
5. A Bottle of prepared Colour.
6. A Bottle of Liquid Gum.
7. A Pair of very fine Scissors.

DOI: 10.4324/9781315399980-106

To the above may be added, for extra purposes, a small Bottle of Gold Powder, and a Bottle of Varnish.

Instructions for Potichomania

1. BEFORE cutting your drawings, you must carefully cover the back of them with inalterable varnish, that the oil paint may not penetrate the paper.
2. When the drawings are dry, you may commence cutting out the figures, flowers, &c., taking care that no white margin is left round them.
3. Having cut out a sufficient number to decorate your Vase, you should first arrange on paper the form in which they shall be placed; for, once fixed, they cannot be removed.
4. When you have done this, you must gum the painted side of the object – place it in the interior of the Vase, taking care that every part is evenly laid.
5. Having ornamented your Vase, pour into it a bottle of the oil colour you have decided on – turn it continually round in the same direction until the colour is equally spread over every part; the remainder being poured out, the Vase is finished, and you have a perfect imitation of Indian, Etruscan, Sèvres, or Japanese *China*.
6. Should a gold edge be desired, you must, before applying the oil colour, mix a little of the gold powder with the prepared gum; then apply it with a camel hair brush evenly round the rim of the Vase.
7. When the inside is perfectly dry, give the whole a layer or two of varnish; this will render the Vase capable of holding water.

89

MRS. [REBEKAH] SKILL, 'INTRODUCTION.', *THE ART OF MODELLING WAX FLOWERS, FULLY AND CLEARLY EXPLAINED, ACCOMPANIED WITH ACCURATE PATTERNS FOR VARIOUS FLOWERS, DECORATIONS FOR TINTING, &C., BY WHICH THE ATTAINMENT OF THIS ELEGANT ART BECOMES SIMPLE AND EASY.*

(London: Simpkin, Marshall, and Co., 1852), pp. 9–19

INTRODUCTION.

THE taste for Floriculture, which has within a few years been so much extended by the Horticultural Meetings and Floral Fêtes, so generally established throughout the country, has given rise to one of the most beautiful of arts – that of imitating in wax the productions of our gardens and greenhouses, as well as those rare and beautiful plants of other climes, for which we are indebted to the exertions of scientific travellers.

This art or accomplishment, of which I propose shortly to treat, is so elegant, cleanly, and delicate, that the most refined lady need not scruple to study or even to practise it in her boudoir: it requires only an examination of Flora's gifts, with delicacy in handling the materials, to bring it to perfection. At the present time, when Fashion exercises such supreme control over the domestic occupations of those ladies who have only their own pleasure to seek in their amusements; and when Berlin work and Crochet have had their full range, it really appears desirable to suggest an employment which, if not quite new, has at least been hitherto regarded as a mystery, only attainable by the expenditure of much time and

DOI: 10.4324/9781315399980-107

money: with the view, therefore, of rendering the art of making WAX FLOWERS more general, the following simple yet efficient directions have been published.

Although it has been said that a close examination of natural flowers is all that is really necessary to lead to perfection in modelling them, it must be admitted that a knowledge of the structure and character of plants, of their scientific arrangement and classification, materially assists us in obtaining a correct idea of those minute parts of a flower which escape the general eye. Botany now forms a part of school education, and thus art and science may mutually aid each other; a young lady may turn from the study of terms and characteristics to the emulation of beauty of form and colouring in nature. The young student need not fear a close examination of her productions, if she bear in mind their scientific classification while at work; she will thus be spared much difficulty.

Flowers are the most beautiful of Nature's adornments; they give life and variety to our gardens and drawing-rooms: but there are seasons when we cannot avail ourselves of these natural beauties, and then a bouquet of wax flowers forms an elegant embellishment to the drawing-room.

To those who are desirous of practising the art of Modelling in Wax, a few hints from one who has had many years' experience in the profession may be acceptable; they may lead persons engaged in more severe studies, or whose leisure time is otherwise engaged, to attempt it as a relaxation.

There can be no doubt that an increased taste for Floriculture has given rise to a desire for imitating in wax some of the beautiful productions of our gardens and greenhouses; this has gradually developed itself very widely amongst persons whose means have enabled them to indulge in so elegant and fascinating a pursuit.

It may, perhaps, be difficult to trace the origin of this increased love of flowers to any other source than to the Floricultural Meetings before mentioned, as the visitors to these places are accustomed to hear the merits of flowers and plants discussed, and to witness perpetually a variety of floral and vegetable productions in a degree of perfection and abundance which, some few years since, from their rarity and costly price, were mostly confined to the hothouses, conservatories, and gardens, of the noble and wealthy, to which very few persons had access. Even when so indulged, it has been regarded merely as a beautiful and gratifying sight; astonishment and delight being the only feelings excited. This is not the case at the present day, owing to the advanced state of horticultural knowledge which has been diffused among the people by their frequent attendance at these meetings. A spirit of emulation has been created and fostered by the liberality of Directors, in awarding prizes of medals and other more acceptable gifts, as an encouragement to the industry and skill of florists, gardeners, and cottagers, of humble means and pretensions, some of whose productions have afforded most convincing proofs of steady perseverance, assisted by a little hor-[ticultural knowledge] that Nature bountifully rewards the exercise[.]

A desire has been felt by many persons for some Guide by which they might be enabled to understand what they see and hear, giving them that slight acquaintance with the leading principles of Botany, which is indispensable towards learning the names and characteristics and explaining correctly the different parts of a plant or flower.

[. . . .]

It is, however, by no means to be inferred, that a very extensive acquaintance with botanical pursuits is absolutely necessary to enable a pupil correctly to imitate in wax any of the productions of our gardens or greenhouses; but a considerable degree of ignorance is manifested by persons who, professing to model flowers, have no more idea of specifying the names, or describing the botanical arrangement, of the various parts of a flower, than they have of any other science.

The art of making Wax Flowers has now become very general, [. . . .] [t]o attain proficiency regular practice is necessary, and with proper directions and good materials this elegant accomplishment becomes interesting – the drawing-room may be ornamented and made cheerful by bouquets of well-made flowers, arranged with due attention to variety in form and harmony of colour; and thus art has this advantage over nature, for we can always secure a fine specimen of a choice and tender plant when, perhaps, the anxious and skilful gardener has had his hopes blighted by some insidious insect at the heart of his finest bloom.

Having from an early age passionately loved flowers, with an opportunity of cultivating them to some extent, it is not surprising that I should feel great pleasure in imitating them in wax. But a few years ago the art as it is now practised was unknown; there were but few persons able to produce tolerable specimens, and those which were exhibited had a very rude and unnatural appearance, with the foliage made of cambric, of a colour as unlike the natural leaves as possible, and deficient also in the various details essential to the natural development of the flowers they attempted to make. It is not so at the present day; the foliage is made of wax, so exactly like nature, that few are able to distinguish that they are imitations.

[. . . .]

It will scarcely be necessary to urge upon the reader the advantages of becoming acquainted with the principles of one of the most beautiful arts of which we have any knowledge, that of imitating in various materials those exquisite productions of nature, Flowers: to do which in wax requires only proper instruction and perseverance for the attainment of excellence; and, as in all other pursuits, the more knowledge of the subject the pupil possesses, the more speedy and certain will be the success.

As before stated, some slight acquaintance with the general principles of Botany is desirable, as any deviation from the laws of nature, must of course destroy the illusion. If the study of Botany and Modelling Flowers are pursued at the same time, the labour will be trifling, and the result satisfactory, as every fresh acquisition will add to the knowledge of both science and art; and that will not easily be forgotten which has been brought into practice as soon as learnt.

Instruction alone will not enable any one to imitate nature, and therefore it is recommended to copy from the living model when practicable; this must be the end and aim of the pupil's exertions; she must remark, not merely the form and peculiarities of the flowers themselves, but their mode of growth, the position of the leaves upon the stem, and, in short, every characteristic of the real flower: to do this the pupil must have a specimen before her.

In the metropolis the facilities are great for the pursuit of this accomplishment, and in the country they are greater: there, every walk may become the source of information and enjoyment, affording the opportunity of learning the nature and character of plants, and of imitating the most beautiful productions of nature. Those only who have sought for happiness in the cultivation of a taste and love for flowers, can justly appreciate the elevating and refining influence which such pursuits have upon the mind.

90

[ANON], 'CURIOSITIES OF INDUSTRY AMONG THE LADIES.'

Chambers's Journal, 7 April 1855, pp. 209–212

I AM a solitary bachelor, leading a bachelor kind of life, which, like all other kinds of life, has its sweets and its – bitters I won't say – but its occasional acids. Well for me that the sweets predominate, and that I am generally inclined to acknowledge their predominance, and make the most of them. I am reclining in my easy-chair before the fire, which I have all to myself; if I enjoy it sometimes a little *à la Trollope,* what matters when nobody looks on? As I lean back, and lift my eyes, not *ad sidera,* but to the marble mantle-piece which crowns the comfortable fireplace, I behold a spectacle by no means either unusual or remarkable in itself, yet exceedingly suggestive to my fancy at this moment, because it conjures up a host of visions of a kind more or less similar, and pregnant with associations not undelightful to recall. That strip of marble slab, some nine inches by fifty in dimensions, upon which now stand a few time-worn and dingy ornaments, worthless in themselves, but invaluable from the memories they awaken, has been in its time the ground of how many patient experiments – the arena of how many innocent triumphs? For how many generations has the domestic mantle-piece been set apart for the exhibition of lady-like skill in the fashionable accomplishments of the day – accomplishments, some of them of a rather equivocal nature, it must be admitted, but interesting in many respects, and affording some curious illustrations of industry in a department which, though familiar to us all, no one, so far as I am aware, has condescended to treat of? Let me be allowed to supply this desideratum, so far as my recollections will suffice for the purpose; and permit me, with the mantle-piece for starting-place, to trace some of the operations of that peculiar species of domestic industry which is as much the subject of fashion as the dress of the fair operatives, and has undergone almost as many mutations and revolutions as feminine costume itself.

The custom of placing a large mirror upon the mantle-piece, now universally prevailing, is of very modern date. It appears, judging from prints of interiors by Hogarth and others, not to have begun so early as a century ago. Then, in houses pretending to gentility, a picture invariably occupied the space which the mirror fills now, and it is pretty certain that the custom was of long standing. There are many houses still existing, which formed part of old London before the Great Fire; and in these the pictures over the mantle-pieces yet remain, painted some of

DOI: 10.4324/9781315399980-108

them on canvas let into the oak-mouldings, and some upon the wainscot itself – being included among the finishing decorations of the building by the original architect. Many of these are of very little merit, but a vast number were painted by Van D'Este; some of whose works are excellent in point of composition and aërial perspective. They are even now so plentiful as to be bought at a low price – their odd shapes, they being of enormous width in comparison with their height, betraying the purpose for which they were painted, and depreciating their value. But even in those palmy days of popular art, the chimney-ornaments stood in front of the picture, just as at a later period they stood, and as they still stand, in front of the mirror. They were not, however, the work of the ladies of the house, but consisted chiefly of foreign rarities, mostly hideous and misshapen gods and idols, with cavernous mouths and corpulent stomachs, modelled in a dark-coloured earth – of imitation mummies and Egyptian deities, with the addition of any *lusus naturæ* that could be picked up, all piled heterogeneously on each side of a central bust of some ancient or historical personage. When the fashion changed, and the mirror supplanted the picture, the multiplication by reflection of all this rubbish – which, for the most part, had but one side fit for view – became offensive; and we observe that it gradually gave place to specimens of China and India ware, bearing a kind of shawl-pattern upon a greenish-white ground. In the days of our great-grandmothers, the possession of a collection of such foreign porcelain was regarded as an evidence of taste, and fabulous sums were given for fresh novelties as they were imported – from enormous punch-bowls and jar-like vases, to diminutive cups no bigger than a tailor's thimble. The mania for this species of goods at that time had an important effect upon our commerce in the East; and there must be something fascinating to a large class in articles of this kind, for to the present day the traffic in them forms a good part of the business of the curiosity-shops. The purchasers, as I have reason to know, are generally people who are well to do, and on the shady side of sixty. Josiah Wedgwood, by the production of his elegant and classical wares, did much to banish the old china from the mantle-piece; but his master-pieces were too expensive for general use; and while they helped to improve the public taste in the matter of chimney-ornaments, they but partially supplied the wants they generated. Now it was that the ladies first came to the rescue, and, taking the mantle-piece under their peculiar charge, commenced a course of experiments and a series of exhibitions, whose several epochs, if one could mark them correctly, would be found as distinctly defined as those of any of the existing or extinct dynasties of Europe with which they have been contemporaneous.

I have no doubt that I was born during the foreign china and punch-bowl era, and I have a distinct recollection of the punch-bowl itself, and the silver punch-ladle, with a guinea let into the bottom of it, and having a handle of twisted whale-bone, with which my honoured parent used to ladle out the inspiriting beverage. But the first mantle-piece upon which I ever cast a gaze of consciousness, had upon it for central ornament a marvellous grotto, built up of sea-shells by the fairy hand of a female cousin; and it was flanked by shells of larger capacity, shaped like monster periwinkles, from which the outer deposit of lime and marine matter had been burned off by the action of aquafortis and spirits of salts. This was the era of shell-cleaning, when the ladies burned the skin off their fingers and holes in their dresses, in developing the mysteries of conchology by the aid of fiery spirits, and the destruction of innumerable tooth-brushes. That pungent odour of spirits of salts is in my nostrils yet, and I never smell it without thinking of the battle of Vittoria, which was fought in that era, and the news of which reached us on the day of a grand triumph achieved by the female cousin aforesaid, who had converted into one huge pearl a mammoth American oyster.

The shells and grottos enjoyed no very durable reign, but gave place, in a few years, to a succession of ephemeral attempts in the natural-history line. Birds of paradise spread their gorgeous tails to the dust, and the dust ruined them in the course of a single summer. The ladies took to stuffing English birds, and exhibiting them in little black boxes with glass fronts; but that process was not considered lady-like, and was surrendered to the barbers and the professors of the art. Something was done in inflated fish-skins, something in gigantic beetles and gaudy butterflies, something in varnished lizards glued to a mossy stone; but nothing of importance was achieved, and so that unsettled era passed away. It was immediately followed by a very brief period of marvels in straw, by which beasts, birds, and landscapes were imitated by a kind of mosaic-work of coloured straws and dried weeds cut into infinitesimal portions. Concurrently with this, came the practice of painting with sands of all tints from Allum Bay. A donkey and panniers painted with sand upon a piece of card-board, and mounted on a little black stand, was accounted a master-piece. Those who could not get over the donkey, could make a cottage, or fill a bottle with coloured sands in wavy strata. The sands ran out, if we remember rightly, about the period of the battle of Waterloo.

With the peace that followed, came more liberal notions of art in connection with chimney-ornaments; and now first dawned the important era of hand-screens. Shaped, as everybody knows, like an open fan, with a long central handle, they presented, upon their virgin milkwhite surfaces, an inviting space for the display of female accomplishments. They came rapidly and universally into vogue. Every lady who could draw, drew her best upon the creamy sheet: she who could paint, painted; and, if the truth must be told, it sometimes happened that she who could do neither, attempted both. Declining such attempts, others mounted the screens with coloured prints, or with the works of water-colour artists, and decked them with gold and silver ornaments, or inscribed them with verses original or select. Screens were the idols of the day; they stood upon every mantle-piece, and the materials for their manufacture were to be found in perplexing abundance among the stocks of every fancy-stationer. They might be bought in every stage of progress – from the blank-sheet of card-board, to the painted and ornamented screen; and you might lavish any sum upon a pair of handles, from eighteen-pence to a couple of guineas. In spite of the conventional group of flowers, consisting of that venerable damask rose, with white ditto, and lily of the valley, they were many of them really pretty things; and they did us a little domestic service, by giving some flavour of art to the pursuits of our home industry. They lasted long; and if they have at length gone out as a fashion, the materials for their fabrication may still be procured at the fancy-stationer's among his dead-stock.

The hand-screens naturally suggested the card-racks and letter-cases, which – neatly trimmed with pink or sky-blue ribbon, enframing a bunch of tender violets half hidden in green leaves, or a cluster of delicate snow-drops, or perhaps a primrose with its crumpled leaf – sometimes formed a handsome and not unsuggestive present to some bachelor friend. The era of hand-screens, card-racks, &c., was in its glory, when, about the time of the trial of Queen Caroline, some considerate and compassionate genius, taking pity upon that portion of the sex who could never hope to draw, through natural incapacity, invented the art and mystery of Poonah-painting. There is, strictly speaking, no art in the practice of this style of painting, and very little mystery; and what there is, is stolen from the stencil-lon. As then practised, it consisted mainly in a series of dusty, smutty operations with powdered black-lead upon white card-board. The pictures were produced by means of dry brushes and stumps, and were all of a striking and portentous character, or they were nothing: they were mostly of an earthquaky complexion, and were for some time the rage with the broken-hearted young ladies of the Byron school, then a very numerous class. Sometimes the subject was a white dove perched on a withered branch, beneath a thunder-cloud as black as Erebus – only, as the fair artists did not draw, but cut the dove from a print with scissors, stuck it on the paper, and scrubbed in the cloud around it, it would happen, through a slip or two in the cutting, that the dove became a duck or a goose, when the effect was not so sentimental. Sometimes the subject was an old stone-cross on a blasted heath, with the black thunder-cloud in the background; but whatever the subject, the thunder-cloud had to be there, or there could be no picture at all. It is impossible to conceive the extent of the mania for this marvellous accomplishment which existed about thirty years ago. The proprietor of a large paper-mill, in the neighbourhood of my then residence, assured me that it had increased the demand for card-board full 200 per cent. – that he had applied the whole resources of his mill, which had been long famous for the manufacture of Bath-post, to the production of card-board, and had only succeeded in meeting the demand by inventing a mode of casting it at once without the necessity of pasting the sheets together. The art was taught in three lessons for a guinea, and for a time the professors grew fat and pursy; but it fell into disrepute almost as suddenly as it rose, partly owing to the fact, that the pictures would not keep, being destroyed by contact with anything; and partly from the conviction, which arose by degrees, that they were not worth keeping. Poonah-painting in another form, and by means of permanent colours, afterwards struggled into birth: it professed to be a royal road to art; but nothing artistic came of it, and that, too, declined.

Next came a series of alarming experiments in the manufacture of artificial rocks, the production of which was a tantalising mystery to the uninitiated. Suddenly the mantle-pieces appeared loaded with little piles of angular rocks, surmounted by a pasteboard tower or turret filled with paper-lights, or pierced to do duty as a clock-tower. There were inkstands imbedded in jagged rocks, flower-vases of rocks, and baskets in abundance formed of rocky crystals. When the secret got wind, it was found that they were produced by immersing a wire frame-work of the object desired in a strong solution of alum, and chemically precipitating the alum, which clung in grotesquely-shaped crystals to the wire, and the work of art was complete. But in a little time the crevices of the rocks were filled with dust, and to wash them clean was to melt them away; and so away they all went, banished to upstairs rooms and cupboards on landing-places. The vacancies they left were speedily filled by castles, martello-towers, &c., flaming in azure and gold; old gateways and sham ruins, elaborately contrived as receptacles for the everlasting paper-lights, which were now industriously cut, curled, and spirally bound with tinsel, and bundled together in castle or fortress, with their party-coloured heads peeping over the battlements.

After that, Japanning came into fashion, and every enterprising young lady felt bound to japan her own dressing-case, work-box, writing-desk, and so on. Plaster of Paris and whiting littered the drawing-room and the boudoir; China-ink and crystal varnish were at a premium; and for some time there was a decidedly Oriental character pervading the paraphernalia of female industry. These productions, which could not be attempted by everybody, were rivalled by ingenious paper-cuttings, which crept by degrees over picture-frames, mirrors, and vases, which they covered like parasitical plants, and served the double purpose of preserving the gilding and exhibiting the ingenious fancies of the fair artists. How many years the changes were rung upon these and similar modes of industrious ornamentation, I do not care to specify. How the japanning was succeeded by the rage for papilions, to which whole holocausts of moths and butterflies were sacrificed – how the spread of geological science brought in a mania for fossil remains – how these were supplanted by imitations of Etruscan ware – and these, again, by the modelling of flowers in wax, and the patient maceration of flowers and plants, and the bleaching and stiffening of their exquisite anatomies, and how worthy triumphs have been won by the talented and the persevering in these last-mentioned pursuits; all this would be long to tell, and need hardly be told to readers of the present day. It is time now that I turn my face from the mantle-piece, and the host of industries it recalls to my mind's-eye, and look around upon another, but still an analogous class of pursuits, which kept pace with them. But I must be brief.

Our great-grandmothers, with the devotion of so many Penelopes, glued themselves to the embroidery-frame. The fruits of their life-long labours, in dim and dusty decadence, still survive in motheaten tapestries, in faded hangings, and on the bottoms of superannuated chairs and ottomans. Another kind of embroidery arose a generation later: it consisted of raised images in silk threads of a brilliant colour upon a satin-ground; many splendid examples of which still remain enshrined in the cabinets of elderly dames. These things were before my time, and I know nothing of them but by tradition. My earliest sympathies with ornamental needle-work are associated with the exploitation of lace-veils, tuckers, and collars by a bevy of five sisters, to whom I had the privilege of being younger brother.

How many patterns have I traced against the window-pane with pencil, and afterwards blackened with pen and ink, when I was a good boy and a 'dear!' And how many have I peremptorily refused to touch when, having got a 'crick in the neck,' I grew sick of it, and was 'a crabbed spite?' I feel some remorse, I confess, as these questions arise. I don't think the lace-veils and tuckers, collars and all that, have died out, or ever will entirely; but the next thing that came up was the netting, with the big balls of cotton-thread and the long ivory pins with bobs at the end, which resulted in no end of window-curtains, &c. The netting bade fair to monopolise the entire energies of the ladies, when all at once arose the glass and steel bead epidemic. This occurred just before the passing of the Reform Bill, and its advent was really a tremendous visitation. Then it was that 'every lady in the land' went suddenly mad for beads – the disease was universal, like the plague entomological in Egypt – not a family escaped the infection. From inquiries I made at the time, I can state with certainty that beads rose with the manufacturers 65 per cent. in value, and they were sold retail by millions and thousands of millions at a profit of 250 per cent. upon the advanced cost. Still, there were not enough in the market; and in numberless cases the dear ladies were vexing and grieving for the want of them, or sallying forth in all weathers to hunt them up at any price however extravagant. Their first use was in the manufacture of bracelets, for which innumerable patterns were sold in the shops. The bracelet could be worked in two modes – either by sewing the beads on a cloth ground, was a simple process enough, or by elaborately netting them together in a small frame by means of mohair and hair-needles, which was an exploit of far more labour and difficulty; but, inasmuch as it exhibited the pattern on both sides, resulted in a product of greater value. From bracelets, the bead-work extended to purses; and from purses, to reticules and bags. The fever then began to abate its virulence, and prevails at the present moment only as an intermittent and perfectly manageable disease.

The Berlin-wool school of art succeeded the bead-work. It was decidedly an advance upon the merely mechanical labours of its predecessor. As a bachelor, I feel bound to speak a word in its praise, if only in gratitude for the elegant pair of slippers which bedeck my toes with all the hues of the rainbow, and enable them to bid defiance to chilblains. I ought to add a word of praise, too, to some neat performances in perforated card-board, sent by my favourite niece to serve the purpose of book-markers; but there is but small space remaining to me, and I must hasten to notice the great Crochet invasion, which, some seven years back, burst like a flood upon the land. When I think of crochet, I am positively in a quiver. Though a bachelor, I have fourteen nieces, and of course they all crochet. The dear girls have deluged me with the fruits of their labours. My head rests at this moment upon a crocheted anti-macassar; I cut my bread from a crocheted bread-cloth; and I cut my cheese from a crocheted cheese-cloth. I sleep under a crocheted coverlet beneath a crocheted canopy; I open my dressing-case upon a crocheted table-cover, and set my shaving-dish upon a crocheted doily. My housekeeper walks off to church on a Sunday afternoon in a crochet-bonnet, her neck encircled by a crochet-tucker, and her somewhat passé face shaded from the sun by a crochet-veil; and I am myself threatened by that merry minx, Margaret Manby, with crochet-frills to my next set of shirts. Of course, being only a bachelor, I cannot enumerate half the doings in crochet; and for this I feel grateful, especially as abundance of information on the subject is to be obtained from other sources by those who want it. There is, as all the world knows by this time, a voluminous library of crochet literature in existence. I confess to having looked into some of the volumes as a matter of curiosity; but they are worse than Greek to me, and I can make nothing of them. They are numerous enough, however, to shew that the cause of crochet maintains a considerable staff of writers; and, looking to the lavish illustrations of artists and engravers, I am sometimes puzzled to think what the antiquaries and archæologists, of a thousand years hence, when poring over the relics of Victoria's reign, will be likely to make of these volumes, if they should chance to light upon them, and what sage theories of explanation they may give rise to. But I must not indulge in these fancies.

Were I just now in a prophetic mood, I might prognosticate the decline and fall of the empire of Crochet, from definite signs and symbols which have lately risen in the horizon. What if I should insinuate that the whole female world is on the point of abandoning the beloved boar's-eye, and rushing headlong into the arms of Potichomanie? Should I be pronouncing a true prophecy? Really, I hardly know what to reply; but this much I do know, and I hasten with all affection to communicate it to my fair friends. Potichomanie has come among us, and is supposed to have been communicated from a foreign vessel which omitted to perform quarantine. It has suddenly broken out in various parts of London, and is observed to prevail in the most aggravated form in those pleasant districts where ladies most resort. In these quarters, glass-pots are the order of the day – pots of all shapes, cylinders, globes, goblets, beakers, flagons, vases lank and lean, long and short, graceful and stout, dropsical and pot-bellied, or slender and slim, classically Greek and Roman, anciently Ninevite and Egyptian, or corpulently and unmistakably British. These it is the function of Potichomanie to transform into unrivalled treasures of skill. The ladies have only to line them with patterns cut from coloured chintz, and ingeniously dove-tailed together, to produce a new species of ceramic art, which promises to surpass all that ancient or modern times have accomplished. The thing is as easy as fibbing. The shopkeepers, good souls! have removed all difficulty. A pair of scissors, a few pots of varnish and adhesive mixtures, and a few brushes with dislocated necks, contrived to spread and plaster round a corner: these things, with a yard or two of guady chintz, and that ardent and fervid genius which all ladies are known to possess, are sufficient to insure the mastery of the whole mystery. Success to Potichomanie! May it prove a curable endemic!

I do not feel called upon to make any reflections upon the above curious matters, which stand confessedly out of the pale of my judgment, and of which it will be seen I know practically very little; but yet a remark or two may not be ill-timed or out of place. Were I disposed to be ill-naturedly satirical, I might congratulate my fair fellow-countrywomen upon the leisure they find for these various employments in addition to the fulfilment of all the obligations which woman owes to the world; but I am *not* disposed that way, and I do not see in the pursuit of any occupation which happens to be temporarily the mode, frivolous though it may appear, the evidence of positive neglect of serious duties. The instinct to be doing something – producing something – is a natural instinct, and is often as strong or stronger in those who are not under the necessity of working for their livelihood as in those who are. It is much better that this instinct should be countenanced and indulged, than that it should be stifled; but what I would deferentially submit is, that very possibly it might be trained to a more lofty and efficient purpose, and made subservient to ends of more importance, than are achieved through the inundation of our dwellings, or the dwellings of our friends, by an everlasting tide of crochet-work, or overloading our mantle-pieces and drawing-room tables by the miracles of Potichomanie.

91

[ANON], 'WEAVING OR PLAITING HAIR ORNAMENTS' AND 'ORNAMENTAL BEAD AND BUGLE WORK.'

Elegant Arts for Ladies (London: Ward and Lock, [1856]), pp. 3–10, 61–63

Figure 91.1 ROULEAU HEAD-DRESS.

HAIRS (says Dr. R. A. H. Hassall) are peculiarly susceptible of being affected by the condition of the health, even more so than the epidermis. If this be vigorous, it will be found that the hairs themselves are thickly and firmly set in the skin: if, on the contrary, the powers of the system be debilitated from any cause, the hair will either fall off spontaneously, or a very slight degree of force will serve to dislodge them from their connections. It has not yet been ascertained by positive

DOI: 10.4324/9781315399980-109

experiment whether the hair is capable of re-formation in those instances in which both bulb and sheath have been removed; it is most probable, however, that where they have been entirely abstracted, no renewal of the hair could ensue.

Hair, that most imperishable of all the component parts of our mortal bodies, has always been regarded as a cherished memorial of the absent or lost. Impressed with this idea, it appears to us but natural, that of all the various employments devised for the fingers of our fair countrywomen, the manufacture of ornaments in hair must be one of the most interesting. Why should we confide to others the precious lock or tress we prize, risking its being lost, and the hair of some other person being substituted for it, when, with a little attention, we may ourselves weave it into the ornament we desire? And the dainty and very tasteful handling hair-work requires, renders it as truly feminine an occupation as the finest crochet or the richest embroidery.

We must commence our instructions by premising that on the length of the lock or tress of hair will depend the use which can be made of it. Hair from one inch to three in length is only adapted for devices. Hair of three to six inches in length may be used for chains, because a chain can be worked in any number of separate portions and united by gold slides; or for ear-rings, made of some very fine plait and worked in two parts. A ring or an ear-ring worked in one hoop requires a length of eight inches. Brooches may be made from hair of various lengths according to the pattern, and also to the size and kind of plait; devices are much used for brooches, and as we have already said, these can be made of quite short hair. A handsome full-sized bracelet requires twenty or twenty-four-inch hair. Of course bracelets can be worked in pieces and united by slides or by caps linked together, and then twelve-inch hair will suffice; or they may be worked on smaller moulds, and several lengths braided or twisted together, in which case eighteen-inch hair will often suffice. Joining hair is a very tedious operation, and, at best, unsatisfactory, for as each hair must be separately fastened on to the one which it is destined to lengthen, the smoothness and neat appearance of the fabric is not improved by the knots, however neat they may be made; while if the ends are cut off closely the knot is liable to give way, and if they are left they give a bristly look to the plait, and totally mar its beauty.

In working hair the great thing to be observed is that there shall be nothing to fray or roughen the strands; therefore it is always best to use the proper hair-work table. This may be made of stained wood or mahogany, and is very simple, consisting only of a circular top about fourteen inches in diameter, and four thin legs. The whole table should be turned and polished, so that it may be *perfectly smooth.* It should stand about three feet in height. In the centre of the top must be a circular hole about five inches in diameter, surrounded by a moulding, which, interiorly, rises about an inch, and exteriorly slopes down to the surface of the table. A small brass hook must be inserted in the inside of this hole just below the moulding.

About three dozen leaden weights, each weighing about three quarters of an ounce, will be required; they must all be equally heavy, and shaped like the following diagram. A skein of strong silk or twist, a little shellac melted and rolled into a stick, and a brass tube or wire of the proper size for the pattern, will complete the list of requisites for the work. These tubes or wires may be obtained at any brass-founders; they should be about ten or twelve inches in length, and *must be perfectly smooth* and polished, both at the ends and over the whole surface.

We now come to the hair: The first thing to be done is to cleanse it, and for this purpose the ends must be evenly arranged and the lock or tress straightened smoothly out; then each extremity firmly bound with thread, care being taken that every hair is secured by the ligature. Dissolve a bit of soda, the size of a bean, in about a pint of water, immerse the hair fairly in it, and boil it for ten or twelve minutes; take it out, shake it, and hang it up to dry in the air. When quite dry it is ready for use. Now, take as many weights as there are strands in the pattern about to be worked; attach about twelve inches of twist to each weight, tying them round the neck, and lay them side by side round the table with the ends of twist hanging down. Take the tress, and without untying the threads which fasten the extremities, draw from it the number of hairs required for a strand; take each hair up separately, and arrange them between the finger and thumb so that all the ends shall be even, and then knot the strand thus formed on to one of the pieces of twist; repeat this until all the strands are formed and each attached to their separate weights, taking care not to disturb or roughen them during the process. Now, stoop down and carefully ascertain that all the hairs in each strand are of equal length; and if this is the case, gather up all the ends between the finger and thumb, bind them firmly together with strong thread, leaving a loop of thread about an inch long hanging, and cement the accumulated ends firmly with shellac.

The loop of thread is then to be put on the hook in the centre of the table, and the weights lifted off one by one and suffered to hang down. Each strand, as it hangs, must now be again examined to see that no hair in it is looser or tigher than the other, but that all are perfectly smooth and firm. If the weights hang more than ten or twelve inches below the top of the table, wind the twist round their necks and so shorten them, as long ends are apt to get entangled while the pattern is being worked; they can afterwards be let down when requisite. Take now some spare weights, and tie them together to form a central balance-weight – about one to every four or five strands is the ordinary proportion – for there must be enough to maintain the balance without straining or cracking the hair; attach this balance weight to the loop of thread (which is now taken off the hook), and suffer it to hang down in the centre of the hole. Select a tube of the requisite size and put it in the hole, suffering one end to rest on the hook, and set to work.

We trust that our readers will pardon this apparent prolixity; but as the beauty of the work depends entirely upon the nicety of the primary proceedings, we have ventured, even at the risk of appearing tedious, to be thus minute in our directions.

ROULEAU HEAD-DRESS.

This pattern requires twenty-four strands, each containing about thirty or thirty-six hairs of eighteen or twenty-four inches in length – the number of hairs depends on their fineness, and the length requisite on the thickness of the *rouleau* they are to be woven on. The following cut will give an idea of the proper mode of arranging the strands on the table.

It will be perceived that they are placed in six groups of four each; each group being lettered *a, b, c, d,* with chalk; and that there is a cross of chalk between two of the groups to mark the commencement of each round.

Instead of the tube ordinarily used for weaving the patterns on, a *rouleau* of satin is here substituted of about an inch and a-half or two inches in circumference; the length being a matter regulated by taste and by the length of the hair at disposal. The satin should match the hair as nearly as may be. The *rouleau* must be evenly made, and should be stuffed with cotton wool, so as to be firm and not hard; a strong wire must be passed through the centre of it to keep it erect while it is being worked over, and to maintain it in shape afterwards. Let the lower end rest on the hook, and, the strands being in due order, commence thus: – 1st Round: Take strand *d,* the one immediately on the right of the cross, and carry it over strands *a* and *b* on the left of the cross, lay it down in the place of strand *c,* and move this latter on to the *d* next to it, while strand *d,* which before was lying there, is to be lifted and carried on to replace strand *c* in the second group to the left, that strand *c* moving into the place of strand *d* next to it, which latter is to be carried on to the third group in a similar manner: work thus through each group until the one immediately on the right of the cross is reached and filled up.

2nd Round: Take strand *a,* immediately on the left of the cross, and carry it over strands *d* and *c* in the group to the right of the cross; lay it down in the place of strand *b,* move this latter on to the *a* next to it, and lift the strand before lying there over *d* and *c* of the second group to the right, and put it down on *b,* removing the strand there already to the *a* next it, and carrying strand *a* on to the third group in a similar manner; so work all the groups round to the cross again.

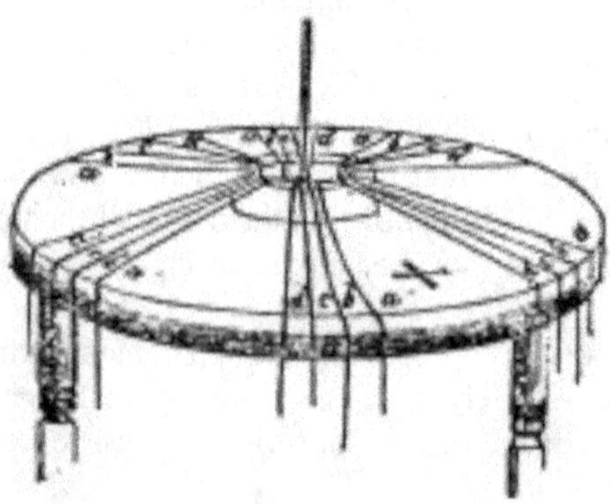

3rd Round is like the first, and worked towards the left.

4th Round is the same as the second, and worked towards the right.

Continue to work these two rounds alternately until the length required is completed. After about eight or ten rounds are worked, the *rouleau* will be sufficiently clasped by the plait to admit of the end being lifted off the hook; it will then maintain itself in the centre. Be careful to keep the strands smooth and in their proper places, as if they get at all out of order the evenness and beauty of the plait is destroyed.

When the requisite length is completed take off the balance weight (which we omitted to say should always be attached to the loop by a doubly-hooked piece of wire); gather the other weights together on to the table, and cut off the hair close to the twist. Without loss of time bind all these ends of the strands neatly and firmly down to the *rouleau* with a few spare hairs, or with some fine silk exactly the colour of the hair; then cut off the loop and cement from the other extremity, and fasten that off in like manner. Sew the two ends together very neatly, and finish off with a gold button and tassel, or one similar in shade to the hair. Where the double *rouleau* (as given in cut) is made, two tassels will be requisite; but a single *rouleau* for the back of the hair only requires one. Where the double *rouleau* is made, the ends of the longest one which are to meet underneath the smaller, or back *rouleau,* may be tapered off to a point.

A very pretty bracelet may be made with this pattern, by working it with sixteen or twenty strands, of about eighteen or twenty-four hairs each, and on a tube three-quarters of an inch in circumference. Three or four separate lengths of about nine inches each must be worked, and these when braided or twisted together make an effective bracelet. Eighteen-inch hair will be requisite. When this pattern is woven upon a tube, we detach the balance-weight; after the completion of the length, cut off the pieces of twist, and bind the extremities of the hair firmly down on to the tube with strong thread; then cut off the loop and cement from the other end, and bind down these hairs in a similar manner. The tube, hair and all, must now be immersed in scalding water, and suffered to remain there for ten minutes or a quarter of an hour, the water being kept up to the same heat all the time. When taken out it must be gently squeezed in a soft silk handkerchief, to remove the superfluous moisture, and then hung up to dry slowly.

The thread is detached from each end when the hair is perfectly dry, and the plait gently slid off the tube. A length of elastic wire (about 8½ inches) must now be drawn through the centre of each plait, and the ends of hair gathered up at each extremity and cemented together to the elastic with shellac. The plaits must next be all cemented firmly together at one end, and braided, or twisted into a cable, and then the other extremities cemented together. It is now ready for the gold cups which are to connect it with the snap or clasp. These may be fixed on with melted cement, or sent to a jeweller to complete.

[SECOND ARTICLE.]

This brooch is to be worked in five lengths, three of which – those for the bows – are to measure three inches each, and the other two (those for the ends) two inches

each. Lighter weights must be used, and for this purpose leaden bullets of a quarter of an ounce each will do, if a groove be made round them to receive the twist.

Twenty-eight strands of six or nine hairs each, depending on the fineness of the hair, must be prepared according to the instructions already given at page 4. These strands are to be arranged in groups of four; each group being lettered *a b c d,* on the table, and a cross is to be made between two of the groups, to mark the place for commencing each round, as in cut of the table and strands in page 5.

1*st Round.* – Commence with the first group immediately on the right of the cross. Take strand *d* (or the fourth one) in the right hand, and strand *c* in the left hand, pass the former *over* the latter, and lay them down in each other's places: take strand *a* in the left hand, and strand *b* in the right hand, and pass the former *under* the latter, moving strand *b* into the place of *a,* while the original strand *a,* instead of being laid down on *b,* is carried over strand *c,* and takes its place, this latter passing under it, and becoming *b.* Proceed now to the second group, and weave it in the same way – viz., passing *d* over *c,* and bringing *a* under *b* and over *c.* Continue thus through each group, until the cross is reached. This round is worked to the *right.*

2*nd Round.* – Take two strands from the group on the right, and two from the one on the left of the cross, and arrange them into a group in the space which intervenes between the two lettered groups, and work them exactly as in the previous round, viz., passing the fourth, or right-hand strand, over the third, and the first, or left-hand strand, under the second and over the third, then raise up two strands in each hand, draw the woven plait gently up to the tube in the centre, and restore the two strands in the right hand to their places on the *a* and *b* of the first group to the right of the cross, and the two in the left hand to the vacant *d* and *c* in the first group to the left of the cross, taking care not to twist or misplace them, but to see that they come straight from the centre.

Proceed now as follows: – Take strands *a* and *b* from the first group to the left of the cross, and strands *d* and *c* from the second group to the left, and arrange these four in the intervening space between the letters on either side, work them in the manner we have just directed, gently draw the knot or plait thus woven up to the tube, and replace the strands; continue to repeat this all round until the cross is reached. This round is worked to the *left*.

These two rounds constitute the whole pattern, and are to be repeated alternately, first working towards the right and using the original groups, and then working towards the left, and compounding each group. Eight-inch hair will be long enough for weaving the brooch. The tube in the centre must not measure more than an inch in circumference.

A bracelet may likewise be made with this pattern by arranging thirty-two or forty strands in groups of four, and putting twice or thrice as many hairs in each strand. A tube of two inches or rather more in circumference, and hair eighteen or twenty inches in length will be requisite.

Figure 91.5 EAR-RING.

The above pattern may be worked in four-inch hair; it is made in two lengths or plaits each measuring an inch and a quarter. Eighteen hairs will be required for each strand, and a fine wire must be substituted for the central tube: the ordinary weights may be used. Draw on the table with white chalk sixteen lines radiating from the centre like the spokes of a wheel. Arrange these lines in pairs, so that each pair shall be equidistant, and exactly parallel with, or opposite to another pair. Letter that pair of lines exactly at the centre of the bottom of the table, or the part close to us, and their opposites, or those exactly at the centre of the top of the table, *a*. Letter the pairs immediately in the centres of the right and the left-hand sides of the table *b:* letter the pair between the bottom *a* and the right-hand *b* and those opposite *c:* letter the pair between the bottom *a* and the left-hand *b* and those opposite *d*.

Having carefully prepared the strands in the proper way, and attached the balance weights, lay a strand on each of the sixteen lines, and commence as follows: –

Take up the two strands or the pair at bottom lettered *a,* and turn them over into the places of the pair at top lettered *a,* laying them down just inside those already there, and lifting those from the top back to fill the vacant lines at bottom; take up the pair from the *b* on the right-hand side, and lay them down inside the pair lettered *b* on the left-hand side, bringing these latter back to fill the vacant lines on the right: now take the pair from the bottom *c,* and transfer them to the position occupied by their opposites, bringing the others back to the empty lines: lastly, work those from the bottom *d* over into the places of the pair opposite to them, and bring those from the upper *d* back: recommence with the bottom *a,* and repeat the pattern until the length is completed, always taking care to lay down the pair of strands carried over inside those we are going to take back. They can be shifted on to the lines with a slight touch of the fingers as we remove the others.

It will be best to stand to work this pattern, as its beauty depends so much upon the strands being lifted clearly and smoothly over, without being pulled, jerked, or twisted, or got at all out of order or place. It will also be advisable to designate the lower *a* in some way, so that we may, by knowing it, work the pairs in their regular order. A capital *A* can be substituted for the small *a;* otherwise, should we be called away while working, and the table be accidentally moved, we may on our return inadvertently reverse the pattern by commencing from the top *a,* and so entirely spoil it.

When done, the plait must be scalded on the wire, dried, slid off, and cemented at either end as neatly as possible. The gold caps and wire for the ear, as well as the drop and slide at the bottom, are of course jewellers' work.

The ear-ring may be worked in a single length of two inches and a half when eight or nine-inch hair can be commanded for the purpose. The ornament at the bottom can then be dispensed with.

Filagree gold-work is, in our opinion, best suited to hair ornaments, as harmonizing most with their lightness of fabric and appearance. But of course these things are matters of taste.

A nice watch-guard may be made from this pattern by using a finer wire, and putting only ten or twelve hairs in each strand. It can be worked with any length of hair, not under five or six inches, as a guard can always be made in separate pieces, and joined together by gold slides. Eight or ten-inch hair is the best for a guard; the great objection to short hair being the expense a number of gold slides entail.

It may at first sight appear that the altering, and twisting, and weaving about of the strands, in order to form a pattern, must be a very tedious and complicated affair; but it is astonishing how soon the fingers habituate themselves to their work, and twine the strands in and out as easily as they propel a crochet-hook through the mazes of some intricate pattern. Nevertheless, we should not advise beginners too rashly to peril the safety of some precious, treasured lock of hair. If our readers will be guided by us, they will take a hat-box or muff-box, and set it on a small round table, and pin to the centre of it, with a strong corking-pin, as many yard-lengths of smooth fine twine as there are strands in the pattern they select to practise on; they will then weight each length as if it were a strand, put a tube or a pencil in the centre, and practise away until a certain degree of proficiency is acquired – for, as in all other things, it is "practice makes perfect."

When the learner begins to feel some little confidence in her skill, let her purchase a small tress of hair at any hairdresser's, and go through the whole process of cleansing it, forming it into strands, arranging the strands on the table, and weaving a pattern with them. Then let her scald the work, suffer it to dry, slide it off the tube, cement it at each end, and she will be enabled to perceive what progress she has actually made, and to judge for herself whether or not she dare venture to trust her skill with the manufacture of the particular tress which she is desirous of weaving into an ornament destined for her own wear, or to be presented to some friend or relative. We do not expect to become at once skilful in embroidery, or learned in the mysteries of crochet; neither can we hope to attain to a proficiency in hair-work without attention and practice. Few things worth knowing, or worth having, are accomplished by a *coup de main.*

PATTERN FOR A WATCH-GUARD.

Draw ten equidistant lines on the table, radiating from the centre; let them be arranged so that five are exactly parallel with the other five, crossing the table in a direct manner.

Make ten strands of eighteen hairs each, and arrange them on the ten lines; put a fine wire in the centre. Letter the lines thus: the central top and bottom lines are both to be *a* (marking the bottom one by a capital *A*); the line immediately to the left of the bottom *A* is to be called *c;* the second to the left is to be *e;* the third to the left *b;* and the fourth to the left *d;* their opposites each receive a similar letter. Thus, commencing from the centre at the bottom, and going round the table towards the left, we find *A, c, e, b, d;* then comes the central top line *a,* and after it *c, e, b, d.* Stand, up and work towards the left, always moving the strands round the table, and never lifting them across.

Move strand *A* half round the table to the place of strand *a* at the top, which latter strand is to traverse the remainder of the circle in order to reach the vacant *A.* Move strand *b* from the right side round to the place of *b* on the left, bringing this latter round the upper half of the circle to the vacuated *b.* Proceed then to the top or right-hand *c,* and work that down to the lower *c,* moving the latter upwards, over the other half of the circle, on to the vacant line; then take the *d*'s, and then the *e*'s, and move them round from right to left; recommence with the *A a,* and repeat until the length is completed, always taking the strands in alphabetical order.

[THIRD ARTICLE.]

TWENTY or thirty-inch hair is requisite for this bracelet, which should be worked on a tube from an inch and a quarter to an inch and three quarters in circumference, the size of the tube being regulated by the length of the hair which is to be used.

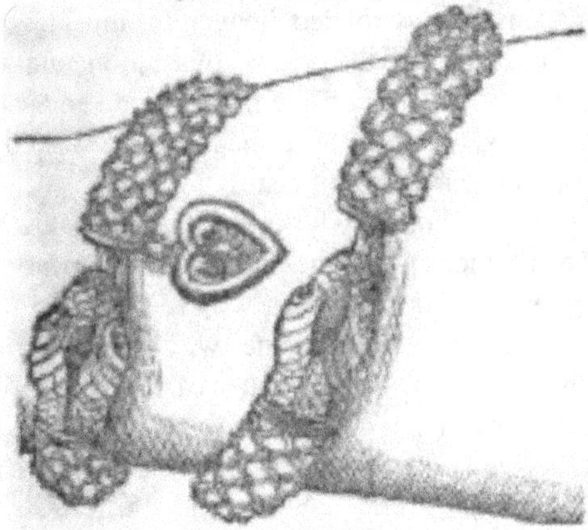

Figure 91.6 HAIR BRACELET.

Prepare thirty-two strands of twenty-four hairs each, in the manner directed at page 4, and arrange them on the table in eight groups of four. Letter each group, *a, b, c, d,* with chalk; make a cross to indicate the commencement of the round, and work as follows: –

1*st Round.* – Lift strand *d,* in the first group to the right of the cross, over strand *c,* and let them change places; lift strand *a* over *b,* and into the place of *c,* moving strand *b* into the place of *a,* and strand *c* into that of *b;* repeat this a second time with these four strands, and then proceed to the next group to the right. Work thus all the way round until the cross is reached, weaving each group twice, and carrying the plait up to the tube.

2*nd Round.* – Take strands *d* and *c* from the left of the cross, and strands *a* and *b* from the right of the cross, and form with these four a group in the space intervening between the letters; take *d* and *c* of the first group to the right of the cross, and *a* and *b* of the second group, and with those four form a new group between the original first and second groups on the right of the cross; do the same all the way round – viz., form a new group in every intervening space between the lettered groups by taking two strands from either side. There will then be eight groups in the eight spaces, and all the letters will be vacant. Commence working with the first on the right of the cross.

Lift the second strand and pass it over the first and then under it, and back into its own place; lift the third strand and pass it over the fourth, and then under it and back into its own place; lift the second strand over the third and let them change places; lift the fourth strand over the third and second and let it become second, while the second becomes third and the third fourth; lift the first strand over the other three and let it become fourth. Weave the next group in like manner, and proceed thus through the whole eight.

When this round is completed, the original groups must be re-formed on the letters by taking the two next strands on either side, having care not to cross, or twist, or intermingle them. These two rounds are to be worked alternately, always weaving towards the right. About seven inches of plait will be requisite for a bracelet. When this length is completed the weights must be detached, the ends of hair bound down to the tube, and the process of scalding and drying gone through; then the work must be gently slid off the tube and the ends cemented, and it will be ready for the snap. A serpent's or bird's head, with jewelled eyes, forms a pretty finish; but this is of course a matter of taste.

Another bracelet may be made with this pattern by substituting a flat tube of about one-fourth of an inch in thickness, and three-fourths of an inch in width, for the round one. Where this is done, it will be necessary to add at least eight more strands, indeed sixteen additional ones will not be too many. As the number of groups will thus be increased, still greater care and attention will be requisite while working, in order to keep the groups distinct and equidistant, and to alter and re-make them correctly at each alternate round, for the least mistake mars the beauty and neatness of the pattern.

Where the bracelet is thus worked flat, a flat clasp or snap, consisting of a device or cipher worked in hair and set in gold, will form an appropriate finish.*

A set of ornaments, *en suite,* may be worked in this pattern – viz., the round bracelet we have already described, finished off with a snake's head and tail; a brooch curved snake-fashion, and having the extremities capped with a similar, though smaller head and tail; and hoop ear-rings.

Thirty-two strands, each consisting of about eight or ten hairs, ten or twelve inches in length, with a tube rather less than an inch in circumference, and the light weights, will be required for the brooch. Twenty-four strands of eight hairs each, and nine or ten inches in length, with a tube measuring nearly three-fourths of an inch in circumference, and the light weights, will be required for each ear-ring.

Where a sufficient quantity of hair, not less than forty or fifty inches long, can be obtained, a graceful ornament for the head, to be worn coronet-fashion, may likewise be made with this pattern. Sixty-four strands, of about thirty-six hairs each, and a tube two inches in circumference, will be required. It must be worked in two lengths, and united in the front by a star or crescent, or some such ornament adapted for the centre of the head; the ends at the back may be finished off in any way, or fastened in with the hair when it is dressed. Of course it will be obvious that the central ornament should be as light as possible.

We may as well state here, that those who intend to work various patterns and ornaments in hair, will find it necessary to have a second top to the table, measuring at least four inches more in diameter than the ordinary one; for it is impossible to work patterns requiring more than thirty-two strands on this latter. They will also need a circular piece of wood exactly fitting into the hole we described in page 4, as being in the centre of the ordinary table; and this piece of wood must be slightly rounded to agree with the elevation there, and have in its middle a round hole the size of a shilling; it must also be perfectly smooth and polished. Whenever fine plaits, as guards, ear-rings, rings, &c., are to be worked, this must be inserted into the table, as the larger opening does not sufficiently steady these more minute fabrics. Substitutes may be found, however, for both the larger top and the central piece; but we do not advise the use of them, because the least roughness or inequality frays and damages the strands greatly.

ORNAMENTAL BEAD AND BUGLE WORK.

THE subjects of the present paper are chiefly ornaments adapted for various purposes of adornment and dress; all of them are useful in their different ways, and such as can be made at home for at least one half what they cost when purchased ready made.

The first cut displays an ornament adapted for dress buttons, for buttons to be attached to velvet as a head-dress, or for attaching to hair-pins to adorn the hair. It is composed of pearls, and may be made of any size, from that of a crown piece to a sixpence.

Four rows of seed pearls, two rows of pearls a size larger, one row about the size of a pea, one row of oblong pearls, a skein of China silk, half a dozen almost flat button moulds, with a hole large enough to admit a quill drilled through the centre of each of them, and half a yard of white sarsenet ribbon, are the requisites.

One of our bead needles, or a straw needle, may be threaded with a long double needleful of the silk, passed through the hole in the centre of the mould, and fastened, by looping the needle through the doubled silk, and the fastening drawn up to the hole, so that the silk proceeds from there, and is at the surface of the mould. Thread five seed pearls and one of the second sized; pass the silk under the mould, and bring it up again through the hole, arrange the beads threaded so as to form one of the lines which radiate from the centre; thread a second line of five seed and one larger pearl, and arrange that into its place. Then thread four seed pearls, and let that row lie between the other two, so as to occupy the space which would otherwise be left vacant. The rows, or radiating lines all round, consist of five seed and one larger pearl, and of four seed pearls placed alternately, until the whole circular surface is filled up. Each row is threaded separately, and the needle brought under the mould and up again through the central hole. When it is necessary to join the silk, the new needleful must be knotted on to the other as close to the end as possible. The work must be held tightly, otherwise the lines will hang loose and get out of place.

When the surface is covered, the needle must be once more brought up through the hole, and a large bead threaded on it, and then the needle passed back again through the hole, and the large bead drawn up so that it may occupy the centre and cover the hole.

The silk has to be fastened on to the edge of the button in order to begin the middle tassel; it is formed by threading a second-sized bead, an oblong bead, twelve seed beads, one second-sized bead, one large one, one second-sized one, and twelve seed beads. We now pass the needle up through the oblong and second-sized pearl, and attach it to the button by looping it through the stitch at the back; we then bring it down again through those two beads, and commence the second loop, which is made by again threading twelve seed, one second-sized, one large, one second-sized, and twelve seed pearls. Once more the needle goes back through the oblong and the second-sized pearl, and is fastened by being looped through one of the upper stitches.

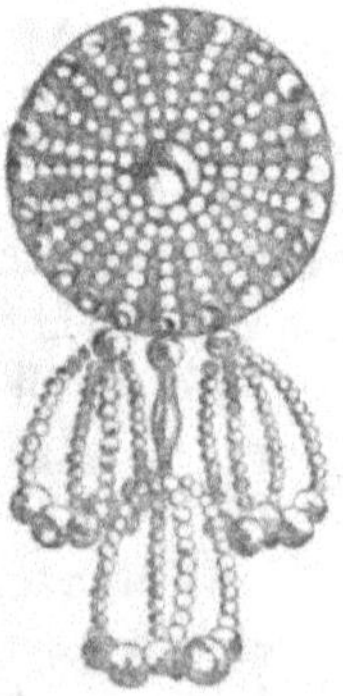

Figure 91.7 ORNAMENT FOR DRESS BUTTONS, ETC.

The two smaller tassels have to be arranged symmetrically on either side, and threaded in a similar way, only omitting the oblong bead.

The number of seed pearls we have directed to be put in the lines, of course will only cover moulds of a certain size: they must be added to or diminished as occasion requires. The tassels, too, can be lengthened or made shorter in like manner. The back of the button is finished off by gumming on a circular piece of the sarsenet ribbon neatly over it.

Our second cut represents a rosette of bugles and beads, adapted for an ornament for the hair, or to be worn in lieu of a broach.

Half an ounce of one-tenth inch bugles, half an ounce of one-fourth inch bugles, a bunch of small cut glass beads, a bunch of cut glass beads a size larger, and a row of large cut glass beads, of the bigness of a pea; some firm yet fine dark wire, a skein of stout silk, and a couple of long hair-pins or sharp steel pins constitute the requisites for making a pair of rosettes. Each rosette consists of three circles of upright loops, one within the other, and a pair of tassels.

The first or outer circle has in it thirteen loops; a length of about a yard of wire is taken, and on it is threaded a second-sized bead, two one-tenth inch bugles and a small bead, two bugles and a bead, two bugles and two beads, three bugles and two beads, two bugles and one bead, two bugles and one bead, and two bugles. These are pushed to within an inch and a half of one end of the wire, and the other end passed again through the first or larger bead, from the outside inwards or towards the bugles, and the loop drawn up firmly and closely. All the loops are alike, and must be arranged so as partially to overlap each other like the petals of a cup-shaped flower. When the requisite number are completed, the extremities must be united and the wires twisted together.

The second circle contains nine loops, requires about three-quarters of a yard of wire, and is threaded thus: one second-sized bead, two one-tenth inch bugles and

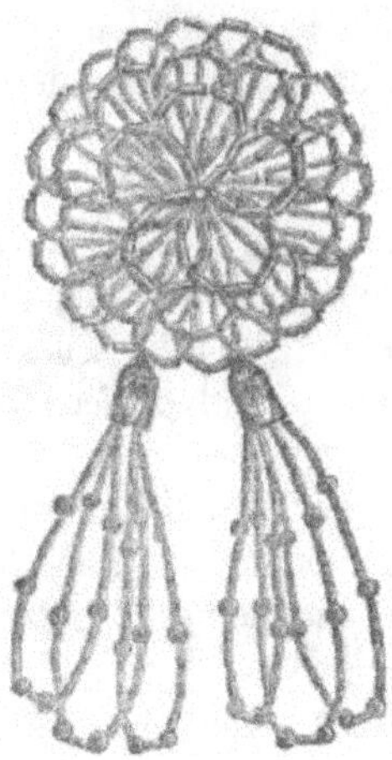

Figure 91.8 ROSETTE OF BUGLES AND BEADS.

a small bead, two bugles and two beads, one bugle and two beads, one bugle and two beads, two bugles and one bead, two bugles.

The third or innermost circle contains only five loops, and requires about half a yard of wire. Each loop has in it one second-sized bead, two one-tenth inch bugles and a small bead, one bugle and two beads, one bugle and two beads, one bugle and two beads, one bugle and one bead, two bugles. Every circle is so formed as to be complete in itself; they are then placed one within the other, and the ends of wire all passed down in the centre. A large cut bead is mounted on about two inches of wire, and being retained firmly in the middle by the ends of the wire being twisted together, is placed in the centre to complete the rosette. The superfluous ends of wire at the back are now to be twisted very neatly together for about half an inch, and the rest cut off; and the twisted ends turned down flat. The rosette is then to be sewn to a button, or a small square of double velvet or silk.

For the tassel, take a good needleful of silk, affix it firmly to the button or square at the back of the rosette, then thread one of our bead needles on it, and commence as follows: – Thread two large beads, three one-fourth inch bugles and a second-sized bead, two bugles and a bead, two bugles and a bead, three bugles, one second-sized, one large, and one second-sized bead, three bugles and two beads, three bugles and a bead, two bugles and a bead, and two bugles. Pass the silk again up the two large beads, thread a sewing needle on it, and attach it by a stitch to the back of the rosette. Thread the silk again in the bead needle, bring it down through the large beads, and make another loop, as before directed. Each tassel should have four loops, and each rosette two tassels pendent from it.

The whole, when completed, must be neatly and firmly sewn on to a long hairpin, if intended for the head, or a sharp steel pin, if destined for the dress. Of course, it will be understood that all the materials employed in a rosette must be of one colour. These ornaments may be made of any size, and with tassels of any length and fullness, by adding to or substracting from the number of beads, and bugles, and loops, we have given. Ours are rather larger than a crown piece when complete, and the tassels about an inch and a half long.

The third cut represents a button worked in turquoise-blue French beads. For a dress trimming of a dozen buttons, six rows of small beads and one of a size larger will be required, also a skein of silk to match, and a dozen button moulds the size of a shilling, flat at the back, slightly raised on the surface, and having a hole drilled through the centre.

They are worked in the same way as our first pattern, viz., in lines or rows radiating from the centre, and having alternately five and four beads in each. One of the larger beads fills up the centre, and the back is finished off by a circular piece of silk gummed on to it.

These buttons may be made in the white, blue, coral coloured, gold, steel, or green pearl glass beads, according to the dress or trimmings with which they are to accord.

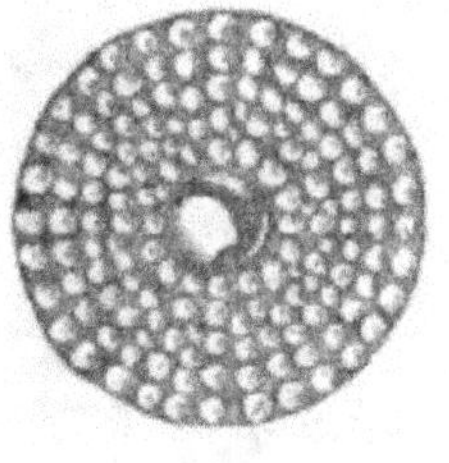

Figure 91.9 BUTTON IN TURQUOISE-BLUE FRENCH BEADS.

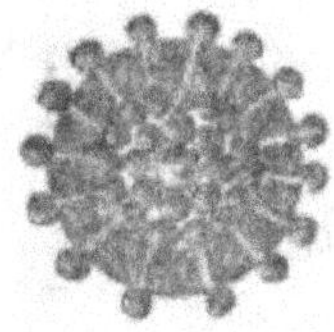

Figure 91.10 BUTTON OF BUGLES AND CUT GLASS BEADS.

The fourth cut illustrates another variety of button, consisting of bugles and cut glass beads worked upon silk buttons. Our pattern is of gray beads and bugles on a gray silk button.

For it we require one-tenth inch bugles, seed beads, and others a size larger; half an ounce of the bugles and a bunch of each size of the beads will suffice for a couple of dozen of the buttons or more. Besides, a skein of sewing silk to match the buttons, and a fine yet strong needle will be necessary. The bugles and beads are threaded by threes, viz., a bead, a bugle, and a bead, and thus sewn on to the button. Eight small beads form the central circle, and a larger one fills this up. All are neatly stitched on in their separate rows or groups. Pattern in such things is a mere matter of taste. There are no arbitrary rules, only all those forming a set should harmonize with each other. The stitches must be as neat as possible, and passed under the silk or at the back of the button.

The oblong or drop-button, of which we give a cut, is worked over a mould pierced down the middle. This one is of cut glass emerald coloured beads, the next size to the seed bead, threaded on green silk; there are alternate rows of fifteen and ten worked according to the directions in our first pattern. It is headed by a cut glass bead the size of a small pea, and terminated by a tassel composed of one of those large beads and four loops of twenty small beads each. A bunch of the smaller beads and a row of the larger ones will make about a dozen of these drop buttons.

Figure 91.11 THE OBLONG BUTTON.

92

[ANON], 'LADY'S CARD-CASE IN GOLD THREAD WITH STEEL BEADS ON KID.'

The Lady's Newspaper, 27 September 1862, p. 201

THE card-case is one of those articles so necessary for use, that it can never be dispensed with, but must in reality be the companion in hand of every morning visit. The design we are now giving is arranged for working on kid, in an outline of gold thread, the interior parts being filled with the very smallest of the cut steel beads that can be procured. The end of the gold thread must be passed through to

Figure 92.1 LADY'S CARD-CASE.

DOI: 10.4324/9781315399980-110

the back of the kid on commencing the outline of the pattern, and the same must be repeated on the return of the gold thread at its conclusion. The border round the edge is formed of a loop of the gold thread, having a single steel bead placed in its centre, carried round with as much regularity as possible. The colour of the kid may be either bronze or grey, either of which contrasts well with the gold and steel colour of the work. When the work has been completed it may be sent to the proper persons for making up, or if in the country, where doing this might be difficult, then the lady herself may stitch it over a cardboard shape, lining the inside with silk, carrying a row of fine steel beads round the edges, as closely as possible together, so as to cover the stitches; sewing up the side and one end in the same way, and only leaving one end open for receiving the cards. The cotton for this beadwork should be No. 40 of Messrs. Walter Evans and Co.'s Boar's-head crochet.

93

[ANON], 'IMITATION WHITE CORAL BASKET.'

Bow Bells, 9 November 1864, p. 357

THE materials required are a piece of white cap wire, which is covered with silk, and rather thick, and some very strong white thread, one pound of *best* plaster of Paris, and two ounces of white wax.

Form the wire into a round of about the size of half-a-crown, and tie the joint firmly together, leaving the first end hanging down a yard long, for a purpose afterwards to be mentioned. Surround this circle with four loops, by continuing the wire and tying with the thread. This part is intended for the centre of the bottom of the basket, from which the work is to be continued in the same way, making loop upon loop in successive rounds. The length of the wire left in these loops varies from three to four inches, but being irregular it cannot be exactly specified, for as the circle enlarges, the number of loops must be increased, by here and there placing two upon one. This basket may be made in various shapes, but as the gipsy is perhaps the most graceful, we shall give it the preference in this description. For this purpose it is necessary to go on enlarging the round until it measures nearly half a yard across. Then, still leaving the wire attached, shape it as gracefully as possible into the required form, slanting it upwards from rather a small bottom into a wide and open shape, having a broad rim, which turns over and hangs down in a pretty and peculiar style. It is in giving its last moulding to this wire shape that the taste of the worker is most called into requisition, and she must look at its contour with an artist's eye, without being discouraged by the irregularities of its component parts, since firmness and form are all that must be considered in this stage of progress. This being done, it is necessary that the handle should be arranged; and now the long end of wire, which will have been left hanging down from the bottom of the basket, is brought into use. This being interlaced through the intervening loops of wire, must be brought out at the same spot where the other end has been left after forming the loops, and the two being securely fastened, must be crossed backwards and forwards over each other in a wide open chain, still firmly tied at each place of junction, until the proper length is completed for making a rather long handle, which is then properly fastened on the contrary side, and the two remaining ends are separately bent in and out until they are lost in the bottom of the basket, to which they thus give additional

DOI: 10.4324/9781315399980-111

finishes. The next portion of the work is to cut a number of lengths of white cotton, varying from three to four inches, and to tie them on to the centres of the loops of the basket, leaving the ends to hang down; which ends are untwisted and opened out, so as to represent the thick knobs of the coral. The same cord is also tied across the openings of the chain handle. All this being done, the basket must undergo its last perfecting of shape, and will then be ready for the next process.

Melt the wax, and mix the plaster of Paris well into it. Take an iron spoon, and first holding the basket with its handle downwards, pour the fluid over every part, twisting and turning the framework round so that it may equalize itself in every curve and corner. Before the wax is quite fixed, bend the ends of cotton cord into those various positions which may best represent the branching out of the coral. Then reverse the basket, and pour the wax over the handle and the interior parts, so that all may be well covered, still twisting it every way to give it a comparatively even distribution, although it is to be remarked that the globular protuberances thus obtained, together with the enlarged ends of the cotton cords, are by no means to be obliterated. The plaster of Paris must be the same as that used by sculptors in making casts, for if that sold in the shops for common purposes is used the beauty of the work will be entirely destroyed.

This basket, filled with artificial fruit or flowers, made either of wax or paper, placed under a glass case, with its stand covered with crimson velvet, is worthy of a place in any drawing-room, and those ladies who take pleasure in ornamenting their homes can scarcely undertake a task which will reward them better.

94

[ANON], 'HOUSEHOLD DECORATIVE ART. II – DIAPHANIE.'

Cassell's Household Guide: Being A Complete Encyclopædia of Domestic and Social Economy, and Forming A Guide to Every Department of Practical Life (London: Cassell, Petter, and Galpin, [1869]), Vol. I, pp. 92–93

II. – DIAPHANIE.

DIAPHANIE is the art of imitating the most beautiful and costly stained glass by the inexpensive and exceedingly simple process of transferring a species of chromo-lithograph in transparent colours to the surface of an ordinary pane of glass, and may be used not only as an embellishment, but as a method of shutting out, and hiding an unsightly view, such as black walls, chimneys, &c., so frequently eye-sores in a town residence.

The art was first practised in France; the original method consisting in printing the subject in colours upon tissue-paper, which paper was permanently fixed upon the glass, by which means the light was intercepted, and the brilliancy and transparency of the colouring destroyed. This system has been improved upon, and by the method now practised, the colours themselves are transferred to the surface of the glass, while the paper is removed, leaving a most perfect imitation of stained glass, upon which neither the violence of the summer sun nor winter frost has any effect. Nor is the art applicable only to windows; it may be used to ornament fire-screens, lamp-shades, Chinese lanterns, and fancy panes in conservatories, and is in fact available for every purpose in which the combination of transparency and ornament enter. The designs used for diaphanie are produced by a new process of lithography, and are mostly copies from well-known and valuable subjects; these you purchase in sheets, and arrange at pleasure, taking care, however, not to mix up designs belonging to different periods. Numbers of beautiful designs are sold at all the paint and oil warehouses, where there is always to be found an extensive choice of subjects, sacred, mediæval, and picturesque, according to the device and subject required. The simplest plan of proceeding is to have a pane of glass to work upon the exact size of that in your window; this, with the design, a few

DOI: 10.4324/9781315399980-112

sheets of lead-foil, a bottle of each transferring varnish, clearing liquid, washable varnish, a roller, and a flat brush, is all that is required.

In the first place, the artist must be very sure that the pane of glass is free from imperfections, such as specks and bubbles, and scrupulously cleansed; of course, if it be already fixed in window frames, you must take it as you find it.

Being assured the glass is all right, lay it flat upon a folded cloth; then trace the outline with a pencil line; those portions where the border ground-work and subject join to serve as a guide for the laying on the lead-foil and the designs which should have previously been cut out. The lead-foil should be cut into strips the width of one-eighth of an inch, though they may be a little wider or narrower, according to the size of the window you desire to decorate, or to the taste of the operator. The lead-foil is to give the effect of the white glass which forms the borders of most coloured glass windows, and when put on the glass it looks quite transparent.

In making the pattern, the designs may be cut out and arranged to show the effect of the composition. Next lay the glass upon the pattern [. . .], and cement upon it the tin-foil previously cut in strips to the proper width; gum is found to be the best cement for laying on the tin-foil. For circles and other shapes the straight strips of foil are cemented, and when nearly dry, stretched with the fingers of one hand, and pressed down with the thumb of the other. No attention need be shown to the creases which may come in the foil, as the smooth handle of a knife or paper cutter, slightly wetted and rubbed over them, flattens and makes the foil flat and even. Having arranged and allowed the foil to be firmly fixed, you can proceed with the laying on of the designs, which should be a little larger than the foiled spaces made ready for their reception, so that the foil may overlap the edges. We cannot enjoin on the beginner too much neatness and care in this operation.

In laying on the designs; the uncoloured part of the paper must be made quite damp with a sponge; then put on the glass and the painted surface a thin coating of the cement. Care must be taken that no air bubbles remain between the glass and the prints, and the papers must be kept damp while the operation is being carried on, for if the cement be allowed to dry, the transparency will be destroyed when the clearing liquid is used. It is a good plan to commence rolling in the centre and working outwards, by which method any superfluity of varnish will ooze out at the edges, and not damage or destroy the surface of the picture. The work having advanced thus far, it should be carefully laid aside for two days at least, or even for three, after which you may begin to remove the paper.

The next operation is to remove the paper; this is done by once more wetting it, then rubbing it gently and evenly with the hand, a sponge, or piece of cloth, the work being kept damp all the while, and great circumspection used, lest by undue pressure any blemish be caused; this must be specially guarded against when, the greater part of the paper having been removed, the painted surface alone is exposed to the hand or cloth, and is liable to scratch or rub off. After the glass has been allowed to dry thoroughly, a thin coating of the clearing liquid is to be applied, and when this has become dry and hard, the work should be re-foiled, over the edges of the transferred picture, following the lines of the first foiling, and proceeding in the manner described before; after which, one or two coatings of the *washable* varnish completes the work, which must dry and harden thoroughly before it is inserted in the frame-work of the window.

This same art may be applied for the adornment of window blinds, &c., upon muslin or silk. The operation consists in stretching either material tightly on a frame, taking the sheets of design, laying the plain side upwards to receive the diaphanous liquid which is put on with a brush; when dry, another coating should be given. A coating of cement should now be applied to the coloured side of the paper, taking great care to press it equally with the roller. There is now nothing left to the completion of the transparency but to varnish it. If the picture be misty, the diaphanous, or clearing liquid, should be used again. Ordinary engravings can be printed on glass in the same manner as the painted designs. The engravings which are to be used should contain no size. The plain side of the picture should be damped with a sponge. Apply to the other a coating of washable varnish; then warm the glass, lay on the print, press with the roller, and place it at some distance from the fire to dry. The next process requires great care, or the beauty of the engraving will be injured. Damp the print again with water, and rub off the superfluous paper after this, and when the miniature has been absorbed, apply the clearing liquid with a camel's-hair brush; and lastly, when it is thoroughly hardened, the washable varnish can be applied, and the work is then finished.

If the learner of the art of diaphanie pays close attention to the exact rules laid down in this article, there will be no difficulty in becoming proficient in this very elegant art, by which every house may be improved in its decorations.

95

[ANON], 'THE FAIR HAND. A STORY FOR GIRLS.'

Our Young Folks Weekly Budget, 5 July 1873, p. 277

"WHAT a nice little hand you have," said Miss Hasbrook to the young girl of whom she was taking a lesson in the art of wax-flower making. "Just the thing for this delicate work."

Agnes Mason looked down at the pretty white hand, of which she was the owner. She was very proud of her hands, and Miss Hasbrook was not by any means the first who had noticed them.

The turquoise ring which looked so neat on her finger had been placed there by one who often spoke of "that lovely little hand," or "that dear, darling little hand."

Agnes was pleasant and good-tempered; in truth she was called a very sweet girl.

Through industry and perseverance she had acquired so much skill in the making of wax flowers, that when she put a specimen in the window of a shop, with her card attached, saying that she would like to give lessons, she received to her great delight two applications.

Now, she thought, she should be able to get some of the articles of dress that other girls had, but that her mother had never felt she could afford to give her.

Mr. Mason was a book-keeper on a small salary; so small, indeed, that he was able to provide but a plain living for his large family; for six children there were, and Agnes was the eldest.

Pleasant and good-tempered we called her, and so indeed she was; but she had one fault, which perhaps more than any other escapes censure, while at the same time it withers and destroys the goodness of the soul. She was very selfish.

There was much to be done in the household where Agnes, seventeen years old, was the eldest daughter. Mary, the next, was four years younger, and then among the little ones, there was no calculating all the matters to be attended to; no anticipating the new garments, the measles, the mumps, and the fits of contrariness.

A great deal of hard work Mrs. Mason had to do, and Agnes, who it would seem might have been so much help, was – it was such a pity – so selfish. She was not indolent, but there were those pretty white hands. Washing, of course, would soak and swell them, and ironing might spread them; even sewing, how it pricked her finger all rough! And so when her mother asked a little assistance she was pretty

DOI: 10.4324/9781315399980-113

sure to make some excuse. She could embroider and make wax flowers, but for this merchandise the market demand did not seem to be great.

Meantime Mrs. Mason, overburdened with care and labour, toiled on day after day, worn out, yet still impelled by the necessity the mother of a large family feels. If her selfish daughter ever gave a little help, it was done so reluctantly that her mother preferred to go on wearily by herself.

"You think, I believe, that your mother is made of iron," she sometimes said, "but you will find she won't last for ever."

And one night, after a day of toil more severe than usual, she said, "I believe my daughter would rather I should wear myself to death than injure in the least her own hands to help me."

Agnes had been engaged all that day upon a work of great utility. She had been embroidering a pair of suspenders for Harry Fleming, because he had given her the turquoise ring. Her mother's words did not at the moment very much trouble her. Little she thought how they would come back to her, for months and years, repeating themselves with a bitter reproach to her sad heart.

The next day Mrs. Mason was too ill to leave her bed. The doctor called it a violent attack of inflammation of the lungs, and said her strength had been overtaxed. The vital force was expended, and in ten days this mother, who had spared not herself for her family, closed her eyes on all care and anxiety.

Agnes had truly loved her mother; and now as she saw the emaciated form lying in the coffin, the sense of grief at her loss, was mingled with a keen self-reproach, the bitterness of which was not understood by those who tried to speak words of comfort to her.

Self-reproach, remorse, how terrible to bear!

Agnes thought of her mother's gentleness and kindness; and then those few words she had spoken the night before she was taken sick would always come into her mind. Her little fair hands awakening the remembrance she would often exclaim, "Oh dear, dear, if only!" and then the tears would roll down her cheeks.

She began to realize too, as she never had done before, how much the comfort and happiness of the family had depended on the dear mother who was gone. And now her heart began to whisper, could not she make some amends for the past, by filling, as far as possible, her mother's place?

She sought the help of God, and by his grace she learned to forget her own self and with cheerful interest to devote herself to the happiness of her father and the little ones.

A short time after this a letter came to Agnes from Harry. In it he said a great many pleasant things; but before he finished he told her that for a long time time he had loved her; and that he hoped she would make him happy by a promise to become his wife.

And what did she say in reply to this? She loved Harry sincerely – so sincerely that she felt she could never marry any one but him.

But what did she reply? If her mother had lived, how happy she should have been; but the past came up sadly before her, and she wrote that there was that in her own heart that told her she belonged now to her father and helpless brothers and sisters, and she could not quite feel it would be right to give herself away. But after saying this somehow there slipped into her letter some little, sweet, gentle expressions, that Harry read over and over again and it seemed to him harder than ever to think of giving her up.

But in writing again he simply told her he should always think of her, and always love her, and then he added he expected the next day to start on a long journey.

Three years passd, and Agnes still "looked to the ways of her household." Many days of wearisome toil she found, but she was happy in the thought that she was doing her duty.

The young sisters were quite tall girls now, and it was the evening of Mary's birthday. Agnes had made an extra loaf of cake, and had said, "We will have a party just among ourselves to-night." The girls had put bright ribbons in their hair, and all wore smiling faces as they sat around the cheerfully lighted tea-table.

And just then there was a ring at the street door, and who should walk in among them, but Harry. He thought how sweet Agnes looked, as she sat at the head of the table: – the dear sister, happy herself in attending to the enjoyment of others.

Harry coveted this prize, and soon declared he could not be refused; and so it came to pass there was a quiet wedding in the household, and then Agness [*sic*] was gone. And Mary in taking her place used to say, she would do the best she could, but she never, never, could be all that Agnes had been.

96

[ANON], 'A SEA-WEED ALBUM.'

The Ladies' Treasury, 1 December 1876, p. 727

MATERIALS. – Two hollow shells of Escallops, quite cleaned from any smell of fish; six shapes of good writing-paper, cut at the edges as in engraving. These are to be sewed together at the points.

The shells must be drilled about the centre of the upper part of the shell. This is to admit of two drawing cords, having a small button at each end; the cord, with buttons attached, is drawn through one shell and through the six papers (which must be pierced exactly opposite the holes in the shells). The cord is then fastened on to the shell with Judson's cement – or it has to be brought through the drilled hole and the end be tied in a knot; but this is apt to interfere with the free drawing of the cord, unless the drilled hole be oval. The second cord is passed through to the opposite shell, and secured in the same manner. This album is a pretty trifle for securing delicate sea-weeds, which, after being washed and floated on to blotting-paper, and dried, can be made to adhere to the writing-paper by the aid of a little weak gum.

DOI: 10.4324/9781315399980-114

97

[ANON], 'USES FOR SHELLS AND SEA-WEEDS.'

The Girl's Own Paper, 13 November 1880, pp. 99–100

THERE seems to be an instinct innate in every mind which prompts one to pick up shells when staying at the sea-side. While taking a walk upon the sands, if we see a pretty shell, an impulse bids us procure it, though we have to jump over or wade through a pool for it, and we know it will be of no use whatever when we have it.

Usually we are tired of carrying our treasures trove, all wet and sandy as they are, before the walk is over, and we throw them back on the sands again with something of relief to be rid of them. Should we manage to convey them in safety to our lodgings, they are laid aside and forgotten till an unpleasant, fishy odour reminds us of their existence, and they are cast away with disgust.

Now, this is a great pity, as even supposing one is not ambitious enough to attempt a collection properly arranged and named, still the most unlearned can make very pretty objects with shells and seaweeds. Collecting shells is a delightful occupation when there is some definite end in view, and the hope of securing fresh varieties adds a new zest to otherwise aimless walks.

A sufficient variety for our purpose can usually be found along the edge of the tide with no other equipment than a basket or one of the little wooden pails without which no child is content. The advantage of a basket is that it saves the trouble of washing the shells separately, a tedious operation in a large collection. By occasionally dipping the basket in the water, the mud and sand will wash through and leave the shells clean. If this be done, however, a small box should be carried, in which to keep any small specimens that might slip through the basket during the washing process.

One needs to be a little more adventurous in collecting sea-weeds. The delicate kinds can only be found in perfection by following the retreating tide step by step. When it is at its lowest ebb, particularly after a storm, you will find a rich harvest of sea-weeds and corallines, chief among the former on our English coasts being the beautiful red rhodosperms.

Most of the red and some of the green sea-weeds lose their bright colour very soon if exposed to the sun and air, changing to a dirty-white hue. It is necessary,

DOI: 10.4324/9781315399980-115

therefore, to collect them as soon as possible after they are deposited by the tide. The bright-coloured lichen-like sponges, so tempting to the inexperienced, which are to be found in the pools at low water, are quite useless for ornamental purposes, as they lose their colour directly.

The different sorts of coralline, common on all our coasts, are very suitable for decoration; one of the most abundantly met with is the sea-hair coralline, so called from its form of growth, in tufts like bunches of hair. Another common one is the sickle coralline; both of these, with any other variety, and all the stiff, bushy sea-weeds that can be found, will be very useful.

It may be interesting to mention here that these corallines, popularly called, and formerly supposed to be sea-weeds, are in reality not so. Each delicate hair-like branch is composed of a series of cells, and each of these is occupied by a tiny living creature, which may be easily seen under a microscope of moderate power. The little inhabitants are generally already dead when the coralline is found on the shore, and from its structure it soon dries and is more lasting in colour and form than most of the sea-weeds.

The true sea-weeds will, some of them, require pressing in the same manner as ferns and flowers [. . .], otherwise they cockle up and lose all their beauty when dry. Any which appear quite limp when taken from the water should be so treated, but before pressing, they must be "floated out," as the process is called. It is done in the following way: – First wash them in clean water, then take each piece separately, and lay it on a plate of clean fresh water, when it will spread out and expand as in its natural state. Take a piece of stout white paper, slip it underneath the sea-weed in the water and gradually withdraw it, arranging the little branches meanwhile with a camel's hair brush, if the movement through the water displaces them at all. They must be put in press between blotting paper, and in a few days will be found dry and adhering to the paper.

On some parts of our coasts nothing but the commonest and plainest kinds of shells are to be found. These should not be neglected, however, as they may be made quite beautiful by rubbing with emery and water. After several applications of this they are finished off with rotten-stone and oil, applied with chamois leather. The process will generally produce a fine polish; but the natural state of the shell, if the pretty ones can be found, is decidedly preferable to any effect obtained by artificial means.

Another way of beautifying shells, such as mussels, some sorts of top-shells and others, is to put them into a cup of vinegar and water, which in the course of a few days will eat off the rough, dingy exterior, and disclose a surface of mother-o'-pearl. They must not be left in too long, nor should the solution of vinegar be very strong, as in either case the shell will dissolve and crumble away altogether.

I have made several exceedingly pretty brackets in the manner to be described, and I am sure that any who follow the directions will be pleased with the result.

Procure some strong mill or cardboard – an old dress box will do admirably; cut out a piece in the shape of a half-moon, the size being regulated by the position to be occupied by the bracket. This is for the top; then cut out another piece for the front, which must be the same length as the rounded part of the top. The lower edge should be shaped in some way.

A small strip for the back may be added for the sake of giving additional firmness, but it must not be as deep as the front, or it will show, and look very unsightly. Cover the top with coloured velveteen or silk, and then stitch the parts firmly together. Make a hole for a nail in the back piece, or else add two little rings at the top to hang it up by.

The bracket itself must be perfectly finished before the ornamentation is begun, as if anything be left till afterwards the shells are likely to be knocked off.

Liquid glue is best to use, and a rather small brush will be necessary.

I put first of all a row of sprigs of coralline all round, projecting over the edge of the bracket, forming a fringe. Then a row of one variety of shells, such as small whelks or cockles, all round inside the fringe of coralline. After this border, a sort of groundwork of the larger shells should be made, leaving the interstices until the last to be filled in with tiny shells and morsels of seaweed. The lovely little pearly galeonna, and the bright pink trough-shells will be at once chosen for these purposes. Should there be a scarcity of bright-coloured specimens, and the bracket looks dull and flat, some little pieces of lichen may be introduced with great advantage; they are of all shades and hues, and can be found on the trees in most country places. They look so much like seaweed that no one will detect the difference, and they add the little touches of colour here and there which are necessary to brighten up the whole.

A favourite, though old-fashioned, way of using these "spoils of the sea" is to take a very small wicker basket, cut it in halves lengthwise, and stitch or glue it on to a piece of cardboard, the hollow side of course inwards. Then fill it with dried or pressed seaweeds, arranging the colours and forms as tastefully as possible, and fastening each piece with gum, either to the basket or to the cardboard, as the position may require. I should have said, however, before the basket is attached, that some sprays of seaweed may be "floated out" on the card, round where the edge of the bouquet is to be. This forms a border and facilitates the arrangement of the rest of the bunch considerably.

A more useful employment of shells, and one, therefore, more to be recommended, is in the conversion of a small wooden box into a pretty work or trinket box. The inside will first require to be lined with silk or coloured material, and the lid attached more securely. Two little hinges may be bought for a trifling sum, and fastened on with tiny nails, or two or three little slips of cloth will do instead of orthodox hinges. A loop of ribbon should also be fastened to the front of the lid, that it may be opened without touching the shells. If they are well glued on, however, they will stand a good deal of wear unless really roughly handled. They are fastened and grouped in the same way as on the bracket. If the box be intended for a present, a pretty idea is to arrange the initials of the recipient in pink or white shells on the lid, the letters being edged with seaweed or very small shells of a different colour, to make them show up well.

The tiniest shells of all may be reserved for the making of birthday and other gift cards; they would be quite lost if employed on any larger objects, but come in beautifully in a wreath of fine and delicate sea-weed on a card of this description, which will form a pleasing memento of a summer holiday at the sea-side.

98

DORA HOPE, 'HOW TO PRESERVE LEAVES AND FLOWERS.'

Silver Sails: Being the Holiday No. of The Girl's Own Paper, [1882], pp. 33–35

DURING a round of calls the other day, I chanced to visit a young lady who had been compelled, through family misfortunes, to begin earning her own living as a governess, and I was rather curious to see how she had been able to accommodate herself to her altered circumstances. Arrived at her humble lodgings, I was shown into a small sitting-room, most plainly and inexpensively furnished, but the first glance round showed me that though she had lost her luxurious surroundings she had by no means lost her love of beautiful things, and seemed somehow to be able to gratify her tastes, for the room was unmistakably that of a refined lady. After a little conversation she told me about all her devices for making her room pretty under difficulties. Little pieces of tasteful needlework, graceful vases, and bright hangings all bespoke the taste of the occupant, but what struck me most was the number and variety of ways in which she had made use of pressed leaves and flowers. Frames, brackets, vases, all were decorated with them. Being sufficiently intimate with her to ask questions, I inquired where and how she had obtained them all, living as she did in a large and smoky town.

"That is easily managed," she replied. "You know as I have always lived in the country till our misfortunes began, I found these interminable streets almost unendurable at first, so I determined to do without everything but absolute necessaries, and so save money to treat myself to half a day in the country pretty often. I am busy with my pupils all the morning, so my little holidays are of short duration, but I follow the excellent example of John Gilpin's wife, and 'Though on pleasure I am bent, I have a frugal mind.' I always take a little basket with me, and a pair of old scissors to cut anything that takes my fancy, as I have a great objection to pricking my fingers by gathering brambles, or cutting them with tough grass stalks, and I come home so laden with treasures that it takes me all the evening to arrange them."

"But are they not faded before you get home?"

"Some of the young fern fronds and delicate flowers would be, but I never go without this old French grammar;" and she began lifting down a number of books to show it to me.

 DOI: 10.4324/9781315399980-116

I began really to fear my young friend's mind had been affected by hard work, and that she had forgotten what she was talking about. I suppose I must have showed my astonishment in my face, for when she turned round to hand me the book and caught sight of my face, she burst out laughing.

"Do not look so dreadfully bewildered," she said, "I am not mad; or, if I am, there is method in my madness. Don't you see that the only way to press very delicate specimens satisfactorily is to begin the operation at once, before they have time to curl up or wither in the least, so I take a book with me and put them in as I gather them, and when I stop to rest I put it down and sit on it, and they are beautifully pressed by the time I get home. Then I take them out and put them into sheets of blotting-paper. Perhaps I ought not to use my grammar," she added, rather sadly, "but it is a sort of reaction; it is so nice to throw off the governess for a little while, and see my beautiful flowers covering those dreadful irregular verbs, which seem made on purpose to try the patience of poor governesses; and it is a very old and dilapidated copy, you see."

"But most of the country round here is so flat," I said, "I cannot think where you find so many varieties."

"It is flat, certainly, and some of it is not at all pretty, but you can get *something* where-ever you go. Last Saturday I found myself in a very uninteresting place, dull fields with nothing picturesque to be seen, but I always think that if one really keeps one's eyes open for beautiful things there are some to be found wherever one goes, so I soon recovered from my disappointment and looked rather more closely than usual; and look here at the splendid collection of buttercups I got, and do you know they press almost better than anything, and keep their colour wonderfully. I declare they are almost brighter than when I gathered them. And as these tiny flowers grow right down amongst the grass, I had walked right across the field trampling on them before I noticed them. I gathered all this quantity and put them in my grammar, and I am going to make a photograph frame of white cardboard, and gum a wreath of those round it and send it to my sister on her birthday with my own photograph in it. The leaves are not very pretty, so as soon as I thought of making the frame I began to hunt about for some moss to use instead of them, and at last I found the very thing I wanted growing down by a ditch. Look, it is in beautiful little branches almost like fern fronds, and such a bright green. You know I can't afford to buy proper presents now, but I do not like to give up keeping birthdays. We always made so much of them at home."

"But you could not have got all this large group anywhere in this neighbourhood," I said, pointing to a splendid bunch in a little wicker basket hanging against the wall.

"No, not quite all; that particular collection is a souvenir of my last summer holiday, when, you know, I went home for a week. Those bulrushes grew in a pond near our house, so did that splendid brown reed grass, and all these other brown headed reeds, whose stalks fortunately are as long as their names, so they make a capital background. I used to find the bulrushes very troublesome, the seed fell so much, but I have tried now dipping the heads in a weak solution of gum, and it is quite successful. I must confess those everlasting flowers are not entirely natural. They had nothing but the common yellow ones in our garden at home, and I got so tired of them that I determined to dye some with Judson's dyes, and that is the result. I flatter myself no one would ever suspect the fraud. Some of the stalks have had to be wired too, as I forgot that everlastings should always be hung up by the stalks, head downwards till they are dry. If that is not done the stalks become soft and will not keep upright."

"But show me where you press these ferns, Ruth," I said. "I see the result of your labours all round, but no sign of the work itself."

"They are in my bedroom, pressing under a large box. At home I always put my sheets of blotting-paper in the linen press, but here of course I have no press, and very little room to spare. I put them under a pile of books first for a few days, as I find it is [...] better not to have too heavy a weight to begin with. I look at them every evening at first, and if the papers are at all damp I change them. After about a week they are not likely to want any more changing, and I put them away under the box."

"And what is that brown paper for?"

"I always use brown paper for the succulent plants. They are difficult to dry, as there is so much sap in them; the best way is to put them between sheets of blotting-paper or coarse brown paper, and cover them with several layers of the same paper, then iron them till the moisture is drawn out of the specimen, and put them to press in fresh dry sheets. For ferns and leaves, newspapers do quite as well as anything else, but flowers need greater care, and ought to be pressed in either prepared botanical paper or blotting-paper, except the hardy kinds, like these buttercups, which keep their colour just as well in brown paper. Here are some of the large ferns," she added, lifting up the loose cushion which covered her little couch. "They were too long to go under my box, so when they were sufficiently pressed I put them under here just to keep them flat."

"When I came in you were busy with a basin of boiling water; had that anything to do with flowers?"

"Not flowers, exactly; but, you know, some kinds of leaves, such as the virginian creeper, always fall off the stalk when they are dried, and I find that dipping them in boiling water before pressing partly prevents that. I have tried the same plan successfully with these very succulent plants. I press them in brown paper, as I told you, and generally iron them, too; but immersing them in boiling water first makes them dry more quickly. Do not imagine," she went on, "that I spend all my time over these leaves. I happened to have a leisure afternoon, and it being too wet for a walk, I took the opportunity to look over and re-arrange my stores; and it is fortunate I did, for I find that some have been put away before they were quite dry, and are becoming mouldy."

"What shall you do with them?"

"They are very common leaves that I can get plenty of, so I shall throw them away, but if they had been rare ones I should wipe each leaf carefully, and put it between fresh sheets of blotting paper. It is no use trying to restore flowers when they are damp, the colour always goes, and nothing can be done with them. But," she added, "stay and have a cup of tea with me, and I will show you all my treasures. I will have the kettle boiling by the time you have got your bonnet off, and you shall have a good rest in my own especial chair, a present from my brothers on my birthday."

So saying, she drew out the favourite chair, and before I had time to refuse had run off with my bonnet and cloak, and in almost less time than it takes to tell she had arranged the tea-things on a little table near me, and we were sitting down for a cosy chat.

"Now," she said, "I am going to talk fast, and tell you all about my plants, or you will say I have kept you under false pretences, and then it will be your turn to tell me about all your doings."

It would take too long to describe all the pretty things she showed me, but I will just mention a few which girls who get a holiday in the country can easily copy. She had made a frame of stout cardboard for one of her own water-colour paintings, and covered it with a wreath of yellow bracken and other fern leaves which had been well pressed and afterwards covered with a coating of varnish – not painter's varnish, but a thinner kind usually sold by stationers. When the varnish was quite dry, the leaves were glued on to the frame, and looked almost like wood-carving.

Next I saw some pieces of cardboard in process of being transformed into a pair of brackets for a bazaar she was anxious to help. These were to be covered with bright-tinted autumn leaves, pressed and varnished in the same way as the ferns. She had a large collection of all kinds: blackberry, sumach, virginian creeper, red beech – all sorts and all colours. She told me that many of the brightest-tinted leaves she noticed were inclined to curl up, and she found it better to soak these in water before pressing them; also some that had very short stalks, or no stalks at all, were fastened to a small length of fine wire before being varnished, both for convenience of handling while wet, and to allow of some of them standing out from the others. The wire extended the whole length of the leaf to support it.

Another idea, which Ruth evidently rather prided herself upon, was to use up any old faded specimens by bleaching them. When dried ferns have been kept in vases for some time, they lose their colour and become brown and shabby; so she dissolved a good teacupful of chlorate of lime in a quart of water, with a few drops of vinegar, and put the old leaves and ferns into the solution, which she had in an inverted bell-glass, so that she could see the progress of the bleaching without disturbing the specimens. They were carefully arranged, stalk downward, as the stalks, being thicker, take longer to bleach than the actual leaves, and the lime settles to the bottom. She told me it did not answer well with thick, strong leaves; maidenhair and other delicate ferns succeed the more.

Two specimen glasses on the mantelpiece were filled with very delicate grasses, which she had gathered by the roadside in her country excursions. She said she gathered every variety she found, only being careful to get them before they were quite ripe, and also to shake them a little to see if the seeds fall much; as those which scatter the seeds easily are only a vexation and not worth carrying home.

She wrapped the bunches of each variety separately in newspapers, and when she wanted them for arranging, shook them out, and put each head singly into the vase. Any attempt to save time by putting two or three heads in together is fatal to the graceful appearance of the group.

"I arranged a very different group of grasses for my landlady's best parlour," said Ruth. "If you like I will run down and get it to show you. While I am going, perhaps you would like to look at my mosses. These bunches have good long stalks, and are of the common hardy kind. I do not press them at all, but hang them wrong side up in bunches to dry, and they are very useful to put round flower-pots, and for Christmas decorations, and to help to fill my grate in the summer."

The other mosses were pressed in the same way as the ferns, and were of all varieties; she appeared to find them very useful for mixing with leaves and cones, on brackets and picture frames, as well as on the small photograph frames and birthday cards. Amongst the bundles of moss there was a cardboard box containing a large variety of lichens, and the tiny grey mosses that grow on the bark of trees. Some of the small scraps were gummed on to pieces of stick and straw, which were evidently prepared for arranging amongst some rustic work. She showed me afterwards a lovely little mirror, destined for the same bazaar as the brackets, with the frame entirely covered with these lichens, and acorns and small fircones, and very beautiful it looked.

I was just wondering what could be the use of a handful of barley and wheat ears, when she came in again, carrying a china vase full of ferns and grasses.

"These," she said, "are not exactly my taste; I like the natural colours better, but my landlady thinks differently. As she said about my first collection: 'It's very nice and pretty like, but it wants a bit of something to brighten it up,' so I have dyed some of these grasses for her with nitric acid. I mix ten parts of water to one part of the acid and just plunge in the grasses, then shake off the liquid, and hang them up to dry. I did these immortelles with borax, as much borax as would colour the boiling water a bright red. I left them in until the flowers had taken the colour, and then hung them up the same as the grass.

"*Apropos* of dyeing, let me advise you to save all your faded old fern leaves and moss, and everything else for Christmas decorations; dipped in a rather strong solution of Judson's dye, they do splendidly for making mottoes and wreaths, and any other decoration you may require. The colour you get is not strictly natural nor very æsthetic, but it is no use having dull colours high upon the walls. It seems absurd to be thinking of Christmas now, in the middle of summer, but now is just the time one ought to think of it, and lay in stores for the endless church and school decorations."

"Is that what these ears of corn are for?"

"Partly, but partly also for some of my little pupils, into whose minds I am trying to instil a love of botany. I give them a few of these ears now and then and we keep them in a specimen glass full of water on the school-room mantelpiece. They begin to sprout in a few days and really look very pretty, besides letting the children see how things grow. But better still, I keep acorns and horse-chestnuts for the same purpose. I fill a glass with water, and then support the acorn at the top of the glass with a piece of wire, or a bent hair-pin, if I have nothing more elegant, so that the water just covers the bottom of the acorn. Chestnuts being larger do not require any support unless the glass is very large. In a short time they begin to grow, and as the leaves unfold at the top the roots grow down into the water, and the children cannot help being interested.

"We are starting a botanical collection too. The little ones are very proud of telling people about their 'herbarium,' though they find the word rather difficult to pronounce. It is a very small collection so far, as we only put in what they get themselves. Of course, I am careful to see that they gather the specimens on a dry day, so that they may press well, and as far as possible when some of the flowers have fallen, and given place to the fruit, so that they may see all the parts of the fructification. We get the small plants with the roots on. They have to be washed and well dried before pressing, and if either the roots or branches are too thick to lie flat on the paper, we pare them off underneath with a sharp knife. I look forward as much as the children do to our botany days since we began the study practically, and instead of sitting over books of theory, we

'Ramble a-field to brooks and bowers,
To pick up sentiments and flowers.' "

It was very reluctantly that I rose to go, for Ruth had evidently plenty more to say on her favourite subject, but the time had flown rapidly, and it was getting late. As I came downstairs she called after me –

"You remember that this is just the best time of year for making skeleton leaves, and they ought to be gathered, like those for pressing, when just in their prime, neither too young and tender, nor withered, and, above all, not wet. The main rules for drying leaves are to gather them at the proper time, and to press them quickly, thoroughly, and with not too heavy a weight at first."

99

[ANON], 'ANSWERS TO CORRESPONDENTS.'

The Girl's Own Paper, 2 January 1886, p. 224

G. R. and P. – Both your questions have been answered more than once. Muriatic acid applied with a small camels' hair brush will remove the rough coating on the outside of shells. It is very burning, so beware how you use it, and lock up the bottle. You should have a basin or saucer of water beside you in which to dip the shell frequently, to wash off the acid before it burns too deeply, or you will soon make perforations. Your hands also should be dipped in the water, and beware how you touch your eyes while using the acid. See vol. ii., pages 176 and 494, for how to press and mount seaweed (monthly parts for December, 1880, and April, 1881), and vol. iii., page 542, for how to preserve their colour (monthly part for May, 1882).

DOI: 10.4324/9781315399980-117

100

JOHN STRANGE WINTER [PSEUD. HENRIETTA ELIZA VAUGHAN STANNARD], *MIGNON'S SECRET*

Seaside Library Pocket Edition (New York: George Munro, 1886), Chapter III, pp. 21–24

And yet this little barrack bairn [. . .] had been lifted altogether out of herself, and filled with a wild dream of ambitious delight that, sooner or later, she would do something for Captain Lucy. But the question was, what should she, or rather what *could* she, do? In her ignorant but grateful heart she cast about to think what the something had best be. Poor child, she thought and thought, and then she sighed to think how much less she knew and could do than others among her fellows. If she were like Polly Armstrong, and could crochet, why, she might make the captain a beautiful antimacassar for his sitting-room. That would be something like a present to give him, and, fired by the constant presence of an elegant specimen of those articles of luxury which covered the little round table in the window of their quarters, and by the remembrance of several superelegant ones which were put away "for best," and only brought to show admiring visitors, or to be used on extra grand occasions, Miss Jack coaxed a penny out of her father, and, with a bent crochet hook belonging to Polly Armstrong, began, under that damsel's tuition, an antimacassar for the ultimate adornment of Captain Lucy's quarters.

For weeks afterward that, to her, herculean task was the effort of her daily life. Never, surely, was such a labor of love undertaken and completed under circumstances so adverse and so trying. In the first place, it was no easy matter for a little girl, who was obliged to keep the whole affair a profound secret at home, to obtain the few pence necessary for the purchase of the cotton with which to make the thing; and then, being obliged to keep it a secret, she was not able to work at it, with her little cramped and unaccustomed fingers, during the long evening hours between dusk and bed-time. Therefore it had all to be done during odd moments and in odd and out-of-the-way corners – sitting on the cold and damp steps leading to the troop-rooms, hiding behind stables or riding-school, only working in comfort on those rare occasions when "mother" was out on a shopping or visiting expedition, or when Polly Armstrong's mother would let Polly bring her into their

DOI: 10.4324/9781315399980-118

quarters to tea. At other times the whole thing reposed in Jack's not too clean or inviting pocket, along with a bit of slate-pencil, two bits of twine, a brass thimble, and a little comb, a Christmas card, and part of a stick of Spanish juice, to the imminent danger of the hook running into her leg, and having to be cut out thereof with the aid of a knife.

But at last, in spite of all let and hinderance, it was finished, and a real antimacassar lay upon the topmost step of the flight of stairs which led to the schoolroom, carefully spread upon an old newspaper. Four or five admiring girls of different ages stood by, while Polly Armstrong smoothed out the fringe with the proud consciousness of being the master-hand, and Jack Henderson gazed at her completed task with shining eyes of rapture. At last she had done something for her captain!

And there, in the midst of the group, lay the work of gratitude, the offering of a thankful heart. The fastidious and those hard to please might have scoffed at it, for it was not very large, nor yet very well done as a specimen of crochet-work. How should it be? Nor yet was it very clean; in fact, it was decidedly dirty, showing plainly enough which of the dragged and irregularly made circles had been added last, as plainly which had been done the first; while the fringe, having been put on last of all, was quite lily-white by comparison with the dinginess of the whole.

But in Jack Henderson's eyes it was without flaw. Polly Armstrong had told her that crochet-work should never be washed before being given away, so she took no heed of the difference of tone which it presented, and beyond it had but one thought: How should she contrive to get it into Captain Lucy's quarters?

101

[ANON], 'EDITORIAL NOTES.'

Pick-Me-Up, 17 August 1889, p. 314

THE peaceful decorum of English home life is threatened by a new form of decorative "fancy work." The Penelope task of cutting holes in strips of linen, for the purpose of sewing them up again, the reckless "enamelling," which attaches the incautious visitor to the chair of the suburban villa, and perfumes his clothing with the nauseous odour of turpentine, the practice of disfiguring door panels, table-tops, and other impossible surfaces with paintings of sprawling flowers; these and other hitherto favourite pastimes for ladies are giving place, we are, assured, to the barbaric art of hypodermic decoration. A trustworthy correspondent tells us that in the shop of a London instrument-maker she was recently shown a small Russia leather case, bearing a silver plate, engraved with the name of a well-known lady of title. The case contained a complete set of tattooing instruments, comprising needles mounted in ivory handles, non-poisonous inks of various colours, a tiny bottle of cocaine, to render the operation painless, and another of glycerine, to allay the resulting inflammation. It was, our correspondent was informed, one of nearly a hundred cases of similar pattern, which have been manufactured to order within the last twelve months.

DOI: 10.4324/9781315399980-119

INDEX

www.ingramcontent.com/pod-product-compliance
Lightning Source LLC
LaVergne TN
LVHW010630300926
849162LV00001B/111
9781138225381